Rehabilitation Counseling
and Emerging Disabilities

Lynn C. Koch, PhD, CRC, is a nationally certified rehabilitation counselor and professor, Rehabilitation Education and Research Program, University of Arkansas, where she has been employed since 2006. Prior to that she was coordinator, Rehabilitation Counseling Program, Kent State University, Ohio, and a faculty member in the Center for Disability Studies. Dr. Koch has authored or coauthored 75 professional journal articles, 16 book chapters, and one book, *Emerging Issues in Rehabilitation Counseling.* She has guest-edited three special issues of professional and academic journals in the field of rehabilitation and allied health professions, including a special issue of *WORK* on emerging disabilities. She also guest-edited a forthcoming special issue of *Rehabilitation Research, Policy, and Education* on psychiatric rehabilitation. Additionally, she has delivered over 85 presentations to consumer, professional, academic, and policymaking audiences. Dr. Koch served as the chair of the National Council on Rehabilitation Education (NCRE) Research Committee for 11 years. She also has served as cochair of the NCRE Psychiatric Rehabilitation Council and has served on the editorial boards of five journals. Dr. Koch was the recipient of the 2014 University of Arkansas College of Education and Health Professions Career Faculty Award; 2013 NCRE President's Award for Exemplary Diligence and Fortitude in Promoting Rehabilitation Research, Education, and Service; the 2008–2009 University of Arkansas Department of Rehabilitation, Human Resources and Communication Disorders' Outstanding Researcher Award; and the 2001 American Rehabilitation Counseling Association Research Award (third place).

Phillip D. Rumrill, Jr., PhD, CRC, is a nationally certified rehabilitation counselor. He is professor and coordinator, Rehabilitation Counseling Program, and director, Center for Disability Studies, Kent State University, Ohio. Dr. Rumrill has authored or coauthored more than 200 professional journal articles; 50 book chapters, monographs, measurement instruments, and training manuals; and 13 books. He has also guest-edited 21 special issues of professional and academic journals in the fields of education and rehabilitation. Dr. Rumrill is a highly sought speaker at national and international conferences in a variety of fields. He has received honors and recognition for his work from such organizations as the International Organization of Social Sciences and Behavioral Research, the Multiple Sclerosis Foundation, the National Council on Rehabilitation Education, the National Association of Student Personnel Administrators, and the National TRIO Foundation. Dr. Rumrill has held distinguished lecturer or visiting scholar appointments at University of Pittsburgh, Ohio State University, University of Hawaii, University of Leeds Medical School in England, University of Glasgow in Scotland, and the Arla Institute of Finland. He coauthored *The Sandwich Generation's Guide to Eldercare,* which won the Gold Medal in the *Foreword Reviews'* INDIEFAB 2013 Book of the Year Awards in the Family and Relationship Books category.

Rehabilitation Counseling and Emerging Disabilities

Medical, Psychosocial, and Vocational Aspects

Lynn C. Koch, PhD, CRC
Phillip D. Rumrill, Jr., PhD, CRC

SPRINGER PUBLISHING COMPANY
NEW YORK

Springer Publishing Company, LLC
11 West 42nd Street
New York, NY 10036
www.springerpub.com

Acquisitions Editor: Sheri W. Sussman
Compositor: Newgen KnowledgeWorks

ISBN: 978-0-8261-2068-7
e-book ISBN: 978-0-8261-2069-4
Instructors' Test Bank and Syllabus ISBN: 978-0-8261-4754-7
Instructors' PowerPoints ISBN: 978-0-8261-4755-4

Instructors' Materials: Qualified instructors may request supplements by e-mailing textbook@springerpub.com

16 17 18 19 20 / 5 4 3 2 1

The author and the publisher of this Work have made every effort to use sources believed to be reliable to provide information that is accurate and compatible with the standards generally accepted at the time of publication. The author and publisher shall not be liable for any special, consequential, or exemplary damages resulting, in whole or in part, from the readers' use of, or reliance on, the information contained in this book. The publisher has no responsibility for the persistence or accuracy of URLs for external or third-party Internet websites referred to in this publication and does not guarantee that any content on such websites is, or will remain, accurate or appropriate.

Library of Congress Cataloging-in-Publication Data
Names: Koch, Lynn C., author. | Rumrill, Phillip D., Jr., author.
Title: Rehabilitation counseling and emerging disabilities: medical, psychosocial, and vocational
  aspects / Lynn C. Koch, Phillip D. Rumrill, Jr.
Description: New York, NY: Springer Publishing Company, LLC, [2017] | Includes bibliographical
  references.
Identifiers: LCCN 2016025747| ISBN 9780826120687 | ISBN 9780826120694 (e-book) |
  ISBN 9780826147547 (test bank and syllabus) | ISBN 9780826147554 (instructor's PowerPoints)
Subjects: | MESH: Disabled Persons—rehabilitation | Counseling—methods |
  Rehabilitation—psychology | Rehabilitation Research | Case Reports
Classification: LCC R727.4 | NLM WB 320 | DDC 362.1/04256—dc23
LC record available at https://lccn.loc.gov/2016025747

Special discounts on bulk quantities of our books are available to corporations, professional associations, pharmaceutical companies, health care organizations, and other qualifying groups. If you are interested in a custom book, including chapters from more than one of our titles, we can provide that service as well.

For details, please contact:
Special Sales Department, Springer Publishing Company, LLC
11 West 42nd Street, 15th Floor, New York, NY 10036–8002
Phone: 877–687-7476 or 212-431-4370; Fax: 212-941-7842
E-mail: sales@springerpub.com

Printed in the United States of America by Bradford & Bigelow.

I dedicate this book to Susan and Kathleen, my two brilliant sisters who provided me with encouragement, support, and advice throughout the process of writing this book; and to the loving memory of my parents, Erlyn and Dan.

Lynn C. Koch

I dedicate this book to Amy, my beautiful wife and one great love; to Rick, my mentor and lifelong friend; to my sons, Stuart, Doug, and Nathan, three fine young men who have filled their dad's heart with pride; to my parents, Shirley and Phil Sr., who instilled in me the importance of hard work and unconditional love; and to the loving memory of my grandparents, Beverly and Harry.

Phillip D. Rumrill, Jr.

Contents

Contributors

Kelly Cichy, PhD, School of Human Development and Family Studies, Kent State University, Kent, Ohio

Alexa Herrera, MEd, School of Lifespan Development and Educational Sciences, Kent State University, Kent, Ohio

Mykal Leslie, MEd, School of Lifespan Development and Educational Sciences, Kent State University, Kent, Ohio

Stephanie L. Lusk, PhD, CRC, Department of Rehabilitation, Human Resources and Communication Disorders, University of Arkansas, Fayetteville, Arkansas

Frank J. Sansosti, PhD, School of Lifespan Development and Educational Sciences, Kent State University, Kent, Ohio

Rachel Timblin, MEd, School of Lifespan Development and Educational Sciences, Kent State University, Kent, Ohio

Melissa D. Wilkins, PhD, CRC, Department of Rehabilitation, Human Resources and Communication Disorders, University of Arkansas, Fayetteville, Arkansas

Foreword

"Emerging disabilities" is a phrase replete with possible meanings and interpretations, all of which have real and substantial implications. Because I was curious how other people might interpret this phrase, in preparation for writing this Foreword I decided to conduct an informal survey among colleagues, students, and rehabilitation professionals. New to many, the phrase evoked a wide range of responses. Some suggested that it referred to rapidly rising prevalence rates among certain disabilities. Frequently identified by those with this view were neurodevelopmental disabilities due to changes in diagnostic criteria among other causes, and chronic conditions or illnesses associated with aging due to the aging of a large segment of the population. A similar response was that the phrase referred to the fact that disabilities previously restricted primarily to specific regions or groups were being seen in new groups, populations, and areas, or becoming more widespread generally. Others suggested that recent social, economic, political, regional, and global events, including war and terrorism, climate change, poverty, and large-scale refugee crises, were leading to conditions that promoted the development of diseases, injuries, or disabilities not previously known. One person took a different approach, and suggested that the term may refer to the emergence of disability within an individual, and the individual's ongoing response to the resulting changes.

The diversity of responses received to this informal survey demonstrated the range of novel disability issues that rehabilitation counselors and other rehabilitation and health professionals are thinking about and dealing with on a daily basis. The survey led to a number of interesting conversations about some things that we all know to be the case, but that we sometimes need to be reminded about, such as that disability does not exist in a vacuum, but arises and is constructed in the complex interactions between people and their social and physical environments; that because disability is a fluid and changing concept, our professional responses must also always be evolving and adapting; and finally, that knowledge and understanding are not static, but must always be advanced and revised.

In the endeavor to be responsive, relevant, effective, and true to our purpose, the rehabilitation counseling profession has never faced a more challenging time. This new century has been characterized by social, political, economic, and technological changes occurring with surpassing speed and consequence. In this period of rapid advancement it is becoming increasingly evident that it is no longer sufficient or effective to apply 20th-century knowledge, skills, and responses in a world in which disabilities are emerging from new situations and sources, having novel impacts, and creating new (or frequently not new) barriers to equality, participation, independence, dignity, and quality of life. New realities are forcing new perspectives, creating new exigencies, and creating new possibilities.

This book has arrived just in time. Koch and Rumrill and their coauthors have created a book that manages to address the complexities and urgencies involved in this diverse set of topics in a way that is comprehensive, thought provoking, informative, and authoritative. This book does several things. It opens our eyes to new realities. It informs our understanding and focuses our response. And it provides a framework for moving forward. It incorporates an ecological perspective throughout, with a thoughtful exploration in each chapter of the reciprocal relationships between the personal and the interpersonal, the social and the physical, and the local and the global. It does not neglect the individual, incorporating personal experiences and perspectives within each emerging context. Finally, it provides our profession a direction forward. In research, in education, and in practice, the authors provide insightful and responsive next steps for the future of our profession. If we are to achieve our purpose as rehabilitation professionals, we must actively strive to be informed and responsive, knowledgeable and effective, and to adapt our profession to the changing needs of those we serve. This book helps us to do this.

Malachy Bishop, PhD, CRC
Professor, Rehabilitation Counseling
Department of Early Childhood, Special Education, and
Rehabilitation Counseling
University of Kentucky

Preface

The nature and scope of disability are constantly changing. New and emerging disability patterns require a re-examination of how disability is defined, evaluated, and treated by rehabilitation counselors working across practice settings. The purpose of this book is to provide a better understanding of emerging disabilities and their impact on all areas of life and to explore implications for rehabilitation counseling practice, policy, and research. This book goes beyond categorizing disability by diagnosis and focusing primarily on diagnoses, symptoms, treatments, and prognoses to examining how factors such as contemporary trends in our global society, causes of emerging disabilities, and societal responses to individuals with these conditions shape the disability experience and impact the rehabilitation counseling process.

In Chapter 1, the authors define emerging disabilities and examine current societal trends that contribute to the onset and diagnoses of chronic illnesses and disabilities that are considered to be emerging in the United States. In this chapter, the authors also provide an overview of medical, psychosocial, and vocational aspects that distinguish emerging disabilities from traditional disabilities. The remainder of the book is divided into three sections. The first section includes four chapters on emerging disabilities with organic causes or unknown etiologies. Chapter 2 examines disabilities and chronic illnesses that are characterized by chronic pain. In Chapter 2, the authors define chronic pain; provide examples of emerging chronic pain conditions and populations in which these conditions are increasing in incidence and prevalence; and explore the medical, psychosocial, and vocational aspects of these conditions. The concluding sections of this chapter review implications for treatment and rehabilitation planning.

In Chapter 3, the authors discuss the increasing rates of two neurodevelopmental disorders—autism spectrum disorder and attention deficit hyperactivity disorder—that are being diagnosed in greater numbers in children. We review the literature that examines potential explanations for these increases; explore the medical, psychosocial, and vocational implications of these conditions; and conclude with recommendations for transition and rehabilitation planning.

Chapter 4 is devoted to understanding chronic illnesses and disabilities associated with aging as well as the varied and complex challenges confronted by aging Americans with disabilities. The authors examine the medical, psychosocial, and vocational aspects of several emerging disabilities that are linked to the aging process. Finally, we examine the role of rehabilitation counselors in providing advocacy, career counseling, case management, and other services to this emerging consumer population.

Chapter 5 examines emerging populations of individuals with psychiatric disabilities: youths and young adults, college students, individuals with psychiatric disabilities and co-occurring medical conditions, individuals with psychiatric disabilities and substance use disorders, and individuals with psychiatric disabilities who are involved in the corrections system. Psychiatric disabilities represent the largest consumer population that rehabilitation counselors serve in a variety of settings. Therefore, a large portion of this chapter is devoted to a review of established and emerging evidence-based practices in psychiatric rehabilitation and how rehabilitation counselors can incorporate these practices into the rehabilitation counseling process to address the medical, psychosocial, and vocational issues experienced by the populations discussed in this chapter.

The second content section of the book (Chapters 6 and 7) examines the role of natural and sociocultural environments in creating new patterns and types of disabling conditions. Chapter 6 focuses on both lifestyle factors and climate change and how these contribute to the onset and/or exacerbation of chronic illness and disability. The authors summarize the literature on the psychological and physical consequences of lifestyle and climate change and provide examples of emerging disabilities linked to these factors. We conclude the chapter with implications for rehabilitation assessment, planning, and placement.

Chapter 7 focuses on physical disabilities, chronic illnesses, and mental health conditions that result from violence. The authors consider the physical and psychological consequences of war, domestic violence, bullying, and workplace microaggressions and incivilities. We also review the literature on trauma-informed approaches to service delivery and the role that rehabilitation counselors play in facilitating recovery from the physical and psychological trauma of violence.

The final section of the book (Chapters 8 and 9) explores implications for rehabilitation practice, policy, and research to better respond to the unique concerns and needs of rehabilitation consumers with emerging disabilities. Chapter 8 compiles information on rehabilitation planning implications from the previous chapters into a holistic framework for reconceptualizing service delivery and facilitating a responsive rehabilitation process that empowers consumers with emerging disabilities to achieve their self-determined goals. The authors recommend emerging and evidence-based practices to include in each phase of the rehabilitation process. Specifically, we address rehabilitation counselor self-reflection and continuing education, outreach and eligibility determination, rehabilitation assessment, rehabilitation plan development and implementation, and rehabilitation services.

Chapter 9 proposes future research directions that will enable rehabilitation counselors to better understand and respond to the complex and unique needs of emerging disability populations. The authors also suggest research topics, designs, and procedures for (a) building upon our knowledge about the rehabilitation needs of emerging disability populations and (b) developing evidence-based practices to facilitate successful rehabilitation outcomes for individuals in these populations.

Taken in aggregate, the nine chapters in this book are intended to provide up-to-date information about the ever-changing disability experience in America. It is our hope that this text will stimulate thought and discussion among prospective and practicing rehabilitation counselors regarding consumers with emerging disabilities and their needs for services and supports. For readers wishing to adopt this book as part of undergraduate or graduate training curricula in the field of rehabilitation, we have developed PowerPoint presentations for class lectures, a sample syllabus, and a bank of test questions for student examinations. **Qualified instructors can request these ancillaries by e-mail: textbook@springer pub.com.**

We wish to thank Sheri Sussman and Mindy Chen of Springer Publishing Company for the opportunity to complete this work. We are indebted to our students, friends, and colleagues who contributed to the writing of this book: Kelly Cichy, Alexa Herrera, Mykal Leslie, Stephanie L. Lusk, Frank J. Sansosti, Rachel Timblin, and Melissa D. Wilkins. We also wish to commend readers for the career choice they have made to provide responsive and effective rehabilitation services in partnership with Americans with disabilities—this is definitely work worth doing! Finally, we wish to express our deep respect and admiration for people living with emerging disabilities, for the courage and strength they exhibit in their quest to lead full, productive, and meaningful lives.

Lynn C. Koch
Phillip D. Rumrill, Jr.

ONE

Introduction to Emerging Disabilities

CHAPTER OBJECTIVES

- *Define emerging disabilities*
- *Examine contemporary societal, global, environmental, and legislative trends that have contributed to the emergence of new causes and types of disabilities as well as the reemergence of disabilities and chronic illnesses in specific populations*
- *Explore medical, psychosocial, and vocational implications of emerging disabilities that distinguish them from traditional disabilities*
- *Examine demographic characteristics of individuals who are most vulnerable to acquiring emerging disabilities*

The spectrum of causes, types, patterns, and outcomes of disability is constantly in flux. Because of the changing demographics of disability populations, stakeholders in rehabilitation counseling are continuously challenged to revise their answers to the question *"How is disability defined?"* In 2014, an estimated 12.6% of Americans had a disability (Krause, 2015), and the number is increasing every year. Disability is gradually becoming viewed as a natural part of the human condition rather than as pathology, a deficit, or an abnormality. Despite these positive developments in the conceptualization of disability, a universal definition of disability does not exist, and disabling conditions that are on the rise in the 21st century are often excluded from definitions and positive conceptualizations of disability. These conditions often have unknown etiologies, are medically debated, are less clearly defined by law and public policy, have higher rates of incidence in already marginalized populations, and/or are underestimated in terms of the severity of their symptoms and the substantial impact of these symptoms on individuals' ability to actively participate in meaningful life activities (Fox & Kim, 2004; Koch, Conyers, & Rumrill, 2012; Nary, White, Budde, & Vo, 2004).

Not only are these emerging disabling conditions increasing in number, but individuals with disabilities and chronic illnesses that defy traditional definitions of disability represent a vastly underserved rehabilitation population who are often in dire need of rehabilitation counseling services. Individuals with emerging disabilities stand to benefit from the same rehabilitation services as those with traditional disabilities (i.e., those that are medically recognized and well understood by rehabilitation, medical, and health care professionals; Fox & Kim, 2004; Koch et al., 2012). However, they often experience a multitude of added barriers to accessing and benefiting from rehabilitation services.

The meaning of disability is mutable and relative to context (Ribet, 2011), and to stay abreast of the constantly changing constellation of disabling conditions, rehabilitation counselors must engage in a process of lifelong learning. If future and current rehabilitation counselors are to successfully partner with consumers with emerging disabilities to address the multitude of barriers these individuals often encounter in living their lives as they choose, they must also be cognizant of external factors associated with the onset, diagnosis, treatment, experience, and consequence of these conditions (Fox & Kim, 2004; Koch et al., 2012). This increased understanding of both emergent developments in causes and types of disabilities and the constantly changing external forces that inhibit or promote participation in rehabilitation programming will enable rehabilitation counselors to then make necessary changes to policies and practices that currently exclude people with emerging disabilities from receiving services and/or that fail to effectively respond to their unique rehabilitation needs.

DEFINING EMERGING DISABILITIES

Emerging disabilities result from diseases or health conditions that are either (a) recently recognized and increasing in prevalence in a population (e.g., chronic Lyme disease, multiple chemical sensitivity [MCS], fibromyalgia, polytrauma) *or* (b) established conditions that are increasing in prevalence in a population or in specific segments of a population (e.g., asthma, autism, type 2 diabetes; Fujiura, 2001). Nary et al. (2004) observed that people with emerging disabilities exhibit less apparent physical disability, even though their conditions can be severe and negatively impact multiple functional domains. They also observed that emerging disabilities are frequently less clearly defined by law and public policy.

Ribet (2011, p. 161) expanded on this definition, defining emergent disability as "a pattern of burgeoning mental and physical conditions which correlates, often strongly, with poverty and various forms of social and political insubordination." In Ribet's definition, emergent disabilities are linked to social inequities based on demographic characteristics of individuals such as race, ethnicity, gender, sexual orientation, gender identity, age, and socioeconomic status as well as the simultaneous interaction of these characteristics. In this definition, emerging disabilities would not be present or as severe if they did not occur in a context of systemic inequities and social injustices resulting from violence, inequitable access to health care, poor nutrition, inadequate housing, employment discrimination, labor exploitation, exposure to environmental hazards, institutionalization, and incarceration. Fox and Kim (2004) also distinguished emerging disabilities from traditional disabilities in terms of social and environmental factors that contribute to their onset, presentation, severity, and consequences. They noted that, in comparison to people with traditional disabilities, people with emerging disabilities face far greater barriers to full inclusion in society; therefore, consideration of social and environmental determinants of disability such as systemic inequities and social injustices is more important than ever before.

In understanding emerging disability populations, it is also important for readers to be familiar with the term *medically unexplained symptoms*. Because many individuals with emerging disabilities experience symptoms with no detectable pathological basis, they must often consult multiple medical specialists who are perplexed by their symptoms and unable to provide them with a definitive medical diagnosis (Koch et al., 2012). In such cases, physicians may conclude that these individuals have medically unexplained symptoms. Medically unexplained symptoms are those "for which conventional biomedical explanation could not be found on routine examination or investigations" (Nimnuan, Hotopf, & Wessely, 2001, p. 366). In a study conducted by Nimnuan et al. (2001) at two general hospitals in southeast London, the researchers found that medically unexplained symptoms were seen across medical specializations and represented the most frequent diagnosis in some of these specializations. More recently, researchers have found that between one third and two thirds of patients seen in general medical clinics do not receive a medical explanation or diagnosis from their treating physicians for their symptoms (Edwards, Stern, Clarke, Ivbijaro, & Kansey, 2010). The most commonly reported medically unexplained symptoms with unknown pathologies are fatigue, pain, heart palpitations, dizziness, and nausea. In some cases, symptoms may be mild and transient, whereas in other cases they are severe, ongoing, and debilitating.

Medically unexplained symptoms challenge the conventional biomedical model of disease that fails to acknowledge the complexity of biopsychosocial factors in the onset and presentation of unexplained symptoms. The biopsychosocial model recognizes that "illness is not an entity independent of social, psychological, and behavioral influences" (Day, Thorn, & Burns, 2012, p. 115). This reconceptualization of illness has led some researchers in the medical sciences to question whether the problem of medically unexplained symptoms is a limitation inherent in traditional medicine, which fails to incorporate a biopsychosocial approach into diagnostics and treatment. It has even been suggested that physicians' inability to diagnose symptoms leads to blaming patients and invalidating their illness experiences rather than examining shortcomings inherent in the biomedical approach to health care (Raymond & Brown, 2000; Van Houdenhove & Luyten, 2004). As McClellan (2012, p. 649) noted:

> Just because scientists don't understand the cause of a disease doesn't mean that it doesn't exist. Back when patient-reported symptoms were all doctors had to go on, MS was known as a "faker's disease." Then magnetic resonance imaging was invented, and doctors could suddenly see detailed high resolution images of the brain lesions that explained the symptoms patients complained about.

Not receiving a diagnosis and explanation of the causes of one's symptoms, which is more likely to happen if the patient is *not* treated from a biopsychosocial framework, can make the symptoms even more distressing for the individual who is experiencing them and can result in adverse psychosocial and functional consequences (Koch et al., 2012). Furthermore, the lack of a definitive medical diagnosis can prevent individuals from qualifying for specific civil rights protections, disability entitlements, and rehabilitation services. Indeed, being told that one's symptoms are medically unexplained or psychosomatic is a far too common experience for individuals with emerging disabilities. Although these individuals experience unexplained symptoms that are not readily diagnosed, these symptoms can cause substantial disruption to their lives and result in numerous functional limitations. In research studies investigating the psychosocial impact of living with chronic illnesses and disabilities that cannot be medically explained or are medically debated, common themes include uncertainty and anxiety, feelings of hopelessness associated with unexplained and continuing declines in individuals' health and functional capabilities, frustration with medical providers' inability to provide a diagnosis, increased stress associated with having their symptoms dismissed and invalidated by physicians and others, exacerbation of symptoms when misdiagnosed and treated for disorders they do not have, and feelings of being misunderstood and socially isolated (Koch et al., 2012).

In addition to recently recognized conditions, established conditions that are growing in incidence and conditions that are difficult to diagnose, another emerging disability population consists of individuals with rare diseases or disorders. The National Organization for Rare Disorders (NORD, 2016) defines a rare disorder as one that affects fewer than 5,000 people in the United States. According to NORD, approximately 7,000 diseases in the United States are considered to be rare disorders. Individuals with these conditions are largely underserved by both health care and rehabilitation systems, in part due to their small numbers and in part due to their marginalized status (Koch et al., 2012). Rare disorders are extremely difficult to diagnose, and specialists and diagnosticians who are knowledgeable about these low-incidence conditions are often limited in number. Even after diagnoses are confirmed, individuals with rare disorders find it difficult to find qualified health care professionals to treat and help them manage their conditions. They also differ from individuals with other disabilities in that they have fewer available resources to cope with their conditions, and, because of the low incidence of rare disorders, individuals with these disorders are not a potent political group (Koch et al., 2012). Finally, because research on rare disorders has primarily focused on the etiology of these conditions and finding cures, there is very limited research on topics such as the quality of life of people dealing with particular rare conditions, their employment outcomes, and rehabilitation interventions that are beneficial to these individuals.

When considering emerging disability populations, we must also take into account the emerging causes of disability (e.g., violence, lifestyle factors, climate change). These causal factors intersect with disability, demographic characteristics of the individual, and social inequities to create unique challenges that must be addressed in rehabilitation plans if individuals with emerging disabilities are to achieve their rehabilitation goals. Unfortunately, rehabilitation interventions often fail to adequately address social and environmental determinants of disability. To remediate this problem, Fox and Kim (2004, p. 325) suggested that "understanding predisposing and sustaining risk factors of persons with emerging disabilities is necessary before system-wide...interventions can be developed."

Finally, in examining emerging disability populations throughout this text-book, we consider populations that are increasingly seeking services from rehabilitation counselors across rehabilitation settings as well as within specific settings. For example, rehabilitation counselors working in vocational settings can anticipate serving growing numbers of older Americans with disabilities as the 77 million members of the baby boom generation continue to age (Wickert, Dresden, & Rumrill, 2013). Yet, rehabilitation counselors have not traditionally provided services to many older individuals in these settings. Furthermore, it has been estimated that 50,000 youths with autism reach adulthood each year (Shattuck et al., 2012), and autism advocates have questioned whether adult service providers are prepared to address the housing, independent living, educational, and employment needs of this burgeoning population of adults with disabilities.

It has also been observed that rehabilitation counselors working across settings are serving growing numbers of individuals with serious mental illness (SMI). For example, McReynolds and Garske (2003) reported that psychiatric disability represented the second most frequently served disability population by the state–federal vocational rehabilitation (VR) program. Rosenthal, Dalton, and Gervey (2007) found that individuals with psychiatric disabilities represented 32.2% of the sample in the Rehabilitation Services Administration's 2001 Case Service Report, making them the largest disability group served during that fiscal year. Additionally, growing numbers of individuals with SMI are attending American colleges and universities (Armstrong & Young, 2015; Byrd & McKinney, 2012). Students with these disabling conditions present unique challenges to post-secondary institutions that are not adequately prepared to provide the necessary support needed for them to achieve their educational goals.

CONTEMPORARY TRENDS LINKED TO EMERGING DISABILITIES

Life in the 21st century is marked by constant change, and contemporary rehabilitation counselors, administrators, educators, policy makers, and researchers must be prepared to proactively respond to these changes. In particular, they must be attentive to the complex rehabilitation needs of emerging disability populations. Kim and Fox (2004) specified trends in the 21st century that have been tied to the "changing pattern of disability" (p. 92) such as violence and abuse, aging, substance abuse and stress, inadequate prenatal care, low birth weight, adolescent pregnancy and child bearing, poor nutrition, environmental hazards, chronic disease, injuries, and childhood abuse or neglect. Koch et al. (2012) discussed trends associated with emerging disabilities such as advances in medical technology, the aging American population, global warming and associated climate changes, violence, poverty, and disability legislation that have led to new patterns of disability and chronic illness. Kim and Fox (2004) and Koch et al. (2012) noted that understanding the roles of sociological, demographic, economic, and other environmental factors in causing and defining newly recognized chronic illnesses and disabilities is more important than ever before. This understanding is a prerequisite to making appropriate adaptations to policies and practices that exclude people with emerging disabilities from receiving services or fail to respond to their unique rehabilitation needs. In the following paragraphs, we examine these and other social and environmental trends that have contributed to the development of emerging patterns and types of disabilities including (a) advances in medicine and assistive technology (AT), (b) globalization, (c) climate change, (d) poverty, (e) violence and trauma, (f) the aging American populace, and (g) disability legislation.

Advances in Medicine and Assistive Technology

Medical advances have led to earlier detection and treatment of life-threatening injuries, diseases, and chronic illnesses, thus increasing the life span of individuals living with these conditions. Advances in emergency medicine have dramatically increased survival rates for individuals with severe, and even catastrophic, injuries. For example, Frain, Lee, Roland, and Tschopp (2012) noted that personnel in current U.S. military operations have acquired disabilities at a rate greater than that of any war since the 1950s, and the authors attributed this outcome to advancements in body armor, the proximity of medical care, and medical innovations that have enabled over 90% of those injured in war to survive their injuries.

Advances in biomedical imaging and laboratory technology have resulted in reduced rates of childhood mortality and increased precision in diagnosing and treating disease in a targeted manner (Falvo, 2014). Likewise, medical advances in cancer diagnostics and treatment have prolonged the lives of cancer survivors to such a degree that cancer, once viewed and treated as a terminal illness, is now considered a chronic illness. Correspondingly, ongoing advances in genome-based (i.e., an organism's complete set of DNA) research have made it possible for scientists and clinicians to gain a better understanding of how genetic factors interact with environmental factors in the onset of diseases such as cancer, diabetes, and cardiovascular disease (National Human Genome Research Institute, 2015). These advances have led to improved screening and diagnostic testing as well as the implementation of more effective, evidence-based treatment approaches tailored to the individual's unique genomic makeup. As a result of these advances, it is anticipated that more individuals will receive earlier diagnosis and treatment for chronic conditions that currently result in long-term disability.

Pharmacological advances have led to more effective treatment of disabling symptoms, fewer side effects of medications, and subsequent improvements in the functional capabilities of individuals with severe disabilities. For example, advances in psychopharmacology have resulted in the development of psychotropic medications that better treat severe and disruptive psychiatric symptoms with fewer side effects. Partially because of these psychopharmacological advances, individuals with SMI are now able to better manage debilitating symptoms that would otherwise prevent them from participating in meaningful life activities, living independently in their communities, participating in postsecondary education, realizing their self-determined recovery and employment goals, and enjoying a high quality of life (Eudaly, 2002; Hartley, 2013; Kiuhara & Huefner, 2008; Megivern, Pellerito, & Mowbray, 2003). As another example, pharmacological treatment of HIV has now resulted in increased life spans for individuals with HIV; because of these advances, the view of HIV as a terminal illness has been changed to that of a chronic illness that can be medically managed (Conyers, 2004a, 2004b).

The field of assistive technology (AT) has, likewise, seen dramatic advances over the past several decades. In fact, Field and Jette (2007) reported that 21,000 assistive devices were available in comparison to 6,000 devices in the early 1980s. Research and development in this area continues at an unprecedented rate, and AT is becoming increasingly customized and portable. Examples of currently available technologies, as well as some that are still in development, include voice recognition software, communication devices based on tracking of individual eye movement, robotic exoskeletons that enable individuals with spinal cord injuries to walk, joy sticks to provide better control of power-assisted wheelchairs, stair climbing wheelchairs, power-assisted propulsion for manual wheelchairs to lower energy expansion and prevent secondary injuries, devices to remotely manage and operate home and office appliances, and prosthetic devices that respond to neural impulses. These advances in medicine and AT have resulted in increased life expectancies, improved functional abilities, and greater opportunities for individuals with disabilities and chronic health conditions to participate in meaningful life activities.

Globalization

Globalization, "the global scale, interconnectedness, and economic intensity of human activity" (McMichael, 2013, p. 1335), has resulted in the worldwide expansion of health risks as well as the potential for permanent disability and chronic illness to be incurred from these health risks. For example, economic, social, demographic, and environmental changes have occurred on a global scale and are linked to increases in the prevalence of obesity; the emergence of infectious diseases; increased rates of cigarette smoking, particularly for populations of people living in poverty; and ongoing and expanding health care disparities. According to Giovanni (2001) many of these health risks are rooted in the globalization of trade, travel, and exchange of information.

The global marketing of brand name beverages and fast foods has contributed to the worldwide epidemic of obesity (Pang & Guindon, 2004). Across the world, traditional foods are being replaced by foods that are high in fat and calories. Relatedly, many industrialized nations have banned the advertising of cigarettes, and tobacco companies are targeting people in poorer countries in their advertising campaigns. Internationally, the high rate of smoking in children and adolescents is a major health concern. Global marketing has also led to higher alcohol consumption, particularly in poorer countries and among younger individuals. These trends have contributed to international increases in rates of conditions such as obesity, diabetes, cardiovascular disease, and cancer. The travel industry has also been globalized, and increasing numbers of individuals are traveling internationally. Increases in global travel have resulted in the spread of communicable diseases into vulnerable, nonimmune populations through travel of infected humans. Indeed, the media has devoted substantial coverage to recent examples of diseases that have spread as a result of international travel including Ebola virus disease, the H5N1 strain of bird flu, and severe acute respiratory syndrome (SARS).

The globalization of ideas and information from sources such as the Internet, satellite television, and social media has now made medical information readily and easily accessible to everyone (Pang & Guindon, 2004). This trend has shaped the widening constellation of disability. With readily available medical information, more and more people are self-diagnosing in the absence of medical validation. Others may self-diagnose, identify courses of treatment, and, with this information in hand, seek out consultation from specialists to confirm their self-diagnoses. Easy access to medical information has contributed to an increasing demand for changes in the roles of physicians and patients. Growing numbers of patients are no longer willing to be passive recipients of medical diagnoses and treatments from the "all-knowing" physician. Now, they are taking more active roles in determining their diagnoses and challenging their providers regarding the best approaches to treatment based on what they have learned by conducting research on the Internet. However, concerns arise regarding unreliable and inaccurate health information that is proliferated through the Internet. In addition to being misleading, this information can also be harmful.

Relatedly, the proliferation of information on the Internet from consumer self-advocacy organizations has reduced some of the stigma associated with disability and chronic illness, thus reducing internalized stigma and increasing the likelihood that individuals with stigmatized conditions will more openly disclose their diagnoses to significant others, disability service providers, and employers. For example, the dramatic increase in the numbers of college and university students who are self-identifying as individuals with psychiatric disabilities is partially attributed to the reduced stigma associated with mental illness that has occurred as a result of powerful antistigma media campaigns that have been launched by consumer advocacy organizations (Eudaly, 2002; Hartley, 2013; Kiuhara & Huefner, 2008; Megivern et al., 2003). Likewise, the proliferation of self-advocacy organizations for individuals with conditions such as chronic Lyme disease, fibromyalgia, and MCS has resulted in increased rates of self-diagnoses in the absence of diagnoses from medical professionals. Individuals with these conditions may now participate in online support groups and chat rooms where they can acquire medical advice from others who have the same condition. Again, the accuracy of information they receive is an issue of concern. This trend challenges rehabilitation and disability agencies and programs for which eligibility criteria are premised on diagnoses from qualified medical professionals. The question arises as to how to respond to growing numbers of individuals who are anticipated to apply for services on the basis of a self-diagnosis. A related concern is how to respond to individuals who do not agree with medical diagnoses and who present with a self-diagnosis that differs from that provided by a medical specialist.

Climate Change

As a result of climate change, we are experiencing dramatic increases in the number and severity of extreme weather events and natural disasters. Although climate change is still debated in the media, research evidence supports that global warming has led to changes in the intensity, duration, and geographical extent of weather events such as heat waves, wildfires, flooding, thunderstorms, ice storms, blizzards, hurricanes, high winds, and tornadoes (Interagency Working Group on Climate Change and Human Health, 2010). These events can exacerbate preexisting chronic health conditions and increase the onset of chronic illnesses such as asthma, respiratory and airway diseases, cancer, and mental health conditions in otherwise healthy individuals. Although most survivors are able to adapt to the consequences of natural disasters resulting from climate change, these can leave others with permanent physical injuries, chronic illnesses, and stress-related mental disorders. Physical injuries (e.g., traumatic brain injuries, fractures, burns, amputations) acquired during these events may result in permanent disability. Many survivors of these events have experienced substantial losses (e.g., destroyed homes; death of family, friends, and pets; destruction of community infrastructure). Reactions to these losses can range from mild stress responses to chronic stress and mental health disorders (Hess, Malilay, & Parkinson, 2008). Individuals who lack the resources to rebuild their lives are especially vulnerable to the negative health consequences of extreme weather events.

Warmer air and ocean temperatures, increased rainfall, and more frequent droughts result in the accumulation of greenhouse gases such as carbon dioxide and methane in the atmosphere (U.S. Environmental Protection Agency [EPA], 2014). The degraded air quality that has resulted from greenhouse gas emissions can exacerbate preexisting conditions such as asthma and other respiratory diseases as well as contribute to the onset of these conditions in otherwise healthy individuals. Also of note when considering environmental causes of chronic illness and disability is the daunting myriad of chemicals to which individuals are exposed on a daily basis in their homes, work settings, and public spaces. Even though most individuals are able to tolerate low-level exposure to these chemicals, others develop severe and ongoing physical reactions that can impede their functioning in multiple domains. Consequently, rehabilitation counselors are serving growing numbers of individuals with disabilities such as asthma and MCS that are triggered by exposure to air pollution and environmental toxins and pollutants such as pesticides, disinfectants, cleaning products, perfumes, cigarette smoke, paint, exhaust fumes, and formaldehyde in home and office furnishings (Gibson, 2006; Gibson, Cheavens, & Warren, 1996; Gibson, Sledd, McEnroe, & Vos, 2011; Koch & Eaton, 2005; Koch, Vierstra, & Penix, 2006; Lamielle, 2003).

Poverty

More than 50 years have passed since President Lyndon Johnson's War on Poverty began, and 15% of Americans still live below the poverty line (Rector & Sheffield, 2014). Rehabilitation research has firmly established that disability results in poverty, with indicators that from one in three to one in five people with disabilities live in poverty. More recently, investigators are exploring the role of poverty as a predisposing factor in the onset of disability and chronic illness. Links have been found between poverty and a variety of chronic illnesses and disabilities (e.g., asthma, diabetes, HIV/AIDS, heart disease; Cha et al., 2015). Individuals living in poverty are also more likely to experience the negative health consequences of climate change and severe weather events (Balbus & Malina, 2009). Of critical concern is the dramatic increase in the rate of children with chronic illnesses, with the majority of this increase occurring in children living in poverty (Perrin, Bloom, & Gortmaker, 2007). Factors associated with poverty that put poor individuals at risk for developing chronic illnesses and disabilities include unsafe housing, health-endangering employment, malnutrition, and poor access to health care and education. Likewise, as disparities in health, health care, and rehabilitation have been illuminated, rehabilitation counselors and researchers are being called upon to examine social justice issues in the rehabilitation process, strategies for implementing rehabilitation services to better serve those most at risk of experiencing social inequities, and ways to develop career trajectories that move individuals out of poverty and into the middle class (e.g., Alston, Harley, & Middleton, 2006; Ratts, Singh, Butler, Nassar-McMillan, & McCullough, 2016; Tarvydas, Vazquez-Ramos, & Estrada-Hernandez, 2015).

Violence and Trauma

Psychological and physical trauma from warfare, violent crime, intimate partner violence, and youth violence can result in permanent physical, cognitive, and psychiatric disabilities. In 2013, three million people, ages 12 years or older, experienced at least one violent victimization (e.g., rape or sexual assault, robbery, aggravated assault, simple assault; Truman & Langton, 2014; U.S. Department of Justice, 2014). Assaults and gun violence can result in injuries to tissue, internal organs, and bones. Assaults are one of the major causes of spinal cord injuries and traumatic brain injuries. Violence is also linked to psychiatric disabilities such as depression, anxiety, and posttraumatic stress disorder (PTSD). Not only is violence a cause of disabilities, but individuals with disabilities are at an increased risk of being victimized by violence (Hughes et al., 2012). Of major concern in the 21st century are the physical and psychological effects of long-term exposure to violence and trauma. This exposure leads to chronic activation of the stress response system and increases the likelihood of developing diseases of the cardiovascular, immune, gastrointestinal, neurohormonal, and musculoskeletal systems (D'Andrea, Sharma, Zelechoski, & Spinazzola, 2011).

As many as 100,000 veterans living in the United States have sustained injuries and permanent disabilities from fighting in U.S. wars between 2001 and 2011 (Frain et al., 2012). Many of these disabilities are acquired from blast-related injuries. As previously stated, approximately 90% of military personnel who acquire these injuries survive, a rate that far surpasses that of survival rates from previous wars. However, these service members must often contend with multiple, severe disabilities and functional limitations. Foremost among these disabilities are polytrauma, traumatic brain injuries, PTSD, and amputations. Moreover, veterans often face significant challenges and are provided with inadequate supports in adapting to civilian life, the consequences of which too often include unemployment, poverty, homelessness, and substance use disorders.

Domestic and intimate partner violence can result in permanent disability from injuries and mental health conditions. Ongoing violence can result in cumulative stress that has been linked to a variety of chronic illnesses including fibromyalgia, irritable bowel syndrome, central nervous system disorders, heart or circulatory conditions, and disorders of the endocrine and immune systems (Briere, Kaltman, & Green, 2008; Crofford, 2007; van der Kolk, 2003). Women with preexisting disabilities may be at risk of experiencing domestic violence because of disability-related factors such as mobility and reliance on others for assistance with activities of daily living (ADLs; Nosek, Hughes, Taylor, & Taylor, 2006) and may sustain secondary conditions or complications of their primary conditions as a result of violent acts.

Peer victimization of school-aged children has received increasing attention in both research and the popular media. The lack of early prevention and intervention for those who have been victimized as children as well as bullies and bully-victims can lead to permanent disabilities and occupational difficulties in adulthood (Faith, Malcolm, & Newgent, 2008; Kumpulainen, 2008). Cyberbullying, a modern-day form of peer victimization, can lead to depression, anxiety disorders, and substance use disorders that often persist into adulthood (Paterson, 2011; Reed, Cooper, Nugent, & Russell, 2016). Children with disabilities are at increased risk of peer victimization, which can lead to secondary mental health conditions such as depression, anxiety, and substance use disorders if early intervention is not provided to cease the victimization of these children (Blake, Lund, Zhou, Kwok, & Benz, 2012; U.S. Department of Education Office for Civil Rights, 2014).

Even chronic exposure to insidious, low-level forms of aggression such as workplace incivility and gender- or racially based microaggressions can have negative effects on physical and mental health. These effects can include increased psychological distress, greater physical health complaints, and higher levels of anxiety and depression (Cortina, Magley, Williams, & Langhout, 2001; Lim, Cortina, & Magley, 2008). Workplace bullying, even when it is subtle, can contribute to stress-related illnesses (Reio & Ghosh, 2009). Additionally, the negative effects of interpersonal mistreatment in the workplace can extend to those who are not direct targets of the mistreatment. Dealing with these daily stressors can have an even more significant impact on physical and mental health than major life stressors (Cortina et al., 2001).

The Aging Populace

Older adults represent a diverse and rapidly growing segment of the U.S. population (Wickert et al., 2013). Americans are experiencing longer life expectancies, and the senior population is larger than it has ever been in history. The number of Americans older than 65 years will double in the next 30 years—and the number of Americans older than 90 years will more than quadruple between 1980 and 2030 (Wickert et al., 2013). Older adults have also been reported to represent over 40% of the American labor force (Copeland, 2014). As a result of the recent economic recession, retirement is no longer an option for many older adults because they do not have the financial resources and benefits to continually support themselves and their families. They must continue to work in order to access income, employment-based health insurance, and 401(k) retirement contributions. In addition to the need for continued employment, older adults must often cope with the added stress of developing functional limitations that interfere with daily living, employment, and overall quality of life. Among adults aged 65 years and older, estimates indicate that as many as 80% have at least one chronic health condition and approximately 60% have two or more chronic health conditions (Wickert et al., 2013). Among the most common of these conditions are vision and hearing loss, arthritis, orthopedic impairments, diabetes, and heart and lung disease. Older adults face other adjustment issues in addition to the onset of chronic illness or disability. These include financial instability, age discrimination, long-term care concerns, caring for grandchildren, and victimization and abuse (Dixon, Richard, & Rollins, 2003; Wickert et al., 2013). These psychosocial challenges can predispose some older adults, especially those who lack the social supports and coping resources to manage these challenges, to mental health conditions such as anxiety, depression, and substance use disorders.

People born with disabilities and those who acquired disabilities in early to middle life are also living longer (Smart, 2009). However, they often experience the effects of aging earlier (in their 40s and 50s) than those without disabilities. In addition, they are likely to develop secondary conditions and long-term complications of treatments (e.g., chemotherapy, radiation, surgeries, medications) for their primary conditions. Common secondary conditions include depression, arthritis, cardiovascular disease, pain, pressure ulcers, fatigue, contractures, spasticity, urinary tract infections, and mobility impairments (Gill, Murphy, Zechner, Swarbick, & Spagnolo, 2009). As another example, individuals with SMI are prone to developing metabolic syndrome as they age (Gill et al., 2009; Newcomer, 2007).

Disability Legislation

The enactment of the 2014 Workforce Innovation and Opportunity Act (WIOA) and the 2008 Americans with Disabilities Act Amendments Act (ADAAA) has expanded definitions of disability to more broadly encompass new patterns and types of disabling conditions, thereby expanding access to VR services (in the case of the WIOA) and civil rights protections (in the case of the ADAAA) for Americans with disabilities (Rubin, Roessler, & Rumrill, 2016). These legislative initiatives are the latest in a long line of laws designed to extend VR services and other protections to people with a wide range of disabling conditions. In 1918, the Soldiers Rehabilitation Act called for the allocation of funding for VR programs for veterans with disabilities, and it was followed by the Civilian Vocational Rehabilitation Act of 1920, which expanded VR services to civilians with physical disabilities. These acts have been followed by the Rehabilitation Act and amendments that have further expanded definitions of disability to include sensory disabilities, developmental disabilities, psychiatric disabilities, and behavioral disorders (Rubin et al., 2016). The Rehabilitation Act Amendments of 1992 emphasized the need to prioritize services to individuals with the most severe disabilities and to address the underrepresentation of racial and ethnic minority groups in state VR programs, thus increasing the numbers of individuals who may otherwise be disqualified for services or fail to achieve competitive employment outcomes.

The WIOA amended the Rehabilitation Act in several important ways, perhaps the most timely being a strengthened emphasis on transition from public schools to adult life for youth with disabilities, improved linkages between state VR agencies and public school special education programs, and an absolute priority on competitive employment in integrated community settings as the preferred placement modality for people with significant disabilities (Rubin et al., 2016). In fact, the WIOA required that most long-term sheltered workshops close their doors by 2016, which required employers, rehabilitation professionals, and people with intellectual and developmental disabilities and their families to reconceptualize what community inclusion really means in 21st-century America. The increased emphasis on transition to integrated adult community settings sets an important agenda for the growing numbers of public school children who are dealing with poverty and lifestyle-related disabling conditions such as asthma, allergies, MCS, and diabetes, as well as for the exponentially increasing number of children who are diagnosed with autism and other neurodevelopmental disorders.

Perhaps the statute that has the most wide-ranging implications for how disability is conceptualized is the Americans with Disabilities Act (ADA) of 1990, coupled with its 2008 amendments through the ADAAA (Rubin et al., 2016). The original ADA provided a three-pronged definition of a qualified person with a disability that includes: (a) a physical or mental impairment that substantially limits one or more major life activities; (b) a record of such an impairment, even in the absence of a current disability; and (c) being regarded as having such impairment even if the individual has no disability. Title I of the ADA afforded protections in the area of employment by prohibiting employers from discriminating against qualified individuals with disabilities and requiring employers to provide reasonable accommodations to qualified individuals unless these cause an undue hardship.

Unfortunately, the original intent and scope of coverage of the ADA was not realized by the enactment of this legislation. In fact, research conducted by investigators in the National Equal Employment Opportunity Commission (EEOC) ADA Research Project found that, in ADA Title I allegations closed by the EEOC between July 26, 1992 and December 31, 2008, merit resolutions favoring the charging party were found in only 22% of all closures (McMahon, 2012). Because various Supreme Court decisions and EEOC interpretations of the ADA narrowed Congress' original intention when crafting the ADA, the 2008 ADAAA was implemented on January 1, 2009 to strengthen the original legislation by broadening its coverage (Burke, Friedl, & Rigler, 2010). The ADAAA includes several major changes that redefine the concept of disability and broaden coverage to individuals who were not protected under the original act. First, the ADAAA includes a statement indicating that "the courts construe the definition of disability in favor of the broadest coverage of individuals permitted by the Act, consistent with the findings and purpose of the ADA" (Burke et al., 2010, p. 67). Second, the ADAAA changed the definition of major life activities to include normal cell growth, endocrinological functioning, neurological functioning, and immune functioning, to name just a few areas, and it listed 13 conditions that are presumptively considered to substantially limit major life activities. The latter provision means that people with presumptively limiting conditions such as blindness, multiple sclerosis, SMI, cancer, diabetes, epilepsy, intellectual disabilities, deafness, spinal cord injuries, and traumatic brain injuries are now automatically considered people with disabilities under the law. Third, whereas mitigating measures (e.g., medications, hearing aids, prosthetics) were used in some court cases under the original ADA to disqualify plaintiffs as people with disabilities, the ADAAA now mandates that these mitigating measures can no longer be considered in determining disability. Finally, episodic and/or temporary conditions were not explicitly covered in the original ADA, but they are now covered in the ADAAA.

The Affordable Care Act (ACA) is also likely to have an impact on the health and functioning of people with emerging disabilities (Rubin et al., 2016; Wickert et al., 2013). The ACA's emphasis on prevention and early intervention is especially important for the growing numbers of Americans who are dealing with chronic health conditions; it may even reduce the numbers of people who are diagnosed with those conditions over time. The removal of annual and lifetime "caps" on health care coverage will help millions of people with severe and catastrophic disabilities continue to receive treatment over the course of their lifetimes, and the ACA's complete prohibition of preexisting condition exclusions ensures that people with chronic health conditions and disabilities can transfer from one employer-based group health insurance plan to another without experiencing an interruption in coverage.

MEDICAL, PSYCHOSOCIAL, AND VOCATIONAL CHARACTERISTICS OF EMERGING DISABILITIES

Although individuals with emerging disabilities experience many of the same barriers to independent living, community integration, education, and employment as individuals with traditional disabilities, they often encounter additional barriers that must be ameliorated if successful rehabilitation outcomes are to be achieved. Furthermore, although individuals with emerging disabilities have the same potential as those with traditional disabilities to achieve successful rehabilitation outcomes, they represent an underserved rehabilitation population. Their underrepresentation can be attributed to a variety of factors including medical controversies regarding the legitimacy of their conditions, lack of awareness on the part of service providers regarding the significance and severity of their disabling conditions, program eligibility criteria that exclude them from receiving rehabilitation services, and failure of individuals with emerging disabilities to apply for services because they do not consider themselves as having disabilities or they are unaware of the availability of rehabilitation services in their communities (Koch et al., 2012). Also noteworthy is the intersectionality of emerging disabilities with race, ethnicity, gender, age, and socioeconomic status. Marginalized populations that have traditionally been underserved by state VR agencies are also overrepresented in emerging disability populations (Fox & Kim, 2004).

Researchers from fields such as rehabilitation, disability studies, health psychology, and nursing (e.g., Arnold et al., 2008; Fox & Kim, 2004; Gibson et al., 2011; Koch et al., 2006; Raymond & Brown, 2000) have investigated the unique psychosocial and vocational implications of living with an emerging disability. Key themes found across samples of individuals with emerging disabilities include: (a) the ongoing struggle of managing a multitude of chronic symptoms and/or functional limitations that substantially impact their quality of life; (b) the added challenge of coping with comorbid medical or mental health conditions; (c) the psychological stress arising from diagnostic uncertainties and medical invalidation of their symptoms; (d) the negative physical and emotional impact of societal stigma and lack of understanding and support from significant others; and (e) the multitude of internal and external barriers to seeking, securing, and maintaining employment. The consequences of these experiences include uncertainty and anxiety; feelings of hopelessness associated with a continuing decline in one's health and functioning without medical explanation; increased stress and feelings of isolation associated with having their symptoms disbelieved or invalidated by others; feelings of rejection and loneliness as a result of the lack of emotional support from significant others who question the validity of their symptoms; and exacerbation of symptoms when undiagnosed or misdiagnosed (Koch et al., 2012). For newly recognized conditions, relatively low prevalence estimates are reported due to lack of universal case definitions, further instilling doubt and disbelief among medical and health care providers, significant others, and diagnosed individuals themselves about the legitimacy of these conditions (Fujiura, 2001). Likewise, the rates of established conditions may be grossly underestimated because of the stigma of self-reporting or the extended length of time that many individuals must live with these conditions before accurate diagnoses and effective treatment are provided.

Multitude, Chronicity, and Severity of Symptoms

Emerging disabilities often affect multiple organ systems and/or functional domains. Consequently, individuals with these conditions experience substantial difficulties in performing ADLs and engaging in other pursuits that bring meaning to their lives (e.g., childrearing, social engagements, recreation and sports, hobbies, community events, worship, education, employment). Individuals with these conditions may experience significant psychological distress in making comparisons of their pre- and postdisability capabilities (Smart, 2009). Emerging disabilities such as fibromyalgia, MCS, chronic Lyme disease, and polytrauma are associated with a vast array of symptoms such as chronic pain, insomnia, fatigue, sleep disturbances, muscle weakness, and cognitive impairments. Emerging disabilities such as autism spectrum disorders (ASD) and attention deficit hyperactivity disorder (ADHD) can also lead to impairments in multiple functional domains, especially learning and social cognitive abilities. One of the most debilitating symptoms associated with many emerging disabilities is pain. Some individuals live with constant pain with unpredictable vacillations in pain intensity. Others experience ongoing intermittent pain that is also difficult to predict. The fatigue associated with chronic pain has been described by many as even more debilitating than the actual pain itself, making it difficult to carry out even the most rudimentary of tasks (Arnold et al., 2008).

The vast majority of emerging disabilities discussed in this textbook are chronic illnesses. Chronic illness represents the leading cause of disability in the United States (Centers for Disease Control and Prevention [CDC], 2015), and although many chronic illnesses are treatable, most cannot be cured. The chronicity of these conditions, along with the lack of a cure, can be experienced by individuals as a devastating loss. Not only must they come to terms with their permanently changed status and identity, they must also make significant adjustments to their daily lives (Smart, 2009). Additionally, they must invest substantial time, physical and emotional energy, and financial resources into managing these conditions. Furthermore, although chronic illnesses may not initially pose substantial limitations to performing ADLs and essential job functions, they can lead to significant disability if not treated early and effectively by medical professionals and if rehabilitation interventions are not implemented before symptoms become severe (Koch, Rumrill, Conyers, & Wohlford, 2013).

Many emerging disabilities are not only chronic, they are episodic and unpredictable. Individuals with these conditions may experience periodic "flare ups" (e.g., fibromyalgia), "attacks" (e.g., chronic migraines), medical crises (e.g., type 2 diabetes), or relapses (e.g., psychiatric disabilities) that make it difficult for them to predict how well they will be able to function from day to day. Daily planning of chores, social activities, and work can thus be emotionally taxing. The unpredictability of these conditions acts as a stressor resulting in uncertainty and feelings of loss of control because individuals never know when an episode or period of symptom exacerbation may occur (Smart, 2009). Smart described the vicious circle of stress and symptom exacerbation for individuals with unpredictable, episodic conditions, noting that the unpredictability of symptoms triggers stress responses that further exacerbate symptoms and lead to additional stress. Smart further noted that each relapse or symptom exacerbation is accompanied by an emotional response. Individuals with episodic courses of illness often have concerns such as "Will treatment be effective? Will this relapse be severe or moderate? How long will this episode last? Will I have my job when I come home from the hospital? Will there be residual effects? Will I return to my past level of functioning? Will my family take me back?" (Smart, 2009, p. 505). These concerns are magnified for individuals with emerging disabilities that are also progressive.

The unpredictable nature of these conditions can result in a lack of social support from others (e.g., family, friends, supervisors, coworkers) who do not understand how individuals with these disabilities can function so well one day and be completely incapacitated the next (Koch et al., 2012). Friends may become frustrated when individuals with unpredictable conditions repeatedly cancel social engagements. Lack of social support is an especially problematic issue for individuals with emerging disabilities that are medically debated because others in their lives may have a difficult time accepting that the individual has a disability if it is not readily diagnosable and labeled. Finally, many of these emerging disabilities (e.g., chronic Lyme disease, chronic migraines, fibromyalgia, MCS) are grossly underestimated in terms of the severity of symptoms and the substantial degree to which they can interfere with the capacities of individuals with these conditions to actively engage in meaningful life activities.

Multimorbidity

In 2012, approximately half of all adults in the United States reported having a chronic health condition, and one out of four adults reported multiple chronic health conditions (Ward, Schiller, & Goodman, 2014). Furthermore, multimorbidity (the presence of more than one chronic illness) has been reported to be present in almost three out of four individuals aged 65 years and older and one in four adults under the age of 65 years (Tinetti, Fried, & Boyd, 2012). Multimorbidity is associated with various emerging disabilities. For example, individuals with chronic pain often have more than one condition that causes pain. People who acquire disabilities from violent acts may have physical disabilities and co-occurring psychiatric disorders and/or substance use disorders. The same holds true for individuals who survive extreme weather events who incur physical injuries that result in permanent disabilities and may also have co-occurring psychiatric disorders such as PTSD, depression, and anxiety. Individuals with SMI experience high rates of metabolic syndrome and reduced life spans because of co-occurring medical conditions (Gill et al., 2009). For individuals with SMI, the onset of these secondary complications can be attributed to a variety of factors including unhealthy lifestyles, lack of access to adequate health care, and long-term adverse side effects of treatments. For some individuals, diagnosis and treatment of the most obvious condition can lead to failure to recognize and treat co-occurring conditions that could be even more problematic in terms of their effects on the individual's functionality. Reported symptoms associated with secondary conditions may be inaccurately attributed by physicians to the primary disability.

Co-occurring mental health conditions are also common among people with emerging disabilities, with high rates of depression, anxiety, and substance use disorders associated with many of these conditions. Psychiatric disabilities can manifest as a result of a variety of contributing factors, including a genetic predisposition to these conditions along with the psychosocial challenges of coping with deterioration in health and functioning, being misunderstood and invalidated by others, and a lack of social support needed to effectively cope with their conditions (Koch et al., 2012). Finally, medical treatments such as surgery and pharmaceuticals can result in secondary complications and side effects that further impair functioning.

Diagnostic Challenges and Medical Skepticism

Diagnostic uncertainties, misdiagnoses, and skepticism on the part of medical providers are frequently associated with emerging disabilities. For many individuals with emerging disabilities, it can take years between the onset of symptoms and an accurate diagnosis and effective treatment of their disabling condition. For example, it has been well documented that, on average, individuals with psychiatric disabilities are not diagnosed and treated for up to 10 years after the onset of symptoms (National Alliance on Mental Illness [NAMI], 2011). Individuals with emerging disabilities such as fibromyalgia and chronic Lyme disease have also reported long prediagnosis periods. In many cases, specific biologic markers indicating the presence of pathology are absent, and diagnoses must be made based on patient self-report and the ruling out of other conditions. Others never receive an accurate diagnosis, and, in the long process of seeking medical validation, become so ill that they must disengage altogether from meaningful life activities such as employment, recreation, socialization, and community engagement (Koch et al., 2012). Even medically validated conditions such as autoimmune disorders can take months to years to accurately diagnose.

Finally, receiving a diagnosis can lead to relief and a sense of validation. However relief may be accompanied by feelings of despair, anxiety, and hopelessness when learning that there is no simple cure (e.g., medication, surgery, treatment) for the condition (Smart, 2009). Once diagnosed, those with conditions such as fibromyalgia, MCS, or chronic Lyme disease that are still medically debated may continue to question the accuracy of the diagnosis and fail to receive the supports they need to cope with their condition. Even medically established conditions with recent dramatic increases in prevalence (e.g., ADHD, autism, bipolar disorder in children) are often disputed among physicians and researchers in the medical sciences in terms of whether these emerging disabilities are actually increasing in incidence or arise from greater awareness, better surveillance, over-diagnosing of these conditions, or reduced stigma in reporting. This skepticism on the part of physicians and researchers can create skepticism on the part of others in the lives of individuals with these conditions and doubts regarding the accuracy of these diagnoses.

In the long process of seeking out a diagnosis and effective treatment, individuals with emerging disabilities often receive treatment from more than one medical specialist and conflicting medical advice about how to manage their symptoms (Koch et al., 2012). Because symptoms may be associated with more than one disease, misdiagnoses may occur and ineffective treatment regimens may be prescribed. In fact, it is not unusual for individuals with emerging disabilities to be prescribed "numerous simultaneous treatments [that result in] worsening of a single disease by treatment of a co-existing one, and treatment burden arising from following several disease guidelines" (Tinetti et al., 2012, p. 2493). Long prediagnosis periods can be both exhausting and discouraging. In seeking out a diagnosis, individuals must expend an extensive amount of time and energy to participate in multiple treatment regimens and often exhaust their financial resources in the process. Job security may be threatened for those who are employed and must take a substantial amount of time off from work to participate in these treatments. Desperate for relief from their symptoms, some individuals may seek out alternative avenues of treatment and may be victimized by charlatans who promise a "cure" if they follow their expensive, nonmedically confirmed treatment approaches.

Fox and Kim (2004) noted that, whereas many individuals with disabilities have historically rejected the medical model that pathologizes disability, those whose conditions are not readily diagnosable fight for verification from the medical community. Medical diagnosis legitimizes their experiences and opens the door to needed services such as health benefits, rehabilitation services, independent living services, and necessary job accommodations from employers. Medical acceptance can also lead to greater social acceptance and validation as opposed to rejection of their disabling conditions from family members and others in their social support networks.

Stigma and Lack of Social Support

Although societal stigmatization has been well documented as a response to disability in general, stigma is an even more pervasive reaction to emerging disabilities, and the negative consequences of this stigma are far reaching. Young, Park, Tian, and Kempner (2013, p. 1) described stigma as "an established construct in the social sciences that describes a characteristic, trait, or diagnosis that discredits individuals and elicits prejudice, discrimination, and loss of status." As previously noted, a common theme across research studies that have investigated the psychosocial aspects of living with a variety of emerging disabilities (e.g., MCS, fibromyalgia, chronic migraine headaches, ADHD) is the negative impact that stigmatization (and the internalization of this stigma) has on their physical and psychological well-being of individuals with these conditions. Both qualitative and quantitative research investigating the psychosocial aspects of emerging disabilities such as asthma, fibromyalgia, Lyme disease, MCS, and fibromyalgia have documented stigma and lack of medical and social acceptance of these conditions as key factors undermining psychosocial adaptation to these conditions. These studies have also documented the negative impact that stigma has on individuals' physical and mental well-being, ability to self-manage their conditions, the number and severity of symptoms they experience, access to employment, and overall quality of life.

Many emerging disabilities have an insidious onset, and as Smart (2009, pp. 477, 479) noted, "more support is usually given for acute-onset disabilities because friends and family can clearly understand a sharp, sudden (often traumatic) onset... those with less ambiguous disabilities and chronic illness are given support and validation, including medical care, time off from work, time to rest, flowers, cards, and the general solicitude of others." Conversely, more ambiguous disabilities are often misperceived by family members, friends, physicians, other health care providers, and employers who fail to understand the severity of their symptoms, refuse to change their expectations of the individual, and withhold emotional and social support. Despite this ambiguity, individuals with emerging disabilities are acutely aware of the disability and its far-reaching impact on their lives (Sim & Madden, 2008).

Often, individuals with emerging disabilities appear to be healthy, and their symptoms are misinterpreted by others as character flaws. For example, individuals with chronic pain (e.g., chronic migraines, fibromyalgia) may be viewed as "weak" or as faking their pain in order to be relieved from performing undesired activities such as household chores or work outside the home (Holloway, Sofaer-Bennett, & Walker, 2007). Likewise, individuals who are injured on the job and experience ongoing pain are often viewed (even by rehabilitation professionals) as malingering for secondary gain (i.e., faking their symptoms so that they can continue to collect Workers Compensation benefits and avoid going back to work). Research investigating the psychosocial consequences of living with MCS has documented the common characterization of these individuals by significant others as psychosomatic or "crazy" (Gibson et al., 2011; Koch et al., 2006). People with obesity and co-occurring type 2 diabetes are often viewed with disdain because of American society's obsession with beauty and healthy living (Smart, 2009), and youths with ADHD may be treated as "lazy" or "uncooperative" when they experience challenges in completing school assignments (American Psychiatric Association [APA], 2013). It can be especially difficult for others to comprehend how individuals with episodic conditions can function normally for a period of time and then be completely incapacitated for days or even months. Due to the unpredictability of their symptoms and the lack of emotional and social support as a coping resource, individuals with emerging disabilities can be at risk of developing secondary health conditions, depression, and anxiety, which can exacerbate the symptoms of their primary conditions and further restrict their functional capacities.

Because many emerging disabilities are hidden, the invisibility of symptoms can lead to further questioning and doubt on the part of the individual, medical providers, family, friends, and employers (Koch et al., 2012). Additionally, individuals with relapsing and episodic disabilities (e.g., asthma, psychiatric disabilities) whose symptoms are in remission (e.g., psychiatric disabilities) may believe that they no longer have a disability and that they can terminate treatment (Smart, 2009). Failure to understand the importance of ongoing treatment and self-management of symptoms, even during periods of remission, can lead to added complications and setbacks that undermine their health and ability to function at their highest levels.

Lack of societal understanding regarding the substantial degree to which newly recognized conditions (e.g., fibromyalgia) can impair functioning; societal failure to accept some conditions as disabilities (e.g., MCS, substance use disorders, chronic Lyme disease); and prejudice and fear regarding emerging disabilities such as SMI, violence-induced spinal cord injuries, and TBIs can often impede individuals with these disabilities from accessing needed social, rehabilitation, medical, and health care services (Fox & Kim, 2004). Stigma is especially an issue of concern for individuals who are believed to have caused their emerging disability by engaging in risky or unhealthy behaviors (e.g., smoking, abusing alcohol and/or drugs, overeating, failing to exercise). These individuals are often blamed for their conditions, and others may lack empathy and be resistant to providing the emotional and social support that these individuals need to cope with their conditions (Smart, 2009). When these individuals are also marginalized due to other personal characteristics (e.g., race, gender, sexual orientation, gender identity, socioeconomic status), the intersection of these multiple identities magnifies the negative attributions others assign to their disabling conditions and can further impair their mental and physical health.

Vocational Challenges

A consistent theme throughout the chapters in this book is the high rate of unemployment, underemployment, and premature disengagement from the workforce experienced by individuals with emerging disabilities. Unemployment can be partially attributed to the multitude of symptoms and/or functional limitations associated with emerging disabilities. Perhaps even more problematic for people with emerging disabilities are the barriers to employment created by external factors such as societal stigma, discrimination, and noninclusive, or even hostile, work environments. Furthermore, because of the disproportionate rates of emerging disabilities in socially and economically disadvantaged populations, discrimination can also occur as a result of membership in these other marginalized groups.

Again, because many emerging disabilities are invisible, misunderstood, medically debated, and stigmatized, employers may be reluctant to hire and provide workplace accommodations for individuals with these conditions (Koch et al., 2012). Employers and coworkers often fail to understand and/or validate the degree to which these conditions create barriers to carrying out essential job functions. Functional limitations may be attributed to undesirable personal characteristics as opposed to effects of their disabling conditions. Consequently, requests for accommodations are treated as unnecessary, even when these accommodations can be made at little to no cost.

Furthermore, individuals with emerging disabilities may not be aware of their eligibility for employment provisions under Title I of the ADA because they do not perceive themselves as having a disability. Even for those who are aware of these provisions, the process of accommodation planning can be fraught with tension, especially for individuals with episodic conditions that are unpredictable. The inability to predict when they might experience new functional limitations, temporary setbacks, exacerbations, or flare-ups makes accommodation planning difficult for both individuals with emerging disabilities and their employers (Koch et al., 2013).

The prospect of disclosing that individuals have a disability as a prerequisite to receiving workplace accommodations may also be fraught with tension. Legitimate concerns regarding disability disclosure arise because individuals with emerging disabilities are acutely aware of the stigma associated with their conditions and may understandably fear negative repercussions if they do disclose (Cole & Cawthon, 2015; Dalgin & Bellini, 2008; Jans, Kaye, & Jones, 2012; Riley & Hagger, 2015). Because they are often members of other marginalized groups prone to discrimination, they may also be concerned that disclosing their status as an individual with a disability will put them at risk of experiencing double discrimination. If they do choose to disclose, they are likely to be perplexed by questions such as what to disclose, when to disclose, how to disclose, and to whom to disclose.

Even when employers are willing to accommodate individuals with emerging disabilities, coworkers may resent these employees and view the provision of workplace accommodations as unnecessary or as giving workers with emerging disabilities an unfair advantage. Negative reactions from coworkers can create a hostile work environment for individuals with emerging disabilities. Working in such an environment can result in substantial work stress, undermine their job performance, negatively impact their overall health and well-being, exacerbate symptoms of their disabling conditions, and contribute to the development of comorbid medical conditions and secondary complications (Cortina et al., 2001; Dillon, 2012; Reio & Ghosh, 2009). Individuals may subsequently be terminated from employment because of poor job performance or voluntarily resign because the exacerbated symptoms of their emerging disabilities have left them incapable of adequately performing their job tasks.

When considering employment implications of emerging disabilities, the developmental stage of the individual with the emerging disability must be taken into account. Youths with emerging disabilities (e.g., asthma, obesity, diabetes, psychiatric disabilities, ADHD, ASD) may be excluded from engaging in normative career-related experiences during critical years when their self-images and work personalities are developing (Ribet, 2011). For example, they may fail to participate in early career development experiences such as household chores, sports, extracurricular school activities, and part-time employment that help them to build the general employment-related skills and the self-confidence to pursue careers of their choice. They may avoid participating in these experiences because of parental overprotection, functional limitations (e.g., poor social skills, physical limitations), a lack of self-esteem, and/or fears regarding the impact of these experiences on their health. Their peers may exclude them from social activities, labeling those with these emerging disabilities as "weak," "frail," "crazy," "dumb," "lazy," or "weird." Youths with emerging disabilities may internalize these labels and fail to perceive themselves as capable of performing in the role of worker.

Poverty also restricts their opportunities to participate in important career development activities because families may not have the resources to financially support their children to engage in these activities. Parents whose children receive entitlement benefits such as Social Security Income (SSI) and Medicaid may discourage these youths from considering employment out of fear that they will lose these much-needed benefits. Additionally, children and youths with some emerging disabilities may not be encouraged by school personnel to develop high career aspirations (Davis, 2015). Finally, many of these children do not receive transition planning services to support them in pursuing postschool outcomes such as a college education or employment. Because of all these factors, youths with emerging disabilities (e.g., ADHD, psychiatric disabilities) are at risk of experiencing undesirable outcomes in later adolescence and adulthood such as dropping out of high school or college, unemployment, substance use disorders, incarceration, declines in their physical and mental health, homelessness, and suicide (Adamou et al., 2013; Davis, 2015; McKeague, Hennessy, O'Driscoll, & Heary, 2015).

For individuals who acquire midcareer emerging disabilities, the prospect of entering or maintaining employment can be fraught with anxiety and even misguided advice. Upon diagnosis, some individuals may be advised by health care professionals that employment is not a feasible goal or, if employed, that they should discontinue working (Koch et al., 2013; Sullivan & Hyman, 2014). This advice is given despite the fact that research has demonstrated that employment is associated with many positive health-related outcomes such as reduced symptoms, treatment adherence, better overall health, fewer hospitalizations, and better health-related quality of life (e.g., Dunn, Wewiorski, & Rogers, 2008; Hall, Kurth, & Hunt, 2013; Hergenrather, Zeglin, McGuire-Kuletz, & Rhodes, 2015; Miller & Dishon, 2006).

Finally, older adults with emerging disabilities must contend with stigma and discrimination associated with their age as well as their disabling conditions (Wickert et al., 2013). Older adults are often perceived by employers as more expensive than younger workers in terms of salaries and benefits. Employers may also have concerns about their ability to be as productive as younger workers. In addition, stereotypes about older workers such as being inflexible, resistant to change, and unable to keep up with emerging technologies in the workplace can make employers reluctant to hire older workers.

POPULATIONS AT RISK OF ACQUIRING EMERGING DISABILITIES

Kim and Fox (2004) found that, in comparison to individuals with traditional disabilities, individuals with emerging disabilities are more likely to be women, economically disadvantaged, older, and members of racial/ethnic minority groups. These individual characteristics intersect with disability characteristics and social and environmental factors (e.g., stigma, discrimination, social injustice, inequities in health and health care, violence, climate change) to magnify the challenges presented by the disabling condition itself. Because the most socially and economically disadvantaged groups in American society are also the most prone to acquiring emerging disabilities, these individuals often encounter "dual" or even "triple" discrimination in all areas of life including housing, community integration, education, and employment. In other words, not only are they discriminated against on the basis of their disability, but they may also be discriminated against because of their race, ethnicity, gender, gender identity, age, socioeconomic status, and/or sexual orientation.

Of all the at-risk populations discussed in this section, those living in poverty experience the highest rates of emerging disabilities as well as greater symptomology and poorest health-related outcomes (Fox & Kim, 2004). People living in poverty are more likely than those living above the poverty line to be victimized by violent crime, to experience the negative health consequences of climate change and severe weather events, and to suffer from the health-related consequences of lifestyle factors that predispose them to emerging disabilities (e.g., asthma, type 2 diabetes). They are predisposed to emerging disabilities due to risk factors such as unhealthy housing, unsafe neighborhoods, poor nutrition, degraded air quality in their homes and communities, indoor and outdoor air pollution, and disparities in access to health care.

Perrin and colleagues (2007) reported that the number of children with chronic health conditions has dramatically increased over the past four decades, and the number of children receiving SSI has more than tripled over the past two decades. Among the conditions that have seen the largest increases in children are obesity, asthma, and ADHD. Children living in poverty are the most susceptible to these conditions. Numerous factors are believed to have contributed to these increases, including increased incidence of low birth weight, maternal cigarette smoking, and reductions in fruit and vegetables in children's diets, along with more consumption of fast foods, displacement of physical activity by television viewing, parental anxiety about children's outdoor play, lack of recreational opportunities (especially in urban areas), and more time spent by children indoors, which exposes them to indoor allergens. Additional contributing factors for children living in poverty include certain infestations created by crowded and unsafe housing and secondary cigarette smoke.

Although rehabilitation counselors typically provide services to adolescents and adults, these dramatic increases in childhood chronic health conditions have significant implications in terms of emerging rehabilitation consumer populations. According to Perrin et al. (2007), asthma persists into adulthood for about 25% of children, and ADHD persists into adulthood for about half of children. Additionally, ADHD is associated with poorer employment outcomes, increased crime and incarceration, increased motor vehicle accidents, and secondary mental health conditions such as anxiety and depression (APA, 2013; McKeague et al., 2015). Obesity that persists into adulthood is linked to type 2 diabetes and increased risk for cardiovascular disease (Cha et al., 2015). Given the persistence of these conditions into adulthood, without rehabilitation services, individuals with these conditions are vulnerable to experiencing unemployment and underemployment, poorer overall quality of life, greater isolation, less community participation, and greater need for support (e.g., health care, housing, employment) from government agencies.

In addition to these chronic health conditions, researchers have reported disproportionate rates of mental health disorders in youths. According to data from the National Comorbidity Study–Adolescent Supplement survey (Merikangas et al., 2010), approximately 20% of American youth are affected by a mental health disorder severe enough to impair their functioning at some point in their lives. About 40% of those reporting a mental health disorder also met criteria for at least one additional mental health disorder. Children whose parents had less education and were divorced were at higher risk than other children in the sample for a mental health disorder.

Women also represent a population that is at an increased risk of acquiring emerging disabilities and chronic illnesses. The incidence of conditions such as autoimmune disorders, depression, anxiety, and PTSD and other trauma- and stressor-related disorders is higher in women than it is in men. Women are also more likely than men to be victims of intimate partner violence, with one in three women worldwide estimated to have experienced physical and/or sexual violence (World Health Organization [WHO], 2013). Women experience higher rates of chronic pain than men, but they are less likely than men to be prescribed pain medications by their physicians (Institute of Medicine [IOM], 2011). In addition, women are more likely than men to be diagnosed with a psychosomatic condition, even when presenting with similar symptoms. Individuals who are determined to have medically unexplained symptoms are also more likely to be female (Nimnuan et al., 2001). They have higher rates of controversial and medically debated conditions such as fibromyalgia. Not only do women experience disparities in their health status compared to men, they also encounter inequities in access to and quality of health care. Women experience greater social, cultural, and economic disadvantages that restrict their access to health care, education, and employment, thus increasing their risk for emerging disabilities (Ribet, 2011). It is also noteworthy that somatic symptoms disorder, a condition that is observed more frequently in primary care than in mental health settings, is diagnosed more frequently in women than in men (APA, 2013). This phenomenon calls into question the role that gender and gender bias play in the validation or invalidation by physicians of medical symptoms reported by women.

Ribet (2011) noted that people of color are another disproportionately represented group in emerging disability populations. For example, Blacks have the highest rates of obesity, hypertension, and diabetes. In comparison to non-Latino Whites, higher rates of PTSD are found among Latinos, African Americans, and American Indians. In comparison to Whites, higher rates of asthma occur among multirace, Black, and American Indian/Alaska Native persons. Compounding the higher rates of emerging disabilities in these populations is the problem of inequitable access to health care for individuals from racial/ethnic minority groups. Health care disparities associated with race and ethnicity have been observed in both the diagnosis and treatment of medical conditions as well as in the quality of care that members of racial/ethnic minority groups receive. As examples, Black patients are more likely than their White counterparts to receive higher cost procedures, even in the presence of adequate health insurance coverage for major diagnostic and therapeutic procedures (IOM, 2011). They are also less likely to receive pain medication.

Lewis and Burris (2012) noted that these inequities are mirrored in the VR system. In fact, rehabilitation researchers have documented that, in comparison to their White counterparts, individuals from racial/minority groups and other underserved populations participate in rehabilitation programs at lower rates, receive fewer services, and experience fewer successful outcomes. Section 21 of the Rehabilitation Act emphasizes these inequities as well as the need for VR systems to employ targeted strategies to eliminate inequities in access, service delivery, and rehabilitation outcomes. In response to Section 21, Lewis and Burris (2012, p. 169) proposed a working definition of disability disparities:

> A disability disparity exists when an underserved, ethnic, or racial minority cultural group's desire is to receive services within the formal

rehabilitation, and disability system (public or private). However, there exists a differential experience based primarily on cultural orientation resulting in a higher incidence of disability, and/or lower participation levels in the formal helping system, and/or fewer successful individual outcomes in comparison to majority cultural groups.

CONCLUSIONS

The world is rapidly changing, and along with these changes, the nature and needs of rehabilitation consumer populations are constantly in flux. Therefore, the purpose of this chapter was to define the concept of emerging disabilities and to provide an overview of the contemporary political, social, and environmental trends that influence the onset of new medical and mental health conditions in the population or increases in incidence of established conditions. We also highlighted some of the unique medical, psychosocial, and vocational characteristics of emerging disability populations. Finally, we examined populations that are most vulnerable to acquiring emerging disabilities. What is particularly noteworthy about these populations is that they represent the most socially and economically disadvantaged groups in American society as well as a vastly underserved rehabilitation population.

In 2004, Fox and Kim (p. 324) recommended that:

> As so-called "emerging disability populations" knock on the door of service providers whose systems are designed to work with "traditional disability populations," greater efforts must be made to more clearly understand what emerging disabilities are in order for these service delivery systems to remain relevant.

More than a decade later, we have seen an increased focus in the scholarly literature on emerging disabilities and innovative practices (e.g., integrated service delivery models, health promotion strategies, illness self-management, trauma-informed service models, evidence-based practices in psychiatric rehabilitation, job retention and career maintenance interventions) that are responsive to their unique rehabilitation concerns. Yet rehabilitation systems are still not fully prepared to effectively address the multifaceted needs of individuals with emerging disabilities. Thus, it is imperative that future rehabilitation counselors acquire the knowledge and skills to respond more effectively to consumers whose disabilities may not match with traditional conceptualizations of disability and whose rehabilitation needs may not be addressed by current rehabilitation service delivery approaches.

In response to Fox and Kim's (2004) recommendation to expend greater efforts toward understanding emerging disabilities, we have devoted the rest of this book to a more in-depth exploration of causes, types, and consequences of emerging disabilities. A substantial portion of each chapter is devoted to innovative strategies that can be incorporated into each phase of the rehabilitation process of service delivery. It is our hope that the information provided in this book will serve as an impetus for future rehabilitation counselors to "lead the charge" (Koch et al., 2012, p. 137) in providing more responsive rehabilitation services to individuals with emerging disabilities.

DISCUSSION QUESTIONS

1. What contemporary trends do you think are the most influential on the way disability is defined, diagnosed, and treated?
2. What are your thoughts regarding the inclusion into the constellation of disabilities those illnesses and conditions that are medically debated, questioned in terms of their legitimacy, or treated as medically undiagnosed symptoms? What changes in disability definitions are needed to include these conditions?
3. Considering the unique medical, psychosocial, and vocational characteristics of emerging disabilities, what are the implications for rehabilitation counseling practice?
4. What are the barriers to participating in rehabilitation programs that are encountered by people with emerging disabilities? What changes in rehabilitation policies, procedures, and processes do you think are necessary to increase access to/participation in rehabilitation programs for individuals with emerging disabilities?
5. What information did you glean from this chapter that is new to you? What topics would you like to learn more about and how can you go about increasing your knowledge regarding these topics?

REFERENCES

Adamou, M., Arif, M., Asherson, P., Aw, T., Bolea, B., Coghill, D., . . . Young, S. (2013). Occupational issues of adults with ADHD. *BMC Psychiatry, 13*, 59. doi:10.1186/1471-244X-13-59

Alston, R. J., Harley, D. A., & Middleton, R. (2006). The role of rehabilitation in achieving social justice for minorities with disabilities. *Journal of Vocational Rehabilitation, 24*(3), 129–136.

American Psychiatric Association. (2013). *Diagnostic and statistical manual of mental disorders* (5th ed.). Washington, DC: Author.

Armstrong, L. L., & Young, K. (2015). Mind the gap: Person-centered delivery of mental health information to post-secondary students. *Psychosocial Intervention, 24*(2), 83–87.

Arnold, L. M., Crofford, L. J., Mease, P. J., Burgess, S. M., Palmer, S. C., Abetz, L., & Martin, S. A. (2008). Patient perspectives on the impact of fibromyalgia. *Patient Education and Counseling, 73*(1), 114–120.

Balbus, J. M., & Malina, C. (2009). Identifying vulnerable subpopulations for climate change health effects in the United States. *Journal of Occupational and Environmental Medicine, 51*, 33–37.

Blake, J. J., Lund, E. M., Zhou, Q., Kwok, O., & Benz, M. R. (2012). National prevalence rates of bully victimization among students with disabilities in the United States. *School Psychology Quarterly: The Official Journal of the Division of School Psychology, American Psychological Association, 27*(4), 210–222.

Briere, J., Kaltman, S., & Green, B. (2008). Accumulated childhood trauma and symptom complexity. *Journal of Traumatic Stress, 21*(2), 223–226.

Burke, L. A., Friedl, J., & Rigler, M. (2010). The 2008 Amendments to the Americans with Disabilities Act: Implications for student affairs practitioners. *Journal of Student Affairs Research and Practice, 47*, 63–77.

Byrd, D. R., & McKinney, K. J. (2012). Individual, interpersonal, and institutional level factors associated with the mental health of college students. *Journal of American College Health, 60*(3), 185–193. doi:10.1080/07448481.2011.584334

Centers for Disease Control and Prevention. (2015). *Chronic disease prevention and health promotion: Chronic disease overview.* Retrieved from http://www.cdc.gov/chronicdisease/overview/index.htm

Cha, E., Akazawa, M. K., Kim, K. H., Dawkins, C. R., Lerner, H. M., Umpierrez, G., & Dunbar, S. B. (2015). Lifestyle habits and obesity progression in overweight and obese American young adults: Lessons for promoting cardiometabolic health. *Nursing & Health Sciences, 17*(4), 467–475. doi:10.1111/nhs.12218

Cole, E. V., & Cawthon, S. W. (2015). Self-disclosure decisions of university students with learning disabilities. *Journal of Postsecondary Education & Disability, 28*(2), 163–179.

Conyers, L. M. (2004a). Expanding understanding of HIV/AIDS and employment perspectives of focus groups. *Rehabilitation Counseling Bulletin, 48*(1), 5–18.

Conyers, L. M. (2004b). The impact of vocational services and employment on people with HIV/AIDS. *Work: A Journal of Prevention, Assessment, and Rehabilitation, 23*(3), 205–214.

Copeland, C. (2014). Labor-force participation rates of the population ages 55 and older, 2013. *EBRI Notes, 35*(4), 2–10.

Cortina, L. M., Magley, V. J., Williams, J. H., & Langhout, R. D. (2001). Incivility in the workplace: Incidence and impact. *Journal of Occupational Health Psychology, 6*(1), 64.

Crofford, L. (2007). Violence, stress, and somatic syndromes. *Trauma, Violence & Abuse, 8*(3), 299–313.

Dalgin, R. S., & Bellini, J. (2008). Invisible disability disclosure in an employment interview: Impact on employers' hiring decisions and views of employability. *Rehabilitation Counseling Bulletin, 52*(1), 6–15.

D'Andrea, W., Sharma, R., Zelechoski, A. D., & Spinazzola, J. (2011). Physical health problems after single trauma exposure when stress takes root in the body. *Journal of the American Psychiatric Nurses Association, 17*(6), 378–392.

Davis, M. (2015). *Research-based employment supports for youth with chronic mental health disorders* [Webcast]. Richmond: Virginia Commonwealth University Rehabilitation Research and Training Center on Work Supports.

Dillon, B. L. (2012). Workplace violence: Impact, causes, and prevention. *Work: A Journal of Prevention, Assessment, and Rehabilitation, 42*, 15–20.

Dixon, C. G., Richard, M., & Rollins, C. W. (2003). Contemporary issues facing aging Americans: Implications for rehabilitation and mental health counseling. *Journal of Rehabilitation, 69*(2), 5.

Dunn, E. C., Wewiorski, N. J., & Rogers, E. S. (2008). The meaning and importance of employment to people in recovery from serious mental illness: Results of a qualitative study. *Psychiatric Rehabilitation Journal, 32*(1), 59–62.

Eudaly, J. (2002). *A rising tide: Students with psychiatric disabilities seek services in record numbers.* Retrieved from https://heath.gwu.edu/files/downloads/psychiatric_disabilities.pdf

Faith, M. A., Malcolm, K. T., & Newgent, R. A. (2008). Reducing potential mental health issues and alcohol abuse through an early prevention model for victims of peer harassment. *Work: A Journal of Prevention, Assessment, and Rehabilitation, 31*(3), 327–336.

Falvo, D. R. (2014). *Medical and psychosocial aspects of chronic illness and disability* (5th ed.). Burlington, MA: Jones & Bartlett.

Field, M. J., & Jette, A. M. (2007). *The future of disability in America.* Washington, DC: National Academies Press.

Fox, M. H., & Kim, K. (2004). Understanding emerging disabilities. *Disability and Society, 19*, 323–337.

Frain, M. P., Lee, J., Roland, M., & Tschopp, M. K. (2012). A rehabilitation counselor integration into the successful rehabilitation of veterans with disabilities. In P. J. Toriello, M. L. Bishop, & P. D. Rumrill (Eds.), *New directions in rehabilitation counseling: Creative responses to professional, clinical, and educational challenges* (pp. 255–281). Linn Creek, MO: Aspen Professional Services.

Fujiura, G. T. (2001). Emerging trends in disability. *Population Today, 29*(6), 9–10.

Gibson, B. E. (2006). Disability, connectivity and transgressing the autonomous body. *Journal of Medical Humanities, 27*(3), 187–196.

Gibson, P. R., Cheavens, J., & Warren, M. L. (1996). Chemical sensitivity/chemical injury and life disruption. *Women & Therapy, 19*(2), 63–79.

Gibson, P. R., Sledd, L. G., McEnroe, W. H., & Vos, A. P. (2011). Isolation and lack of access in multiple chemical sensitivity: A qualitative study. *Nursing & Health Sciences, 13*(3), 232–237.

Gill, K. J., Murphy, A. A., Zechner, M. R., Swarbrick, M., & Spagnolo, A. B. (2009). Co-morbid psychiatric and medical disorders: Challenges and strategies. *Journal of Rehabilitation, 75*(3), 32.

Hall, J. P., Kurth, N. K., & Hunt, S. L. (2013). Employment as a health determinant for working-age, dually-eligible people with disabilities. *Disability and Health Journal, 6*(2), 100–106.

Hartley, M. T. (2013). Investigating the relationship of resilience to academic persistence in college students with mental health issues. *Rehabilitation Counseling Bulletin, 56*(4), 240–250. doi:10.1177/0034355213480527

Hergenrather, K. C., Zeglin, R. J., McGuire-Kuletz, M., & Rhodes, S. D. (2015). Employment as a social determinant of health: A review of longitudinal studies exploring the relationship between employment status and mental health. *Rehabilitation Research, Policy & Education, 29*(3), 261–290.

Hess, J. J., Malilay, J. N., & Parkinson, A. J. (2008). Climate change: The importance of place. *American Journal of Preventive Medicine, 35*(5), 468–478.

Holloway, I., Sofaer-Bennett, B., & Walker, J. (2007). The stigmatisation of people with chronic back pain. *Disability and Rehabilitation, 29*(18), 1456–1464.

Hughes, K., Bellis, M. A., Jones, L., Wood, S., Bates, G., Eckley, L.,...Officer, A. (2012). Prevalence and risk of violence against adults with disabilities: A systematic review and meta-analysis of observational studies. *The Lancet, 380*(9845), 899–907.

Institute of Medicine. (2011). *Relieving pain in America.* Washington, DC: National Academies Press.

Interagency Working Group on Climate Change and Human Health. (2010). *A human health perspective on climate change: A report outlining the research needs on the human health effects of climate change.* Retrieved from https://www.niehs.nih.gov/health/assets/docs_p_z/interagency_climate_508.pdf

Jans, L. H., Kaye, H. S., & Jones, E. C. (2012). Getting hired: Successfully employed people with disabilities offer advice on disclosure, interviewing, and job search. *Journal of Occupational Rehabilitation, 22*(2), 155–165.

Kim, K., & Fox, M. H. (2004). Knocking on the door: The integration of emerging disability groups into independent living. *Journal of Vocational Rehabilitation, 20,* 91–98.

Kiuhara, S. A., & Huefner, D. S. (2008). Students with psychiatric disabilities in higher education settings. *Journal of Disability Policy Studies, 19*(2), 103–113.

Koch, L., Conyers, L., & Rumrill, P. (2012). The nature and needs of people with emerging disabilities. In P. J. Toriello, M. L. Bishop, & P. D. Rumrill (Eds.), *New directions in rehabilitation counseling: Creative responses to professional, clinical, and educational challenges* (pp. 116–139). Linn Creek, MO: Aspen Professional Services.

Koch, L., & Eaton, B. (2005). Multiple chemical sensitivity and rehabilitation planning implications. *Journal of Applied Rehabilitation Counseling, 36*(1), 24–29.

Koch, L., Vierstra, C., & Penix, K. (2006). A qualitative investigation of the psychosocial impact of multiple chemical sensitivity. *Journal of Applied Rehabilitation Counseling, 37*(3), 33–40.

Koch, L. C., Rumrill, P. D., Conyers, L., & Wohlford, S. (2013). A narrative literature review regarding job retention strategies for people with chronic illnesses. *Work: A Journal of Prevention, Assessment, and Rehabilitation, 46,* 125–134.

Krause, L. (2015). *Disability statistics annual report.* Durham: University of New Hampshire.

Kumpulainen, K. (2008). Psychiatric conditions associated with bullying. *International Journal of Adolescent Medicine and Health, 20*(2), 121–132.

Lamielle, M. (2003). *Multiple chemical sensitivity and the workplace.* Voorhees, NJ: National Center for Environmental Health Strategies, Inc.

Lewis, A. N., & Burris, J. L. (2012). The multicultural rehabilitation counseling imperative in the 21st century. In P. J. Toriello, M. L. Bishop, & P. D. Rumrill (Eds.), *New directions in rehabilitation counseling: Creative responses to professional, clinical, and educational challenges* (pp. 164–208). Linn Creek, MO: Aspen Professional Services.

Lim, S., Cortina, L. M., & Magley, V. J. (2008). Personal and workgroup incivility: Impact on work and health outcomes. *Journal of Applied Psychology, 93*(1), 95.

McKeague, L., Hennessy, E., O'Driscoll, C., & Heary, C. (2015). Retrospective accounts of self-stigma experienced by young people with attention-deficit/hyperactivity disorder (ADHD) or depression. *Psychiatric Rehabilitation Journal, 38*(2), 158–163. doi:10.1037/prj0000121

McMahon, B. T. (2012). An overview of workplace discrimination and disability. *Journal of Vocational Rehabilitation, 36*(3), 135–139.

McMichael, A. J. (2013). Globalization, climate change, and human health. *New England Journal of Medicine, 368*(14), 1335–1343.

McReynolds, C. J., & Garske, G. G. (2003). Psychiatric disabilities: Challenges and training issues for rehabilitation professionals. *Journal of Rehabilitation, 69*(4), 13–18.

Megivern, D., Pellerito, S., & Mowbray, C. (2003). Barriers to higher education for individuals with psychiatric disabilities. *Psychiatric Rehabilitation Journal, 26*(3), 217–231.

Merikangas, K. R., He, J., Burstein, M., Swanson, S. A., Avenevoli, S., Cui, L.,…Swendsen, J. (2010). Lifetime prevalence of mental disorders in US adolescents: Results from the National Comorbidity Survey Replication–Adolescent supplement (NCS-A). *Journal of the American Academy of Child & Adolescent Psychiatry, 49*, 980–989.

Miller, A., & Dishon, S. (2006). Health-related quality of life in multiple sclerosis: The impact of disability, gender and employment status. *Quality of Life Research, 15*(2), 259–271.

Nary, D. E., White, G. W., Budde, J. F., & Vo, H. Y. (2004). Identifying the employment and vocational rehabilitation concerns of people with traditional and emerging disabilities. *Journal of Vocational Rehabilitation, 20*(1), 71–77.

National Alliance on Mental Illness. (2011). *State mental health cuts: A national crisis.* Retrieved from http://www2.nami.org/ContentManagement/ContentDisplay.cfm?ContentFileID=126233

National Council on Disability. (2009). *Invisible wounds: Serving service members and veterans with PTSD and TBI.* Retrieved from https://www.ncd.gov/publications/2009/March042009

National Human Genome Research Institute. (2015). *A brief guide to genomics.* Retrieved from http://www.genome.gov/18016863

National Organization for Rare Disorders. (2016). *Resources and FAQs.* Retrieved from http://rarediseases.org/for-patients-and-families/information-resources/resources-faqs

Newcomer, J. W. (2007). Metabolic syndrome and mental illness. *The American Journal of Managed Care, 13*(7S), S170–S177.

Nimnuan, C., Hotopf, M., & Wessely, S. (2001). Medically unexplained symptoms: An epidemiological study in seven specialties. *Journal of Psychosomatic Research, 51*(1), 361–367.

Nosek, M. A., Hughes, R. B., Taylor, H. B., & Taylor, P. (2006). Disability, psychosocial, and demographic characteristics of abused women with physical disabilities. *Violence Against Women: An International and Interdisciplinary Journal, 12*(9), 838–850.

Pang, T., & Guindon, G. F. (2004). Globalization and risks to health. *EMBO Reports, 5*(1S), S11–S16.

Paterson, J. (2011). Bullies with byte. *Counseling Today, 53*(12), 44.

Perrin, J. M., Bloom, S. R., & Gortmaker, S. L. (2007). The increase of childhood chronic conditions in the United States. *JAMA, 297*(24), 2755–2759.

Ratts, M. J., Singh, A. A., Butler, S. K., Nassar-McMillan, S., & McCullough, J. (2016). Multicultural and social justice counseling competencies: Practical applications in counseling. *Counseling Today, 58*(8), 40.

Raymond, M. C., & Brown, J. B. (2000). Experience of fibromyalgia: Qualitative study. *Canadian Family Physician, 46*, 1100–1106.

Rector, R., & Sheffield, R. (2014). *The war on poverty after 50 years.* Retrieved from http://www.heritage.org/research/reports/2014/09/the-war-on-poverty-after-50-years

Reed, K. P., Cooper, R. L., Nugent, W. R., & Russell, K. (2016). Cyberbullying: A literature review of its relationship to adolescent depression and current intervention strategies. *Journal of Human Behavior in the Social Environment, 26*(1), 37–45.

Reio, T. G., & Ghosh, R. (2009). Antecedents and outcomes of workplace incivility: Implications for human resource development research and practice. *Human Resource Development Quarterly, 20*(3), 237–264.

Ribet, B. (2011). Emergent disability and the limits of equality: A critical reading of the UN convention on the rights of persons with disabilities. *Yale Human Rights and Development Law Journal, 14*, 101–150.

Riley, G. A., & Hagger, B. F. (2015). Disclosure of a stigmatized identity: A qualitative study of the reasons why people choose to tell or not tell others about their traumatic brain injury. *Brain Injury, 29*(12), 1480–1489.

Rosenthal, D., Dalton, J., & Gervey, R. (2007). Analyzing vocational outcomes of individuals with psychiatric disabilities who received state vocational rehabilitation services: A data mining approach. *International Journal of Social Psychiatry, 53*(4), 357–368.

Rubin, S., Roessler, R., & Rumrill, P. (2016). *Foundations of the vocational rehabilitation process* (7th ed.). Austin, TX: Pro-Ed.

Sim, J., & Madden, S. (2008). Illness experience in fibromyalgia syndrome: A metasynthesis of qualitative studies. *Social Science & Medicine, 67*(1), 57–67.

Smart, J. (2009). *Disability, society, and the individual* (2nd ed.). Austin, TX: Pro-Ed.

Sullivan, M. L., & Hyman, M. H. (2014). Return to work as a treatment objective for patients with chronic pain? *Journal of Pain Relief, 3*(1). doi:10.4172/2167-0846.1000130

Tinetti, M. E., Fried, T. R., & Boyd, C. M. (2012). Designing health care for the most common chronic condition: Multimorbidity. *JAMA, 307*(23), 2493–2495.

Truman, J. L., & Langton, L. (2014) *Criminal victimization, 2013.* U.S. Department of Justice. Retrieved from http://www.bjs.gov/content/pub/pdf/cv13.pdf

U.S. Department of Education Office for Civil Rights. (2014). *Responding to bullying of students with disabilities.* Retrieved from http://www2.ed.gov/about/offices/list/ocr/letters/colleague-bullying-201410.pdf

U.S. Department of Justice. (2014). *Crime in the United States, 2013.* Uniform Crime Report. U.S. Department of Justice–Federal Bureau of Investigation. Retrieved from http://www.fbi.gov/about-us/cjis/ucr/crime-in-the-u.s/2013/crime-in-the-u.s.-2013/violent-crime/violent-crime-topic-page/violentcrimemain_final.pdf

U.S. Environmental Protection Agency. (2014). *Climate change indicators in the United States: Lyme disease.* Retrieved from http://www.epa.gov/climatechange/science/indicators/health-society/lyme.html

van der Kolk, B. A. (2003). The neurobiology of childhood trauma and abuse. *Child and Adolescent Psychiatric Clinics of North America, 12*(2), 293–317.

Van Houdenhove, B., & Luyten, P. (2005). Beyond dualism: The role of life stress in chronic pain. *Pain, 113*(1–2), 238–239.

Ward, B. W., Schiller, J. S., & Goodman, R. A. (2014). Multiple chronic conditions among US adults: A 2012 update. *Preventative Chronic Disease.* doi:10.4172/2167-0846.1000130

Wickert, K., Dresden, D., & Rumrill, P. (2013). *The sandwich generation's guide to eldercare.* New York, NY: Demos Health.

World Health Organization. (2012). *Intimate partner violence.* Retrieved from http://apps.who.int/iris/bitstream/10665/77432/1/WHO_RHR_12.36_eng.pdf

Young, W. B., Park, J. E., Tian, I. X., & Kempner, J. (2013). The stigma of migraine. *PLOS ONE, 8*(1), e54074.

TWO

Chronic Pain

CHAPTER OBJECTIVES

- *Define chronic pain, types, and causes*
- *Describe medical characteristics of two emerging chronic pain conditions (i.e., chronic migraines, fibromyalgia) and discuss symptomology, diagnosis, and treatment issues associated with these conditions*
- *Explore the medical, psychosocial, and vocational aspects of chronic pain*
- *Examine the characteristics of populations most likely to experience chronic pain*
- *Present recommendations for providing responsive rehabilitation counseling services to the growing numbers of individuals living with chronic pain who are served by rehabilitation counselors across all employment settings*

CASE ILLUSTRATION: LINDA

Linda is a 52-year-old White female who is employed full time as a director of communications in a college of arts and sciences at a medium-sized university. Approximately 7 years ago, she began experiencing pain in her neck and left shoulder after lifting and carrying a heavy suitcase. She ignored the pain for several months (thinking she had simply strained a muscle, and it would resolve on its own) until it spread to other parts of her body and began to cause extreme fatigue and difficulty sleeping. At this point, she made an appointment with her primary physician who ordered x-rays and diagnosed her with degenerative disc disease (which he told her was common and nothing to worry about). He prescribed muscle relaxants that did nothing to alleviate her pain so Linda returned to her physician who then set her on a long course of numerous failed treatments (e.g., physical therapy, spinal manipulations, acupuncture, psychotherapy). Finally, her primary physician referred her to a rheumatologist who diagnosed her with fibromyalgia (FM) and treated her with Lyrica and Cymbalta for the pain and trazodone to help her sleep. These medications helped somewhat with the widespread body pain, fatigue, and sleep disturbances, but the pain in her neck and shoulders continued to worsen until it became excruciating. She returned to her primary physician once again and he ordered an MRI and referred her to a neurosurgeon. The MRI revealed that extensive degeneration in two of her cervical discs was responsible for her excruciating pain, and Linda underwent a three-level anterior cervical discectomy and fusion. The surgery helped to ease the pain somewhat, but most days it still remains in the moderate to severe range.

Linda has been employed in her current position for the past 12 years. In this position, she is responsible for publicizing faculty and student accomplishments through news releases, social media websites, digital message boards, and weekly internal newsletters. She spends, on average, 6 hours a day working at her computer. During the rest of the workday, she interviews faculty and students (either in person or over the telephone) for news stories or goes to campus and community events and research sites to gather data for her stories and photograph faculty and students. Linda loves her job but is having difficulty keeping up with the pace of her work. Although she never lets her pain prevent her from going to work, it does interfere with her concentration and memory (especially later in the day), accuracy in writing news stories, length of time it takes to complete projects, and ability to meet deadlines. She reports feeling very anxious about her capacity to continue working because she cannot financially afford to lose her job. In addition to normal expenses, she and her spouse pay tuition for their two children who are going to college out of state.

Linda also feels despondent because of her inability to do anything when she gets home from work but lie on the couch in misery. She hates that she cannot enjoy her weekends because she has to spend most of her time in bed recovering from the workweek. She has become isolated from her friends and extended family because she can no longer participate in evening or weekend social gatherings. As a consequence, she has lost contact with the majority of her social network. Linda also feels guilty about the strain her conditions have put on her spouse who is also employed full time and has had to take over all household duties. Her desire is to continue working until she reaches retirement age but also to have a life outside of work like she did prior to the onset of her chronic pain.

Chronic pain, the leading cause of disability in the United States, is a pervasive public health problem that takes a considerable toll on the physical, emotional, economic, social, and vocational well-being of affected individuals. Recent estimates indicate that 30% to 40% (100 million) adults in the United States experience chronic pain, a figure that exceeds the total number of Americans living with diabetes, heart disease, and cancer combined (Gatchel, McGeary, McGeary, & Lippe, 2014). Chronic pain costs society billions of dollars in health care expenditures and lost productivity. In 2011, the Institute of Medicine (IOM) estimated that the annual economic cost attributable to chronic pain was $261 billion to $300 billion for health care and $297 billion to $336 billion for lost productivity.

The IOM (2011) has indicated that the number of Americans with chronic pain is expected to continue to increase in the foreseeable future for several reasons. First, the rapid aging of the U.S. population is likely to result in increases in the numbers of individuals with conditions associated with chronic pain (e.g., diabetes, cardiovascular diseases, arthritis, cancer). Second, increasing rates of obesity predispose large numbers of Americans to chronic pain conditions such as diabetes-associated neuropathy and orthopedic problems. Third, because of advances in emergency medicine, individuals with catastrophic injuries, who until fairly recently would have died from these injuries, are now surviving, but often with lifelong chronic pain. Relatedly, modern medicine has increased the life spans of individuals with serious illnesses, but many of these individuals must contend with debilitating pain. Fourth, the majority of surgical procedures are now performed on an outpatient basis, thus increasing the risk of unmanaged acute postsurgical pain that could evolve into chronic pain. Fifth, greater public awareness of chronic pain conditions and new treatments for these conditions could inspire people who never sought care for their chronic pain to seek treatment. Finally, the Affordable Care Act could increase access to diagnosis and treatment for those with chronic pain who prior to the implementation of this act did not have the financial resources to seek care.

DEFINITIONS, TYPES, AND CAUSES OF CHRONIC PAIN

The International Association for the Study of Pain (IASP, 2015, para. 3) defines pain as "an unpleasant sensory and emotional experience associated with actual or potential tissue damage, or described in terms of such damage." Chronic pain, sometimes referred to as persistent pain, is "ongoing or recurrent pain, lasting beyond the usual course of acute illness or injury healing, more than 3 to 6 months, and which adversely affects the individual's well-being" (American Chronic Pain Association [ACPA], 2015, p. 10). Unlike acute pain that serves as a warning signal to protect individuals from further harm, chronic pain is harmful in and of itself (IOM, 2011).

The ACPA (2015) classifies pain as (a) nocioceptive, (b) neuropathic, or (b) mixed or undetermined. Nocioceptive pain occurs as a result of ongoing nonneural tissue damage, and results from activation of nocioceptors (IASP, 2015). Nocioceptors are "high-threshold receptors of the peripheral somatosensory nervous system that are capable of transducing and encoding noxious stimuli" (IASP, 2015, p. 1). Neuropathic pain results from damage to the brain, spinal cord, or peripheral nerves. Neuropathic pain is "generated independently by the nervous system, resulting from the culmination of physiological processes that are set in motion by persistent nocioceptive or inflammatory processes" (Fine, 2011, p. 999). Many chronic pain conditions have no known etiology or occur as a result of a combination of nocioceptive and neuropathic pain. The IASP (2015) indicates that when individuals report pain in the absence of tissue damage or unknown etiology, *it should be accepted as pain*.

The IOM (2011) identifies sources of chronic pain such as underlying diseases or medical conditions that can result in pain that persists after the disease has been cured (e.g., shingles) or worsens as the disease progresses (e.g., cancer). Individuals with diseases or medical conditions such as low back pain and osteoarthritis experience both persistent pain and flare-ups of worsening pain. Chronic pain may result after surgery when immediate acute pain following the surgery becomes chronic or when nerve damage occurred during the surgery. It can also result from inflammation as occurs in conditions such as rheumatoid arthritis and gout. Another type of chronic pain, central pain syndrome, can develop with chronic illnesses and disabilities such as stroke, multiple sclerosis, Parkinson's disease, brain tumors, limb amputations, brain injuries, and spinal cord injuries (ACPA, 2015). Central pain syndrome is a neurological condition that results from dysfunction in the central nervous system (CNS; i.e., brain, brainstem, spinal cord). It may be months or years after the damage to the CNS before central pain syndrome develops.

When acute pain becomes chronic, it becomes a medical condition in and of itself (Brennan, Carr, & Cousins, 2007; Fine, 2011; IOM, 2011). As Fine (2011, p. 996) noted,

> When left untreated, pain can become more complex in in its pathophysiology than the pain caused by the original injury or disease. These changes can involve structural and functional alterations in the nervous system such that pain ceases to be symptomatic of the initial cause and becomes an entirely separate condition.

Although the etiology of chronic pain is unknown, Gatchel et al. (2014) summarized neuroscience research that is beginning to uncover some of the processes that occur in the development of chronic pain. For example, chronic pain can cause prolonged activation of the stress regulation system, thereby causing breakdowns of the muscles, bones, and neural tissues. This breakdown, in turn, creates increased pain and a vicious circle of pain-stress-reactivity. Prolonged activation of the stress regulation system results in increased cortisol secretion, and while cortisol secretion is an adaptive response that mobilizes energy when one is stressed or in danger, prolonged cortisol secretion can cause detrimental effects to the body such as muscle atrophy, impairment of growth and tissue repair, and suppression of the immune system. Neuroscience has also revealed the potential common pathogenesis shared by chronic pain and co-occurring psychiatric conditions (i.e., the same neurotransmitters, namely norepinephrine and serotonin, are involved in both chronic pain and mood disorders). Neuroimaging techniques have identified brain regions involved in cognitive and emotional processes (e.g., attention, empathy, anticipation, reward, control) that modulate pain as well as anatomical changes in the brains of people with chronic pain (IOM, 2011).

Chronic pain can range from mild to severe and fluctuate from day to day or even throughout a single day. Common conditions that result in chronic pain, in addition to those cited earlier in this chapter, include headaches, arthritis, FM, low back pain, other musculoskeletal disorders, trauma, heart disease (angina), complex regional pain syndrome, repetitive stress injuries, shingles, and irritable bowel syndrome (IOM, 2011). Chronic pain has negative effects on physical, cognitive, and emotional functioning (Fine, 2011). Individuals with chronic pain may experience difficulties with stamina, sitting or standing for prolonged periods, and strenuous physical activities. They may also experience disruptions in concentration, memory, and attention. Fatigue and sleep disturbances may exacerbate the pain and lead to further impairment. Other symptoms of chronic pain include allodynia, which occurs when individuals experience pain from stimuli such as soft touch that normally do not produce pain, and hyperalgesia, an exaggerated response to stimuli that are typically only mildly painful (Gatchel et al., 2014). Chronic pain can impair functioning in multiple functional domains including activities of daily living, occupational functioning, recreation and leisure activities, social interactions, sexual functioning, and family relationships.

Furthermore, chronic pain can result in neurological changes in the brain and increase the risk for hypertension due to "altered processes in pain pathways and cardiovascular function that normally overlap" (Fine, 2011, p. 988). Finally, the emotional stress of living with chronic pain can be quite profound in terms of its effect on quality of life and can lead to psychological symptoms such as depression and anxiety (Gatchel et al., 2014).

Currently, no objective medical tests are available to diagnose chronic pain. Instead, physicians take a pain history that relies on patients' descriptions of the type of pain (e.g., stabbing, throbbing, sharp, dull, piercing) they are experiencing, its location(s), whether the pain is constant or episodic, and other symptoms (National Institutes of Health [NIH], 2011). Physicians may also perform diagnostics to rule out other conditions that could be the source of pain. Based on the results of these evaluations, treatment plans are developed that typically include a combination of both nonpharmacological and pharmacological approaches, with the goal of returning patients to a pain level that is less disruptive to their daily lives (ACPA, 2015).

EXAMPLES OF EMERGING CHRONIC PAIN CONDITIONS

Chronic Migraines

More than 37 million Americans experience migraine headaches (Lipton, 2015; Lipton et al., 2007). Although previously believed to be caused by dilation and constriction of blood vessels in the head, migraines are now considered to be a neurological disorder with a genetic basis. The pain associated with migraines is often excruciating, and during migraine attacks individuals may be completely incapacitated. Migraines are categorized as episodic and chronic (Lipton & Silberstein, 2015). Episodic migraines occur on fewer than 15 days per month and can progress to chronic migraines. Chronic migraines occur 15 days or more per month for at least 3 months, with features of migraine occurring at least 8 days per month (Lipson, 2015). As many as 3% of Americans are estimated to have chronic migraines (Lipton, & Silberstein, 2015); however, because chronic migraines are underdiagnosed and undertreated, the prevalence is likely to be considerably higher (Lipton, 2015).

Chronic migraines, in comparison to episodic migraines, are associated with "a substantially greater personal and societal burden, more frequent comorbidities, and may be associated with brain abnormalities that are persistent and perhaps progressive" (Lipton, 2015, p. 104). The two major subtypes of migraines are migraine with aura and migraine without aura (Lipton, 2015). However, these subtypes are not mutually exclusive because individuals who experience auras may also have migraines without aura. Approximately 36% of people with migraine headaches experience auras. Auras are warning signs that a migraine attack is pending. Auras typically occur about 30 minutes before the onset of a migraine attack. Auras are characterized by vision changes, sensory symptoms, or language disturbances. Vision changes include blurred vision, blind spots, or seeing flashes or jagged light in peripheral vision. Sensory changes may be experienced as numbness and tingling, and language disturbances include difficulty with verbal and written expression and problems understanding words written or spoken by others.

During migraine attacks, individuals experience symptoms such as throbbing, pulsating pain; photophobia (light sensitivity); sound sensitivity;

sensitivity to smells; nausea; vomiting; pain on one side; and visual changes (Lipton & Silberstein, 2015). These attacks can last from several hours to days and vary in intensity of pain and associated symptoms, often rendering individuals completely incapacitated. Migraine attacks are followed by a postdromal phase in which the individual experiences exhaustion that extends the period of time during which the ability to function is impaired. Other functional domains that can be impaired during migraine attacks include writing, comprehension, motor abilities, and difficulties moving. Chronic migraines also increase risk for cardiovascular and respiratory diseases (Lipton, 2015).

Although the causes of migraines are unknown, certain migraine triggers have been identified. These triggers are listed in Table 2.1. Because there are no biomarkers for chronic migraines, diagnosis is made based on a clinical history, physical examination, and diagnostic tests to rule out other headache disorders (Katsarava, Buse, Manack, & Lipton, 2012). Treatment for chronic migraines focuses on pain relief, restoration of function, and reduction of headache frequency (Lipton & Silberstein, 2015). Treatment, as described by the National Institute of Neurological Disorders and Stroke (NINDS, 2015), includes pharmacological interventions and nonpharmacological interventions to both prevent migraine attacks and provide relief during migraine attacks. Preventive medications are taken on a regular basis and include the same medications used to treat epilepsy, high blood pressure, and depression. Medications taken during migraine attacks include sumatriptan, ergo derivatives, and analgesics such as ibuprofen and aspirin. Nonpharmacological interventions include patient education, stress reduction, and lifestyle changes. Stress reduction strategies include exercise, relaxation techniques, and biofeedback. Keeping a daily pain diary can help to identify triggers and subsequent lifestyle changes (e.g., eating regularly, weight loss, smoking cessation, adequate hydration, developing a consistent

TABLE 2.1 Migraine Triggers

- Stress or anxiety
- Certain foods (e.g., chocolate, cheese, processed foods)
- Food additives (e.g., monosodium glutamate, aspartame)
- Weather changes
- Lack of sleep
- Not getting enough to eat
- Hormonal fluctuations
- Bright lights, loud sounds, and strong smells
- Alcohol or caffeine withdrawal
- Smoking
- Certain medications
- Intense physical activity

Source: Agency for Healthcare Research and Quality (2012); Lipton and Silberstein (2015).

sleep schedule, discontinuing use of certain medications) to prevent migraine attacks. Treatment may also include pharmacological and nonpharmacological interventions for co-occurring conditions that are common among individuals with chronic migraines such as sleep disorders, depression, obesity, hypertension, and chronic neck pain.

Fibromyalgia

In recent years, there has been an escalation in health care provider office visits by people with fibromyalgia (FM), leading to an increased recognition of FM as a common medical condition (Skaer, 2014). FM is a chronic pain disorder with estimates indicating that it affects between 5 and 6 million Americans (Arthritis Foundation, 2013; Skaer, 2014). FM is characterized by widespread musculoskeletal pain, fatigue, memory problems, and mood changes (Arthritis Foundation, 2013; Grodman et al., 2011). Individuals with FM can also experience sleep disturbances, memory and concentration difficulties (i.e., "fibro fog"), tension and migraine headaches, irritable bowel syndrome, bladder spasms and the urge to urinate frequently, dizziness, restless legs, and paresthesia (Arthritis Foundation, 2013).

The severity of FM pain varies across individuals, and although some only experience mild symptoms that are easily managed, others experience moderate to severe symptoms that can substantially disrupt their lives (Arthritis Foundation, 2013). FM pain often initially occurs in one region of the body (e.g., neck, shoulders) and later spreads to other regions. Tender areas across the body cause pain when touched. People with FM often experience flare-ups (i.e., "fibro flares") that are characterized by a temporary worsening of their symptoms that can last from a single day to months. A variety of triggers of flare-ups have been identified including time of day, activity level, weather, sleep patterns, and stress levels.

The cause of FM is unknown; however, researchers have speculated about a variety of potential factors such as an injury, trauma, or infection that alters the way the CNS responds to pain; psychological trauma that leads to biochemical changes in the muscles and later to the CNS; injury to the CNS that interferes with brain wave patterns related to pain; and hormonal changes or infections (Arthritis Foundation, 2013). Advances in neuroimaging have demonstrated that when small amounts of pressure or heat are applied to tender points, regions of the brain that receive pain signals demonstrate much higher amounts of pain in people with FM as compared to those without FM.

Grodman et al. (2011) summarized research being conducted to understand the pathogenesis of FM. Serotonin deficiency and an excess of substance P (i.e., a neuropeptide that is released by specific sensory nerves that transmits pain signals to the brain) have been found in the spinal fluid of individuals with FM. Deficiencies in serotonin may be related to sleep difficulties, and excesses of substance P could result in an enhanced sensitivity to pain. Abnormalities in the central sensitization of pain have been identified as another potential explanation for the heightened sensitivity to pain stimuli experienced by people with FM. Other explanations have been that abnormal pain amplification at the level of the spine accounts for the increased pain. The tender points in FM may be caused by muscular pathology, and decreased growth hormone, which is necessary for muscular function. These could account for the extended muscular pain experienced after exercise. Additionally, research is being conducted to determine if family history and genetics play a role in the onset of FM.

No diagnostic tests are available for FM. However, tests may be used to rule out other conditions (e.g., hypothyroidism, rheumatoid arthritis, lupus) that have symptoms similar to FM (Arthritis Foundation, 2013). Instead, diagnosis of FM is made based on a thorough health history and medical exam. Although diagnosis was previously based on both a history of widespread chronic pain and greater than 11 of 18 possible tender points on physical examination, in 2010 the American College of Rheumatology (ACR) developed new criteria for diagnosing FM (Grodman et al., 2011; Skaer, 2014). These criteria require that diagnosis of FM is to be made using a symptom severity (SS) scale and widespread pain index (WPI). The SS scale score is the sum of severity of three symptoms (fatigue, waking unrefreshed, cognitive symptoms) plus the extent of somatic symptoms in general. Somatic symptoms can include "muscle pain, irritable bowel syndrome, fatigue/tiredness, thinking or remembering problems, muscle weakness, headache, pain/cramps in the abdomen, numbness/tingling, dizziness, insomnia, depression, constipation, pain in the upper abdomen, nausea, nervousness, chest pain, blurred vision, fever, diarrhea, dry mouth, itching, wheezing, Raynaud's phenomenon, hives/welts, ringing in ears, vomiting, heartburn, oral ulcers, loss of/change in taste, seizures, dry eyes, shortness of breath, loss of appetite, rash, sun sensitivity, hearing difficulties, easy bruising, hair loss, frequent urination, painful urination, and bladder spasms" (Wolfe et al., 2010, p. 607).

The WPI is a diagnostic tool used by physicians to determine the number of areas on the body where pain has occurred over the last week (Wolfe et al., 2010). Nineteen body areas are included, and individuals can receive a score of 0 to 19. To make a diagnosis of FM, the individual must receive a score greater than 7 on the WPI and greater than 5 on the SS scale or between 3 and 6 on the WPI or greater than 9 on the SS scale. In addition to these criteria, symptoms must have been present for at least 3 months, and the patient must not have another disorder that could explain the symptoms.

Although there is no cure for FM, treatment that includes a combination of medications and illness self-management strategies has been demonstrated to be effective at reducing symptoms of FM. The U.S. Food and Drug Administration (FDA) has approved several medications for treating the pain associated with FM. These medications and their intended purposes are listed in Table 2.2.

In addition to FDA-approved medications for FM, several off-label medications have been found to be effective in treating symptoms. Off-label medications are those that are prescribed for indications other than their intended use (Wittich, Burkle, & Lanier, 2012). These include tricyclics and cyclobenzaprine to relieve pain and improve sleep; selective serotonin reuptake inhibitors (SSRIs) to relieve pain and improve mood; nonsteroid anti-inflammatory drugs (NSAIDs) in modest doses to provide some pain relief; and opioid pain relievers and tranquilizers for severe cases, although these tend to be less effective for FM than they are for other pain conditions, and long-term use can have negative effects on organs and nervous and digestive systems. Other off-label medications for FM include gabapentin, venlafaxine, tizanidine, cannabinoids, gamma-hydroxybutyrate, and low-dose naltrexone (Arthritis Foundation, 2013, p. 9)

Nonpharmacological treatments include exercise programs to increase blood flow to affected areas, prevent muscle atrophy, and release endorphins

TABLE 2.2 FDA-Approved Medications for Treating Fibromyalgia

Duloxetine (Cymbalta)	Raises levels of neurotransmitters (i.e., norepinephrine and serotonin) known to lower pain transmission
Milnacipran (Savella)	Raises levels of neurotransmitters (i.e., norepinephrine and serotonin) known to lower pain transmission
Pregabalin (Lyrica)	Reduces levels of neurotransmitters (e.g., glutamate, substance P) that increase pain transmission

FDA, Food and Drug Administration.
Adapted from the Arthritis Foundation (2013, pp. 8–9).

to improve pain and mood; psychoeducation to equip individuals with the skills to effectively manage their pain and live satisfying lives; and relaxation techniques to reduce muscle tension and anxiety (Arthritis Foundation, 2013). Some individuals with FM also find complementary therapies such as acupuncture, gentle massage, heat, hydrotherapy, tai chi, biofeedback, changes to their diet, cranial sacral therapy, transcutaneous electrical nerve stimulation (TENS), meditation, yoga, and chiropractic interventions to be helpful (Arnold et al., 2008).

PSYCHOSOCIAL ASPECTS OF CHRONIC PAIN

Unrelenting pain can take a tremendous emotional and physical toll on the individual. As described by Cowan (2011, p. 4), chronic pain is "a constant companion that interferes with every thought, word, and deed." In *The Pain Chronicles* written by Melanie Thernstrom (2011, p. 5), the author describes the experience of living with chronic pain as follows:

> Usually, pain subsides; one wakes from it as from a nightmare, trying to forget it as quickly as possible. But what of pain that persists? The longer it endures, the more excruciating the exile becomes. *Will you ever go home?* You begin to wonder, home to your normal body, thoughts, life?

Chronic pain can make it difficult for individuals to continue performing in valued roles such as family member, friend, and employee because of lack of energy, exacerbation of pain, and/or fears of exacerbating their pain (IOM, 2011). When individuals are unable to continue performing in roles that they value, they may struggle to balance this loss with maintaining a strong sense of self (Toye & Barker, 2010). Tasks (e.g., activities of daily living, job tasks) that, prior to the onset of chronic pain, were easily accomplished may be difficult to impossible, and those with chronic pain may experience psychological distress as they make comparisons between their prior abilities and their current abilities (Day, Thorn, & Burns, 2012). Individuals with chronic pain may also experience significant anxiety about their impaired ability to carry out the multitude of daily activities (e.g., work, household management, childcare) that modern life demands. Fears about the future, the further diminishing of functional capacities, the ability to continue working, increasing pain, and worsening of associated symptoms are also common. Compounding the aforementioned problems, many individuals with chronic pain never visit a health care professional because of a fatalistic belief that no one can relieve their suffering (Brennan et al., 2007).

Constantly feeling tired and fatigued can be another source of significant psychological distress (Arnold et al., 2008; Sim & Madden, 2008), particularly for individuals who maintained very active lifestyles prior to the onset of pain. Participation in activities such as work and social engagements may be curtailed by some individuals with chronic pain because of unpredictable fatigue. In addition, individuals may fear that these activities will worsen their condition when, in reality, these activities could potentially alleviate some of their pain and contribute to a better sense of emotional well-being (Thernstrom, 2010). Likewise, some individuals may avoid exercise out of fear that they will further injure themselves or experience additional pain. Deconditioning and guarding of the afflicted area can result in muscle atrophy, which can further impair mobility and cause greater pain (IOM, 2011; Thernstrom, 2010).

Most individuals with chronic pain also have more than one chronic pain condition and/or co-occurring disorder (e.g., anxiety, depression, substance use disorder). For example, individuals with FM may also have additional chronic pain conditions such as rheumatoid arthritis, osteoarthritis, or lupus (Arthritis Foundation, 2013). Given the suffering caused by chronic pain, it is not surprising that between one third and one half of individuals with chronic pain have co-occurring depression (Thernstrom, 2010). However, the relationship between chronic pain and depression is more complex than it appears on the surface. Researchers have studied depression as both an antecedent and a consequence of chronic pain. According to Thernstrom (2010, p. 157) the two are "biologically entwined diseases with a common pathophysiology stemming from a common genetic vulnerability." Research has resulted in the discovery of the similar effects that both chronic pain and depression have on the neurotransmitters serotonin and norepinephrine. Abnormalities in these neurotransmitters play a role in both mood disorders and the gate-control mechanisms of pain.

Other studies are investigating inflammation as a link between chronic pain and depression (NIH, 2015). According to these studies, people with severe depression feel more intense pain because they have higher than normal levels of cytokines. Cytokines are proteins that can cause pain by promoting inflammation, to protect an injured area or infection by destroying, removing, or isolating it.

The psychosocial challenges of living with chronic pain are numerous. Foremost among these challenges are the lack of understanding that the general public has about chronic pain. Individuals with chronic pain may isolate themselves from others who lack empathy and understanding of what it is like to live a life characterized by pain. Social isolation is compounded if the pain is unpredictable (Arnold et al., 2008). For example, individuals with FM and chronic migraines cannot always predict when they will have flare-ups or migraine attacks. This unpredictability may lead these individuals to limit or totally discontinue participation in activities that bring them pleasure, a sense of accomplishment, or social connectedness. They may need to repeatedly cancel plans with friends due to unpredictable flare-ups or onset of symptoms, and friends may disbelieve or misinterpret their reasons for cancellation as a form of social rejection and stop inviting them to social engagements, thus further contributing to the feelings of isolation. Those with chronic pain may not be able to participate in family activities (e.g., dinners, outings, school events, sporting events in which their children participate) to the extent they were able to prior to the onset of chronic pain. Personal feelings of guilt and anxiety as well as anger and resentment among family members can result in role tension, family conflict, reduced sexual activity, and ineffective communication (Holloway, Sofaer-Bennett, & Walker, 2007).

Psychosocial challenges also arise from diagnostic uncertainties and invalidation of one's complaints (Holloway et al., 2007; Sim & Madden, 2008; Toye & Barker, 2010). Individuals with chronic pain often spend years consulting with multiple specialists (Sim & Madden, 2008), some of whom dismiss their reported symptoms, others of whom tell them there is nothing that can be done, and still others of whom diagnose their symptoms and set them on a path of treatment that fails to result in any relief of their pain or, in worse case scenarios, exacerbates their pain (Hansson, Fridlund, Brunt, Hansson, & Rask, 2011). Even conditions such as FM and chronic migraines that have been medically recognized for decades are not viewed by all physicians as legitimate chronic illnesses (Thernstrom, 2010).

The treatments (e.g., physical therapy, spinal manipulations, surgical procedures, psychotherapy) prescribed for chronic pain may extend over a substantial period of time (Jensen & Turk, 2014) and require a considerable financial, emotional, time, and behavioral commitment without positive outcomes. Frustration, self-blame for not achieving desired effects of these treatments, fears about worsening symptoms, concerns that they are dying, feelings that they are "going crazy," and anger toward medical and health care providers for failing to provide effective treatments are also common reactions (IOM, 2011).

Receiving a diagnosis is often accompanied by mixed feelings of relief, validation, anxiety, and uncertainty about the future (Raymond & Brown, 2000). Coming to terms with the fact that pain will continue indefinitely is a difficult process, often accompanied by significant psychological distress. Given the ambiguity of chronic pain and the absence of objective medical tests to diagnose chronic pain conditions, many individuals refuse to accept that they have a condition of unknown etiology with no cure. Consequently, "their lives become dominated by attempts to become pain free" (IOM, 2011, p. 44). Understandably, these individuals may develop depression, and a disturbing research finding is that individuals with chronic pain and co-occurring depression are more likely than individuals without these conditions to experience suicidal ideation, suicide attempts, and completed suicides (Thernstrom, 2010). The more severe the pain, the more likely they are to contemplate, attempt, and/or complete suicide.

It is not only the medical community that creates significant psychosocial challenges for individuals with chronic pain. Medical invalidation leads to societal invalidation, stigma, and rejection (Holloway et al., 2007). Because chronic pain is invisible and often associated with episodic flare-ups or unpredictable vacillations in severity of pain, others may not believe the pain is real. This response may, in turn, lead individuals with chronic pain to also question if their pain is real (Toye & Barker, 2010). As Smart (2009) noted, the ambiguity of invisible and episodic disabilities often results in the attribution of bad motives (e.g., attention-seeking, exaggeration of pain, secondary gain) to individuals with these conditions. Because of these negative attributions, individuals with chronic pain may go to great efforts to hide their pain. Others may also struggle with issues related to self-presentation (Hansson et al., 2011; Toye & Barker, 2010). On the one hand, they do not want to appear too healthy because then they will not be perceived as having a chronic pain condition. Conversely, if they present themselves as too unhealthy, they may be viewed as exaggerating their pain or malingering.

A multitude of myths govern how people (including health care providers and individuals with chronic pain themselves) view and respond to chronic pain. As observed by Brennan et al. (2007, p. 217), "for too long, pain and its management have been prisoners of myth, irrationality, ignorance, and cultural bias." In their article advocating for pain management as a fundamental human right, these authors describe the cultural, religious, attitudinal, educational, economic, and political sources from which these myths arise as well as how damaging these myths are to individuals with chronic pain. First and foremost among these sources is the biomedical model that still dominates much of the practice of medicine with its foci on disease, pathology, and curing acute illnesses. The biomedical model fails to address important issues for individuals with chronic pain such as the chronicity of their conditions and their overall quality of life. The biomedical model also focuses exclusively on objective, quantitative measurements in making diagnoses rather than on qualitative patient self-reports. Individuals with chronic pain, who also ascribe to the biomedical model, may question the validity of their pain when objective tests to diagnose their conditions are lacking (Toye & Barker, 2010)

Another myth that springs from the biomedical model is that if the cause of chronic pain cannot be determined, the pain is not real, and the individual who seeks treatment for chronic pain is either malingering to get out of unpleasant activities or has a psychosomatic condition that should be treated by a mental health professional (Hansson et al., 2011; Holloway et al., 2007). This myth prevails among physicians, health professionals, and the general public. Rehabilitation counselors are not exempt from being negatively influenced by this myth. In fact, it is not uncommon for rehabilitation counselors who provide services to injured workers to view those clients who report continuing pain after their injury has healed to be malingering so that they can continue to receive financial compensation for their work-related injuries and avoid going back to work.

Another prominent myth is that if the individual looks "normal," she or he must not be in pain (Hansson et al., 2011; Sim & Madden, 2008; Toye & Barker, 2010). The fact that someone does not have outward signs of pain and appears to be comfortable is not evidence of the absence of pain. People with chronic pain often go about their normal daily activities despite their pain. In research conducted by Toye and Barker (2010), individuals with persistent unexplained back pain described how this myth put them in the position of constantly having to prove their pain was legitimate. Individuals with chronic pain may also struggle to find the right words to describe their pain to others so that the amount of physical suffering they experience is not dismissed or invalidated (Sim & Madden, 2008).

"Religion, philosophy, and folklore have 'saturated pain with meaning'" (Brennan et al., 2007, p. 207). These teachings suggest that suffering is a natural part of human life and builds character. Relatedly, the assignment of redemptive qualities to those who "suffer in silence" and views of pain as a sign of strength result in societal perceptions of those who complain of pain as having weak characters (Brennan et al., 2007). This myth can be especially harmful if it influences individuals in terms of how they respond to their pain (i.e., ignoring it versus seeking treatment). The "no pain, no gain" adage that dominates contemporary American culture is also detrimental to the physical and psychological well-being of individuals with chronic pain. Directly linked to this adage is the myth that one should just "push through" the pain and continue what she or he is doing. The fact is that knowing one's limits and pacing oneself accordingly are important components of pain management. For individuals with chronic pain, pushing themselves beyond these limits will only serve to exacerbate their pain. Finally, given the rapidly aging population, a myth that warrants special consideration is that pain is a natural part of the aging process (Thielke, 2012). Believing this myth may have the harmful result of ignoring the pain instead of seeking early intervention to identify the source of the pain, receive treatment, and potentially prevent what may be a life-threatening condition.

Myths also prevail regarding the treatment of chronic pain. For example, "opiophobia" and "opioignorance" prevent individuals from accessing medications (i.e., opioids) that, for some, can improve their symptoms, enable them to function in valued roles, and enhance their quality of life (Brennan et al., 2007; Thernstrom, 2010). Prosecution of physicians for prescribing opioids, concerns about patient potential for dependence and abuse, and fears of regulatory scrutiny have led to reluctance, and even refusal, on the part of physicians to prescribe opioid analgesics to any patients, regardless of the potential of these medications to alleviate suffering (Brennan et al., 2007; Roskos, Keenum, Newman, & Wallace, 2007; Thernstrom, 2010). Brennan et al. (2007) suggested that there is a need for opioid control to prevent abuse and diversion to be better balanced with the need to ensure that these medications are available for those who need these medications for pain management purposes.

Thernstrom (2010) noted that myths about opioids arise from the confusion between physical dependence and addiction, concerns that these medications will sedate individuals to such a degree that they will be unable to function, and fears about the heightened risk of accidental death from respiratory depression that is caused by opioids. Dependence can occur with long-term opioid use. Dependence is the body's adaptation to a drug, requiring larger doses to achieve the desired effect (tolerance), and resulting in withdrawal symptoms if the drug is abruptly ceased (ACPA, 2015). However, some individuals benefit from the same dosage for years. Conversely, addiction occurs when individuals engage in compulsive drug use, regardless of the negative impact the individual's drug use has on work, social, and family functioning (Thernstrom, 2010). Addiction is characterized by an inability to stop using the drug, and, depending on the drug used, tolerance and withdrawal. With respect to the concerns about sedation, drowsiness is a temporary side effect, and individuals with chronic pain develop a tolerance to drowsiness, and many are actually able to function better once the sedative effects wear off (ACPA, 2015). Respiratory depression is a serious side effect of opioids. However, to avoid the risk of accidental death from respiratory depression, practice guidelines for prescribing physicians require them to take thorough medication and health histories, carefully monitor patients, and educate them about avoiding use of other drugs (sedative-hypnotics, benzodi-azepines, antidepressants, muscle relaxants, alcohol) that can depress breathing.

Because of the "opioid backlash," individuals who complain of chronic pain and the need for painkillers are often treated as "drug seekers" and are denied the very medications that could significantly improve their ability to function as well as improve their overall quality of life (Thernstrom, 2010). The failure of physicians to treat individuals with chronic pain with appropriate pain medications has been described as a moral issue and a violation of both medical ethics and human rights (Brennan et al., 2007; IOM, 2011; Thernstrom, 2010). It has even been suggested that "unreasonable failure to provide adequate pain relief constitutes negligence" (Brennan et al., 2007, p. 212).

With regard to all of these misconceptions about opioid analgesics, rehabilitation counselors should be aware that many organizations such as the American Academy of Pain Medicine (2013) and the ACPA (2015) have developed guidelines for prescribing opioids for pain management with common elements across guidelines. First, guidelines recommend prescribing opioids only after other pharmacological treatments have failed. Guidelines also recommend the careful assessment of risk factors (e.g., individual or family history of addiction; serious problems with anxiety, depression, and other mental health disorders; childhood history of abuse) for addiction should be conducted before prescribing opioids. These guidelines also require physicians to closely monitor for pain and any drug-related behaviors. On an ongoing basis, prescribing physicians must evaluate the patient's degree of pain relief, ability to perform activities of daily living, adverse side effects of medications, and abnormal drug-related behaviors. They must also evaluate the patient for medication benefits such as significant increases in his or her level of functioning, reduction or elimination of pain complaints, more positive and hopeful attitudes, and safe management of side effects. This ongoing evaluation includes urine testing at random intervals to screen for other drugs prior to prescribing opioids.

Guidelines also indicate that patients should be given opioid contracts with conditions they must abide by to continue to receive treatment. Opioid contracts outline specific instructions and information about such treatment issues as appropriate use of opioids, risk factors and side effects, safeguarding medication from inadvertent or intentional use by others, tolerance and withdrawal, prohibited behavior, terms of treatment, breaches of contract that could result in treatment termination, emergency issues, and legal considerations such as actions to take if medications are stolen (Roskos et al., 2007). Finally, guidelines include safe and effective methods for discontinuing opioids. In conclusion, although opioids pose serious risks and have many potentially negative side effects, physicians and patients with chronic pain must balance the potential risks with the benefits as well as the use of alternative medications to determine if opioid therapy, in combination with nonpharmacological treatments, is the most beneficial course of action (ACPA, 2015).

VOCATIONAL ASPECTS OF CHRONIC PAIN

Chronic pain can interfere with participating in employment in numerous ways. First and foremost, some individuals with chronic pain do not believe that beginning, returning to, or continuing work is a feasible goal for them. In these instances, their treating physicians may have told them that they are not able to work, and, when they hear these words from a professional they hold in high esteem, they are highly likely to develop the belief that they are permanently vocationally disabled (Sullivan & Hyman, 2014). Many others want to enter, return to, or maintain employment but have numerous symptoms in addition to pain that present barriers to working. Commonly reported symptoms include fatigue, muscle weakness, reduced mobility, sleep disturbances, motor difficulties, and memory and concentration difficulties (Grodman et al., 2011; IOM, 2011). Stamina is often reduced, and many individuals with chronic pain do not get adequate sleep. Poor sleep hygiene can impair concentration, memory, and thought processes (Muller et al., 2015). Fatigue caused both by pain and lack of adequate sleep can make it difficult to complete even the simplest job tasks. Working in extreme heat or cold can also exacerbate pain and other symptoms. For individuals with chronic migraines, functional impairments are most likely to be problematic in work environments that contain elements (e.g., fluorescent lighting, smoke, smells, noise) that could trigger a migraine attack (Job Accommodation Network, 2015). Chronic pain can also create interpersonal challenges with coworkers, supervisors, and customers because of stigma, irritability associated with the chronic pain one is experiencing, overreliance on coworkers to assist with tasks that exceed the individual's capabilities, and experiences of having one's pain invalidated (Shaw et al., 2012).

To preserve employment, individuals with chronic pain must often make substantial changes to how they perform the essential functions of their jobs (Rakovski, Zettel-Watson, & Rutledge, 2012; Skaer, 2014). Others must change to different positions or occupations to maintain employment. Even so, frequent absenteeism and compromised work productivity can occur as a result of fatigue, pain, sleep disturbances, and co-occurring anxiety or depression. In addition, it is not uncommon for employees with chronic pain to reduce their work hours. For example, Skaer (2014) reported that many employees with FM reduce their work hours by 50% to 75%.

In 2012, the IOM estimated the annual value of lost productivity due to chronic pain at approximately $300 billion. Chronic pain has been identified as the most common reason for disability leave from work (Grodman et al., 2011). Additionally, in comparison to individuals without chronic pain, rates of unemployment are markedly higher in samples of individuals with chronic pain, and the highest rates are experienced by individuals with severe chronic pain. Skaer (2014) noted that unemployment rates for individuals with FM are reported in the literature to be as high as 80.6%. Conversely, Grodman et al. (2011) cited research indicating that 34% to 77% of women with FM were successful in preserving their jobs despite their pain, especially when their employers were willing to provide scheduling modifications and other reasonable accommodations.

In addition to high rates of unemployment, adults with chronic pain are absent from work more often than those without chronic pain. They also have higher rates of presenteeism (i.e., reduced performance while at work; Fine, 2011), and, once again, the highest rates of both absenteeism and presenteeism are among those with severe chronic pain. Given the debilitating nature of chronic pain and the negative effects of pain on stamina, energy level, and cognitive and social functioning, it is not surprising that unemployment, absenteeism, and presenteeism are common problems for people with chronic pain. Added to these problems, the extensive myths associated with chronic pain may influence employer and employee behaviors in a manner that creates employer trepidation about hiring individuals with chronic pain, reluctance to accommodate them, and hostile work environments (Holloway et al., 2007).

CHARACTERISTICS OF INDIVIDUALS LIVING WITH CHRONIC PAIN

The IOM (2011) has summarized data on the demographic characteristics of individuals most likely to experience chronic pain. Not surprisingly, the highest rates of chronic pain are experienced by the most socially and economically disadvantaged members of society. In addition to higher rates of chronic pain, these individuals also experience health care disparities that prevent them from receiving both early intervention for acute pain and effective treatment for chronic pain.

Women experience higher rates of chronic pain than men, and certain disorders are more prevalent in women than men (IOM, 2011). For example, FM is more commonly diagnosed in women than men, and although the onset of FM typically occurs between the ages of 30 and 50, it can also occur in children, especially adolescent females (Arthritis Foundation, 2013). FM is also more prevalent in lower socioeconomic status populations, and several factors have been postulated to explain why this occurs. Among these factors are that these populations tend to work in jobs (e.g., manual labor) that may increase the likelihood of acquiring injuries and pain, have a tendency to be overweight (a risk factor for pain), and perform more housework (Grodman et al., 2011). In addition, individuals in these populations may be less able to afford and access preventive health care and early treatment for pain, thereby increasing the likelihood of developing FM. Chronic migraines are also more commonly experienced by women (Katsarava et al., 2012; Lipton & Silberstein, 2015). In attempting to understand why higher rates of chronic pain are reported by women, several possible explanations have been posed: (a) gender role stereotypes making it more socially acceptable for women to report chronic pain; (b) women are exposed to more risk factors; and (c) women are more vulnerable to developing certain types of pain. Of these three explanations, the vulnerability hypothesis has received the most research support (IOM, 2011). In addition to higher rates of chronic pain, women, in comparison to men, are also more likely to be undertreated for chronic pain and, in seeking treatment, to have their pain characterized by physicians as hormonal or "all in their heads" (Haley & Lawhead, 2015).

Individuals from diverse racial and ethnic groups experience higher rates of chronic pain than Whites. For example, African Americans report greater pain after surgical procedures and in association with a variety of specific medical conditions such as AIDS, angina pectoris, arthritis, headache, and some musculoskeletal conditions (IOM, 2011). In comparison to Whites, African Americans receive lower rates of clinician assessment of pain and higher rates of undertreatment (Haley & Lawhead, 2015), even when expressing similar painful symptoms. They are less likely to be prescribed analgesic medication or to receive surgery that could alleviate their pain. In one study cited by the IOM, the researchers found that

African Americans and individuals of lower socioeconomic status who acquired on-the-job low back injuries were less likely than other workers to receive treatment or compensation. American Indians and Alaska Natives report markedly higher rates of overall pain and pain related to specific sites (e.g., severe headache or migraine, low back pain, neck pain, joint pain). They also experience disproportionate rates of diseases and conditions that can cause pain such as diabetes, arthritis, and obesity.

Factors that place Hispanics at risk for chronic pain include lower education and income levels, higher rates of being overweight, lack of health insurance, lack of a usual source of care, limited English proficiency, and poor communication with health care providers. Interestingly, however, some research has demonstrated that Mexican Americans, the largest Hispanic group in the United States, report lower rates of pain than non-Hispanic Blacks and Whites (IOM, 2011).

Approximately 50% of older adults living independently in their communities and 75% to 85% of older adults in care facilities experience chronic pain (NIH, 2011). Older adults may believe that pain is a natural part of the aging process and, consequently, may not seek treatment because of their belief in this myth (Sofaer et al., 2005). Additionally, fears of losing their independence may preclude seeking help for pain, and many older adults may adapt to their pain using their own self-prescribed pain management techniques. Psychosocial factors that may compound their pain include a lack of social support from family, bereavement, loss of home or job, and failing health. Like women and individuals from racial and ethnic minority groups, older adults who do seek treatment are also undertreated for their pain (IOM, 2011), and this undertreatment has serious health consequences such as decreased mobility, social isolation, depression, anxiety, and sleep disturbances.

Factors that have been identified as potential contributors to the lower rates of clinician assessment and undertreatment of pain in all the populations described include both patient and clinician barriers (IOM, 2011). Patient barriers include lack of a usual source of care, low levels of trust in clinicians, poorer expectations of treatment outcomes, language barriers, and communication difficulties. Physician barriers include racial, ethnic, gender, and age stereotyping; biases and prejudices against these groups; and greater clinical uncertainty when interacting with culturally diverse patients.

REHABILITATION COUNSELING IMPLICATIONS

Counselor Awareness and Self-Reflective Practice

Because myths about chronic pain are so prevalent, rehabilitation counselors must carefully examine their own potential biases and misconceptions about chronic pain, its causes, and treatment. Then, they should engage in thoughtful reflection about how their attitudes might impact their interactions with consumers with chronic pain. Important questions rehabilitation counselors can ask themselves in the self-reflective process include: What have been my personal and professional experiences interacting with individuals with chronic pain? How have I interpreted their pain and its causes? How do I respond to their complaints about symptoms? Do I respond with compassion and empathy or do I tend to be suspicious of their motives because I don't really believe their pain is real or as bad as they say it is? What cultural myths about chronic pain have shaped my thinking and what can I do to change my thinking? What are some of my biases and misunderstandings about treating chronic pain? Do I view some chronic pain conditions as legitimate disabling conditions and others as not legitimate? What sources of information can I seek out to challenge my biases and better educate myself about chronic pain? What professional biases have governed the way in which consumers with chronic pain are viewed and treated within the setting where I work? How can I work with supervisors and other rehabilitation counselors in my professional setting to make changes to better serve consumers with chronic pain?

By asking themselves these questions, rehabilitation counselors can identify areas in which continuing education is warranted. Additionally, if biases are self-identified that could interfere with service delivery, rehabilitation counselors may want to consider strategies for combatting these biases that include learning from individuals with chronic pain themselves about their experiences. One strategy could be to obtain permission to attend pain support group meetings to hear personal accounts of what it is like to live with chronic pain. Other firsthand accounts can be obtained by reading qualitative studies about the lived experiences of individuals with chronic pain. Another useful resource is the *Pain Matters* website at painmatters.com. It includes a documentary on chronic pain and short video clips of individuals living with chronic pain. If, in reflecting about their own potential sources of bias, rehabilitation counselors determine that many of these arise from their professional training or misperceptions from within their particular employment setting, they can then advocate for in-service training for all staff.

Outreach and Eligibility Determination

Because many individuals with chronic pain may not identify themselves as disabled, outreach is needed to inform them about the availability of rehabilitation services and programs. Outreach should be specifically targeted to both potential rehabilitation consumers and their physicians. Physicians may need information about the health-related benefits of work because these providers may advise patients against working. Likewise, because many individuals with chronic pain also receive care from emergency departments at local hospitals (IOM, 2011), informational brochures can be placed in emergency waiting rooms. Rehabilitation counselors can also provide outreach to self-advocacy and support groups by attending meetings to educate group members about the availability of services.

Of utmost importance when meeting with individuals with chronic pain for initial interviews is to focus on building a trusting relationship. Keeping in mind that many individuals with chronic pain have had numerous encounters with service providers who minimized, dismissed, invalidated, and/or misdiagnosed their conditions, rehabilitation counselors must avoid approaching the initial session with suspicion, and, instead, ensure that they empathically listen to these consumers and validate their experiences. Although some consumers may be malingering for secondary gain, they represent a very small minority.

The vast majority of individuals with chronic pain continue, or desire to resume, participation in socially sanctioned roles and activities despite the overwhelming disruption to every aspect of their lives that is caused by chronic pain. Thus, the rehabilitation counselor should be attuned to the strength and resiliency that these individuals bring to the rehabilitation counseling process.

In a similar vein, cancellations, missed appointments, or rescheduling of appointments should not be automatically attributed to a lack of motivation or uncooperativeness. Rather, pain, particularly for those who are not being effectively treated, may interfere with the ability of these consumers to attend appointments. Alternatively, they may have little faith that participating in rehabilitation counseling services will lead to positive outcomes due to a long history of repeated failures of professionals to effectively treat their pain. In these cases, counseling and guidance should be provided to address these issues, provide consumers with hope, and determine alternatives to in-person appointments if necessary.

Eligibility determination may be complicated when medical records and specialty consultations indicate that individuals have chronic pain of an unknown origin. In these cases, it is extremely important that rehabilitation counselors conduct thorough intake interviews that focus on the impact of pain on major life activities. Rehabilitation counselors should collect intake information about the location, distribution, severity, chronicity, and effects of chronic pain on activities of daily living and employment; co-occurring conditions; current and previous treatments received for pain and the consumer's satisfaction with these treatments; psychosocial factors such as family relationships, support systems, employment history, receipt of disability compensation, and primary sources of income; goals the consumer would like to achieve; and rehabilitation services he or she desires.

Based on intake information, a determination should be made regarding the need to obtain specialist evaluations. When additional medical evaluations are indicated to make eligibility decisions, rehabilitation counselors should keep in mind that a variety of specialists treat chronic pain and should ensure that referrals to the appropriate specialists are made. Staffings with medical consultants can reduce the likelihood of costly expenditures resulting from inappropriate referrals, and, more importantly, can reduce consumer stress and anxiety associated with having to endure multiple specialist evaluations. Likewise, when documentation to establish service eligibility requires classification of the individual's reported condition into a specific disability category, agencies and programs should consider adding "chronic pain" as its own category, if one does not already exist, to ensure that these individuals are not denied much needed services.

Finally, rehabilitation counselors working in vocational settings must be cognizant that employment can serve to either enhance or further impair individual functioning. For some with chronic pain, working full time can exhaust all of their physical, emotional, and cognitive resources or exacerbate their pain to such a degree that all time off from work is spent recovering from pain. For these individuals, other important aspects of their lives (e.g., parenting, interpersonal relationships, leisure activities, community involvement, volunteering) may be neglected because all of their energy is devoted to working. Rehabilitation counselors should carefully explore with these consumers both the risks and benefits of employment; their perceptions regarding the impact of working on their overall quality of life; how workplace accommodations might increase their reserves for participating in other valued life activities; and employment alternatives such as part-time work, telecommuting, or job sharing. If individuals determine that employment is not a feasible goal, referrals should be made to other appropriate service providers such as benefits counselors to assist with obtaining disability compensation and/or to independent living counselors to identify home modifications and other services that could minimize the pain they experience in carrying out activities of daily living.

REHABILITATION ASSESSMENT AND PLANNING

Currently, the most widely used framework for understanding and treating chronic pain is the biopsychosocial model. This model describes chronic pain and disability as "a complex and dynamic interaction among physiological, psychological, and social factors that perpetuate, and even worsen, one another resulting in chronic and complex pain syndromes" (Gatchel et al., 2014, p. 120). Physiological factors include genetic predispositions and neural and biochemical mechanisms in pain processing. Psychological factors include emotional (e.g., depression, anxiety, fear, anger) and cognitive (e.g., pain appraisal, fear avoidance beliefs, perceived self-efficacy) responses to pain. Social factors include "activities of daily living, environmental stressors, interpersonal relationships, family environment, social support/isolation, social expectations, cultural factors, medicolegal/insurance issues, previous treatment experiences, and work history" (Gatchel et al., 2014, p. 583). The biopsychosocial model serves as a framework for holistically evaluating and treating chronic pain from an interdisciplinary perspective. It responds to each person's unique experience of pain and offers an individualized approach to providing targeted interventions to remediate the combination of biological, psychological, and social factors that exacerbate pain and undermine one's ability to function. Rehabilitation counselors should be highly effective at implementing this model because it closely aligns with the holistic approach that is the hallmark of rehabilitation counseling. Treatment of chronic pain from a biopsychosocial framework involves a variety of pharmacological and nonpharmacological interventions provided by a number of medical and health care specialists. Treatment may be provided in primary care settings, specialist offices, or interdisciplinary pain centers (IOM, 2011). Unfortunately, most current treatments of chronic pain have limited effectiveness, and, although they can mitigate pain to some degree, they do not resolve it (Thernstrom, 2010). However, research continues to advance understanding of chronic pain and identify new forms of treatment (Haley & Lawhead, 2015). Advances in neuroimaging and genetics testing, for example, may one day make it possible to better diagnose chronic pain and identify interventions that can be specifically tailored to the individual patient (Jensen & Turk, 2014).

In identifying potential biopsychosocial interventions to include in the rehabilitation plan, the rehabilitation counselor must carefully evaluate what treatments the consumer is already receiving and his or her assessment of the effectiveness of these treatments. Then, together, the rehabilitation consumer and counselor can collaboratively identify those interventions that the consumer wants to continue receiving as well as additional interventions that may prove beneficial. These decisions should be flexible and based on consumer preference (Jensen & Turk, 2014). In making these determinations, consumers should be advised of both the risks and benefits of all interventions and encouraged to visit potential service providers and treatment settings before making treatment decisions. Many of the interventions described in this chapter require a substantial time commitment, investment of energy, ongoing practice, and willingness to make significant life changes. Thus, consumers must be strongly invested in taking the steps toward change that are necessitated by selected interventions if successful outcomes are to occur. Reassurance should be provided that the services included on the rehabilitation plan will be periodically reviewed with the consumer to determine if amendments are necessary. If a service included on the rehabilitation plan does not lead to improvement in pain and functioning, alternative treatments should be explored (Jensen & Turk, 2014).

Finding well-qualified professionals to deliver these interventions can be a challenge (Jensen & Turk, 2014). Although many individuals with chronic pain can be effectively treated in primary and specialty care settings, others may be best treated in interdisciplinary treatment programs that include physicians who are board certified in pain care. Unfortunately, the Commission on the Accreditation of Rehabilitation Facilities has only accredited about 122 pain treatment facilities, and only 3,488 physicians were board certified in pain care between 2000 and 2009 (IOM, 2011). Moreover, Jensen and Turk (2014) stated that the availability of appropriately trained therapists to provide psychological interventions to individuals in chronic pain is often limited to large urban areas and university centers. The websites of professional associations and licensing and certification bodies are good sources for identifying qualified practitioners in or near the rehabilitation consumer's community. Medical consultants can assist the rehabilitation counselor with making appropriate referrals to qualified providers, as can consumer self-help and advocacy organizations. In some communities, particularly smaller cities and rural communities, these professionals may not be available, thus restricting options and necessitating exploration of alternatives.

REHABILITATION SERVICES

Counseling and Guidance

Counseling and guidance are provided throughout the rehabilitation process to all consumers. However, consumers with chronic pain present with unique characteristics, challenges, and rehabilitation needs that have major implications for the consumer–counselor working alliance, rehabilitation process, and rehabilitation outcomes. Individuals with chronic pain are most likely to respond positively to counseling and guidance with a focus on (a) providing ample opportunities to openly discuss their struggles in living with chronic pain; (b) validating their concerns regarding the multitude of psychosocial challenges that accompany chronic pain; (c) empathically listening to their anxieties and fears about their future while also inspiring hope; and (d) treating them as equal partners in identifying strategies to manage pain (Hansson, 2011).

An important part of the counseling and guidance process is to help facilitate psychosocial adaptation to disability. However, it is vital that rehabilitation counselors understand that individuals with chronic pain must adapt to their disabilities every day. Each day requires psychosocial adaptation to fluctuations in pain intensity, variations in the degree to which pain interferes with daily life, and shifting emotional responses to one's pain. Likewise, stigma and discrimination are important issues to tackle in counseling and guidance. Negative, invalidating reactions from others can create substantial psychological distress that can exacerbate pain and further increase psychological distress, thus creating a vicious cycle. Rehabilitation counselors can disrupt this cycle by providing consumers with a safe space to share their experiences of stigmatization and discrimination, partnering with them to educate and equip others with accurate information, and assisting these consumers to develop skills to advocate for their rights. Rehabilitation counselors may also need to assist consumers in educating family members about chronic pain and how family members can better support consumers to effectively cope with their pain and achieve their rehabilitation goals.

During counseling and guidance sessions, rehabilitation counselors should be alert to symptoms of depression and anxiety that may necessitate referral to an outside mental health professional. However, rehabilitation counselors should also be aware that any suggestion of referral to a mental health specialist could be interpreted by consumers as further invalidation of their pain. Thus, rehabilitation counselors should provide a rationale for making this referral that is grounded in the understanding that *pain is real*. They should also make it clear that their reasoning for recommending a referral for mental health assessment and treatment stems from the recognition of the significant degree to which pain interferes with life activities rather than from a belief that symptoms are "all in the consumer's head." Finally, rehabilitation counselors should discuss with consumers the potential benefits that mental health services could offer in alleviating symptoms such as anxiety and depression that can increase their pain.

Pharmacological and Surgical Interventions

Many medications are available to treat chronic pain, and most individuals with chronic pain take more than one medication (Jensen & Turk, 2014). Among the most frequently used medications are nonopioid analgesics such as acetaminophen; NSAIDs (e.g., ibuprofen, aspirin); opioids; and medications used for other indications (e.g., anticonvulsants, psychotropics; ACPA, 2015). Serotonin and norepinephrine reuptake inhibitors and muscle relaxants are additional medications that may be prescribed for chronic pain. Individuals may also be prescribed medication for sleep disorders and anxiety as well as for other co-occurring conditions such as depression, diabetes, and hypertension.

Cannabis use for medical purposes is currently legal in 23 states and the District of Columbia (Lusk, Paul, & Wilson, 2015). However, federal law still considers cannabis use illegal. The use of cannabis to treat chronic pain is controversial, but tetrahydrocannabinol (THC), the active ingredient found in cannabis, can decrease pain, muscle spasms, headaches, migraines, insomnia, stress, and anxiety (ACPA, 2015; Lusk et al., 2015). Medical cannabis has been used to treat various chronic pain conditions such as FM, rheumatoid arthritis, and neuropathic pain (Lusk et al., 2015). Still, cannabis can have significant negative effects on various bodily systems (e.g., CNS, mental health, cardiopulmonary, reproductive, endocrine systems) and can lead to addiction (ACPA, 2015; Luske et al., 2015). Some physicians refuse to prescribe medical cannabis but do not object to its use with other pain medications. Others will prescribe it, and some will refuse to prescribe other pain medications (especially opioids) if the patient is using cannabis (ACPA, 2015). Although strong empirical support is lacking to validate the use of medical cannabis to treat chronic pain, many experts and consumers advocate for medical cannabis as a safer alternative to treating pain with fewer side effects than other current pain medications (Bostwick, 2014), and research is emerging to examine its efficacy and safety in treating chronic pain.

Regional anesthetic interventions are invasive procedures for administering medications directly to the pain site (ACPA, 2015). These procedures include sacroiliac joint injections, epidural steroid injections, nerve blocks, and spinal analgesic infusion pumps. Even more invasive surgical procedures may be indicated if all other pharmacological and nonpharmacological treatments have failed. These procedures include spinal decompression procedures (i.e., laminectomies and discectomies), disc replacement, spinal fusion, and nerve decompression (i.e., for carpal tunnel syndrome or trigeminal neuralgia).

Medications, regional anesthetic interventions, and more invasive surgical procedures are all limited in their effectiveness, have serious side effects, and may benefit some individuals but not others (ACPA, 2015). Therefore, in considering various pharmacological and surgical options, rehabilitation consumers should have a solid understanding of the risks, benefits, and success rates of each option. Because health literacy is low among most Americans (Roskos et al., 2007), rehabilitation counselors can help consumers to understand written instructions (e.g., medication guidelines, opioid contracts, preoperative and postoperative instructions) from treating physicians and to develop assertiveness skills so they can confidently communicate with their physicians when they have questions or need clarification regarding physicians' communications. Additionally, rehabilitation counselors can encourage consumers to bring companions with them to take notes during medical appointments.

Cognitive Behavioral Therapy

Cognitive behavioral therapy (CBT) is currently the most widely used nonpharmacological intervention to facilitate psychosocial adaptation to chronic pain (Jensen & Turk, 2014). By challenging problematic appraisals of one's ability to manage the many life changes associated with chronic pain and teaching new skills to manage these changes, CBT can be a useful intervention for individuals with chronic pain. A variety of CBT techniques have applications to facilitating effective coping with chronic pain. These techniques are frequently included as components of interdisciplinary pain management programs (Turk, Wilson, & Cahana, 2011) but may also be offered in other contexts (e.g., individual psychotherapy sessions).

Cognitive techniques in CBT focus on challenging thoughts and beliefs (e.g., attributions of pain, efficacy in coping with pain, expectations about how pain will affect one's abilities, personal control) that may influence emotional and physiological responses to chronic pain (Jensen & Turk, 2014; Vlaeyen & Morley, 2015). The focus of cognitive approaches is to help individuals shift from a stance of hopelessness and helplessness to one of belief in their ability to actively and resourcefully cope with pain (Turk et al., 2011). For example, cognitive restructuring identifies and challenges unrealistic thoughts, distortions, and/or catastrophic beliefs about one's pain that create passivity, reactivity, dependency, and hopelessness (Turk et al., 2011). By challenging these negative cognitions and replacing them with more realistic ones, individuals are able to increase both their self-efficacy and active participation in managing pain. This technique can also be effective in managing co-occurring conditions such as anxiety and depression.

Behavioral techniques in CBT focus on assisting individuals with chronic pain to develop specific skills to manage their pain. Examples of these techniques include pacing/energy conservation, behavioral activation, and problem solving (Lee, Chan, Chronister, Chan, & Romero, 2009; McCracken & Turk, 2002; Turk & Wilson, 2009; Turk et al., 2011). These techniques focus on managing one's activity levels, thereby, reducing flare-ups of symptoms such as pain, fatigue, and cognitive difficulties. Pacing/energy conservation activities include keeping pain diaries to record the impact of daily activities on symptoms and functionality; performing the most demanding work tasks or home chores during times of the day when feeling the most rested and/or pain free; delegating tasks to others during times of increased pain, fatigue, or cognitive difficulties; and alternating throughout the day between performing more demanding tasks and less demanding tasks.

Behavioral activation strategies include pleasant events scheduling, progressive muscle relaxation, and meditation (Wetherell et al., 2011). These techniques can decrease pain and reduce symptoms such as anxiety and depression by increasing opportunities for positive reinforcement and shifting focus from the pain to enjoyable external stimuli. Problem solving training teaches individuals the steps of identifying the problem, generating potential solutions, deciding on solution(s) to be implemented, implementing the solution(s), and evaluating the effects of the solution on solving the problem. For individuals with chronic pain who must often manage multiple symptoms and engage with numerous health care and rehabilitation service providers, problem-solving skills can empower them to take charge of their own treatment and rehabilitation.

Although CBT has long been considered the "gold standard" of psychological interventions for chronic pain (Day et al., 2012), and CBT techniques are embedded in rehabilitation counseling practices, CBT is not without its limitations. A substantial research base has established the positive effects of CBT on various health and disability outcomes. However, a limitation of this research is that, even in randomized clinical trials, the effects of CBT interventions on studied outcomes are small to moderate (Wetherell et al., 2011). Likewise, these interventions may be effective for some individuals but not others (Jensen & Turk, 2014). Furthermore, cognitive techniques may be met with defensiveness and resistance from rehabilitation consumers with chronic pain who have long histories of being invalidated by others and told that their symptoms are "all in their head." These individuals have often experienced substantial losses (i.e., they have lost the support of family and friends, are in constant pain, are invalidated by medical professionals, must deal with daily rejection and hostility from others such as classmates and coworkers, have experienced significant reductions in their health and functioning, are unemployed or at risk of becoming unemployed, and are facing financial destitution). Their difficulties do not arise from cognitive distortions; rather, they arise from their symptomology and external sources of stress. Additionally, as Day et al. (2012, p. 118) pointed out:

> The question has been raised as to whether explicitly changing the content of cognitions per se is necessary to reduce distress and increase function. Future research may show that the key cognitive process of change in CBT is not changing thought content, but rather engendering more emotional distance from one's maladaptive thoughts.

As a result of this concern, a "third wave" of CBT has emerged that includes mindfulness-based and acceptance-based approaches (Day et al., 2012).

Mindfulness Practices

Mindfulness-based therapies have become increasingly used to treat chronic pain (Day et al., 2012; Marchand, 2012). Mindfulness is the practice of focusing attention on one's moment-to-moment experiences in a way that is characterized by curiosity, lack of judgment, and openness to the experiences (Marchand, 2012; Rosenzweig et al., 2010). Attention is given to uncomfortable bodily sensations (e.g., pain), thoughts, and emotions. However, mindfulness approaches differ from CBT in that attempts to change these experiences are not made. Rather, the intent is to develop self-acceptance and compassion, "not to continually strive for pleasant experiences or to push aversive experiences away but rather to accept things as they are" (Marchand, 2012, p. 235). Three variations of mindfulness practices include Zen meditation, mindfulness-based stress reduction (MBSR), and mindfulness-based cognitive therapy (MBCT; Marchand, 2012). These techniques are similar in that they all teach mindfulness techniques; however, Zen meditation focuses exclusively on mindfulness practices, and the other two couple mindfulness with traditional CBT techniques (e.g., psychoeducation about stress, coping skills training, assertiveness training, cognitive therapy).

The underlying mechanisms of mindfulness approaches are not clearly understood, but these are believed to be both psychological and biological in nature (Marchand, 2012). From a psychological perspective, mindfulness techniques are believed to shift perspective so that individuals are able to detach from their own thoughts and emotions, and, consequently, recognize, for example, that they are not their pain or their depression, but rather these are experiences. Becoming less identified with distressful experiences and emotions and less egocentric can subsequently lead to decreased distress when the ego is threatened. Analytical self-focused rumination is replaced with detachment and can be effective in reducing symptoms of pain as well as co-occurring depression and anxiety. An increased ability to tolerate unpleasant sensations, thoughts, emotions, and experiences can also result because of enhanced desensitization of these experiences. The cognitive and behavioral flexibility learned from these techniques can lead to more adaptive responses in terms of managing one's pain. Recent research has also demonstrated that mindfulness techniques can lead to changes in both brain function and structure. These physiological changes appear to be linked to altered activation of the stress-response system and include improvements in blood pressure, cortisol levels, and immune function. Although research on the effectiveness of mindfulness strategies is still relatively new, the outcomes are at least as good as CBT outcomes.

Acceptance and Commitment Therapy

Acceptance and commitment therapy (ACT) is a form of CBT that uses mindfulness strategies and behavioral interventions to assist individuals to develop psychological flexibility (Hayes, Strosahl, & Wilson, 2012). Psychological flexibility is the opposite of psychological rigidity, which is believed to be a major contributor to problems such as depression, anxiety, and pain. Psychological flexibility enables individuals to approach life from a more centered, engaged, and open stance. Psychological flexibility involves six core processes: acceptance, diffusion, the self-as-context, flexible attention to the present moment, chosen values, and committed action. These processes are described in Table 2.3.

ACT differs from traditional CBT in its assumption that "attempts to change certain aversive internal experiences, such as chronic pain, are likely to be futile at best, and at worst may contribute to increased distress and interference" (Wetherell et al., 2011, p. 2098). Through ACT, individuals learn to willingly observe and experience both pain and their thoughts and feelings about their pain without trying to censor or change these. Through this process, painful sensations and unpleasant thoughts and emotions are defused, and individuals develop the realization that they can live with their pain while also committing to making changes in their lives to realize their values-based goals. ACT can be delivered in individual or small group sessions as well as larger workshops. Individuals can also learn how to use ACT through workbooks and other media. Specific techniques used in ACT include exposure, instruction, behavioral activation, skills training, mindfulness,

---

TABLE 2.3 Six Core Processes of Acceptance and Commitment Therapy

- Acceptance of and willingness to experience uncomfortable thoughts, emotions, memories, cognitions, sensations) without treating theses as "literal truths that rule the word" (Hayes et al., 2012, p. 65).

- Attention to unwanted thoughts, emotions, memories, and sensations without trying to suppress, control, or change these, but rather to observe and experience these in a defused fashion with genuine curiosity and acceptance.

- Connection with self in the present moment (i.e., the I-here-now experience) to correct for over-identification with one's self-story and to explore thoughts, feelings, and sensations in a defused and accepting manner.

- Development of flexibility in attentional processes and ability to come back to the present moment.

- Connection with positive qualities of the present moment that are intrinsically linked to one's values.

- Linkage of specific actions to one's chosen values and successively building larger patterns of effective values-based actions.

Source: Hayes et al. (2012).

use of metaphors, visualization exercises, behavioral homework assignments, and techniques for building a strong therapeutic alliance (McCracken & Vowles, 2014). Research to date has demonstrated that ACT has positive effects on physical and social functioning and reduces pain-related medical visits. Overall, ACT has been found to be as effective as traditional CBT (McCracken & Vowles, 2014; Wetherell et al., 2011).

Complementary Health Approaches

The National Center for Complementary and Integrative Health (2016) defines complementary health approaches as those that are developed outside, but used in conjunction with, mainstream Western medicine. Complementary health approaches include natural products such as herbs, vitamins, minerals, and probiotics. They also include mind and body approaches such as acupuncture, yoga, spinal manipulation, meditation, massage therapy, relaxation techniques (e.g., breathing exercises, guided imagery, and progressive muscle relaxation), tai chi, healing touch, hypnotherapy, and movement therapies. Other approaches include traditional healers, Ayurvedic medicine, traditional Chinese medicine, homeopathy, and naturopathy.

Complementary health approaches are often used by people with chronic pain and may include yoga, spinal manipulation, massage therapy, heat and cold applications, meditation, acupuncture, herbal medicines, vitamins, and minerals (IOM, 2011). These approaches, however, like more traditional therapies, are not without their risks. Research on several natural products has demonstrated that they do not work, and little is known about the effects of these products on the human body. Likewise, herbal medicines, vitamins, and minerals may be contraindicated with other medications.

Just as in making referrals to providers of conventional medicine, rehabilitation counselors should ensure that practitioners who provide complementary health approaches have appropriate training and credentials. Rehabilitation counselors should also ensure that consumers using these therapies consult with their primary physicians to make sure they are safe and not contraindicated with other treatments.

Pain Self-Management

Bishop, Frain, Rumrill, and Rymond (2009, p. 121) defined self-management as "the skills necessary to carry on an active and emotionally satisfying life in the face of a chronic condition." In a meta-analysis of self-management programs for individuals with chronic musculoskeletal pain conditions, the six core skills that were emphasized included problem solving, decision making, resource utilization, formation of a patient–provider working relationship, action planning, and self-tailoring (i.e., individuals choose self-management skills based on their preferences; Du et al., 2011).

Pain self-management also involves applying techniques learned from CBT, mindfulness, and ACT practitioners to one's daily life. These techniques may include deep breathing, getting an appropriate amount of sleep, regular exercise, smoking cessation, mindfulness meditation, healthy diets, yoga, participation in hobbies or activities that reduce stress, interacting with others to reduce isolation, and keeping pain diaries to identify triggers and make behavioral modifications to minimize or avoid triggers. Research on formal programs to teach pain self-management demonstrates small to moderate effects in improving pain and disability on a long-term basis.

Because chronic pain effects virtually every aspect of one's life and treatment, usually involving multiple specialists, is often insufficient, "the burden of controlling pain falls most heavily on people in pain and their families" (IOM, 2011, p. 170). Therefore, assessing rehabilitation consumers' pain-management skills and assisting them to further develop those skills through counseling and guidance and/or the procurement of specific services (e.g., pain management programs, smoking cessation programs, weight loss programs, physical therapy evaluations to assist with developing appropriate exercise programs) is an imperative function of rehabilitation counselors.

Self-Help and Support Groups

According to Munir, Randall, Yarker, and Nielson (2009), social support can serve as a buffer against the stress of living with chronic health conditions and can also enhance feelings of emotional well-being. Because, as we have established in prior sections of this chapter, individuals with chronic pain often lack social support, interventions to assist them in developing peer supports can be a crucial rehabilitation service. Research on the efficacy of peer support interventions has yielded mixed results in terms of their impact on important outcomes for individuals with chronic pain (e.g., symptom reduction, overall physical and mental health, efficacy in illness self-management, coping, life satisfaction). However, these groups can reduce one's sense of isolation, invalidation, and alienation. Individuals with unexplained chronic pain have described how meeting with peers helped to confirm the legitimacy of their pain (Toye & Barker, 2010). Peer support and self-help groups can also enhance self-esteem and perceived social supports. They can provide individuals with informational and instrumental assistance that is not available from health care providers. Members also have the opportunity to observe and model effective coping strategies. However, these groups are not without their disadvantages. For example when group members experience setbacks, exacerbation of symptoms, or relapses, it can be distressing for other members of these groups. Likewise, individuals who need support in continuing to work may not find benefit from participating in groups in which other members are not working.

Wakefield, Bickley, and Sani (2013) observed that group membership in a peer support or self-help group, in and of itself, is not enough to ensure positive outcomes. Rather, group identification, described as a sense of belonging coupled with a sense of commonality with other group members, is necessary to achieve the benefits of this type of intervention. Rehabilitation counselors obviously have an obligation to discuss with consumers both the risks and benefits of peer support and self-help groups and help those interested to identify appropriate pain support groups in their local communities or on the Internet if local community groups are not available.

Job Development and Placement

Job development and placement activities conducted with consumers with chronic pain are individualized and targeted at finding positions that match the consumer's interests, desires, and skills. In this way, the process is no different than it is for any rehabilitation consumer. However, additional considerations in identifying appropriate job matches for consumers with chronic pain include the occupational stress factors and organizational culture of specific work settings, workplace policies regarding medications used to treat chronic pain, and the job retention needs of these consumers.

Occupational stress can exacerbate pain and decrease work productivity. Therefore, in considering placement options, rehabilitation counselors should engage consumers with chronic pain in a thorough assessment of their individualized stress vulnerabilities as well as worksite assessments of occupational stressors (Merz, Bricout, & Koch, 2001). This assessment will enable the rehabilitation counselor to match individual consumers with positions in companies where the stressors that are most individually problematic are minimal and to identify potential worksite accommodations that could be implemented to reduce job stress. Peer and supervisor support, employer flexibility, employee resilience, and the ability to manage pain while meeting the demands of employment can increase the likelihood that employees with chronic pain will maintain employment (Shaw et al., 2012).

Both practical support (i.e., giving information and advice) and emotional support (i.e., demonstrating sympathy and understanding) from employers, especially from line supervisors, have been found to be associated with developing self-efficacy in managing symptoms at work (Munir et al., 2009). Self-efficacy beliefs, in turn, positively influence illness self-management behaviors. To create a supportive work environment, employers must overcome misunderstandings and stigma about chronic pain. Rehabilitation counselors can play a pivotal role in educating employers and coworkers about chronic pain, dispelling myths, and explaining how workplace accommodations can make it possible for individuals with chronic pain to effectively perform the functions of their jobs. Among the most pressing training needs that employers are likely to have are (a) targeted training for managers and supervisors to address strategies for accommodating workers with chronic pain; (b) training that offers specific examples of workplace accommodations and supports along with information about how to implement and evaluate these strategies; (c) assistance with developing clear policies and processes for implementing return to work after extended absence due to illness; and (d) information about specific accommodations for workers such as flex hours, job share programs, and work from home (Wong, 2006).

Another important consideration in job development and placement for some consumers with chronic pain is how the use of certain medications (e.g., opioid analgesics, cannabis) may restrict job options. For example, individuals who take opioid analgesics are restricted from occupations such as those that require driving, use of dangerous equipment, or operation of heavy equipment. Individuals who use medical cannabis may be precluded from working for companies that have drug-free office policies (Lusk et al., 2015). These are important considerations to explore with consumers during the job development and placement process but also earlier on in the rehabilitation planning process when they are considering various treatment and employment options.

A substantial literature base has emerged that addresses how vocational rehabilitation (VR) systems, rehabilitation counselors, and employers can better respond to the job retention and career maintenance needs of consumers with chronic illness (e.g., Allaire, Niu, & LaValley, 2005; Bishop et al., 2009; Koch, Rumrill, Conyers, & Wohlford, 2013; Roessler, 2002; Roessler & Rumrill, 1994; Rumrill & Roessler, 1999). Because individuals with chronic pain often incur their pain from injuries sustained on the job or have conditions (e.g., FM, chronic migraine) with typical onset during their prime working years, job retention may be an especially pressing issue for these employees. Proactive accommodations planning and workplace support have been identified as strategies to facilitate job retention (Koch et al., 2013).

Proactive planning requires that individuals develop a comprehensive understanding of their pain conditions, triggers of symptoms, strategies to minimize flare-ups, and the potential impact of their pain condition or illness on future job performance. It also involves modifying behaviors both at home and on the job to prevent early departure from the work force. For workers with chronic health conditions, such as chronic pain, both practical support (i.e., giving information and advice) and emotional support (i.e., demonstrating sympathy and understanding) from employers, especially from line supervisors, have been found to be associated with developing self-efficacy in managing symptoms and medications at work (Munir et al., 2009). Self-efficacy beliefs, in turn, positively influence illness self-management behaviors. To create a supportive work environment for employees with chronic illnesses, employers must overcome misunderstandings and stigma about chronic illness. Here again, rehabilitation counselors can play a pivotal role in educating employers about chronic illness, its impact on employment, and workplace accommodations.

In addition to these job retention strategies, research has documented that even minimal, periodic follow-up from rehabilitation counselors can prevent consumers with chronic health issues such as persistent pain from prematurely exiting the workforce (Allaire et al., 2005; Roessler, 2002). Another alternative recommended by Koch and Rumrill (2001) is the provision of career maintenance clubs facilitated by rehabilitation counselors to combine education and peer support in the promotion of job retention and career advancement. These clubs can provide a safe space where employed individuals with chronic pain can discuss their struggles at work while receiving emotional support from each other, collectively explore strategies for addressing these struggles, and share job accommodations ideas with each other. Although research is needed to evaluate the effect of career maintenance clubs on outcomes such as job retention, job satisfaction, worker productivity, and pain symptomology, such an intervention holds potential promise in supporting workers with chronic pain to sustain employment and advance in their careers.

Accommodation Planning

Accommodation planning is an essential service for individuals with chronic pain who often require adjustments to both the manner in which job tasks are performed and to their workstations. The accommodation planning process begins by first assessing consumers' knowledge about Title I of the Americans with Disabilities Act Amendments Act (ADAAA) and educating them about their rights and responsibilities as afforded by this legislation. Then, the rehabilitation counselor and consumer can develop an individualized accommodations plan that identifies specific barriers as well as strategies to ameliorate those barriers so that the consumer is able to perform the essential functions of the job. Work environments and the demands of the consumer's job must be assessed to determine potential accommodations that are currently needed and may eventually be needed. This process requires a unique set of skills (e.g., communication, problem solving, negotiation, self-advocacy) that can be developed with the utilization of a variety of accommodations planning tools that have been demonstrated to be effective with chronic illness populations (Roessler, 1995).

Shaw et al. (2012) noted that, although many workers with chronic pain experience substantial difficulties carrying out the essential functions of their jobs, others manage their pain quite well and do not need formal job accommodations. For those who do need formal accommodations, the first step is to identify specific barriers to job satisfactoriness and satisfaction. The second step is to identify how they can apply pain management strategies used in other contexts to work settings to ameliorate barriers. Shaw et al. recommended that in assisting individuals to implement pain self-management strategies on the job, three areas of workplace concerns must first be evaluated: (a) the physical demands of the job and the individual's perceived limitations; (b) workplace leeway in modifying or customizing job tasks; and (c) workplace roles and relationships. Job types and work environments in which individuals are most likely to implement effective pain management strategies are those in which physical demands are easily modifiable, substantial flexibility is provided in terms of carrying out job demands, and ample support and assistance are provided by employers and coworkers.

A variety of pain management strategies can be implemented on the job (Shaw et al., 2012). For example, pacing and energy conservation can be used to reduce fatigue and perform the most physically or mentally demanding job tasks when one has the most energy to do so. Likewise, mindfulness strategies can be generalized to the work setting to develop awareness of bodily sensations, thoughts, and feelings while performing specific job functions and identifying needed changes to body mechanics, one's workstation, and how essential functions are performed. Other strategies include breaking down work assignments into manageable tasks, alternating between demanding and less demanding tasks, and self-awareness of one's limitations so that he or she can seek out help from coworkers in completing tasks that increase pain. Strategies used at home can also enhance functioning on the job. These include getting adequate sleep, stretching before getting out of bed in the morning, delegating chores to others, or giving up activities to free up time and energy to devote to work. In exploring potential pain management strategies that could be used at work, the rehabilitation consumer should be treated as the best expert.

In addition to the application of pain management strategies to the job site, the Job Accommodation Network (JAN) provides numerous ideas for accommodating workers with chronic pain (Loy, 2013). JAN's accommodation ideas for reducing fatigue and weakness include reduction or elimination of physical exertion and workplace stress, allowance for periodic breaks away from the employee's workstation, flexible work schedule and leave time, self-paced workload, accessible entry into building and parking near the entrance, automatic door openers, and relocation of work stations so they are closer to office equipment and breakrooms. Accommodation ideas for reducing muscle pain and stiffness include providing employees with an ergonomic workstation and ergonomic chair (e.g., sit-lean stools) that allow for periodic alterations between sitting and standing; reducing repetitive work tasks or alternating these tasks with other tasks; provision of lifting aids and carts; modification of worksite temperature; use of fans, air conditioners, and heaters at the work station; and telecommuting or work from home when weather is extremely hot or cold. Finally, accommodation ideas for depression and anxiety include proactive planning for use of on-the-job stress management strategies before problems arise, allowance for phone calls to be made while on the job to physicians and other support providers, allowance for time off to attend medical appointments, and use of a service animal on the job to reduce stress. JAN (2013) also provides examples of accommodations that can be made for workers with specific chronic pain conditions. For example, accommodations for individuals with chronic migraines focus primarily on making changes to the work environment to control triggers of migraine attacks. To control lighting triggers, accommodations that can be helpful include adding filters to fluorescent lights to create more natural lighting, changing lights altogether, providing antiglare filters for computer monitors, providing a liquid crystal display monitor that has a better refresh rate, moving the workstation to an area that allows for personal adjustment to appropriate lighting, allowing the employee to wear sunglasses or antiglare glasses in the work area, and allowing the employee to telecommute. To minimize noise triggers, JAN recommends accommodations such as moving the employee's workstation away from noisy, high traffic areas; providing an environmental sound machine to mask distracting sounds; providing the employee with noise canceling headsets; providing sound absorption panels; and encouraging coworkers to keep non–work-related conversation to a minimum. Job accommodations that can be implemented to minimize smell triggers include implementing a fragrance-free office policy, allowing the employee to telecommute, relocating the employee's work station to an area where the fragrances are not as strong, and providing air purification systems. Other accommodation ideas for workers with migraines are similar to those that can be implemented for any worker who experiences chronic pain. In addition to using JAN as a resource for identifying accommodation ideas, ergonomic assessments can be conducted to determine how to design workstations to minimize pain and maximize productivity.

Once individualized accommodation plans have been developed, rehabilitation counselors can assist consumers to develop appropriate communication skills to disclose their need for accommodations, request specific accommodations from employers, and determine courses of action to take if their requests are denied. Practicing these skills in role plays can create confidence in consumers' ability to approach employers. In some cases, the rehabilitation counselor may want to jointly meet with the employer and the employee to help facilitate the process. Follow-along support for both the employee and the employer may also be needed to evaluate the effectiveness of accommodations, problem solve, and determine if any additional accommodations are needed.

CONCLUSIONS

Chronic pain is a complex, misunderstood, undertreated, and growing problem in contemporary American society. Chronic pain, in all its forms, can cause significant suffering, prevent individuals from participating in meaningful life activities, and substantially reduce their quality of life. Chronic pain is also cloaked with myths and stereotypes that can contribute to medical undertreatment and restrict access to social supports, rehabilitation, and disability compensation. Chronic pain is especially problematic for socially and economically disadvantaged groups such as women, members of racially and ethnically diverse groups, those living in poverty, and the elderly.

Although the causes of chronic pain are still uncertain, the predominant model used as a framework for assessing and treating chronic pain is the biopsychosocial model. This model views chronic pain as a disorder that affects the whole individual and promotes treatment approaches that respond to the biological, psychological, and social aspects of pain. Biopsychosocial treatment approaches include both pharmacological and nonpharmacological interventions. Most approaches have been found to be minimally to moderately effective, but research continues to develop better understanding of chronic pain and to identify more effective treatment modalities.

Individuals with chronic pain may be a particularly challenging rehabilitation consumer population because of the severity of their symptoms, the large degree to which these impair functioning, the lack of a cure for their chronic pain, and the futile efforts that many individuals have invested in pursuing treatments that prove to be marginally effective at best. Many of these individuals have a long history of being invalidated, dismissed, and/or misdiagnosed. Understandably, they may expect the same response from rehabilitation counselors. Consequently, the best approach to individualized rehabilitation planning with consumers with chronic pain begins with validating their pain and then developing a thorough understanding of how pain affects their day-to-day living. Following these steps, the rehabilitation counselor and consumer can identify pain coping strategies already used to enhance their ability to participate in meaningful life activities and, in vocational rehabilitation planning, how these might be applied to occupations of interest to these consumers. The rehabilitation consumer and counselor can then proceed to the step of jointly identifying and supplementing these strategies with rehabilitation services to even further improve functioning. The process moves on to providing preliminary and long-term follow-along services to facilitate independent functioning and employment in work settings that are inclusive, attentive to minimizing occupational stressors through flexibility and emotional and practical support, and responsive to ideas for modifying how individuals with chronic pain perform the essential functions of their jobs.

DISCUSSION QUESTIONS

1. What myths have influenced your perceptions of people with chronic pain? What information presented in this chapter has challenged you to reconsider your perceptions?
2. Describe the psychosocial and vocational challenges that you think present the greatest barriers to quality of life and employment for people with chronic pain?
3. What do you think are the most important considerations for forming strong working alliances with clients with chronic pain?

4. What are the most important implications for rehabilitation planning discussed in this chapter?
5. At the beginning of the chapter we described Linda's case. Do you think her desires to continue working and resume a life outside of work are feasible? Why or why not? What objectives, services, and reasonable accommodations would you include in Linda's rehabilitation plan to assist her to maintain employment and improve her overall quality of life?

REFERENCES

Agency for Healthcare Research and Quality. (2012). *Migraine in adults: Preventative pharmacologic treatments.* Retrieved from https://www.effectivehealthcare.ahrq.gov/ehc/products/313/1453/migraine-report-130408.pdf

Allaire, S. H., Niu, J., & Lavalley, M. P. (2005). Employment and satisfaction outcomes from a job retention intervention delivered to persons with chronic diseases. *Rehabilitation Counseling Bulletin, 48*(2), 100–109.

American Academy of Pain Medicine. (2013). *Use of opioids for the treatment of chronic pain.* Retrieved from http://www.painmed.org/files/use-of-opioids-for-the-treatment-of-chronic-pain.pdf

American Chronic Pain Association. (2015). *ACPA resource guide to chronic pain medication & treatment.* Retrieved from https://theacpa.org/uploads/documents/ACPA_Resource_Guide_2015_Final%20edited%20(3).pdf

Arnold, L. M., Crofford, L. J., Mease, P. J., Burgess, S. M., Palmer, S. C., Abetz, L., & Martin, S. A. (2008). Patient perspectives on the impact of fibromyalgia. *Patient Education and Counseling, 73*(1), 114–120.

Arthritis Foundation. (2013). *Fibromyalgia.* Retrieved from http://www.arthritis.org/about-arthritis/types/fibromyalgia

Bostwick, J. M. (2014). The use of cannabis for management of chronic pain. *General Hospital Psychiatry, 36*(1), 2–3. doi:10.1016/j.genhosppsych.2013.08.004

Brennan, F., Carr, D. B., & Cousins, M. (2007). Pain management: A fundamental human right. *Anesthesia and Analgesia, 105*(1), 205–221.

Cowan, P. (2011). Living with chronic pain. *Quality of Life Research: An International Journal of Quality of Life Aspects of Treatment, Care and Rehabilitation, 20*(3), 307–308. doi:10.1007/s11136-010-9765-7

Day, M. A., Thorn, B. E., & Burns, J. W. (2012). The continuing evolution of biopsychosocial interventions for chronic pain. *Journal of Cognitive Psychotherapy, 26*(2), 114–129.

Du, S., Yuan, C., Xiao, X., Chu, J., Qiu, Y., & Qian, H. (2011). Self-management programs for chronic musculoskeletal pain conditions: A systematic review and meta-analysis. *Patient Education and Counseling, 85*(3), e299–e310. doi:10.1016/j.pec.2011.02.021

Fine, P. G. (2011). Long-term consequences of chronic pain: Mounting evidence for pain as a neurological disease and parallels with other chronic disease states. *Pain Medicine, 12*(7), 996–1004.

Gatchel, R., McGeary, D., McGeary, C., & Lippe, B. (2014). Interdisciplinary chronic pain management: Past, present, and future. *American Psychologist, 69*(2), 119–130.

Grodman, I., Buskila, D., Arnson, Y., Altaman, A., Amital, D., & Amital, H. (2011). Understanding fibromyalgia and its resultant disability. *IMAJ: Israel Medical Association Journal, 13*(12), 769–772.

Haley, C., & Lawhead, J. (2015). *Pain matters* [Documentary]. Alexandria, VA: Summer Productions.

Hansson, K. S., Fridlund, B., Brunt, D., Hansson, B., & Rask, M. (2011). The meaning of the experiences of persons with chronic pain in their encounters with the health service. *Scandinavian Journal of Caring Sciences, 25*(3), 444–450. doi:10.1111/j.1471-6712.2010.00847.x

Hayes, S. C., Strosahl, K. D., & Wilson, K. G. (2012). *Acceptance and commitment therapy: The process and practice of mindful change* (2nd ed.). New York, NY: Guilford Press.

Holloway, I., Sofaer-Bennett, B., & Walker, J. (2007). The stigmatisation of people with chronic back pain. *Disability and Rehabilitation, 29*(18), 1456–1464.

Institute of Medicine. (2011). *Relieving pain in America.* Washington, DC: National Academies Press.

International Association for the Study of Chronic Pain. (2015). *IASP taxonomy.* Retrieved from http://www.iasp-pain.org/Taxonomy#Pain

Jensen, M., & Turk, D. (2014). Contributions of psychology to the understanding and treatment of people with chronic pain: Why it matters to all psychologists. *American Psychologist, 69*(2), 105–118.

Job Accommodation Network. (2015). *Accommodations and Compliance Series: Employees with migraine headaches.* Retrieved from http://askjan.org/media/Migraine.html

Katsarava, Z., Buse, D. C., Manack, A. N., & Lipton, R. B. (2012). Defining the differences between episodic migraine and chronic migraine. *Current Pain and Headache Reports, 16*(1), 86–92. doi:10.1007/s11916–011-0233-z

Koch, L. C., Rumrill, P. D., Conyers, L., & Wohlford, S. (2013). A narrative literature review regarding job retention strategies for people with chronic illnesses. *Work: A Journal of Prevention, Assessment, and Rehabilitation, 46*, 125–134.

Lee, E., Chan, F., Chronister, J., Chan, J. Y., & Romero, M. (2009). Models, research, and treatment of coexisting depression for people with chronic illness and disability. In F. Chan, E. Da Silva Cardoso, & J. A. Chronister (Eds.), *Understanding psychosocial adjustment to chronic illness and disability: A handbook for evidence-based practitioners in rehabilitation* (pp. 75–107). New York, NY: Springer Publishing Company.

Lipton, R. (2015). Risk factors for and management of medication-overuse headache. *Continuum: Lifelong Learning in Neurology, 21*(4), 1118–1131.

Lipton, R., Bigal, M., Diamond, M., Freitag, F., Reed, M., & Stewart, W. (2007). Migraine prevalence, disease burden, and the need for preventive therapy. *Neurology, 68*(5), 343–349.

Lipton, R., & Silberstein, S. (2015). Episodic and chronic migraine headache: Breaking down barriers to optimal treatment and prevention. *Headache: The Journal of Head & Face Pain, 55*, 103–122.

Loy, B. (2013). *Accommodation and Compliance Series: Employees with chronic pain.* Retrieved from https://askjan.org/media/ChronicPain.html

Lusk, S., Paul, T. M., & Wilson, R. (2015). The potential impact of the legalization and decriminalization of marijuana on the vocational rehabilitation process. Why the buzz? *Journal of Applied Rehabilitation Counseling, 46*(2), 3–12.

Marchand, W. R. (2012). Mindfulness-based stress reduction, mindfulness-based cognitive therapy, and Zen meditation for depression, anxiety, pain, and psychological distress. *Journal of Psychiatric Practice, 18*(4), 233–252. doi:10.1097/01.pra.0000416014.53215.86

McCracken, L. M., & Turk, D. (2002). Behavioral and cognitive-behavioral treatment for chronic pain: Outcome, predictors of outcome, and treatment process. *Spine, 27*(22), 2564–2573.

McCracken, L. M., & Vowles, K. E. (2014). Acceptance and commitment therapy and mindfulness for chronic pain: Model, process, and progress. *American Psychologist, 69*, 178–187.

Merz, M. A., Bricout, J. C., & Koch, L. C. (2001). Disability and job stress: Implications for vocational rehabilitation planning. *Work: A Journal of Prevention, Assessment, and Rehabilitation, 17*, 85–95.

Muller, V., Brooks, J., Tu, W., Moser, E., Lo, C., & Chan, F. (2015). Physical and cognitive-affective factors associated with fatigue in individuals with fibromyalgia: A multiple regression analysis. *Rehabilitation Research, Policy & Education, 29*(3), 291–300. doi:10.1891/2168–6653.29.3.291

Munir, F., Randall, R., Yarker, J., & Nielsen, K. (2009). The influence of employer support on employee management of chronic health conditions at work. *Journal of Occupational Rehabilitation, 19*(4), 333–344.

National Center for Complementary and Integrative Health. (2016). *Complementary, alternative, or integrative health: What's in a name?* Retrieved from https://nccih.nih.gov

National Institute of Neurological Disorders and Stroke. (2015). *Migraine information page.* Retrieved from http://www.ninds.nih.gov/disorders/migraine/migraine.htm

National Institutes of Health. (2011). *Relieving pain in America: A blueprint for transforming prevention, care, education, and research.* Retrieved from http://www.national academies.org/hmd/Reports/2011/Relieving-Pain-in-America-A-Blueprint-for-Transforming-Prevention-Care-Education-Research.aspx

National Institutes of Health. (2015). *Health literacy.* Retrieved from https://obssr-archive.od.nih.gov/scientific_areas/social_culture_factors_in_health/health_literacy/index.aspx

Rakovski, C., Zettel-Watson, L., & Rutledge, D. (2012). Association of employment and working conditions with physical and mental health symptoms for people with fibromyalgia. *Disability & Rehabilitation, 34*(15), 1277–1283. doi:10.3109/09638288.2011.641658

Raymond, M. C., & Brown, J. B. (2000). Experience of fibromyalgia: Qualitative study. *Canadian Family Physician, 46*, 1100–1106.

Roessler, R. T. (1995). *The Work Experience Survey.* Fayetteville, AR: Arkansas Research and Training Center in Vocational Rehabilitation.

Roessler, R. T. (2002). TWWIIA initiatives and work incentives: Return-to-work implications. *Journal of Rehabilitation, 68*(3), 11–15.

Roessler, R. T., & Rumrill, P. (1994). Strategies for enhancing career maintenance self-efficacy of people with multiple sclerosis. *Journal of Rehabilitation, 60*(4), 54.

Rosenzweig, S., Greeson, J., Reibel, D., Green, J., Jasser, S., & Beasley, D. (2010). Mindfulness-based stress reduction for chronic pain conditions: Variation in treatment outcomes and role of home meditation practice. *Journal of Psychosomatic Research, 68*(1), 29–36. doi:10.1016/j.jpsychores.2009.03.010

Roskos, S. E., Keenum, A. J., Newman, L. M., & Wallace, L. S. (2007). Literacy demands and formatting characteristics of opioid contracts in chronic nonmalignant pain management. *Journal of Pain, 8*(10), 753–758. doi:10.1016/j.jpain.2007.01.005

Rumrill, P. D., & Roessler, R. T. (1999). New directions in vocational rehabilitation: A career development perspective on closure. *Journal of Rehabilitation, 65*(1), 26–30.

Shaw, W. S., Tveito, T. H., Geehern-Lavoie, M., Huang, Y. H., Nicholas, M. K., Reme, S. E.,... Pransky, G. (2012). Adapting principles of chronic pain self-management to the workplace. *Disability and Rehabilitation, 34*(8), 694–703.

Sim, J., & Madden, S. (2008). Illness experience in fibromyalgia syndrome: A metasynthesis of qualitative studies. *Social Science & Medicine, 67*(1), 57–67.

Skaer, T. L. (2014). Fibromyalgia: Disease synopsis, medication cost effectiveness and economic burden. *Pharmacoeconomics, 32*(5), 457–466. doi:10.1007/s40273-014-0137-y

Smart, J. (2009). *Disability, society, and the individual* (2nd ed.). Austin, TX: Pro-Ed.

Sofaer, B., Moore, A. P., Holloway, I., Lamberty, J. M., Thorp, T. S., & O'Dwyer, J. (2005). Chronic pain as perceived by older people: A qualitative study. *Age and Ageing, 34*(5), 462–466.

Sullivan, M. L., & Hyman, M. H. (2014). Return to work as a treatment objective for patients with chronic pain? *Journal of Pain Relief, 3*(1), 1–3.

Thernstrom, M. (2010). *The pain chronicles: Cures, remedies, spells, prayers, myths, misconceptions, brain scans, and the science of suffering.* New York, NY: Farrar, Straus and Giroux.

Thielke, S. (2012). Aging: Are these 4 pain myths complicating care? Is pain a natural part of aging? Does "toughing it out" make pain more tolerable? Read on to see what the evidence really says regarding 4 common misconceptions about pain and aging. *Journal of Family Practice, 61*(11), 666–671.

Toye, F., & Barker, K. (2010). "Could I be imagining this?"—The dialectic struggles of people with persistent unexplained back pain. *Disability & Rehabilitation, 32*(21), 1722–1732. doi:10.3109/09638281003657857

Turk, D. C., & Wilson, H. D. (2009). Pain, suffering, pain-related suffering—Are these constructs inextricably linked? *The Clinical Journal of Pain, 25*(5), 353–355. doi:10.1097/AJP.0b013e31819c62e7

Turk, D. C., Wilson, H. D., & Cahana, A. (2011). Treatment of chronic non-cancer pain. *The Lancet, 377*(9784), 2226–2235. doi:10.1016/S0140–6736(11)60402–9

Wakefield, J. H., Bickley, S., & Sani, F. (2013). The effects of identification with a support group on the mental health of people with multiple sclerosis. *Journal of Psychosomatic Research, 74*(5), 420–426. doi:10.1016/j.jpsychores.2013.02.002

Wetherell, J., Afari, N., Rutledge, T., Sorrell, J., Stoddard, J., Petkus, A., ... Hampton Atkinson, J. (2011). A randomized, controlled trial of acceptance and commitment therapy and cognitive-behavioral therapy for chronic pain. *Pain, 152*(9), 2098–2107.

Wittich, C., Burkle, C., & Lanier, W. (2012). Ten common questions (and their answers) about off-label drug use. *Mayo Clinic Proceedings, 87*(10), 982–990. doi:10.1016/j.mayocp.2012.04.017

Wolfe, F., Clauw, D. J., Fitzcharles, M. A., Goldenberg, D. L., Katz, R. S., Mease, P., ... Yunus, M. B. (2010). The American College of Rheumatology preliminary diagnostic criteria for fibromyalgia and measurement of symptom severity. *Arthritis Care & Research, 62*(5), 600–610.

Wong, L. (2006). *A report on a survey of certified human resources professionals regarding episodic disabilities.* Retrieved from http://pubs.cpha.ca/PDF/P41/24475.pdf

THREE

Neurodevelopmental Disabilities: Autism Spectrum Disorder and Attention Deficit Hyperactivity Disorder

Coauthored by Frank J. Sansosti With Contributions From Alexa Herrera

CHAPTER OBJECTIVES

- *Define neurodevelopmental disorders*
- *Examine the medical, psychosocial, and vocational aspects of two neurodevelopmental disorders that are increasing in the U.S. population—autism spectrum disorder (ASD) and attention deficit hyperactivity disorder (ADHD)*
- *Identify populations at risk of being diagnosed with ASD or ADHD*
- *Distinguish key considerations for outreach, eligibility determination, and rehabilitation assessment and planning*
- *Consider services to be included in the rehabilitation plan to facilitate goal achievement for consumers with ASD or ADHD*
- *Examine evidence-based practices in job development, placement, and retention*

CASE ILLUSTRATION: CONNER

Conner is a 24-year-old White male who is currently in treatment with a mental health counselor for depression. His counselor referred Conner to a state vocational rehabilitation (VR) agency to be evaluated for attention deficit hyperactivity disorder (ADHD) and to receive vocational testing and career counseling to assist him to identify and work toward a vocational goal. Although Conner never been formally diagnosed, the counselor thinks that many of the issues he discusses in counseling may be attributed to ADHD. For example, he reports feeling depressed because he "has no life" and he "feels like a loser." He does not socialize outside of his family and would like to have a girlfriend but states that he has a difficult time forming relationships because other people find him annoying. Conner lives with his parents, who pay for his mental health counseling, and he reports feeling bored, restless, and wanting a steady job so he can move into his own apartment. He has a limited work history and is currently unemployed. His only vocational activities include doing odd jobs for his family, babysitting for his older sister's children, and mowing lawns in the summer for a family friend who has a lawn service business.

Conner is a high school graduate but reports that he hated school and received failing grades in some courses that he had to repeat during the summer. He indicates that he barely passed his other courses, with the exception of a photography class in which he received a final grade of A. Although he had substantial academic difficulties in school, he never received a diagnosis or services to address his difficulties. He had problems completing assignments, struggled with maintaining attention, and became easily frustrated. He was repeatedly reprimanded by his teachers for talking incessantly, leaving his desk during seated assignments and lectures, disrupting other students while they were working on assignments, and interrupting students and teachers when they were talking. In addition, he indicates that his peers rejected him. When his mental health counselor asked him about his vocational interests, he stated that he had none. However, upon further inquiry, he stated that he enjoys watching television dramas such as *Code Black*, *Chicago Fire*, and *Chicago Med* and thinks he would be a good emergency medical technician. However, he doubts his ability to successfully complete the postsecondary training required to qualify for this occupation.

Neurodevelopmental disorders are conditions with typical onset in early childhood development, often manifesting before the child enters grade school (American Psychiatric Association [APA], 2013). These disorders are characterized by deficits that impair personal, social, academic, and/or vocational functioning. Neurodevelopmental disorders can cause delays in achieving developmental milestones and frequently co-occur (e.g., Autism Spectrum Disorder [ASD] and Intellectual Disability). Neurodevelopmental disorders in the *Diagnostic and Statistical Manual of Mental Disorders* (5th ed. [*DSM-5*]; APA, 2013) include Intellectual Disabilities, Communication Disorders, Autism Spectrum Disorder (ASD), Attention Deficit Hyperactivity Disorder (ADHD), Specific Learning Disorder, Motor Disorders, and other neurodevelopmental disorders

Among the neurodevelopmental disorders, ASD and ADHD represent those with the most dramatic increases in diagnoses in recent years (Holwerda, van der Klink, Boer, Groothoff, & Brouwer, 2013). Shattuck, Narendorf, Cooper, Sterzing, Wagner, and Taylor (2012) reported estimates indicating that approximately 50,000 youths with ASD reach adulthood each year. The Centers for Disease Control and Prevention (CDC, 2016a) reported that ADHD diagnoses have steadily increased since 1997. Both ASD and ADHD typically affect individuals across the life span and can result in severe functional limitations that continue into adulthood. Consequently, rehabilitation counselors can anticipate serving growing numbers of individuals with these two neurodevelopmental disorders. This chapter focuses on emerging developments in the understanding of both ASD and ADHD and evidence-based practices for responding to the rehabilitation needs of consumers who have these conditions.

AUTISM SPECTRUM DISORDER

Traditionally, the term *autism* was used to describe individuals who demonstrated deficits in social development and communication and a range of repetitive behaviors or restricted interests. However, since the late 1970s, the categorization of individuals with autism has been recognized as a spectrum of disorders, currently referred to as *autism spectrum disorder* (ASD) or the autism spectrum. The *DSM-5* (APA, 2013) represents ASD as a single diagnostic category to describe a group of neurodevelopmental disabilities characterized by (a) deficits in social communication and social interactions across multiple contexts and (b) restricted interests or repetitive behaviors.

Across the spectrum, characteristics of ASD manifest uniquely as a collection of symptoms that rarely are the same from one individual to another. At one end of this spectrum are individuals characterized by severe deficits "requiring very substantial support" (Level 3; APA, 2013, p. 52). Such individuals typically display severe deficits in social communication and/or interactions, extremely limited or unintelligible speech, and inflexible behaviors that interfere with functioning (e.g., displays of repetitive behaviors such as hand flapping or rocking). For individuals with more severe forms of ASD, intellectual disabilities may be present. At the other end of the spectrum are those individuals with difficulties in social communication and restricted behaviors/interests "requiring support" (Level 1; APA, 2013, p. 52). Individuals at this level often demonstrate an ability to speak in full sentences and engage in conversation, but display odd or atypical attempts/responses to social interactions (i.e., a long-winded, pedantic communication style), difficulty switching between activities, rare or unique special interests (e.g., deep-fry cookers, trains, vacuums, tractors, engines), and problems with planning and organization. Despite the presence of such social and behavioral difficulties, individuals with higher functioning ASD demonstrate no significant delays in the development of language or cognitive abilities.

Within the past two decades, the number of individuals identified as having ASD has increased substantially. Traditionally, ASD was considered a low-incidence disability, occurring in only four to six of every 10,000 (or one in approximately 1,600) live births (Lotter, 1967). However, the CDC (2016b) recently released prevalence rates from data collected by the Autism and Developmental Disabilities Monitoring (ADDM) Network, indicating that one in 68 individuals met criteria for an ASD. This new estimate represents a nearly 30% increase from the one in 88 reported in 2008 and continues to reinforce the notion that ASD is the fastest growing developmental disability in the United States. Although it remains unclear why such dramatic increases are occurring in the number of individuals with ASD, it is likely that some of the increase may be due to heightened awareness, improved assessment tools, differences in access to services, and inclusion of a broader spectrum of symptomatology (Mahjouri & Lord, 2012).

Although individuals with ASD will vary greatly from each other, they all will experience impaired social communication skills of one kind or another. In fact, deficits in social communication and social interactions are the defining characteristics of ASD (APA, 2013; Volkmar, Reichow, Westphal, & Mandell, 2014). In general, individuals with ASD have a weakness in understanding nonverbal cues such as facial expressions, gestures, and tone of voice. Such a weakness makes it difficult to decipher thoughts, feelings, intentions, and perspectives of others. This means that individuals with ASD likely will have difficulty interpreting when another person is upset, happy, or uninterested. Furthermore, it is unlikely that an individual with ASD will engage in expected nonverbal behaviors when communicating. That is, he or she may demonstrate poor eye contact (or have a stiff, staring gaze), display awkward or clumsy body posture and limited or inappropriate facial expressions, and/or fail to use gestures while interacting and communicating with others.

Individuals with ASD also express limited social and emotional reciprocity. Often unresponsive to auditory cues (e.g., their name being called, requests from another person), some individuals appear to be unaware of the people and circumstances that surround them. In fact, it is not uncommon that individuals with ASD are described as in their "own little world" (Volkmar et al., 2014). These individuals may prefer to engage in solitary activities or take part in activities from the periphery rather than actively participating in games or group activities with others (APA, 2013; Volkmar et al., 2014). Moreover, they may not share feelings of enjoyment about their interests, activities, or accomplishments.

An important aspect of social and emotional reciprocity in which individuals with ASD demonstrate impairment is in the ability to consider others' perspectives and to appreciate the fact that other individuals think, feel, and view the world differently than they do, a concept commonly referred to as *mindblindness* (Charman, Swettenham, & Baron-Cohen, 1997). In individuals with higher functioning ASD, such mindblindness often is manifested in a one-sided social approach to others whereby they overly pursue a topic of interest (e.g., Hoover vacuum cleaners, dinosaurs) regardless of the other individual's interests or reaction (APA, 2013). For example, an individual with ASD may continue to talk about the latest Spiderman movie while seemingly ignoring the listener's signs of boredom (e.g., rolling of the eyes, looking away) or attempts to leave. This failure may appear as disregard for others' feelings and may come across as insensitive. However, this is not the individual's intention. Instead, individuals with ASD have a poor capacity to recognize, relate to, and understand the feelings of others, making it difficult for them to understand why others do not share their level of passion.

Taken together, individuals with ASD frequently demonstrate unawareness of how to engage and respond socially. As a result, they likely will violate many social conventions and engage in a large amount of socially inappropriate behavior(s) at one time or another. For example, an individual with ASD may infringe upon another's personal space (e.g., touching a T-shirt bearing a logo the individual likes) and may be unable to refrain from asking extremely personal questions (e.g., "Did you brush your teeth this morning?") or to keep thoughts and/or opinions to themselves (e.g., blurting out "You have really ugly shoes"). In addition, these individuals often are confused as to why their behavior(s) may affect others as they do. A lack of understanding of the social world, combined with socially inappropriate behavior(s), often results in numerous social errors.

Individuals with ASD frequently display behaviors, interests, and activities that are not only restricted and repetitive in nature, but also abnormally intense or focused (APA, 2013). These patterns of behavior, interests, and activities can be separated into two distinct groups: "lower-level" and "higher-level" behaviors (Turner, 1999). Lower-level behaviors are characterized by stereotyped motor movements or atypical, involuntary actions (e.g., hand flapping, object spinning).

Conversely, more advanced, higher-level behaviors include insistence on following elaborate routines and focusing on circumscribed interests (e.g., arranging objects by order of color, eating exactly five Pringles at lunchtime).

With regard to lower level behaviors, individuals with ASD may engage in rigid motor mannerisms. These behaviors may include spinning, finger flapping, clapping, hand flapping or twisting, pacing, stereotyped walking, and/or complex whole-body movements (APA, 2013; South, Ozonoff, & McMahon, 2005). Often, these repetitive movements—frequently referred to as "self-stimulatory" or "self-stimming" behaviors—denote expressions of excitement, happiness, frustration, and/or agitation. These behavioral difficulties are not performed intentionally. Rather, they are due to difficulty in identifying and describing emotions (Fitzgerald & Bellgrove, 2006), as well as the individual's sense of loss of control or inability to predict outcomes (Koerner & Dugas, 2008; Wigham, Rodgers, South, McConachie, & Fresston, 2015). That is, lower-level behaviors likely occur in highly stressful periods that are difficult to interpret or that evoke anxiety and/or confusion.

When examining higher-level behaviors, individuals with ASD often display an inflexible adherence to seemingly nonfunctional routines or rituals, desiring sameness and requiring environmental predictability (APA, 2013). Moreover, change, surprise, chaos, and uncertainty are not easily tolerated, and the lack of predictability or sameness can cause feelings of stress and/or anxiety (Lidstone et al., 2014). Individuals with ASD function best when they can predict what is going to occur within the environment. By engaging in routines or ritualistic behaviors, individuals with ASD attempt to control their environment.

Perhaps the most interesting feature of rigid behavior displayed by individuals with higher functioning ASD is their obsessive and, at times, all absorbing interests. These individuals may collect volumes of detailed, factual information and trivia related to a relatively narrow topic (e.g., roller coasters, NASCAR racing, telephone pole insulators). It is not uncommon for interests to change once an individual collects all the information available regarding a specific topic. Regardless of the topic or the frequency by which it may change, individuals with higher functioning ASD tend to focus most of their social advances and conversations on their specific topic of interest (Ozonoff et al., 2002) and talk about it to the point that they annoy others.

Individuals with ASD often respond unusually to sensory stimuli, such as sound, light, touch, texture, taste, smell, pain, and temperature, reacting in either hypersensitive (i.e., oversensitive) or hyposensitive (i.e., undersensitive) ways (Hilton et al., 2010). For example, some individuals with ASD may have a high threshold for withstanding painful bumps or bruises, yet they may be extremely sensitive to clothing touching their skin (e.g., the tag on the back of their shirt) or people touching them (e.g., giving them a hug or a kiss). The most common oversensitivity for these individuals is specific sounds (Tomchek & Dunn, 2007). Many individuals with ASD have a propensity to be overly startled by sudden noises. Moreover, they may perceive sounds of a certain pitch to be unbearable or notice very faint sounds that others might not hear, such as a siren in the distance. Additionally, many individuals with ASD may withdraw from certain stimuli due to overloading the senses.

On the other hand, individuals with ASD also may demonstrate a lack of sensitivity to various stimuli. This typically occurs when responding to particular sounds, such as their names being called. They also may be unusually able to endure pain and tolerate cold weather. In fact, some sensory stimuli may evoke pleasure, such as cool air coming from an air conditioner or the smell of perfume. Generally, individuals with ASD appear to be confused by and fail to understand why others do not have the same level of sensitivity to stimuli that they themselves do. In addition, the way in which individuals with ASD respond to different sensory stimuli, whether fearful or not, can frequently cause problems in daily living situations (Hilton et al., 2010).

Diagnosis of ASD occurs in two steps: (a) a developmental screening and (b) a comprehensive diagnostic evaluation (CDC, 2016b). The developmental screening occurs at regularly scheduled well-child visits to determine if there are any developmental delays in learning, speaking, behaving, and moving. Data for the screening are derived from physicians' observations and input from parents or guardians. ASD can be detected at 18 months or younger so specific screening for ASD begins when the child is 18 months old. If problems are detected in developmental screenings, the physician will complete a comprehensive evaluation that may also include a hearing and vision screening, genetic testing, other medical testing and/or referral to a specialist (e.g., developmental pediatrician, child neurologist, child psychiatrist, or psychologist).

In some cases, individuals may not be diagnosed until adulthood (APA, 2013). These individuals may be prompted to seek out a diagnosis because of the diagnosis of ADHD in a child who is a family member or because of difficulties in work or relationships. Obtaining a detailed developmental history for purposes of diagnosis may be difficult, and clinicians must rely on the adult's self-reports of functional difficulties. When clinicians determine that clinical diagnostic criteria are met, ASD diagnoses may be made in adulthood as long as there is no evidence of good social and communication skills in childhood.

Early intervention is central to the effective treatment and management of ASD. Numerous educational, behavioral, and communication interventions have been developed to improve communication skills, social functioning, and academic achievement and to decrease maladaptive behaviors (CDC, 2016b; Hsia et al., 2014). No medications are available to treat ASD; however, children, youths, and adults may take medications to treat and manage specific ASD symptoms (e.g., irritability, sleep difficulties, high energy levels) and and/or co-occurring disorders such as depression, anxiety, and seizure disorders.

ATTENTION DEFICIT HYPERACTIVITY DISORDER

Attention deficit hyperactivity disorder (ADHD) is a common neurodevelopmental disorder that is defined in the *DSM-5* as "a persistent pattern of inattention and/or hyperactivity-impulsivity that interferes with functioning or development" (APA, 2013, p. 59). The three subtypes presented by individuals with ADHD are (a) combined, (b) predominately inattentive, and (c) predominately hyperactive/impulsive. The predominately inattentive subtype is characterized by symptoms such as failure to closely attend to details; making careless mistakes in school or work assignments; difficulty sustaining attention during lectures, lengthy readings, or conversations; appears not to be listening when spoken to directly; difficulty following through with instructions and completing school or work assignments;

difficulty organizing tasks as exemplified by behaviors such as poor management of sequential tasks, problems keeping materials and belongings in order, disorganized work, poor time management, and failure to meet deadlines; avoidance, dislike, and/or reluctance to perform tasks that require sustained mental effort; often losing things (e.g., school or work materials, paperwork, eyeglasses, wallets, keys, cell phones) that are necessary to perform tasks; becoming easily distracted by extraneous stimuli; and forgetful in daily activities such as returning phone calls, paying bills, and/or keeping appointments. The hyperactive/impulsive subtype is characterized by symptoms such as frequent fidgeting, hand tapping, or inability to sit still; leaving seats in classroom or workplace situations when they are expected to remain in place; frequently feeling restless; frequent inability to quietly engage in play or leisure activities; inability or discomfort with remaining still for extended periods of time such as in restaurants or in lengthy work meetings; talking excessively; difficulty waiting for their turn while waiting in line or in conversations; blurting out answers before questions have been completed; interrupting or intruding into or taking over what others are doing without their permission (APA, 2013).

ADHD symptoms initially appear early in childhood, and diagnosis requires the presence of several symptoms before the age of 12 (APA, 2013). Diagnosis also requires that symptoms be present in more than one setting (e.g., home, school, work). ADHD may be diagnosed as mild, moderate, or severe depending on number and severity of symptoms and the degree to which they impair social or occupational functioning. ADHD typically persists into adolescence and adulthood and can result in marked impairment in social and vocational functioning. For example, in comparison to their peers, adolescents with ADHD score lower on standardized tests, have higher absenteeism rates, are at greater risk for dropping out of high school, and are less likely to pursue postsecondary education (DuPaul, Weyandt, & Janusis, 2011). Those who do pursue postsecondary education have lower grade point averages (GPAs) than their peers, as well as demonstrate higher dropout and academic probation rates. As they begin adulthood, they tend to have few friends, engage in impulsive decision making, have poor driving records and more motor vehicle accidents, experience difficulties in romantic relationships, and have higher rates of criminal activity (APA, 2013; Fedele, Hartung, Canu, & Wilkowski, 2010; McKeague, Hennessy, O'Driscoll, & Heary, 2015).

Population estimates regarding the prevalence of ADHD vary depending on the population sampled, reporting mechanisms, and the diagnostic criteria used to determine estimates (Adamou et al., 2013). However, most estimates indicate that the prevalence of ADHD in school-aged children is between 5% and 12% (Adamou et al., 2013; APA, 2013; CDC, 2016a; Holwerda et al., 2013). Worldwide prevalence estimates of ADHD in adulthood typically range from 2.5% to 5%. ADHD prevalence estimates, like ASD prevalence estimates, have increased over the years, and some question whether this increase reflects a true growth in prevalence or is the result of other factors such as changes in diagnostic criteria, increased public awareness, greater access to services, policy changes in special education, and the influence of the pharmaceutical industry on diagnostic practices (CDC, 2016a; Polanczyk Willcutt, Salum, Kieling, & Rohde, 2014). The validity of research into ADHD rates has also been called into question because of the variability of estimates reported across studies and differences in sources of information (e.g., parental reports, teacher reports, self-reports, physician reports, estimates based on different diagnostic criteria across studies) used to determine estimates. In fact, Polancyzk et al. (2014) found no evidence to support that rates of ADHD are increasing in the population when standard diagnostic procedures were used to determine rates. Despite doubt regarding increasing rates of ADHD, recent data from the National Survey of Children's Health indicate that the proportion of children who have ever been diagnosed with ADHD has increased from 7.8% in 2003 to 9.5% in 2007 to 11.0% in 2011 (CDC, 2016a). Of those diagnosed with ADHD, 69% were currently taking ADHD medication.

Although the precise cause of ADHD is unknown, researchers are investigating three potential factors: (a) abnormalities in the brain; (b) hereditary factors; and (c) functional differences (Adamou et al., 2012). Impairment in executive functioning is now considered to be the underlying cause of symptoms associated with ADHD (Field, Parker, Sawilowsky, & Rolands, 2013). Executive functioning is the "self-regulating mechanism for organizing, directing, and managing other cognitive activities, emotional responses, and overt behaviors" (Field et al., 2013, p. 67). The skills involved in executive functioning that are challenging for individuals with ADHD include (a) activation (i.e., organizing and initiating tasks); (b) focus (i.e., sustaining and shifting attention); (c) effort (i.e., regulating alertness and adjusting speed of processing); (d) emotions (i.e., managing frustrations and controlling intense emotional responses); (e) memory (i.e., retaining, retrieving, and working with information); and (f) action (i.e., initiating, monitoring, and adjusting effort) (Field et al., 2013; Parker, Field Hoffman, Sawilowsky, & Rolands, 2011).

The American Academy of Pediatrics (AAP) has recently developed new clinical guidelines for the diagnosis and treatment of children with ADHD (CDC, 2016a). The AAP guidelines are based on *DSM-5* (APA, 2013) criteria for diagnosis of children aged 4 to 18 who present with academic or behavioral problems and symptoms of inattention, hyperactivity, or impulsivity in more than one setting (e.g., school, home). In making diagnoses, clinicians gather information about observations from parents, guardians, teachers, and/or other school or mental health professionals who are involved in the child's education or care. In making diagnoses, other conditions are ruled out, and clinicians also assess the child or adolescent for conditions that co-occur with ADHD (e.g., anxiety, depression, oppositional defiance disorder, conduct disorders, learning and language disorders, other neurodevelopmental disorders, tics, sleep apnea). AAP guidelines indicate that ADHD should be treated as a chronic condition.

Early intervention and service provision throughout primary and secondary education are hallmarks of effective treatment for children and youths with ADHD and can facilitate better outcomes in adulthood (DuPaul et al., 2011). The most commonly used interventions are a combination of pharmacological and nonpharmacological interventions. FDA-approved psychostimulants (e.g., methylphenidate) are the most commonly prescribed medications. Doses of medication are titrated (adjusted) to achieve maximum benefit with minimal adverse effects. Nonpharmacological interventions include evidence-based parent- or teacher-administered behavior strategies. Home–school communication between teachers and parents or adult guardians is critical to ensure that these strategies are consistently being implemented in both settings. Likewise, partnerships among teachers, parents, and school psychologists (who recommend strategies) are critical.

Diagnosis of ADHD in adults is typically made by a licensed mental health professional or physician based on a thorough clinical evaluation. The clinical evaluation includes a comprehensive diagnostic interview, a detailed history of current and past functioning, information from spouses, partners, or family members, *DSM-5* symptom checklists, standardized behavior rating scales, cognitive assessment, and other psychometric testing that the diagnostician deems necessary (Children and Adults with Attention Deficit Hyperactivity Disorder [CHADD], 2015). Adults must have at least five of the *DSM-5* symptoms present, and, in the same manner of diagnosing ADHD in children, clinicians rule out other disorders and assess for the presence of co-occurring conditions in adults. Treatment for adults, like treatment for children, typically involves psychostimulant medications as well as cognitive behavioral therapy. Cognitive behavioral approaches include education about ADHD, attention management training, behavioral management training, social skills training, stress management training, anger management training, and problem solving training (Wadsworth & Harper, 2007).

PSYCHOSOCIAL ASPECTS OF ASD AND ADHD

Adolescence is characterized by an intense desire for peer group acceptance and belonging. Concerns about "fitting in" and conforming to social norms are typical during this developmental stage (McKeague et al., 2015). Unfortunately, children and youths with ASD and ADHD may be regarded by their peers as "freaks" or "weirdos." They are often stigmatized by their peers, bullied, teased, and/or rejected (APA, 2013). Youths with ASD report having few friends and do not rely on friendships as a source of support (Wehman et al., 2014). Likewise, research has documented that, in comparison to children without ADHD, those with ADHD are more likely to be socially rejected by their peers and have greater difficulties in establishing friendships (DuPaul et al., 2011). Symptomatic behaviors associated with ASD and ADHD (e.g., social skills deficits) contribute to these negative perceptions and rejection by peers. Relationship difficulties can cause feelings of isolation, being different, and feeling left out, and these difficulties often persist into adulthood. Family discord can occur in response to ADHD behaviors, and as adults, individuals with ADHD are likely to experience substantial interpersonal conflict (APA, 2013).

The sense of being different from others can result in negative self-evaluations, self-blame, and internalized stigma. However, McKeague et al. (2015) found in a qualitative investigation of psychosocial issues for youths with ADHD and depression that some youths respond to peer stigmatization with anger and a sense of injustice at being mistreated, and by standing up for themselves. These authors also discovered that disclosure was a major psychosocial issue for adolescents in their study because of their desire to hide their disorders from others to avoid stigmatizing reactions. However, as they made transitions from childhood to adolescence to adulthood, met other individuals like themselves, and developed stable groups of friends, their concerns about how others perceived them decreased, and they were more likely to disclose. It is not only peers that stigmatize individuals with these neurodevelopmental disabilities, teachers may also perceive labels such as ASD and ADHD unfavorably (DuPaul et al., 2011) and automatically anticipate that children with these labels will be difficult to manage in the classroom.

Stereotypes, misperceptions, and stigma can also have a negative impact on individuals with ASD and ADHD. ADHD, in particular, has been "under the spotlight of public scrutiny" in recent years (Admou et al., 2013, p. 3), and the general public's perception of children with ADHD is of "a rampant child, rowdy and disobedient; brought on by the consumption of chemical additives" (Admou et al., 2013, p. 2). Recent debates regarding the legitimacy of ADHD diagnoses have stigmatized ADHD treatment, treatment providers, and individuals with ADHD (Walkup, Stossel, & Rendleman, 2014). As a consequence, providers are de-incentivized from offering appropriate treatment, and individuals with ADHD are inhibited from seeking treatment.

The inability of individuals with ADHD to complete tasks (e.g., classroom and work assignments) that require sustained attention and effort is often misinterpreted by others as "laziness, irresponsibility, or failure to cooperate" (APA, 2013, p. 63). These public perceptions can undermine the mental and physical health of individuals with ADHD when these individuals also question the legitimacy of their disabilities and fail to seek treatment, rehabilitation, postsecondary classroom accommodations, and workplace accommodations as a result. Individuals with ASD are also affected by stigma, and they may develop compensatory strategies to mask their difficulties but suffer from the stress and constant effort of trying to maintain a socially acceptable façade (APA, 2013).

Both ASD and ADHD can be accompanied by co-occurring psychiatric disabilities. Within the last decade, more research and clinical information has indicated that many individuals with ASD may be more susceptible to anxiety and other affective mood problems. In fact, both families and educators have reported that individuals with ASD have substantially more problems with internalizing symptoms as compared to their typically developing peers (Merikangas et al., 2010). Anxieties may begin to emerge at early ages due to: (a) preoccupation with possible violations of routines and rituals; (b) being placed in situations without clear schedules or expectations; and/or (c) anticipation of failed social encounters. Over time, such anxieties may evolve into more depressive symptoms during adolescence and early adulthood. Depression typically occurs when individuals with ASD begin to develop a greater insight into their differences from others and experience a growing desire for friendships (Eussen et al., 2013). It has been suggested that feelings of victimization and chronic frustration from repeated failure to engage others socially may contribute to the development of both depression and anxiety disorders in individuals with ASD (Bauminger, Shulman, & Agam, 2003). In fact, increased prevalence of anxiety and depression has been reported among individuals with ASD (e.g., Somonoff et al., 2008; van Steensel, Bögels, & Perrin, 2011). Such problems likely directly interfere with these individuals' ability to enter into and sustain mutually enjoyable relationships with their peers (Hedley & Young, 2006).

Research has also documented a high rate of co-occurring psychiatric disabilities among individuals with ADHD. In fact, it has been discovered that as many as 90% of adults with ADHD have co-occurring psychiatric disorders (Gjervan, Torgersen, Nordahl, & Rasmussen, 2012). These include anxiety disorders, mood disorders, substance use disorders, and antisocial and other personality disorders (Adamou, 2013; Gjerven et al., 2012). Left untreated, psychiatric comorbidities can amplify the difficulties that individuals with ADHD experience in social interactions, education, and employment. ADHD can also co-occur with other neurodevelopmental disorders including ASD.

In addition to co-occurring psychiatric disabilities, ample research has suggested that sleep disturbances are common among individuals with ASD (e.g., Polimeni, Richdale, & Francis, 2005; Tudor, Hoffman, & Sweeney, 2012). Individuals with ASD may have greater frequencies of and more types of sleep problems than typically developing individuals. For example, Polimeni et al. (2005) indicated that individuals with ASD were more sluggish and disoriented and had slower reactions and speech after waking than typically developing individuals. In addition, parents report that sleep disturbances in individuals with ASD regularly include difficulties in falling asleep, frequent and longer lasting nighttime awakenings, night terrors and sleep-walking, earlier morning awakenings, shorter overall sleep duration, and lower sleep quality (e.g., Polimeni et al., 2005; Tudor et al., 2012). Unfortunately, disordered sleep can have a significant negative impact on the daytime functioning of individuals with ASD, including elevated behavioral outbursts, daytime drowsiness, and learning difficulties (Tudor et al., 2012).

VOCATIONAL ASPECTS OF ASD AND ADHD

It is reported that more than 90% of individuals with ASD are unemployed upon exiting high school (Schall, Wehman, & McDonough, 2012). Other research estimates employment rates among individuals with ASD ranging from 10% to 50%. With such a high unemployment rate, it can be expected that young adults with ASD are especially vulnerable within the work environment. Adult outcome studies throughout the world continue to report low employment rates, wages, and hours worked for individuals with ASD (Chen, Leader, Sung, & Leahy, 2015). Data from the National Longitudinal Transition Study-2 (NLTS2) continuously report that young adults with ASD demonstrate the lowest employment rates among people with disabilities (Chen et al., 2015). In fact, job attainment (at least once since high school graduation) is always significantly lower for individuals on the spectrum (37% to 45%) than it is for those with other disabilities (60% to 72%; Chen et al., 2015). Similarly, the rate at which individuals on the spectrum held paid employment during the first 6 years following high school graduation was 55%, the lowest rate when compared to their peers with learning disability (LD; 94%), intellectual disability (ID; 69%), and speech/language impairment (SLI; 86%; Chen et al., 2015). Roux and colleagues (2013) analyzed the same data set (NLTS2) and found that young adults with ASD also earned a significantly lower wage (mean of $8.10/hour) than their peers with other disabilities (emotional disability [ED], $11.90; LD, $11.20; SLI, $12.00). Furthermore, the amount of hours worked was another troubling statistic. About one fifth of the individuals with ASD worked full time (>35 hours per week), which was about one half the rate of the ID group (40%) and about one third of the rate of the ED (61%), LD (73%), and SLI (63%) groups (Roux et al., 2013). Other studies using the Rehabilitation Services Administration's 911 dataset (RSA-911) reported similar findings (Chen et al., 2015).

Adults with ADHD also experience high unemployment rates. Estimates of employment among individuals with ADHD range from 22% to 54% (Holwerda et al., 2013). Young adults with ADHD who are employed typically work part time, in lower status jobs, earn lower wages, and have unstable work histories. Other work-related problems for individuals with ADHD include poor job performance, more workplace accidents and injuries, and greater absenteeism than workers without ADHD (Adamou et al., 2013; Holwerda et al., 2013).

In a Dutch study of predictors of finding and maintaining work for adolescents and young adults with ASD and attention deficit disorder (ADD), Holwerda et al. (2013) found that being male was a predictor of finding and maintaining work for individuals with ADD but not for individuals with ASD. For both samples, living independently, expectations to be able to work full time, high perceived support from parents, and positive attitudes of parents regarding work were related to finding work but not maintaining work. However, higher age and positive attitudes regarding work did predict maintaining employment for both individuals with ADD and ASD.

The steps prior to obtaining a job are a taxing process and the difficulties that individuals with ASD and ADHD experience during this process can significantly limit their job options. Prior to obtaining a job, one must undergo the lengthy and overwhelming job application process. This process typically consists of job searching, resume building, and interviewing. Individuals with ASD and ADHD may experience a multitude of difficulties throughout this process, which can significantly limit their job options.

Müller and colleagues (2003) interviewed adults with ASD and asked about their experiences not only within the workplace, but also with the obstacles they faced prior to beginning a job. Respondents reported difficulty with coordinating the job search process as a whole. For example, knowing how to begin looking for a job, how to initiate job contacts, and how to follow up with contacts were identified as problematic. Another study found individuals with ADHD likely to be disorganized and sporadic in coordinating the job search and to have difficulties forming working alliances with placement specialists (Adamou et al., 2013).

Once a job is identified, the next step is to submit an application and a résumé. Individuals with ASD reported this step as a daunting task due to the uncertainty of what employers were looking for, which experiences and skills to highlight, and the degree of details to provide (Müller et al., 2003). Individuals with ASD also reported their reluctance to initiate phone conversations. Specifically, the anxiety experienced during or prior to the conversation often resulted in the avoidance of telephone conversations all together. Job seekers with ADHD are likely to have problems with the tedious task of completing job applications and resumes, may fail to complete all items on application forms, or may inaccurately complete them because of failure to properly read the questions or to reflect on their answers (Adamou et al., 2013). These challenges in completing job applications arise from ADHD characteristics such as attention difficulties, impatience, and poor understanding of social conventions.

An interview is the next major step in the job acquisition process. It is very important to make a good impression during the interview and to demonstrate good communication skills with a potential employer. Individuals with ASD noted that they felt very awkward and tense during interviews. They also often did not know how to answer interview questions directly or were uncertain about how much detail to provide. In the job interview, individuals with ADHD often come across as very talkative and friendly, may overstate their qualifications for the position, and may respond to interviewer questions with some inaccuracies about their history (Adamou et al., 2013).

Unfortunately, obtaining a job is not the end of the struggle. The work environment is a challenging place for individuals on the spectrum as well as individuals with ADHD. The various behaviors exhibited by individuals with either of these neurodevelopmental disorders could potentially block them from successful employment outcomes. Social skills are vital within many aspects of life, including the workplace. Individuals on the spectrum experience difficulty with social communication, which often contributes to the inability to retain a job. Examples of these difficulties include rudely terminating or interrupting conversations, inability to communicate needs, lack of spontaneous speech, and inappropriate use of trendy language phrases. Some other social communication deficits are the inability to "read between the lines," misunderstanding facial expressions and tones of voice, and asking too many questions (Müller, 2003). Social immaturity and social naïveté were also identified as difficulties for people with ASD in the workplace. Examples include poor hygiene and grooming skills, inability to understand others' emotions, and acting inappropriately with individuals of the opposite sex (Müller, 2003). Those with ADHD also experience social interaction deficits that can impair vocational functioning (e.g., appearing not to be listening when spoken to, missing appointments, talking excessively, butting into conversations, using others people's things without asking, intruding on or taking over what others are doing; APA, 2013.)

Individuals with ADHD may initially present as highly motivated workers. However, if the job is not a good match with their interests and abilities, symptoms of their ADHD may begin to impair their job performance (Adamou et al., 2013). These symptoms and examples of the negative impact they can have on job performance include inattention to detail that can lead to making mistakes; impulsivity that can lead to poor decision making; hyperactivity that can be disruptive to coworkers; distractibility that interferes with staying on task, especially when tasks are tedious or boring, and can result in making mistakes; and disorganization and time management problems that interfere with meeting deadlines (Adamou et al., 2013).

As mentioned previously in this chapter, individuals with ASD exhibit many challenging behaviors that make it difficult for them to adapt within the work environment. Examples include phenotypic behaviors, ritualistic activities, inflexible routines, yelling, tantrums, limited attention to tasks, hyperactivity, uncooperative behaviors, obsessive behaviors, aggression, property destruction, and self-injurious behavior. Individuals who display more challenging behaviors have poorer employment outcomes (Chen et al., 2015). Behavior problems were also noted as the most common reason for termination and were the least tolerated by employees and coworkers. Although many of these behaviors may go unnoticed for a while, there are clear antecedents that can trigger the behaviors. Examples include sensory issues, misunderstanding during conversations, and unanticipated changes in the routine or schedule.

Education level and improved employment outcomes are not directly related for individuals with ASD. Unfortunately, obtaining a college degree does not guarantee adequate employment in a relevant field, as college graduates with ASD are still frequently unemployed or underemployed (Chen et al., 2015). In 2014, Baldwin and colleagues reported that 45% of the adults on the spectrum were overqualified for the job that they were performing. Likewise, individuals with ADHD are often overqualified for the jobs they perform, and these jobs are often incompatible with their intellectual abilities, which, in most cases, are in the average to above-average range (Gjerven et al., 2012).

CHARACTERISTICS OF INDIVIDUALS WITH ASD AND ADHD

ASD is reported to occur in all racial, ethnic, and socioeconomic groups (Durkin et al., 2010). However, ASD, is almost five times more likely to occur in males (one in 42) than in females (one in 189; CDC, 2016b), which has been suggested to be due to a specific gene (PTCHD$_1$) mutation on the X-chromosome (Noor et al., 2010). Males are also more likely than females to be diagnosed with ADHD, with a 2:1 ratio in children and a 1.6:1 ratio in adults (APA, 2013). Females, however, are more likely than males to develop inattentive features as their primary presentation. Males are more likely to develop combined features of inattention and distractibility/hyperactivity (Gjerven et al., 2012).

REHABILITATION COUNSELING IMPLICATIONS

Over the years, an increased recognition of the need for VR services among individuals with ASD has developed. An encouraging statistic revealed by Schaller and Yang (Chen et al., 2015) indicated that 66% of individuals with ASD who utilized VR services achieved successful employment. Lawer and colleagues (2009) reported that 42% of service users with ASD obtained employment when they exited the VR system; this was the highest success rate among all participants with disabilities in their study. Relatedly, increased attention in the professional literature has focused on the substantial challenges that individuals with ADHD experience in the employment arena. Given the evidence that VR services have a positive impact on employment outcomes for individuals with ASD, as well as the literature on the numerous barriers to employment experienced by individuals with ADHD that could be ameliorated by rehabilitation services, it stands to reason that if appropriate rehabilitation services and supports are provided to these individuals, it could directly contribute to better outcomes with future endeavors. Therefore, we discuss important considerations to keep in mind throughout the rehabilitation counseling process when providing services to individuals with ASD and ADHD.

Counselor Awareness and Self-Reflective Practice

When considering rehabilitation counseling services for individuals with ASD and ADHD, several areas of reflective practice warrant attention. First and foremost, rehabilitation counselors should thoughtfully consider their views regarding the vocational potential of individuals with these disabilities. Because of the multitude of functional domains that these disorders may affect, rehabilitation counselors should be cautious not to underestimate their strengths or prematurely restrict vocational options as they work with these consumers to identify employment goals. Relatedly, rehabilitation counselors should keep in mind the heterogeneity of both these populations in terms of their skills, functional limitations, compensatory strategies, interests, and preferences. Additionally, they should consider how functional deficits in settings that do not provide a good person–environment match may be assets in settings that *do* provide a good person–environment match.

Another important area of reflection is counselors' attitudes regarding family involvement in the rehabilitation counseling process. Rehabilitation counselors may become understandably frustrated with family members who are either uninvolved or overinvolved in the process. If this is the case, rehabilitation counselors can challenge negative attitudes by putting themselves into the positions of family members to better understand all the factors that could contribute to lack of involvement or over-involvement. For example, rehabilitation counselors should not automatically assume that parents who are not involved in the transition and rehabilitation processes are uninvested in their children's welfare. Perhaps, their work hours conflict with being able to attend transition and rehabilitation meetings, they may lack transportation to appointments, or they cannot afford to pay for childcare so that they can attend appointments. Conversely, when families seem overinvolved (e.g., they speak for their children instead of letting their children speak for themselves), rehabilitation counselors should keep in mind that parents are understandably protective of their children, and they are not going to automatically trust an unknown service provider. Additionally, parents and guardians have, in many cases, had to expend substantial efforts to get their children's educational, health, and transition needs met. They may, subsequently anticipate that they will have to do the same with the rehabilitation counselor. Therefore, to counter these negative anticipations, as much attention should be paid to developing empathy for family members as is paid to establishing rapport with rehabilitation consumers.

Outreach and Eligibility Determination

Early detection and treatment of both ASD and ADHD is associated with improved adult outcomes (e.g., employment, independent living, community engagement, social functioning; Adamou et al., 2013; Gjerven, Torgersen, Nordahl, & Rasmussen, 2012; Wehman et al., 2014). Early delivery of rehabilitation services is also likely to improve adult outcomes. Outreach to schools to identify students with ASD and ADHD who stand to benefit from transition services that incorporate early and ongoing career development activities is imperative. Also, early planning and preparation for transitioning to adult services can help to ease the transition, particularly for those with ASD or ADHD who have difficulties with handling change.

Because individuals with ASD and ADHD are predisposed to co-occurring psychiatric disabilities, it is important that during the initial interview rehabilitation counselors screen for comorbidities and make appropriate referrals for evaluation and treatment. Additionally, it is important for rehabilitation counselors to be aware of the ways in which co-occurring psychiatric conditions may present themselves. Characteristics of these conditions may include a worsening in behavior, inattention, social withdrawal, overreliance on obsessions and compulsions, hyperactivity, aggressive or oppositional behavior, agitation, and/or changes in eating and sleeping (Eussen et al., 2013). Adults who apply for rehabilitation services who suspect that they have ASD or ADHD but have never been formally diagnosed should be queried during the intake interview about functional difficulties that they are currently experiencing and referred for a comprehensive evaluation by a qualified neuropsychologist, psychologist, or psychiatrist to establish eligibility for services and identify potential rehabilitation service needs.

Rehabilitation Assessment and Planning

As is true in providing services to all rehabilitation consumers, it is important that rehabilitation assessment and planning take an individualized approach, especially because of the heterogeneity of individuals diagnosed with ASD and ADHD. Because no two individuals with ASD or ADHD will display the same characteristics or level of impairment to an equal degree, consideration of each consumer's uniqueness must be at the forefront in exploring individual strengths, interests, and preferences. When designing/implementing individualized supports and services for individuals with ASD and ADHD, rehabilitation counselors should strive to create as many opportunities for these consumers to exert greater control through *choice making*—the process of allowing an individual to select an activity among several alternatives. However, especially if they are younger with more severe functional limitations, these consumers may have had limited experiences with decision making and may need training in decision making and self-determination. In these cases, decision making may need to involve the presentation of options by the rehabilitation counselor. For example, an individual with ASD may be given the choice of whether to complete one of two work-required tasks. The expectation remains that the individual will complete both activities, but the individual with ASD directs the order regarding which to do first. Related to the importance of choice making, rehabilitation counselors should also incorporate the individual's *preferences*—those objects, tasks, and/or activities most appealing and naturally rewarding—into all aspects of the rehabilitation planning process. When choice making and preference can be incorporated into rehabilitation planning, individuals with ASD and ADHD may exert more control over their lives, thereby decreasing problematic behaviors and increasing time engaged in social contexts (Powell-Smith & Vaughn, 2006).

Rehabilitation Services

Unfortunately, research has yet to identify a single intervention that is appropriate and effective for all individuals with ASD across various educational and vocational contexts (Crosland & Dunlap, 2012). Rather, examination of the extant literature has outlined various tools within a toolbox of evidence-based approaches that are necessary for effective programming for individuals with ASD (e.g., Crosland & Dunlap, 2012; Iovannone, Dunlap, Huber, & Kincaid, 2003; Lee & Carter, 2012). Various approaches are also available for effective programming for individuals with ADHD (DuPaul et al., 2011). This chapter posits that rehabilitation counselors should build an approach that utilizes a combination of evidence-based practices when designing and implementing a variety of rehabilitation plans for individuals with ASD and ADHD. Specifically, it is important that such plans include each of the following strategies: (a) individualized instruction that incorporates choice and preference; (b) functional programming (i.e., viewing challenging behavior[s] as instructional needs; developing instructional priorities that emanate from the environment); (c) systemic instruction provided within a structured environment; and (d) collaboration with families, school personnel, and other service providers. Such programming should steadily expose individuals with ASD and ADHD to cues, prompts, and interesting and motivating stimuli, as well as employ consistent feedback and repeated exposure in order to be most effective. The incorporation of these characteristics in social skill, behavioral, and even academic and employment plans not only will permit rehabilitation counselors to support the needs of individuals with ASD and ADHD, but also promote positive outcomes.

Research endorses the idea that interventions for individuals with ASD and ADHD should include personalized elements in order to increase motivation and engagement when learning new skill sets (e.g., DuPaul et al., 2011; Koegel, Shirotova, & Koegel, 2009; Lanou, Hough, & Powell, 2012; Wehman et al., 2014). The incorporation of individualized supports that align with the interests and strengths of the individual promote higher levels of engagement, which may be a predictor of positive outcomes during, and in some cases, after a treatment, education, transition, or employment plan (Logan, Bakeman, & Keefe, 1997). Evidence-based practices can include individualized elements such as specific hand gestures as a response cue that the individual finds engaging (i.e., high-five), using a favorite character to teach a skill, or even incorporating a particular strength in circumscribed interests (e.g., deep-fry cookers). Regardless, rehabilitation plans should take the role of being custom designed in order to cater to individual needs and skill level.

In order to create individualized supports that incorporate choice and preference for the individuals with ASD and ADHD, rehabilitation counselors and transition team members should:

- Identify individualized intervention components that will increase engagement and motivation to succeed.
- Identify individualized goals that prioritize the most prominent needs.
- Provide opportunities for the individual (or caregivers) to advocate for choice and preference into any part of the rehabilitation plan (when applicable).
- Provide individuals with ASD and ADHD with the support they need throughout their lives to experience positive outcomes throughout adulthood. Access to vocational services and interventions has been shown to benefit people with ASD and to extend their abilities for working and living independently (Chen et al., 2015). Individuals with ADHD are also likely to experience these benefits of vocational services. Schall and colleagues (2012) mentioned the importance of emphasizing employment in high school before graduation. High school internships can provide individuals with ASD and ADHD with the experiences they need to better transition into employment after graduating from high school.
- Using effective social skills and knowing how to behave in a variety of social situations can make the difference in successful outcomes in the workplace as well as at home and in the community (DuPaul et al., 2011; Schall et al., 2012). Individuals with ASD and ADHD need to be taught social skills early in life to better assist the transition process from school to college or a career. Using practices such as role playing, counseling, behavior rehearsal, and targeted instruction on social skills frequently results in overcoming the problems associated with poor social skills.

⬤ It is imperative to educate students with disabilities within the least restrictive environment to the maximum extent appropriate. Providing young students with ASD and ADHD the access to the general curriculum will allow them to interact with students in the school, participate in extracurricular activities, and abide by the school rules (DuPaul et al., 2011; Schall et al., 2012). Having this foundation will increase the competence of individuals with ASD and will predict better outcomes when in the workplace and in the community.

COUNSELING AND GUIDANCE

Counseling and guidance are always individualized to the unique characteristics, rehabilitation needs, and preferences of each rehabilitation consumer. Rehabilitation consumers with ASD and ADHD are also very heterogeneous populations that represent great diversity in the number and severity of symptoms they experience, their strengths, rehabilitation needs, and self-determined goals. With these caveats in mind, we highlight several general considerations for providing counseling and guidance to individuals with these neurodevelopmental disabilities.

Because ASD is characterized by functional difficulties in social communication, the rehabilitation consumer–counselor interaction may be difficult for both parties. However, several considerations for improving communications with consumers with ASD can substantially improve the partnership and increase the potential for successful outcomes (A. Greene, Director, University of Arkansas Autism Support Program, personal communication, December 18, 2015). First, because many individuals with ASD prefer structure and sameness, it will be important to hold all counseling sessions in the same place and to follow the same structured format for conducting the session. Second, individuals with ASD tend to be fairly concrete and have difficulty with the nuances of language. Therefore, rehabilitation counselors should try to avoid sarcasm and use of idioms (e.g., "it's raining cats and dogs"). Consumers with ASD can also experience difficulties with expressive and receptive nonverbal social cues. They may not be able to interpret the rehabilitation counselor's nonverbal facial expressions and body language, and at the same time, their nonverbal expressions may not match what they are thinking and feeling. Therefore, counselors should communicate directly with consumers with ASD and directly ask these consumers what they are thinking and feeling. When these consumers are making social mistakes, it is also important for rehabilitation counselors to directly (and compassionately) point out these mistakes rather than ignoring them or responding to these mistakes with nonverbal cues. For example, if an individual is standing too close to you, rather than backing away as a nonverbal communication of your discomfort, it is important to verbally communicate your discomfort: "I feel uncomfortable when you stand so close to me. Could you please back up two steps?" As another example, if the consumer does not respond to your nonverbal cues that the counseling session is over; the rehabilitation counselor could state at the next appointment, "We have five more minutes before our appointment is over." Finally, a typical symptom of ASD is an obsessive focus on one particular area of interest that often dominates the person's conversations with others. If this occurs in rehabilitation counseling sessions and prevents the rehabilitation counselor and consumer from accomplishing the tasks that are the focus of the session, it needs to be directly addressed with the consumer. For example, if the consumer keeps going off topic and discussing her or his specific interest, the counselor can respond by saying, "We're off topic;

let's go back to talking about what we are here to accomplish." The rehabilitation counselor can also address this issue by reserving the last 5 minutes of each session to talk about the consumer's interest. This technique validates that the consumer's interests are important to the counselor but not at the expense of the work that needs to be accomplished during the session.

Rehabilitation counselors should also recognize when the consumer is demonstrating "self-stimulatory" or "self-stimming" behaviors that denote expressions of excitement, happiness, frustration, and/or agitation. It is important to understand that if these behaviors occur during a counseling session, they are not performed intentionally. Rather, they are due to difficulty in identifying and describing one's emotions (Fitzgerald & Bellgrove, 2006) as well as the individual's sense of loss of control or inability to predict outcomes (Koerner & Dugas, 2008; Wigham et al., 2015). That is, lower level behaviors likely occur in highly stressful periods that are difficult to interpret or that evoke anxiety and/or confusion. Thus, these may be signals that the rehabilitation counseling session is highly stress-provoking for the individual with ASD, and actions (e.g., inviting the consumer to bring a friend or advocate to the next session, providing more structure in future sessions, limiting the amount of time in sessions) should be taken to reduce the consumer's stress.

Wadsworth and Harper (2007) provided some helpful guidance for counseling individuals with ADHD. First and foremost, the focus of counseling and guidance should be on empowering these individuals to manage their symptoms and functional difficulties so that they can live fulfilling lives. Due to long histories of academic and vocational failures and troublesome relationships, adults with ADHD may experience self-blame, frustration, and helplessness. Consequently, they may avoid any situation that has historically been problematic for them. Because of these negative past experiences, they may also have negative expectations of failure in the counseling relationship and rehabilitation process. Rehabilitation counselors should, in these cases, assist the consumer to reframe his or her negative experiences as symptoms of the disorder rather than personal failures. They should also offer ongoing support and encouragement as consumers with ADHD learn and practice new skills to replace those in which they have deficits.

These authors also recommended that structured, directive counseling approaches are likely to be more effective in working with rehabilitation consumers with ADHD than insight-oriented, nondirective approaches (Wadsworth & Harper, 2007). Counseling approaches should focus on establishing clear guidelines regarding the rehabilitation process, the importance of being on time for appointments, and both the rehabilitation consumer's and counselor's responsibilities. At the same time, the consumer may perceive the rehabilitation counselor as too controlling. To counter this negative perception, the rehabilitation counselor can emphasize that the rehabilitation consumer is an equal partner who has the final say regarding service options and rehabilitation goals. This emphasis, if repeatedly stated and coupled with questions about what the consumer's preferences are, could assuage the consumer's perception of the rehabilitation counselor as being too controlling.

Wadsworth and Harper (2007) also delineated ADHD symptoms that may be observable in counseling sessions and cautioned rehabilitation counselors not to misinterpret these as disinterest, lack of motivation, uncooperativeness, defiance, and/or immaturity. Examples of these symptoms include long pauses in speech, stopping in the middle of a sentence, forgetting what they were saying, asking the rehabilitation counselor to repeat what she or he was saying, staring into space rather than looking at the rehabilitation counselor, interrupting the rehabilitation counselor when he or she is speaking, and wandering around or leaving the rehabilitation counselor's office.

Because negative expectations of individuals with ASD and ADHD can create barriers to employment, rehabilitation counselors should ensure that they encourage these individuals to focus on their skills and positive individual traits (Holwerda et al., 2013). Developing a list of these skills and traits can facilitate change from negative expectations to positive expectations. However, consumers may initially have difficulty identifying these traits. In these cases, rehabilitation counselors, family members, and transition team members may need to initially provide examples of traits that they have observed to help the client to then self-identify traits. Another important focus of counseling should be placed on facilitating the development of self-determination skills.

Finally, rehabilitation counselors should keep in mind that transitional periods (e.g., from high school to college or work; from college to work) can be challenging times for all youths and young adults, but these can be even more challenging for youths with neurodevelopmental disorders. Wehman et al. (2014) observed that many youths with ASD leave high school unprepared for adulthood with respect to employment, postsecondary education, and community living. They may lack the autonomy or independence to effectively transition into adult roles, and as a consequence may continue to rely on family for basic needs, financial support, housing, supervision, and companionship.

FAMILY INVOLVEMENT

The families of children, adolescents, and young adults with ASD or ADHD most often have the greatest insight into their children's needs, styles, strengths, and interests. As such, families should be included as active partners in the rehabilitation process—from rehabilitation assessment and plan development to implementation—to the highest degree possible. Parental input offers a unique and critical viewpoint that can provide insight into the individual's developmental history and interpretation of abilities, along with services and interventions provided to the individual in the past (Sansosti, Powell-Smith, & Cowan, 2010). Family and parent engagement increases the frequency of learning opportunities for the individual and can help to maintain and generalize skill sets learned across settings (e.g., home, community) throughout the individual's entire day (Barton & Harn, 2014). Research also has shown that challenging behaviors may decrease and engagement with tasks may increase when parents are included in the execution of interventions (Lequia, Machalicek, & Lyons, 2013). As such, it is beneficial for rehabilitation counselors to view families as essential partners in rehabilitation planning and delivery of supports and services.

Prior to engaging families, rehabilitation counselors should consider several circumstances. If the rehabilitation consumer is a legal adult, he or she must first be consulted to determine if he or she wants family members to be involved, to identify specific members to be involved, and to determine the degree of family involvement the consumer desires. Second, a partnership is a reciprocal relationship that involves listening and sharing, *not* telling a family what to do. Rehabilitation counselors should continue to offer expertise, but encourage members of the family (as well as the individual, when appropriate) to offer their expertise—knowledge of their child! Third, it is important that rehabilitation counselors recognize that family members may not know how to participate in their child's transition. They may be hindered by their own experiences, or lack of experiences, collaborating with professionals, or, more likely, feel ineffective and/or alienated (especially those from different cultural or linguistic backgrounds). Fourth, rehabilitation counselors should make a concerted effort to understand the particular family dynamics that may influence availability and/or involvement. Issues such as work schedules, transportation issues, family characteristics, and/or other stressors influence the ability of families to have time to be consistently involved (Crosland & Dunlap, 2012; Iovannone et al., 2003). Rehabilitation counselors should account for such dynamics in a nonjudgmental manner, and make appropriate accommodations to account for each family's unique constraints. Fifth, rehabilitation counselors should be aware that parent involvement tends to decrease with the increasing age of their son or daughter, but the need for parental involvement for individuals with neurodevelopmental disorders likely increases. As such, rehabilitation counselors should do their best to consider methods for offering families assistance during the complex time of adolescent development/young adulthood. Once such considerations are accounted for, efforts to create a more collaborative partnership between home and community should be of primary focus. Such efforts can incorporate either passive or active approaches, both of which aim to increase the capacity of families and agencies to engage in transformational projects that have the power to influence change and enhance programming.

EDUCATIONAL AND TRANSITION SERVICES

Services that will increase employability, capacity to live independently in their communities, and ability to achieve other desired adult outcomes should begin early in the education of children with ASD and ADHD. Wehman et al. (2014) reported that children and youths with ASD receive most of their education in special education settings, report low rates of participation in their own transition planning, and have a curriculum that includes primarily nonacademic/nonvocational courses despite the fact that they may have remarkably high grade point averages in comparison to their peers with other disabilities. These inadequate school experiences leave youths with ASD unprepared to successfully transition into adult roles. To remediate this problem, Wehman et al. (2014) provided several recommendations:

- Increase inclusion of these students in general education classes.
- Incorporate training in high school curricula on self-determination.
- Encourage students to establish goals that include 2-year or 4-year colleges or postsecondary vocational training.
- Provide opportunities for students to dually enroll in postsecondary classes while they are still receiving individualized education plan (IEP) services in high school and where they can receive educational coaching.
- Ensure that students participate in paid employment with intensive job coaching and support before they leave high school. "Such experience will allow these students to demonstrate their capacities and to engage supervisors and co-workers in ways that point to their high value in competitive employment" (Wehman et al., 2014, p. 7).
- Provide systematic instruction to increase functional literacy, self-care, life skills, independence, and self-determination.

- Provide peer mentoring and structured social skills training with an emphasis on real-world applications such as engagement in extracurricular activities.
- Increase access to professional speech and behavioral therapies that focus on functional adaptation in natural community settings and work environments.

Wehman et al. (2014, p. 7) also recommended that because "technology is exploding, and youth with ASD are embracing it," technology can be used in school, work, home, community, and recreation to address the communication and transition challenges these youths face.

Perhaps the most important feature of transition planning for individuals with ASD is the provision of systematic instruction occurring within a structured environment. Systematic instruction involves the process of carefully planning for all aspects of a given transition plan. When a transition plan is designed systematically it will: (a) identify the overall goals for a given transition plan/intervention (e.g., increase the number of social initiations); (b) detail the instructional procedures (e.g., use of computer-assisted social skills lessons); (c) outline the implementation procedures (e.g., provide direct lessons three times per week, supplemented by computer-assisted social skills training three times per week for a period of 8 weeks); (d) identify activities to ensure skill maintenance and generalization; and (e) specify the procedures for data collection and evaluation (e.g., behavior will be rated each day; data will be reviewed each week). In essence, transition plans that are systematic are those that have clear, purposeful objectives that focus on detailed aspects of the intervention and use meaningful data to monitor outcomes. It is important that rehabilitation counselors and other transition team members use, to the maximum extent possible, carefully developed plans that can be evaluated through data-driven practices (e.g., progress monitoring) to determine if the individual evinces gains in various domains of functioning (Sansosti & Powell-Smith, 2006; Sansosti et al., 2010). By carefully targeting essential skills to be taught, planning specifically when and how the skills will be taught, and determining data collection methods, rehabilitation counselors and transition team members will have effective programs that engage students with ASD (Iovannone et al., 2003) and that are legally defensible (Yell, Katsiyannis, Drasgow, & Herbst, 2003).

In addition to being systematic, a transition plan for an individual with ASD should be employed in a highly structured environment. An organized teaching environment is imperative for teaching skills to individuals with ASD because of difficulties they likely have restricting attention to relevant stimuli and engaging in learning new tasks and skills. As such, any intervention should be delivered in a manner that elicits, facilitates, enhances, and/or supports the acquisition of specific skills. By creating a highly predictable environment, individuals with ASD will demonstrate improved ability to attend to important stimuli in the environment, thereby promoting learning and decreasing the amount of time engaging in nonfunctional stereotypical behavior (Barton & Harn, 2014). One method for ensuring a structured environment for individuals with ASD is the use of visual supports/media. In fact, strategies that incorporate visual presentation are considered to be one of the most effective methods for assisting individuals with ASD (National Autism Center [NAC], 2009; Nikopoulos & Nikopoulos-Smyrni, 2008). The use of visual supports utilizes pictures, photographs, lists, or other visual material (e.g., computers, mobile technologies) that prompt the individual with ASD to engage in a particular behavior or prepare him or her to engage in a particular activity or task (Sansosti & Powell-Smith, 2006). Through the use of visuals, individuals with ASD require less verbal reminders and they increase their level of independence. Without visual aids, some individuals with ASD may engage in stereotypical and/or inappropriate behavior(s), whereas others may do nothing or spend their time focusing on details of a task, making them forget the task entirely.

DuPaul et al. (2011) described classroom interventions targeted at maladaptive behaviors, self-regulation, academic abilities, and social skills that should be incorporated into the IEPs of children and youths with ADHD. To address behavioral issues, they recommended the implementation of both antecedent- and consequence-based strategies. Antecedent-based strategies include posting classroom rules in full view of all students and strategically reviewing these rules. In addition, rules can be printed on an index card and affixed to the desks of children with ADHD. These authors also recommended that frequent praise be provided to students with ADHD when they follow the rules. Modifications to the length or content of assignments are another antecedent-based strategy that can reduce time off task and disruptive behaviors. Again, consistent praise for staying on task and completing assignments reinforces these behaviors. Another strategy is to give students choices in homework assignments. Contingent positive reinforcement in the form of tokens or teacher praise can also be effective. Time-outs can be effective as well if the classroom is viewed by the student with ADHD as a positive environment. If it is not, time-outs could reinforce maladaptive behaviors. Self-regulation interventions focus on teaching students to monitor behaviors such as staying on task and completing assignments. Academic interventions focus on providing direct instruction in relevant skills (e.g., note taking) that are necessary for academic achievement. Classroom peer tutoring can be an effective approach that also assists students with ADHD in developing appropriate social skills. Social skills training with specific strategies for maintenance and generalization outside of the classroom is also recommended. Involving peers without ADHD in all phases of social skills instruction and practice meets these criteria.

In addition to providing remediation to ameliorate ADHD symptoms, McKeague et al. (2015) pointed out the need to initiate school-wide antistigma campaigns so that peers and teachers better understand ADHD, the importance of inclusion, respect for diversity, and how they can become involved in collaborating with students with ADHD to reduce stigmatizing attitudes and negative behaviors (e.g., bullying, teasing, name-calling, ignoring), and increase opportunities for these students to develop friendships with their peers without ADHD. Student leaders, teachers, IEP team members, and, most importantly, students with ADHD themselves can partner to develop, implement, and evaluate the outcomes of these campaigns. Antistigma campaigns also have applications to students with ASD.

POSITIVE BEHAVIORAL SUPPORTS

Individuals with ASD often exhibit problem behavior(s) that can be stereotypical and regimented in nature while also being disruptive to others. To address such behavioral difficulties, it is essential that rehabilitation counselors and other transition team members use an approach to address problem behaviors in a way that not only reduces the behaviors, but also develops prosocial skills through nonaversive procedures. One approach is positive behavioral support (PBS; Carr et al., 1999). PBS is the process of systematically identifying problem behaviors and their antecedents, developing an understanding of the function of an individual's behavior, developing hypotheses, and teaching new, functional skills to achieve socially important behavior change (Sugai et al., 2000). Primarily, interventions under the components of PBS will focus on preventing problem behaviors from occurring and teaching replacement behaviors (e.g., teaching an individual to request help instead of turning over desks when frustrated). The educative approach of PBS encourages positive interactions rather than simply decreasing or eliminating problem behaviors.

Most germane to this chapter are the essential components of functional programming that should be part of any treatment plan. Specifically, transition team members should utilize the following criteria when developing and implementing effective plans for individuals with ASD: (a) prevent problem behaviors from occurring by first gathering data on the *antecedents* (What happens immediately before the behavior occurs?) and *consequences* (What happens immediately after the behavior occurs?) of behavior; (b) teach replacement behaviors (i.e., new skills that provide access to a desirable outcome through the use of socially appropriate and functional alternatives rather than engaging in some form of the inappropriate behavior); and (c) provide contingent positive reinforcement (e.g., attention, access to desirable items/activities) *immediately* following the desired behavior and when it is *contingent* on the emission of that behavior (Sansosti et al., 2010). Positive behavioral supports also have applications to transition planning with youths with ADHD and to providing on-the-job services in supported employment for both individuals with ASD and ADHD that prevent problematic work behaviors and reinforce appropriate work behaviors.

POSTSECONDARY SUPPORTS AND SERVICES

Growing numbers of students with ASD and ADHD are attending American colleges and universities. Because these students experience poorer outcomes than their peers without these neurodevelopmental disabilities, despite the fact that they have the potential to succeed, postsecondary supports and accommodations are often needed. Postsecondary supports and accommodations that have been identified as instrumental to the academic success of students with ADHD include course-specific strategy instruction for academic achievement, assistive software programs for enhancing reading comprehension, extended time on tests in distraction-free environments (e.g., testing centers), books on tape, and note taking assistance (DuPaul et al., 2009). However, as DuPaul et al. noted, there is a need for systematic research to document the impact of these supports and accommodations on postsecondary outcomes.

Growing numbers of colleges and universities across the United States have established programs for students with ASD to provide services above and beyond what most campus disability services offices are able to offer. These programs range from summer transition programs for incoming college students with ASD to services and supports provided throughout students' academic enrollment. Although each program is unique, Table 3.1 provides a list of services that are frequently provided across programs.

Students in these programs typically meet with their peer and academic advisors on a weekly basis or more frequently during stressful times such as midterms and finals. A downside of these programs is that they cost a fee (typically $2,000 to $3,000 a semester) in addition to tuition. However, some programs do offer scholarships. Research is needed to demonstrate the effectiveness of these programs.

TABLE 3.1 Services and Supports Provided by Postsecondary Programs for Students With Autism Spectrum Disorder

- Individualized planning for university-based supports and services

- Academic coaching (i.e., individuals with at least a bachelor's degree in education, counseling, rehabilitation, speech communications, or a related field who receive training from program staff) to address issues related to executive functioning (e.g., organization, time management, study skills, stress management); assist students with classroom accommodations; and facilitate meetings with professors and other members of the academic community

- Peer mentoring (i.e., undergraduate students who receive training from program staff) and coaching to assist students with social integration into the postsecondary setting (e.g., social skills, friendships, joining clubs, going to sporting events)

- Career planning and vocational services

- On-campus and community internships for juniors and seniors to gain work experience, develop appropriate work skills, learn the "unspoken rules" of workplace cultures, and receive corrective feedback from a job or academic coach

- Collaboration with other university services (e.g., accommodations, tutoring, writing centers, student affairs)

- Psychoeducational and peer support group meetings

- Living learning environments in residence halls

Source: Autism Speaks (2015).

ADHD coaching is a relatively new intervention for improving executive functioning skills and enhancing self-regulation that has received increasing research attention in recent years (Field et al., 2013; Parker et al., 2013). The focus of coaching is on the development of specific executive functioning skills such as goal setting, confidence building, organizing, problem solving, and persistence at completing tasks. ADHD coaches work with students to set goals based on an accurate self-awareness of their ADHD, its symptoms, and how symptoms affect how they think and behave. In goal-setting, coaches foster goal achievement by helping students to develop greater self-awareness by teaching strategies to stop, reflect, and take action. They also work with students to identify both individual and environmental factors that support or restrict goal achievement and work with them to develop strategies to activate supportive factors and ameliorate restrictive factors. This process is directed by the student with ADHD, who is held accountable for achieving her or his goals. However, ADHD coaches offer suggestions and guidance, set structure, provide support, and help students implement strategies for skill building. They also teach and foster development of appropriate social skills, self-reliance, and self-advocacy.

In ADHD coaching, coaches use specific types of questioning to elicit student involvement in identifying their own self-determined goals, recommend strategies, model effective executive functioning, and elicit students' own ideas about effective strategies as they increase their capacity to improve their executive functioning and self-regulation skills (Field et al., 2013; Parker et al., 2013). Students develop their own goal-directed action plans with the coach's support, guidance in plan development, and monitoring of the plan. The action plan includes specific action steps to achieve goals. For example, if the student's goal is to achieve a 3.0 GPA for the semester, action steps might include blocking out a specific amount of study time per day in a distraction-free environment.

In research conducted by Field et al. (2013), the researchers evaluated a coaching intervention that consisted of 24 weeks of 30-minute sessions with coaches that were conducted by telephone. Students were also able to e-mail or contact coaches by telephone if needed between sessions. Students with ADHD who participated in the intervention experienced significantly higher scores in learning study, self-regulation, and well-being than students with ADHD in a comparison group. Although the research on the effects of ADHD coaching on variables associated with academic persistence and postsecondary goal achievement is still relatively limited, preliminary evidence does demonstrate that it is effective at improving overall executive functioning and time management skills in particular, increasing persistence in academic programs, facilitating self-determined academic goals, reducing daily anxiety and stress, and contributing to a greater sense of well-being (Field et al., 2013; Parker et al., 2013). ADHD coaching is a specialty within the broader field of coaching. The International Coach Federation details the qualification and credentialing of coaches and has a registry of coaches that can be accessed at www.coachfederation.org/credential/landing .cfm?ItemNumber=3343&navItemNumber=3379.

Job Development and Placement

Because early intervention is a key factor associated with positive adult outcomes, career development activities that are age-appropriate should be incorporated into the IEPs of children with ASD and ADHD long before formalized job development and placement services are implemented. These activities include participation in chores at home and in school, social skills training and opportunities to practice these skills in real-world contexts, participation in school clubs and athletics, adult and peer mentors, self-determination training, and work-related experiences such as volunteering, job shadowing, part-time employment, and work studies. These activities will enable children and youths to explore their interests, develop prevocational and vocational skills, and, perhaps most importantly, envision themselves as future employees. Rehabilitation counselors working for agencies and programs that provide services to children and youths with disabilities can be instrumental members of IEP teams and ensure that career development experiences are incorporated into the IEP plans of children and youths of all ages.

In exploring job opportunities with individuals with either ADD or ADHD, rehabilitation counselors should keep in mind that characteristics that may be deficiencies in some employment settings may be assets in other settings. For example, individuals with ADHD are likely to perform better in occupations in which they can be creative, work independently at their own pace without having to continually report to a supervisor, work in novel settings, perform actives that they are passionate about, and carry out nonrepetitive tasks that involve generating new ideas (Verheul et al., 2015).

Obtaining and maintaining employment is a construct that predicts quality of life for adults in general. Furthermore, paid employment is a source of pride and meaning for people with and without disabilities (Burgess & Gutstein, 2007).

Individuals with ASD and ADHD may require support throughout employment to achieve desirable outcomes. Supported employment is arguably the single most influential practice that results in employment for youth with ASD (Schall et al., 2012). Specifically, supported employment assists people with severe disabilities through customized, intensive, and ongoing support that contributes to achieving and maintaining employment in competitive work settings (Chen et al., 2015). Although research on supported employment for individuals with ASD is sparse, those with severe disabilities are also likely to benefit from supported employment. Business partnerships are a collaborative effort to increase the employment of individuals with disabilities. This form of supported employment is utilized to assist workers in specialized business (e.g., Walgreens, Bank of America, Marriot Bridges) until the employee is independent (Schall et al., 2012). Customized employment is another model of supported employment that allows a person with ASD or ADHD to negotiate a personalized job independently or through a job negotiator. The job negotiator meets with the employer and arranges a job for the individual. In an example provided by Schall and colleagues (2012) the job negotiator met with the owner of a sandwich shop and arranged for the individual to prepare vegetables for sandwiches, stock the drink cooler, and deliver orders within a 4-block radius of the store. These tasks served the needs of the business and the employment needs of the individual with ASD (Schall et al., 2012).

Finally, self-employment allows some individuals with ASD and ADHD to develop a community-based or home-based business that reflects their personal strengths. Self-employment provides individuals with the freedom to develop their own business, define their job, and make their own hours. A notable example provided by Schall and colleagues (2012) is Poppin' Joe's Kettle Korn in Louisburg, Kansas, where a young man with ASD owns and operates a successful kettle popcorn business. Verheul et al. (2015) noted that some of the characteristics (e.g., risk takers, creative, action-oriented, resilient in the face of adversity) of ADHD are also characteristics of entrepreneurs. These authors further noted, "when they manage to develop 'resilience' mechanisms to cope with their 'weaknesses,' individuals who exhibit behavior associated with ADHD may even outperform others in particular work environments, for example, in jobs that require fast decision making or creativity" (Verheul et al., 2015, p. 86). The authors referred to David Neeleman, founder of JetBlue Airlines, and Paul Orfalea, founder of Kinko's, as examples of successful entrepreneurs with ADHD.

With these considerations in mind, rehabilitation consumers who want to pursue self-employment should be provided assistance (e.g., entrepreneurial mentors) with evaluating the feasibility of their business ideas. An excellent resource for these consumers is SCORE (businessadvising.org), a nationwide organization that has chapters across the United States with business mentors that provide free advising and consultation to prospective entrepreneurs. They can assist with evaluating if a business idea is marketable, developing business plans, identifying sources for start-up funding, and other aspects of starting a new business.

Finally, rehabilitation counselors and employment specialists can assist employers in hiring and retaining workers with ASD and ADHD by developing tools to better understand these neurodevelopmental disabilities, how to accommodate these workers, and effective strategies for supervising and evaluating employees with ASD and ADHD.

Accommodation Planning

First and foremost in the accommodation planning process is the need for individuals with ASD and ADHD to receive training regarding their rights and responsibilities under the Americans with Disabilities Act. In an investigation of workplace discrimination and ASD, Van Wieren, Reid, and McMahon (2008) found that an extremely low number of ASD discrimination complaints were received by the Equal Employment Opportunity Commission (EEOC) and speculated that this could indicate a particular need to educate individuals with ASD about their rights and options to file discrimination complaints. These authors also suggested that individuals with ASD may not recognize discrimination when it occurs or know what actions to take if they do recognize it.

In the process of identifying functional limitations and potential accommodations, the rehabilitation counselor or placement specialist can initiate this step with consumers by exploring functional difficulties and corresponding accommodations they have used in secondary and postsecondary classrooms and/or previous employment to determine if any of these can be applied to new positions. These ideas can then be supplemented by additional ideas generated from the rehabilitation consumer and counselor. Whetzel (2014) offered numerous accommodation ideas for workers with ASD that can be retrieved from the Job Accommodation Network (JAN) at askjan.org/media/downloads/ASDA&CS. For example, to address communication difficulties, the author recommended ideas such as providing advance notice of topics to be addressed at meetings or allowing employees to provide written, instead of oral, responses at meetings. Examples of accommodations for atypical body movements include allowing employees to use items such as squeeze balls for self-stimulation and providing structured breaks for physical activity. To accommodate sensory issues, accommodation ideas include changing the lighting for individuals with fluorescent light sensitivity, moving individuals with noise sensitivity to quieter offices or workstations, and (to accommodate fragrance sensitivities) instituting fragrance-free office policies or allowing telework. To accommodate stress management difficulties, ideas include providing praise and positive reinforcement and the use of a support animal.

Adamou et al. (2013) recommended accommodations that are neither expensive nor time-consuming that employers can easily implement to address work-related problems and improve the job performance of workers with ADHD. These accommodation ideas can also be implemented to address deficits in executive functioning for workers with ASD and are described in Table 3.2.

Because of the communication difficulties associated with both ASD and ADHD, requesting accommodations may be a particularly daunting prospect. Pre-interview practice with scripts and role-plays can be useful in these cases. One of the most effective approaches is for placement or employment support specialists to partner directly with the employee and employer to identify, implement, and evaluate reasonable accommodations.

TABLE 3.2 Job Accommodations for Workers With Attention Deficit Hyperactivity Disorder

Functional Limitation	Accommodation
General	Regular meetings, reviews, and structured feedback
	Verbal information supplemented with clear, concise written instructions
Attention	Private office, location of workstation in quieter area, flex-time to work at quieter times of day, and headphones
Impulsivity	Buddy system to help remain focused
Hyperactivity	Allowing productive movements at work, encouraging employees to remain active, including structured breaks in long meetings
Disorganization, time management problems	Alarms or beepers, structured notes, and agendas, regular supervision or mentoring, delegation of more tedious tasks to coworkers, incentives and awards for task completion and overcoming memory problems

Source: Adamou et al. (2013).

CONCLUSIONS

With increasing rates of ASD and ADHD being diagnosed in children, youths, and adults, it is anticipated that growing numbers of individuals with these neurodevelopmental disorders will seek out rehabilitation counseling services. Rehabilitation counselors must be (a) knowledgeable about these neurodevelopmental conditions and (b) adequately prepared to provide effective rehabilitation counseling services to consumers with these conditions. Characteristics of ASD and ADHD that warrant consideration in the rehabilitation counseling process are the heterogeneity of individuals with each of these conditions in terms of degree and severity of impairment, the functional domains affected by each condition (particularly executive functioning and social communications), the need to take on a life-span perspective and provide services in an early intervention context to improve adult outcomes, and other conditions that commonly co-occur with ASD and ADHD.

Although research on ASD and ADHD has focused primarily on employment barriers and less on rehabilitation counseling interventions to ameliorate these barriers, preliminary evidence has demonstrated support for the effectiveness of such interventions as positive behavioral supports, postsecondary programs for youths with ASD, ADHD coaching, and supported employment. Rehabilitation counselors should stay abreast of ongoing research to evaluate these interventions to ensure that they are including evidence-based approaches in the rehabilitation plans of individuals with ASD and ADHD. Rehabilitation counselors must also take into consideration the importance of family involvement in the transition and rehabilitation of youths with ASD and ADHD. We have made several recommendations for ensuring that family members are treated as equal, valued members of team-based treatment planning. However, we recommend continued education in the area of family involvement because family members can be instrumental to the success of all rehabilitation consumers, not just those with ASD and ADHD.

DISCUSSION QUESTIONS

1. What misperceptions do you have about people with ASD and ADHD? What information presented in this chapter has challenged you to reconsider your perceptions?
2. Describe the psychosocial and vocational challenges that you think present the greatest barriers to quality of life and employment for people with neurodevelopmental disabilities.
3. What do you think are the most important considerations for forming strong working alliances with clients with neurodevelopmental disabilities?
4. What are the most important implications for rehabilitation planning discussed in this chapter?
5. At the beginning of the chapter we described Conner's case. What are the first steps you would take with Conner to establish eligibility for VR services and identify his rehabilitation needs? Do you think his goal of becoming an emergency medical technician is feasible? Why or why not? What objectives, services, and reasonable accommodations would you include in Conner's rehabilitation plan to assist him to identify an employment goal and to secure and maintain a position that is compatible with his skills and interests?

REFERENCES

Adamou, M., Arif, M., Asherson, P., Aw, T., Bolea, B., Coghill, D.,...Young, S. (2013). Occupational issues of adults with ADHD. *BMC Psychiatry, 13*, 59. doi:10.1186/1471-244X-13-59

American Psychiatric Association. (2013). *Diagnostic and statistical manual of mental disorders* (5th ed.). Washington, DC: Author.

Autism Speaks. (2015). *Autism.* Retrieved from https://www.autismspeaks.org

Barton, E. E., & Harn, B. (2014). *Educating young children with autism spectrum disorders: A guide for teachers, counselors, and psychologists.* Thousand Oaks, CA: Corwin.

Bauminger, N., Shulman, C., & Agam, G. (2003). Peer interaction and loneliness in high-functioning children with autism. *Journal of Autism and Developmental Disorders, 33*, 489–507.

Burgess, A. F., & Gutstein, S. E. (2007). Quality of life for people with autism: Raising the standard for evaluating successful outcomes. *Child and Adolescent Mental Health, 12*(2), 80–86.

Carr, J. E., Horner, R. H., Turnbull, A. P., Marquis, J. G., McLaughlin, D. M., McAtee, M. L.,... Braddock, D. E. (1999). *Positive behavior support for people with developmental disabilities: A research synthesis.* Washington, DC: American Association on Mental Retardation.

Centers for Disease Control and Prevention. (2016a). *Attention-deficit/hyperactivity disorder (ADHD): Data & statistics.* Retrieved from http://www.cdc.gov/ncbddd/adhd/data.html

Centers for Disease Control and Prevention. (2016b). *Autism spectrum disorder (ASD): Data & statistics.* Retrieved from http://www.cdc.gov/ncbddd/autism/data.html

Charman, T., Swettenham, J., & Baron-Cohen, S. (1997). Infants with autism: An investigation of empathy, pretend play, joint attention, and imitation. *Developmental Psychology, 33*, 781–789.

Chen, J. L., Leader, G., Sung, C., & Leahy, M. (2015). Trends in employment for individuals with autism spectrum disorder: A review of the research literature. *Review Journal of Autism and Developmental Disorders, 2*, 115–127.

Children and Adults with Attention Deficit Hyperactivity Disorder. (2015). *Diagnosis of ADHD*. Retrieved from http://www.chadd.org/Understanding-ADHD/For-Adults/Diagnosis-of-ADHD.aspx

Crosland, K., & Dunlap, G. (2012). Effective strategies for the inclusion of children with autism in general education classrooms. *Behavior Modification, 36*, 251–269.

DuPaul, G. J., Weyandt, L. L., & Janusis, G. M. (2011). ADHD in the classroom: Effective intervention strategies. *Theory into Practice, 50*(1), 35–42. doi:10.1080/00405841.2011.534935

Durkin, M. S., Maenner, M. J., Meaney, F. J., Levy, S. E., DiGuiseppi, C., Nicholas, J. S.,… Schieve, L. A. (2010). Socioeconomic inequity in the prevalence of autism spectrum disorder: Evidence from a U.S. cross-sectional study. *PLOS ONE, 5*, 1–8.

Eussen, M. L. J. M., Van Gool, A. R., Verheij, F., De Nijs, P. F. A., Verhulst, F. C., & Greaves-Lord, K. (2013). The association of quality social relations, symptom severity and intelligence with anxiety in children with autism spectrum disorders. *Autism, 17*, 723–735.

Fedele, D. A., Hartung, C. M., Canu, W. H., & Wilkowski, B. M. (2010). Potential symptoms of ADHD for emerging adults. *Journal of Psychopathology & Behavioral Assessment, 32*(3), 385–396. doi:10.1007/s10862-009-9173-x

Field, S., Parker, D. R., Sawilowsky, S., & Rolands, L. (2013). Assessing the impact of ADHD coaching services on university students' learning skills, self-regulation, and well-being. *Journal of Postsecondary Education and Disability, 26*(1), 67–81.

Fitzgerald, M., & Bellgrove, M. (2006). The overlap between alexithymia and Asperger's syndrome. *Journal of Autism and Developmental Disorders, 36*(4), 573–576.

Gjervan, B., Torgersen, T., Nordahl, H. M., & Rasmussen, K. (2012). Functional impairment and occupational outcome in adults with ADHD. *Journal of Attention Disorders, 16*(7), 544–552.

Hedley, D., & Young, R (2006). Social comparison processes and depressive symptoms in children and adolescents with Asperger syndrome. *Autism, 10*, 139–153.

Hilton, C. L., Harper, J. D., Kueker, R. H., Lang, A. R., Abbacchi, A. M., Todorov, A., & LaVesser, P. D. (2010). Sensory responsiveness as a predictor of social severity in children with high functioning autism spectrum disorders. *Journal of Autism and Developmental Disorders, 40*, 937–945.

Holwerda, A., van der Klink, J. L., de Boer, M. R., Groothoff, J. W., & Brouwer, S. (2013). Predictors of sustainable work participation of young adults with developmental disorders. *Research in Developmental Disabilities, 34*(9), 2753–2763. doi:10.1016/j.ridd.2013.05.032

Hsia, Y., Wong, A., Murphy, D., Simonoff, E., Buitelaar, J., & Wong, I. (2014). Psychopharmacological prescriptions for people with autism spectrum disorder (ASD): A multinational study. *Psychopharmacology, 231*(6), 999–1009.

Iovannone, R., Dunlap, G., Huber, H., & Kincaid, D. (2003). Effective educational practices for students with autism spectrum disorders. *Focus on Autism and Other Developmental Disabilities, 18*(3), 150–165.

Jensen, M., & Turk, D. (2014). Contributions of psychology to the understanding and treatment of people with chronic pain: Why it matters to all psychologists. *American Psychologist, 69*(2), 105–118.

Koegel, R. L., Shirotova, L., & Koegel, L. K. (2009). Brief report: Using individualized orienting cues to facilitate first-word acquisition in non-responders with autism. *Journal of Autism and Developmental Disorders, 39*, 1587–1592.

Koerner, N., & Dugas, M. J. (2008). An investigation of appraisals in individuals vulnerable to excessive worry: The role of intolerance of uncertainty. *Cognitive Therapy and Research, 32*, 619–638.

Lanou, A., Hough, L., & Powell, E. (2012). Case studies on using strengths and interests to address the needs of students with autism spectrum disorders. *Intervention in School & Clinic, 47*, 175–182.

Lawer, L., Brusilovskiy, E., Salzer, M. S., & Mandell, D. S. (2009). Use of vocational rehabilitative services among adults with autism. *Journal of Autism and Developmental Disorders, 39*, 487–494.

Lee, G. K., & Carter, E. W. (2012). Preparing transition-age students with high-functioning autism spectrum disorders for meaningful work. *Psychology in the Schools, 49,* 988–1000.

Lequia, J., Machalicek, W., & Lyons, G. (2013). Parent education intervention results in decreased challenging behavior and improved task engagement for students with disabilities during academic tasks. *Behavioral Interventions, 28,* 322–343.

Lidstone, J., Uljarevi, M., Sullivan, J., Rodgers, J., McConachie, H., Freeston, M., … Leekam, S. (2014). Relations among restricted and repetitive behaviors, anxiety and sensory features in children with autism spectrum disorders. *Research in Autism Spectrum Disorders, 8*(2), 82–92. doi:10.1016/j.rasd.2013.10.001

Logan, K. R., Bakeman, R., & Keefe, E. G. (1997). Effects of instructional variables of engaged behavior of students with disabilities in general education classrooms. *Exceptional Children, 63,* 481–497.

Lotter, V. (1967). Epidemiology of autistic conditions in young children: Prevalence. *Social Psychiatry, 1,* 134–137.

Mahjouri, S., & Lord, C. E. (2012). What the DSM-5 portends for research, diagnosis, and treatment of autism spectrum disorders. *Current Psychiatric Reports, 14,* 739–747.

McKeague, L., Hennessy, E., O'Driscoll, C., & Heary, C. (2015). Retrospective accounts of self-stigma experienced by young people with attention-deficit/hyperactivity disorder (ADHD) or depression. *Psychiatric Rehabilitation Journal, 38*(2), 158–163. doi:10.1037/prj0000121

Merikangas, K. R., He, J., Burstein, M., Swanson, S. A., Avenevoli, S., Cui, L., …Swendsen, J. (2010). Lifetime prevalence of mental disorders in US adolescents: Results from the National Comorbidity Survey Replication–Adolescent Supplement (NCS-A). *Journal of the American Academy of Child & Adolescent Psychiatry, 49,* 980–989.

Müller, E., Schuler, A., Burton, B. A., & Yates, G. B. (2003). Vocational supports for individuals with Asperger syndrome. *Journal of Vocational Rehabilitation, 18,* 163–165.

National Autism Center. (2009). *Findings and conclusions of the National Standards Project: Addressing the need for evidence-based practice guidelines for autism spectrum disorders.* Randolph, MA: Author.

Nikopoulos, C. K., & Nikopoulou-Smyrni, P. (2008). Teaching complex social skills to children with autism: Advances in video modeling. *Journal of Early and Intensive Behavior Intervention, 5,* 30–43.

Noor, A., Whibley, A., Marshall, C. R., Gianakopoulos, P. J., Piton, A., Carson, A. R., … Vincent, J. B. (2010). Disruption at the PTCHD1 locus on Xp22.11 in autism spectrum disorder and intellectual disability. *Science Translational Medicine, 2,* 49–68.

Ozonoff, S., Dawson, G., & McPartland, J. (2002). *A parents' guide to Asperger syndrome and high-functioning autism.* New York, NY: Guilford Press.

Parker, D. R., Field Hoffman, S., Sawilowsky, S., & Rolands, L. (2011). An examination of the effects of ADHD coaching on university students' executive functioning. *Journal of Postsecondary Education & Disability, 24*(2), 115–132.

Parker, D. R., Field Hoffman, S., Sawilowsky, S., & Rolands, L. (2013). Self-control in postsecondary settings: Students' perceptions of ADHD college coaching. *Journal of Attention Disorders, 17*(3), 215–232.

Polanczyk, G., Willcutt, E., Salum, G., Kieling, C., & Rohde, L. (2014). ADHD prevalence estimates across three decades: An updated systematic review and meta-regression analysis. *International Journal of Epidemiology, 43*(2), 434–442.

Polimeni, M. A., Richdale, A. L., & Francis, A. J. P. (2005). A survey of sleep problems in autism, Asperger's disorder, and typically developing children. *Journal of Intellectual Disability Research, 49,* 260–268.

Powell-Smith, K. A., & Vaughn, B. J. (2006). Families of children with disabilities. In G. G. Bear & K. M. Minke (Eds.), *Children's needs III: Development, prevention, and intervention* (pp. 689–704). Bethesda, MD: National Association of School Psychologists.

Roux, A. M., Shattuck, P. T., Cooper, B. P., Anderson, K. A., Wagner, M., & Narendorf, S. C. (2013). Postsecondary employment experiences among young adults with autism spectrum disorder. *Journal of the American Academy of Child & Adolescent Psychiatry, 52*(9), 931–939.

Sansosti, F. J., & Powell-Smith, K. A. (2006). High-functioning autism and Asperger's syndrome. In G. G. Bear, & K. M. Minke (Eds.), *Children's needs III: Development, prevention, and intervention* (pp. 949–963). Bethesda, MD: National Association of School Psychologists.

Sansosti, F. J., Powell-Smith, K. A., & Cowan, R. J. (2010). *High functioning autism/Asperger syndrome in schools: Assessment and intervention.* New York, NY: Guilford Press.

Schall, C., Wehman, P., & McDonough, J. L. (2012). Transition from school to work for students with autism spectrum disorders: Understanding the process and achieving better outcomes. *Pediatric Clinics of North America, 59*(1), 189–202.

Shattuck, P. T., Narendorf, S. C., Cooper, B., Sterzing, P. R., Wagner, M., & Taylor, J. L. (2012). Postsecondary education and employment among youth with an autism spectrum disorder. *Pediatrics, 129*(6), 1042–1049. doi:10.1542/peds.2011–2864

Somonoff, E., Pickles, A., Charman, T., Chandler, S., Loucas, T., & Baird, G. (2008). Psychiatric disorders in children with autism spectrum disorders: Prevalence, comorbidity, and associated factors in a population-derived sample. *Journal of the American Academy of Child & Adolescent Psychiatry, 47*, 921.

South, M., Ozonoff, S., & McMahon, W. M. (2005). Repetitive behavior profiles in Asperger syndrome and high-functioning autism. *Journal of Autism and Developmental Disorders, 35*, 145–158.

Sugai, G., Horner, R. H., Dunlap, G., Hieneman, M., Lewis, T. J., Nelson M. C., ... Ruef, M. (2000). Applying positive behavior support and functional behavior assessment in schools. *Journal of Positive Behavior Interventions, 2*, 131–143.

Tomcheck, S. D., & Dunn, W. (2007). Sensory processing in children with and without autism: A comparative study using the short sensory profile. *American Journal of Occupational Therapy, 61*, 190–200.

Tudor, M. E., Hoffman, C. D., & Sweeney, D. P. (2012). Children with autism: Sleep problems and symptom severity. *Focus on Autism and Other Developmental Disabilities, 27*, 254–262.

Turner, M. A. (1999). Annotation: Repetitive behavior in autism: A review of psychological research. *Journal of Child Psychology and Psychiatry, 40*, 839–849.

van Steensel, F. J., Bögels, S. M., & Perrin, S. (2011). Anxiety disorders in children and adolescents with autistic spectrum disorders: A meta-analysis. *Clinical Child and Family Psychology Review, 14*, 302–317.

Van Wieren, T., Reid, C., & McMahon, B. (2008). Workplace discrimination and autism spectrum disorders: The National EEOC Americans with Disabilities Act Research project. *Work: A Journal of Prevention, Assessment, and Rehabilitation, 31*(3), 299–308.

Verheul, I., Block, J., Burmeister-Lamp, K., Thurik, R., Tiemeier, H., & Turturea, R. (2015). ADHD-like behavior and entrepreneurial intentions. *Small Business Economics, 45*(1), 85–101. doi:http://dx.doi.org/10.1007/s11187–015-9642-4

Vlaeyen, J. S., & Morley, S. (2005). Cognitive-behavioral treatments for chronic pain: What works for whom? *Clinical Journal of Pain, 21*(1), 1–8. doi:10.1097/00002508-200501000-00001

Volkmar, F. R., Reichow, B., Westphal, A., & Mandell, D. S. (2014). Autism and the autism spectrum: Diagnostic concepts. In F. R. Volkmar, R. Paul, S. J. Rogers, & K. A. Pelphrey (Eds.), *Handbook of autism and pervasive developmental disorders: Diagnosis, development, and brain mechanisms* (Vol. 1). Hoboken, NJ: Wiley.

Wadsworth, J. S., & Harper, D. C. (2007). Adults with attention-deficit/hyperactivity disorder: Assessment and treatment strategies. *Journal of Counseling & Development, 85*(1), 101–109.

Walkup, J. T., Stossel, L., & Rendleman, R. (2014). Beyond rising rates: Personalized medicine and public health approaches to the diagnosis and treatment of attention-deficit/hyperactivity disorder. *Journal of the American Academy of Child & Adolescent Psychiatry, 53*(1), 14–16. doi:10.1016/j.jaac.2013.10.008

Wehman, P., Schall, C., McDonough, J., Kregel, J., Brooke, V., Molinelli, A.,…Thiss, W. (2014). Competitive employment for youth with autism spectrum disorders: Early results from a randomized clinical trial. *Journal of Autism and Developmental Disorders, 44*(3), 487–500. doi:10.1007/s10803-013-1892-x

Whetzel, M. (2014). Interviewing tips for applicants with autism spectrum disorder (ASD). *Journal of Vocational Rehabilitation, 40*(2), 155–159. doi:10.3233/JVR-140668

Wigham, S., Rodgers, J., South, M., McConachie, H., & Fresston, M. (2015). The interplay between sensory processing abnormalities, intolerance of uncertainty, anxiety and restricted and repetitive behaviours in autism spectrum disorder. *Journal of Autism and Developmental Disorders, 45*, 943–952.

Yell, M. L., Katsiyannis, A., Dragsow, E., & Herbst, M. (2003). Developing legally correct and educationally appropriate programs for students with autism spectrum disorders. *Focus on Autism and Other Developmental Disabilities, 18*, 182–191.

FOUR

Disabilities Related to Aging

Coauthored by Kelly Cichy and Mykal Leslie

CHAPTER OBJECTIVES

- *Describe changes in the age demographic of the American populace that will steadily increase the number of elderly people in the United States for the next 30 years*
- *Examine the relationship among aging, health, and disability*
- *Describe the characteristics and needs of people who have frequently occurring aging-related disabling conditions such as dementia, rheumatoid arthritis, and stroke*
- *Describe the implications of aging-related emerging disabilities to counseling practice in all aspects of the rehabilitation process*

CASE ILLUSTRATION: ADALINE

Adaline is an 80-year-old Caucasian woman who has lived in the Great Lakes Region of the Midwestern United States her entire life. She graduated from high school in 1954, was married in 1958, and had her first child, a daughter named Rhonda, in 1961. She had her second child, Steve, in 1965. Adaline, along with her older sister, cared for their mother in her home until she passed away at the age of 100.

Following her retirement from a shipping/clerical support position with the same company for more than 35 years, Adaline worked at several part-time jobs, including one as a cafeteria worker in an elementary school. In her early 50s, Adaline began experiencing joint pain, swelling, and stiffness in both her wrists and hips. Her pain was accompanied by fatigue, loss of appetite, and weight loss. Work activities such as standing, bending, lifting, and writing became increasingly difficult for Adaline. Adaline was referred by her primary care physician to a rheumatologist, who diagnosed her with rheumatoid arthritis (RA) at age 55. She began working fewer hours at that time, and she began a course of treatment that included physical therapy and anti-inflammatory and antirheumatic medications. Adaline reluctantly stopped working altogether in her late 60s due in part to the increased severity of her RA episodes.

Adaline considers herself an independent woman. She and her husband, David, divorced in 1967, following which she lived alone until 2015. During that time, she lived next door to her older sister, who is now 84, who in recent years helped Adaline manage her increasingly severe RA symptoms. She also had several friends who would visit her often and assist her with errands. Her son Steve lives 90 miles away from the town where Adaline lived most of her life. Her daughter Rhonda lives in California. Over the past few years, Adaline had gradually exhibited increasing signs of dementia, as evidenced by her short-term memory loss; inability to make rational decisions; difficulties performing such tasks as overseeing her bank account, taking her medication, and caring for her home; and her increasing habit of misplacing personal items. She developed some effective coping mechanisms, and, although she was aware of many of her limitations, she continually expressed a desire to remain independent.

Adaline's friends and family noticed her decline in functional abilities and were concerned about her well-being living alone. One indication of her diminishing ability to live independently came when she was still driving and got lost on her way to her son's home, a destination she had driven to dozens of times over the previous 10 years. She also ran a stop sign while driving with her son in the car. On another occasion, a family friend reported that she found Adaline wandering in the local cemetery, unable to find her car after visiting her mother's grave. At the insistence of her children, Adaline reluctantly gave up driving following these incidents. She then relied upon her sister and neighbors to take her shopping and run other errands.

Recognizing her diminishing ability to live independently and manage her own affairs, Steve and Rhonda sought assistance for their mom from a variety of local agencies. Although she did not like the idea, Adaline had an assessment conducted by the Area Agency on Aging in her county. The caseworker provided resources to Adaline and her children to begin to develop a plan to ensure that she remained in a safe environment given her ongoing and increasing functional deficits.

At the time of her assessment, Adaline was being treated by several different physicians including a primary care physician, an endocrinologist for diabetes that she developed at age 76, a rheumatologist for RA, a gynecologist, and a cardiologist. As her psychosocial symptoms increased, it became more challenging for her and her also-aging sister to effectively manage all of her medical care. At one point, her sister realized that Adaline had taken her medications outside of her prescribed dosage and had ill effects as a result. Her children spoke to her about seeing a geriatric specialist to undergo a complete medical evaluation and receive a diagnosis as to why she was exhibiting these increasing symptoms. Another objective for seeing a geriatric specialist was to have one provider oversee all her medical care including medication management and treatment.

Reluctantly, and only after strenuous urging by Steve, Rhonda, and her sister, Adaline consented to the appointment with the geriatric specialist. Neurological testing, including an MRI scan, revealed a diagnosis of vascular dementia. The geriatric specialist told Adaline, Steve, and Rhonda in no uncertain terms that she was no longer able to be alone in her home. Adaline wished to remain in her home, so Steve and Rhonda sought the assistance of a home health agency. For several months, Adaline received assistance at home from the agency, albeit reluctantly, while Steve began to oversee her financial and medical affairs. Because Adaline

was no longer able to independently manage her medication regimen, this responsibility was assumed by the home health agency on a daily basis. Steve traveled
90 miles to Adaline's home once each week to check on her, and her older sister,
Carol, visited her at least once per day. Her friends and neighbors continued regular contact with Adaline, often taking her to visit their home or to attend community events.

As Adaline's symptoms increased, it became increasingly difficult for Steve to
tend to her from a distance while meeting the needs of his own family, and Steve
and Rhonda decided that it was time to move Adaline closer to one of them. The
financial cost of in-home care, which by this time she needed on a 24-hour basis,
was certainly a consideration, but more importantly Steve and Rhonda believed
that Adaline needed more local support than her neighbors and her also-aging
sister could provide. Steve lived in the same state, so it was decided that Adaline
would move to Steve's community.

Steve arranged for Adaline to move into an assisted living facility less than a
mile from his home. Steve and Rhonda had been exploring this as an option for several months and met with staff members of the assisted living facility on multiple
occasions to plan the transition process. Adaline's level of dementia did not allow
her to participate much in the decision to move her to the assisted living facility in
Steve's community, but she definitely did not favor the idea at first. Steve, Rhonda,
and Adaline's sister Carol consulted with Adaline's geriatric specialist throughout
the transition into Adaline's new home. Part of the transition plan was that Steve
would spend the first several nights with her in her new apartment to make her
feel more comfortable. Carol and Rhonda, who visited from California for 2 weeks
during Adaline's move, stayed with Adaline during the day, so for the first several
days she was with family at all times in her new surroundings. Adaline and her
family met the staff and other residents of the assisted living facility, which made
everyone more comfortable with Adaline's move to her new home.

Adaline transitioned as well as could be expected into the assisted living facility. Being closer to his mom and seeing her every day, Steve and his family began
to see the severity of her dementia on a daily basis. Although the initial plan was a
temporary one in theory, Adaline's family quickly realized that going back to her
home and living alone was no longer an option. One year later, Adaline continues
to live in her assisted living apartment and keeps busy every day with activities
including going out to restaurants, attending symphony concerts, shopping, and
participating in the many events that occur at the assisted living facility.

Although Adaline's family has had to adjust to seeing her dementia take a
stronger hold on her as time goes by, an adjustment process Steve and his wife
describe as very much like grieving, they are satisfied knowing she is in a safe
place near their home, which makes it possible for them to see her on a daily
basis. She has also developed a very close relationship with her grandchildren,
who enjoy visiting her and including her in their school and sports activities.

For the first time in American history, people aged 65 and over will soon outnumber children under the age of five (Hooyman, Kawamoto, & Kiyak, 2015). This
demographic shift in the population toward older ages is often referred to in the

professional literature as *population aging,* and it is colloquially described as the "Graying of America." Population aging, however, is a worldwide phenomenon, and the trend is accelerating in most industrialized countries, including the United States, Australia, Canada, France, Germany, Japan, New Zealand, and the United Kingdom (Anderson & Hussey, 2000).

The continued aging of the 77 million members of the American baby boom generation (born between 1946 and 1964), coupled with advances in medical treatment that have significantly increased life expectancies, means that the number of Americans over the age of 65 will double in the next 30 years—and the number of Americans over the age of 90 will more than quadruple between 1980 and 2030 (Wickert, Dresden, & Rumrill, 2013).

The growth in the aging population has a number of important implications for society, and rehabilitation counselors will play an increasingly important role in working to address the unique challenges and opportunities that are inherent in this demographic shift. Therefore, the goals of this chapter are threefold: (a) to describe general trends in population aging and the implications of population aging for individuals, families, and society; (b) to describe the specific impact of population aging on public health, health care, and disability; and (c) to describe the unique implications of emerging age-related disabilities, including the changing role of rehabilitation counselors in addressing these growing needs.

THE GRAYING OF AMERICA

By 2020, approximately 17% of the U.S. population will be 65 or older and 3.7% will be 80 or older (Anderson & Hussey, 2000). By 2050, the number of Americans aged 65 and older is expected to double and is projected to total 88.5 million (Vincent & Velfkoff, 2010). By 2030, it is estimated that nearly one in five Americans will be aged 65 or older, as all of the baby boomers will have moved into the ranks of the older population (Vincent & Velkoff, 2010). These changes in the aging population are attributed to increases in life expectancy thanks to advances in medical technology and treatment, the baby boom between 1946 and 1964 during which 77 million living Americans were born, trends in immigration, and changes in fertility patterns.

In 2013, the life expectancy at birth in the United States was 78.8 years (76.4 for males; 81.2 for females), which represented an increase of 1.9 years for males and 1.5 years for females between 2003 and 2013 (National Center for Health Statistics, 2015). Increases in life expectancy are due to a number of factors, including reductions in acute diseases, decreases in infant mortality, decreases in female mortality at childbirth, and advances in the prevention and treatment of chronic diseases. From 2003 to 2013, the infant mortality rate decreased by 13% (National Center for Health Statistics, 2015), and today women no longer routinely die giving birth (Hooyman et al., 2015). Due to the development of vaccinations, a number of acute diseases like polio have all but been eradicated (Hooyman et al., 2015), and medical advancements, new technologies, and prescription medications allow individuals to survive and manage chronic conditions, including heart disease, diabetes, and even some types of cancer for longer periods of time than ever before (Graffigna, Barello, Wiederhold, Bosio, & Riva, 2013). Increases in life expectancy are also traced to general declines in certain poor health behaviors such as cigarette smoking that represent significant risk factors for morbidity and mortality (National Center for Health Statistics, 2015).

It is important to acknowledge, however, that during the same time frame in which we have seen an increase in life expectancy and decline in cigarette smoking, other risk factors for chronic disease and disability (e.g., obesity, poor nutrition, sedentary lifestyle) have increased from 14.8% between 1988 and 1994 to 20.4% between 2009 and 2012 (National Center for Health Statistics, 2015). Further, when the United States is compared to other developed countries, results reveal that life expectancies in the United States are not rising as fast, in part due to increasing rates of poverty, chronic health conditions, and increasing economic disparities between the richest and poorest citizens (The Commonwealth Fund, 2011; Muennig & Glied, 2010).

Moreover, gender and racial disparities in life expectancies persist. At older ages, women outnumber men, with two thirds of all Americans over the age of 80 being women (Wickert et al., 2013). Women who reach the age of 85 have an additional life expectancy of 6.8 years, compared to 5.7 additional years for men who live to 85 (Federal Interagency Forum, 2012; U.S. Census Bureau, 2011). Although the reasons for women's longer life expectancies are not entirely clear, both biological and lifestyle factors have been found to be contributors (Federal Interagency Forum, 2012). For example, genetic theory suggests that females' two X chromosomes are protective in infancy through late life, making females more physiologically robust (Hooyman et al., 2015). Lifestyle factors such as women's greater likelihood of engaging in preventive health care, avoiding high-risk behaviors, and lower rates of substance abuse also contribute to their longer life expectancies (Federal Interagency Forum, 2012; Hooyman et al., 2015).

Life expectancy also differs substantially by race/ethnicity, and racial disparities in health and well-being between African Americans and European Americans are substantial and well documented (Haas & Rohlfsen, 2010; Williams, 2005; Williams & Mohammed, 2009). Life expectancy for African Americans, though increasing in absolute terms in recent years, is lower at every decade of life than it is for European Americans (Levine & Crimmins, 2014). Even after considering socioeconomic status, African Americans remain at increased risk of morbidity and mortality (Williams & Jackson, 2005) and report lower levels of psychological well-being compared to European Americans (Hughes & Thomas, 1998; Williams & Harris-Reid, 1999). At all income levels, African Americans face chronic stressors such as discrimination, economic strains, and stressful life events, as well as unequal access to health care and preventive health services (Levine & Crimmins, 2014; Sinn, 2011). Although these racial disparities are found for both African American men and women, the death rate for African American men remains higher at every age. Among African American elders, the "oldest old" African American women (85 and older) are the fastest growing group and also have the highest prevalence of health problems, functional limitations, and disability (Hooyman et al., 2015). Life expectancy and rates of chronic disease also vary by socioeconomic status, with low-income and less educated older adults in all racial/ethnic groups experiencing lower life expectancies and higher rates of chronic disease (Dupre, 2007; Geruso, 2012; Hayward, Miles, Crimmins, & Yang, 2000). Disabling chronic conditions also occur earlier in life among African Americans, Latinos, and American Indians. In general, however, life expectancies are increasing among Americans in virtually every racial/ethnic group and in every socioeconomic stratum (Wickert et al., 2013).

As life expectancies have increased, the United States has seen a corresponding decline in the fertility rate and the birth rate (Hamilton, Martin, & Ventura, 2013), which decreases the proportion of younger people in the American populace and therefore increases the proportion of older people. Fertility has declined from the mid-1960s to the present, and trends suggest that U.S. birth rates will continue to fall (Stulik & Vollmer, 2015). The decline in birth rates reflects changing social and demographic conditions, including the availability of birth control, the postponement of marriage and childbearing in order to pursue higher education and career development, and increases in labor force participation among women (Rubin, Roessler, & Rumrill, 2016). Together, these factors have led to Americans having fewer children than preceding generations did, thereby contributing to population aging and its implications for individuals, families, and society.

IMPLICATIONS OF POPULATION AGING

The shift toward increasing numbers of older adults brings with it a multitude of challenges related to the personal, social, vocational, residential, and health care needs of our elderly loved ones. It is important for rehabilitation counselors to understand the impact that population aging has had and will continue to have on family interaction and socialization, the American economy, and our health care and social service systems.

Informal Eldercare

Informal eldercare is defined as unpaid care provided to a person by friends or family members, most often by a spouse or children (Freedman, Akyan, Wolf, & Marcotte, 2004; Silverstein & Giarrusso, 2010; Wolff & Kasper, 2006). Wickert et al. (2013) pointed out that elderly Americans often outlive their financial resources, which places a tremendous burden on families to provide for their elderly loved ones' needs. As the baby boom generation continues to age, the inventory of family members who are available to provide informal eldercare is expected to decline, because the baby boom generation had fewer children than their parents did. Compounding the informal eldercare problem is the historically high divorce rate among the baby boom generation, which reduces the availability of spouses to provide needed care. Also, because women live longer than men on average, elderly women are likely to be widowed and living alone as the years pass and their health declines (Ryan, Smith, Antonucci, & Jackson, 2012).

These trends underscore the need for older baby boomers to participate in advanced planning and to explore nontraditional ways to meet their caregiving demands. Although disadvantaged when it comes to receiving support from spouses and children, baby boomers do have more siblings than previous or subsequent generations. Therefore, as in Adaline's case presented at the beginning of this chapter, sibling relationships could represent alternative sources of informal eldercare, provided that one's sibling is in good health and not in need of care himself or herself (Ryan et al., 2012). Further, due to remarriage rates among those in midlife (Brown & Lin, 2012), baby boomers may also begin to rely on stepchildren for support in later life. Recent research, however, indicates that filial obligations to provide care to parents are not as strong in stepfamilies as it is in biological families (Coleman, Ganong, Hans, Sharp, & Rothrauff, 2005). Together, these findings suggest that baby boomers may be disadvantaged in terms of receiving informal care in later life, leaving them more reliant on formal services, the cost of which often exceeds their means. Increasingly, however, baby boomers are beginning to systematically plan for their future care needs because of the well-documented increases in life expectancy. For older cohorts, including the parents of baby boomers, life spans into the 80s and 90s were not expected, so they did not tend to make deliberate plans for their future care. Wickert et al. (2013) chronicled the challenges that multiple generations of Americans face in caring for their elderly loved ones in *The Sandwich Generation's Guide to Eldercare*, which provides practical strategies to assist families in planning for, administering, and financing eldercare in ways that reflect the elderly person's wishes and honor his or her status in the family.

Work and Retirement

Population aging also has important implications for work and retirement. By necessity, people are putting off retirement until later in life than ever before (Strauser, 2013); by 2030, one in 10 American workers will be over the age of 60 (Anderson & Hussey, 2000). The United States has the highest workforce participation rate in the world among people 60 years of age and older, as well as the highest average age of retirement (Anderson & Hussey, 2000). Staying in the workforce may provide financial and health care–related advantages for aging Americans in terms of funding formal care services and maintaining a comfortable standard of living (Ryan et al., 2012), but it also means that growing numbers of older workers will be coping with age-related health conditions that will need to be accommodated if they plan to continue their careers past traditional retirement age. Also, even with workers putting off retirement until later in life than ever before, the large and increasing numbers of Americans living into their 80s and 90s means that the ratio of retirees to workers in the labor force will continue to grow for the next 30 years or so, which will leave proportionally fewer workers to support the American economy.

Social Insurance Programs

One of the consequences of the dwindling ratio of workers to retirees in the American economy is that revenues to support pay-as-you-go entitlement programs such as the Social Security retirement pension and Medicare stand to decrease considerably over time (Wickert et al., 2013). However, the larger number and proportion of retirees over the next several decades means that many more Americans will be seeking to draw benefits from these programs over a longer period of time than ever before. Therefore, Social Security programs will be severely hampered between now and 2050 by decreased employee contributions in real dollars and by significantly increased demand for Social Security income maintenance and health insurance benefits.

AGING, HEALTH, AND DISABILITY

In the United States the greatest challenges associated with population aging stem from the public health significance of the growing older adult population. Experts agree that one of the most important health care problems in American history will be how the national economy supports the medical, psychological, and community living needs of the baby boom generation as its members continue to age for the next 30 or more years. Even today, the oldest old, those 85 and over, are the fastest growing age group in the country (Wickert et al., 2013). By 2050, nearly a quarter of the older adult population will be 85 years of age or older, and they are projected to multiply more than four times in number from 1990 to 2030. Although improvements in health care and disease prevention have allowed Americans to live longer, healthier lives, the oldest old are at increased risk of having multiple chronic health conditions and higher rates of disability (Smart, 2009). Further, one third to one half of total health care expenditures in the United States goes to fund care and services for people over the age of 65 (Anderson & Hussey, 2000), and the oldest old utilize health care services at much higher rates than younger people. Although those 85 and over account for 1.5% of the current American population, they use 16.1% of Medicare expenditures (Wang, 2004). The oldest old, particularly women, are also increasingly likely to reside in high-cost long-term care (LTC) facilities (He, Sengupta, Velkoff, & De Barros, 2005), a trend that will likely continue for the next several decades. Although women live longer than men, they also experience more nonfatal chronic conditions (e.g., arthritis, osteoporosis, cataracts), which limit their functioning and quality of life (Bird & Rieker, 2008; Read & Gorman, 2010). At the oldest ages, women are also more likely than their male counterparts to require assistance in performing activities of daily living, with 72% of women age 85 and older reporting disabilities as per definitions set forth in the Americans with Disabilities Act Amendments Act (Hooyman et al., 2015).

In fact, for both men and women, research indicates that the incidence of disability increases as a linear function of age beginning in early adulthood. Wickert et al. (2013) reported a disability rate of 6% among American 20-year-olds and 30-year-olds, a 10% rate among 40-year-olds, and a 15% rate among 50-year-olds. By age 60, almost a quarter of Americans have disabilities, and the disability rate continues to increase to 31% by age 70, 48% by age 80, 61% by age 85, and more than 75% by age 90. An examination of disability prevalence in individuals over age 90 by Berlau, Corrada, and Kawas (2009) showed a rapid increase in disability in the oldest old, with nearly 100% of centenarians experiencing difficulty with one or more activities of daily living. The disability-as-a-function-of-age phenomenon is particularly true for the current generation of older Americans. According to research examining period and cohort effects of aging and disability in the United States, the number of older Americans with disabilities and the proportional disability rate has steadily increased over the last few decades (Lin, Beck, Finch, Hummer, & Master, 2012).

The most common chronic health conditions for people over the age of 65 include arthritis, hypertensive disease, heart disease, hearing impairments, musculoskeletal impairments, chronic sinusitis, diabetes, and visual impairments. Disabling conditions that are most feared by senior citizens include Alzheimer's disease and dementia, stroke, cancer, physical disability that prevents independence and autonomy (e.g., arthritis, Parkinson's disease), heart disease, chronic pulmonary disorder, deafness, and blindness. Similarly, the leading causes of death in Americans over the age of 65 are heart disease (32%), cancer (22%), stroke (8%), chronic respiratory disease (6%), flu/pneumonia (3%), diabetes (3%), and Alzheimer's disease (3%; Wickert et al., 2013).

Population aging is associated with a growing burden of chronic disease and disability, and the prevalence of the majority of risk factors for chronic disease rises with age (Prince et al., 2015). Specifically, advanced age is associated with an increase in physical inactivity, total cholesterol, fasting blood glucose, and blood pressure; smoking is more common among people of younger ages (Prince et al., 2015). Further, increased life expectancy has contributed to an increased incidence and prevalence of several disabling conditions, including hypertension, ischemic heart disease, stroke, diabetes, visual impairments, musculoskeletal conditions, arthritis, cancer, and dementia (Chatterji, Byles, Cutler, Seeman, & Verdes, 2015; Prince et al., 2015). For example, the economic burden of diabetes is forecast to increase by 96% from 2004 to 2030, with this endocrine disease's largest increase in prevalence observed among people over the age of 70 (Prince et al., 2015). More than 7 million Americans are currently living with dementia, and that number is expected to more than double by the year 2050 (Wickert et al., 2013). More than two thirds of Americans who are legally blind are over the age of 65, a proportion that is projected to increase to four fifths by 2035 (Rubin et al., 2016).

MEDICAL, PSYCHOSOCIAL, AND VOCATIONAL ASPECTS OF EMERGING AGE-RELATED DISABILITIES

Dementia

Dementia, a term referring to the death of or failure in the function of the nerve cells in the brain, is an increasingly prevalent and highly disabling condition for adults over the age of 65. Due to the wide range in functionality of neurons, the breakdown of these cells can create a vast array of impairments including limitations in basic activities of daily living such as eating, drinking, walking, communicating with others, self-care, motor skills, cognitive abilities, and decision making (Wickert et al., 2013). Usually progressive, dementia ranges in its impact from mild to severe depending mostly on how long the person has been dealing with the condition (National Institute on Aging, 2016).

The most common form of dementia is Alzheimer's disease, which accounts for about 60% to 80% of all dementia diagnoses. Other forms of dementia include vascular dementia or "poststroke dementia," dementia with Lewy bodies (DLB), mixed dementia, Parkinson's disease dementia, frontotemporal lobar dementia, Creutzfeldt–Jakob disease, and normal pressure hydrocephalus. Signs and symptoms of Alzheimer's disease include memory loss that disrupts daily activities; inability to make plans or solve problems; inability to complete daily tasks such as dialing a phone; confusion related to time and place; trouble understanding visual images and determining color or contrast; new problems with words in speaking and writing; misplacing items; poor social judgment; withdrawal from social situations; and personality or mood changes such as becoming easily frustrated, fearful, or anxious (Alzheimer's Association, 2016; Wickert et al., 2013).

Alzheimer's disease is an irreversible, progressive brain disorder that slowly destroys higher cognitive functioning such as memory and thinking skills and eventually affects a person's ability to perform even the simplest tasks (National Institute on Aging, 2016). According to the National Institute on Aging (2016), Alzheimer's symptoms are most likely to first occur in the person's mid-to-late 60s. Time from diagnosis to death can be as little as 3 or 4 years for individuals diagnosed over the age of 80, whereas individuals may survive as long as 10 or more years if they are diagnosed at a younger age (National Institute on Aging, 2016). Although the course of Alzheimer's disease varies from person to person, it is typically a slow and progressive disease that is categorized into three stages: early, middle, and late.

The early stage of Alzheimer's disease is characterized by a gradual onset and a few early symptoms that may include memory loss, lack of interest in social activities, difficulty with activities of daily living, and depressive episodes (Wickert et al., 2013). Once diagnosis is conferred, the individual and his or her caregivers must make several adjustmental decisions, including telling others about the diagnosis and arranging supports.

During the middle stage of Alzheimer's, a person typically experiences ongoing changes in personality as well as behavior that ultimately result in a diminished ability to live independently. Some common symptoms of this stage include irritability, depression, anxiety, paranoia, sudden mood swings, verbal outbursts, aggressive behavior, increased forgetfulness, constant repetition of words or stories, getting lost or disoriented, and difficulties making rational decisions. A person in this stage may require assistance with tasks that were previously routine activities of daily living such as bathing, grooming, meal preparation, dressing, and cleaning (Wickert et al., 2013).

The last stage of Alzheimer's disease is characterized by difficulties in eating and drinking, as well as with bowel and bladder functioning and skin and body health. At this point, 24-hour care may be required due to the individual's inability to communicate effectively, remember friends and family, use the bathroom independently, and make sound judgments regarding his or her personal safety. People in late-stage Alzheimer's disease may inquire about friends or relatives who have passed away years before and may exhibit irrational or violent behavior not consistent with their former personality (Alzheimer's Association, 2016; Wickert et al., 2013).

There is currently no cure for Alzheimer's disease; in fact, it is the only condition in the top ten causes of death in America that cannot be prevented, cured, or slowed (Alzheimer's Association, 2016). Treatment, therefore, tends to focus on symptom management through the use of a variety of different medications. It is common to include psychotropic medications in the treatment process such as antidepressants, antianxiety medications, and antipsychotics (Wickert et al., 2013).

It is estimated that there are currently 5.3 million Americans living with Alzheimer's disease, with 5.1 million of those individuals being aged 65 and older and women with the diagnosis outnumbering men 2:1 (Alzheimer's Association, 2016). According to the Alzheimer's Association (2016), the disease is the sixth leading cause of death in the United States, and one third of individuals aged 65 and older have either Alzheimer's or another form of dementia at the time of their death. The total medical cost associated with all forms of dementia in the United States in 2015 was $226 billion, a figure that is expected to rise to a staggering $1.1 trillion by 2050 (Alzheimer's Association, 2016).

Although the actual prevalence rates of Alzheimer's disease and other forms of dementia may be even higher than reported because many cases of dementia, especially in the early stages, go undiagnosed, the numbers of confirmed diagnoses continue to rise in the United States each year. A study of the changes in incidence rates of age-related diseases in the United States from 1992 to 2005 revealed an overall increase in the incidence rate of Alzheimer's disease by an average of 3.96% per year (Akushevich, Kravchenko, Ukraintseva, Arbeev, & Yashin, 2013). In fact, it is estimated that, as the number and proportion of Americans over the age of 65 continue to increase, the number of Americans with Alzheimer's disease will reach 7.1 million—a 40% increase—by 2025. By 2050, estimates indicate that some 14 million Americans will be living with Alzheimer's (Wickert et al., 2013).

Rheumatoid Arthritis

Rheumatoid arthritis (RA) is a disabling autoimmune disease in which the body's immune system mistakenly attacks the joints, causing swelling and pain in and around affected areas (Arthritis Foundation, 2016). RA is a chronic, long-term disease, and, if left unchecked, the swelling caused by RA in the lining of the joints, also known as the synovial membrane, can lead to damage of the cartilage and bone surrounding the joint and deformity of the joint itself (Centers for Disease Control and Prevention [CDC], 2016a). RA is classified as a systemic disease due to its effect on multiple bodily systems including inflammation in the cardiovascular and respiratory systems (Arthritis Foundation, 2016).

RA is the most common type of autoimmune arthritis, and it is most often diagnosed between ages 30 and 70, with onset occurring most often for individuals in their 60s (CDC, 2016a). It is estimated that 1.5 million Americans are living with RA, which translates to a 0.6% national prevalence rate, whereas international RA prevalence rates range from 0.4% to 1.3% (CDC, 2016a). Research indicates that the rates of RA are currently on the rise in the United States. The most recent data on the incidence of RA come from the Rochester Epidemiology Project, a longitudinal study of the trends in incidence and prevalence of RA in the United States from 1995 to 2007. Findings indicated that, although there was a drastic decrease in the incidence of RA in the four decades leading up to the 1990s, there has been a modest and steady increase in the incidence of RA in the past few decades, particularly in women who demonstrated a 2.5% average annual rate increase (Myasoedova, Crowson, Kremers, Therneau, & Gabriel, 2010). Of particular importance for the aging population, data indicated that RA incidence increased with age, peaking between ages 65 and 74 (Myasoedova et al., 2010).

RA is costly on both personal and public levels. According to the U.S. Medical Expenditure Panel Survey (MEPS), the total medical costs associated with RA were $22.3 billion in 2011, with earning losses due to RA totaling $1,212 per person (Kawatkar et al., 2012; Simons, Rosenblatt, & Trivedi, 2012). One study reported that the total RA-attributable costs to society, including costs to patients, employers, family members, and the government, totaled $39.2 billion in 2005 (Birnbaum et al., 2010). For an individual diagnosed with RA, estimated median lifetime costs of the disease range from $61,000 to $122,000 (Gabriel, Crowson, Campion, & O'Fallon, 1997).

Some common warning signs of possible RA include joint pain, tenderness, and/or stiffness lasting 6 weeks or longer, morning stiffness for 30 minutes or longer, more than one joint affected, small joints such as wrists affected, and the same joints on both sides of the body being affected. In addition to joint pain, many people experience fatigue, loss of appetite, and a low-grade fever. RA is an episodic disorder, which means that symptoms and effects may come and go with exacerbations, also known as flares, lasting anywhere from several days to months at a time. Prolonged inflammation due to RA can have severe repercussions throughout the body, affecting functioning of the eyes, mouth, skin, lungs, blood vessels, and blood itself (Arthritis Foundation, 2016).

RA is categorized into three distinct courses: monocyclic, polycyclic, and progressive. The monocyclic course is characterized by having one episode that ends within 2 to 5 years of the initial diagnosis, possibly resulting from early diagnosis and aggressive treatment. A polycyclic course indicates that the disease activity fluctuates over the course of the condition. The progressive course is indicated when the RA continues to increase in severity over time and does not dissipate. The characteristic bone and cartilage damage typically occurs fastest within the first year of onset in RA (CDC, 2016a).

Although there is no cure for RA, treatment has advanced drastically in the past few decades. Current medications allow individuals with RA significant symptom relief, with some individuals remaining in an indefinite asymptomatic remission status (Ruderman & Tambar, 2013). Treatment approaches for RA are aggressive and begin immediately upon diagnosis. Disease-modifying anti-rheumatic drugs (DMARDs) have proven successful in relieving RA symptomology and even slowing the progression of the disease. DMARDs are typically prescribed in addition to nonsteroidal anti-inflammatory drugs (NSAIDs) or low-dose corticosteroids in order to alleviate swelling, pain, and fever (Ruderman & Tambar, 2013). In addition to medication, RA treatment often includes education regarding lifestyle changes that may contribute to successful disease management such as exercise, stress management, and eating a healthy diet (National Institute of Arthritis and Musculoskeletal and Skin Diseases, 2014).

The effects of RA span well beyond the realms of physical and medical functioning. RA's significant impact on an individual's psychosocial and vocational functioning is well documented. Research comparing the quality of life of people with RA to the quality of life of other people indicated that those with RA were 40% more likely to report fair or poor general health, 30% more likely to need help with personal care, and twice as likely to have a health-related activity limitation (Dominick, Ahern, Gold, & Heller, 2004). In fact, people with RA demonstrate significant losses in function compared to individuals without arthritis in the domains of work, leisure, and social relations (CDC, 2016a).

RA can be a significant source of work limitation and a major reason for disengagement from the labor force, a problem that is likely to increase as the American workforce continues to age and more older workers acquire this highly intrusive disease in future decades (Baldwin et al., 2012). Factors associated with loss of employment for people with RA include increasing age, nonprofessional positions, less education, and number of days of work missed due to RA symptoms. Individuals with RA working in jobs that are less physically demanding and more flexible tend to demonstrate better vocational outcomes (Baldwin et al., 2012). With the increasing need for the aging population in America to work well into traditional retirement age, the issue of early retirement is particularly noteworthy for people with RA. Research reveals that 26.3% of people with RA retire early due to illness, compared to an illness-related early retirement rate of only 3.4% among people without arthritis. Vocational rehabilitation (VR) services have been shown to be an effective intervention when utilized prior to work disability, but services for people with RA are more likely to be provided after job loss has occurred, at which point the likelihood of regaining employment for VR consumers with RA is no higher than the likelihood of re-employment for those with RA who are not referred for services (Crockatt, Targett, Cifu, & Wehman, 2009). In addition to lack of timely access to VR services, workers with RA report limited use of workplace accommodations. An examination of worksite barriers facing people with RA revealed that, even though more than two thirds of respondents reported 10 or more vocational barriers, only 38% used any type of job accommodations (Allaire, Li, & LaValley, 2003).

Given that 20% to 40% of those diagnosed with RA leave the workplace within 3 years of diagnosis, early vocational intervention is especially important (Crockatt et al., 2009). An aggressive treatment approach within the first 3 months of onset including DMARDs along with workplace accommodations, especially work station modifications, can greatly increase the likelihood of employment retention (Crockatt et al., 2009). Other effective accommodations for workers with RA include use of assistive technology, regular breaks during the workday, changes in scheduling, performing work in a different way, reassignment of job functions, and reassignment to another position (Crockatt et al., 2009). Perhaps even more important to job retention for people with RA than the specific workplace accommodations implemented are employer support, a positive work environment, transportation assistance, and support from coworkers and health care professionals (Varekamp, Haafkens, Detaille, Tak, & van Dijk, 2005).

Stroke

Stroke, also known as cerebrovascular accident (CVA), is a term that refers to a group of conditions characterized by neurological deficits due to an interruption in cerebral blood flow (Zhang, Chapman, Plested, Jackson, & Purroy, 2012). The interruption occurs when a blood vessel in the brain is either blocked or ruptured, thus depriving brain cells of blood and consequently oxygen, which leads to cell death (American Stroke Association, 2016). A stroke caused by a brain aneurysm burst or a weakened blood vessel leak is referred to as a hemorrhagic stroke, the least common of the two types of strokes but the most likely to be fatal. A stroke due to a blood vessel in the brain being blocked by a blood clot is known as an ischemic stroke; this type accounts for 87% of all strokes (CDC, 2016b). The residual effects of a stroke vary greatly, depending on the person's prestroke health status, the area of the brain that is affected, and the amount of cerebrovascular damage that is caused (National Stroke Association, 2016).

The most common effects of stroke include hemiparesis (weakness on one side of the body), hemiplegia (paralysis on one side of the body), dysarthria (difficulty speaking or slurred speech), dysphagia (trouble swallowing), fatigue, loss of emotional control and changes in mood, memory loss, poor judgment, issues with problem-solving, personality changes, inappropriate language or actions, decreased field of vision, and difficulties with visual perception (American Stroke

Association, 2016). Several complications of stroke are specific to the side of the brain that is affected; for instance, aphasia (difficulty in speaking or comprehending spoken language) and behavior becoming more cautious are common accompaniments of a left-brain injury, whereas one-sided neglect (lack of awareness of the left side of the body), trouble understanding facial expressions and tone of voice, and behavior becoming more impulsive are typical of right-brain injuries. Due to the brain's contralateral functionality, the physical effects of any brain injury manifest on the side of the body opposite to the injury. Many individuals who sustain strokes also experience neuropsychiatric sequelae such as apathy, depression, anxiety, posttraumatic stress disorder (PTSD), irritability, pseudobulbar affect, and denial (American Stroke Association, 2016).

In addition to the overwhelming individual complications of stroke, there are significant macro-level medical, social, and economic implications of this condition. The worldwide prevalence of stroke in 2010 was 33 million people, 16.9 million cases of which involved people having their first stroke. Each year, approximately 800,000 Americans suffer a new or recurrent stroke, and there are more than 7 million (2.5%) people living in the United States who have survived a stroke (American Stroke Association, 2016; Wang, Kapellush, & Garg, 2014; Zhang et al., 2012). Stroke is the second leading cause of death in the world, accounting for 11.8% of deaths globally, and it is the fifth leading cause of death in the United States, accounting for 129,000 deaths every year (American Stroke Association, 2016). The rates of stroke in the United States are highest in the Southeast, which has come to be known as the "Stroke Belt," where prevalence is 125% higher than the rest of the country even after adjusting for age and gender (Liao, Greenlund, Croft, Keenan, & Giles, 2009). The risk of stroke is nearly doubled for African Americans in comparison to their Caucasian counterparts, and it increases as a function of age with two thirds of stroke hospitalizations occurring in individuals aged 65 years and older (CDC, 2016b). The total cost of stroke in the United States is an estimated $34 billion each year in health care services, medications, and missed days of work (CDC, 2016b).

Preventive measures and medical advances have resulted in the prevalence of stroke in the United States remaining relatively stable over time and the mortality rate decreasing significantly. An examination of the changes in incidence of stroke over time revealed an average annual decrease of 2.89% from 1992 to 2005 (Akushevich et al., 2013). In regard to mortality rate, over the last decade, the death rate from stroke has fallen by 34% and the absolute number of stroke deaths has decreased by 18% (American Stroke Association, 2016). Therefore, even as the number of strokes each year slightly decreases, the proportion and total number of people who survive strokes has drastically increased. This means that there are far more individuals in the United States living with the complications of stroke than ever before. Moreover, with the growing elderly segment of the American populace, the number of people who will be seeking medical, psychosocial, and vocational rehabilitation services for this age-related condition will continue to increase for decades to come.

Given the wide range of functional limitations caused by stroke, the powerful negative impact that this condition has on survivors' psychosocial functioning and quality of life is not surprising. A review of the literature pertaining to the psychosocial impact of stroke by Thompson and Ryan (2008) identified four dominant themes: coping, adapting, and adjusting; role, identity, and work; emotional issues and poststroke fatigue; and sexual function and sexuality. Individuals who had survived strokes reported significant changes in everyday functioning, including the loss of valued roles, difficulty leaving the house, lack of participation in leisure activities, difficulty with communication and memory, and deterioration of important relationships. Despite the negative impact of stroke in almost every aspect of life, the authors noted that strong predictors of successful poststroke adjustment included maintaining or restoring a sense of meaningfulness, optimism, and control, as well as the presence of hopeful thinking, optimism, self-efficacy, and a sense of coherence when experiencing functional impairment (Thompson & Ryan, 2008).

Additional research indicates that community involvement and quality of life are most significantly affected among stroke survivors who experience the highest number of stroke-related deficits, particularly depression and hemiplegia. A study of health-related quality of life (HRQoL) in stroke survivors over age 60 revealed that more stroke deficits were associated with lower HRQoL (Min & Min, 2015). The effect was most evident for individuals experiencing hemiplegia, one of the most common stroke complications, which creates problems with mobility, produces pain and discomfort, and can hinder independence during activities of daily living (Min & Min, 2015). Bujick and Koopmans (2014) investigated the quality of life of older adults who had completed stroke rehabilitation and found that the presence of neuropsychiatric sequelae, specifically depressive symptoms, negatively affected quality of life; conversely and not surprisingly, high functional independence was associated with high quality of life.

The impact of stroke is also highly evident in the world of work. Stroke is one of the most common causes of work disability worldwide, and it is the leading cause of adult disability in the United States (National Stroke Association, 2016). As many as 70% of working-age stroke survivors have some type of impairment to their work capacity, and only about 40% of individuals employed at the time of stroke are able to successfully return to work (Conroy, Milani, Levine, & Stein, 2009). The most recent research suggests that between 22% and 53% of stroke survivors are able to successfully return to work between 6 and 12 months poststroke and only 19% are able to successfully sustain that employment and remain in the workforce after 5 years (Wang et al., 2014).

Extant poststroke research has identified several critical factors influencing the return to work process. According to Conroy and colleagues (2009) key issues associated with return to work likelihood include age, severity of stroke and nature of residual impairments, psychological factors, socioeconomic status, financial and family obligations, educational level, and prestroke occupation type. Another recent study revealed a higher probability of return to work for stroke survivors with shorter lengths of stay in the hospital, with less severe strokes, with an absence of severe physical and cognitive impairment, with high ability to perform activities of daily living, with a more supportive work environment, and with more flexible professional level jobs (Wang et al., 2014).

Age has repeatedly been identified as a key factor in an individual's intent to return to work after a stroke. For those nearing retirement age, suffering a stroke can be a catalyst for making the decision to retire. Given that the incidence of stroke increases with age, it is not surprising that many individuals who have the financial means to stop working do so following a stroke, especially if they were planning to retire in the near future before the stroke occurred (Conroy et al., 2009; Saeki, 2000).

However, leaving the workforce prematurely due to stroke (or any other disabling condition, for that matter) may deleteriously affect the person's sense of self-worth; retirees who sustained strokes shortly before exiting the workforce frequently report feeling that they are a burden on their families, that their lives lack a strong purpose and direction, and that they are not contributing fully to society (Conroy et al., 2009).

For those stroke survivors who choose to return to employment, early intervention and management of workplace barriers is crucial. Slowly reintegrating individuals into the workplace after stroke is important because of the extended recovery period associated with poststroke treatment (Conroy et al., 2009; Saeki, 2000). Domains of functioning including cognition, language, communication, physical strength and coordination, and perceptual abilities require varying degrees of time for recovery, often making immediate return to full-time employment a difficult proposition (Conroy et al., 2009).

There is no clear-cut successful formula for helping stroke survivors return to work, but, just as the complications of stroke are highly individualized, the more individualized the rehabilitation plan is, specifically in regard to the person's limitations, accommodation needs, and rehabilitation goals, the better. In general, employer support and willingness to modify working conditions or environments are predictive of successful return to work plans (Saeki, 2000). Taking advantage of volunteer and part-time work opportunities and gradually transitioning to full-time work can be a helpful strategy, and the importance of long-term part-time work or even volunteer activities cannot be overlooked in helping people re-establish a sense of purpose and psychosocial well-being (Conroy et al., 2009). For positions that are physically demanding, creative job accommodation strategies or even a change of position to a less labor-intensive role may be necessary (e.g., transitioning from performing electrical work to teaching electrical work in a classroom). Given the high prevalence of fatigue in stroke survivors, accommodations such as increased breaks, flexible scheduling, and mobility aids should be considered as part of the return-to-work plan. Finally, given that stroke often compromises one's ability to drive, transportation to and from work and for required on-the-job travel is often an important return-to-work issue.

REHABILITATION COUNSELING IMPLICATIONS

Counselor Awareness and Self-Reflective Practice

Rehabilitation counselors are subject to the same biases and misperceptions about aging, health, and disability that exist in the general public. Hence, it is important that they examine their perceptions of older individuals and the issues they face in health care, family interaction and socialization, employment, and community living. Counselors should first examine their own experiences with aging and declining health within their own families, considering to what extent their elderly loved ones were treated with the dignity, respect, and compassion they deserve. Counselors should also explore their beliefs regarding who should be financially responsible for eldercare in contemporary society—the individual himself or herself, family members, private insurers, the government—and the extent to which the wishes of the elderly person should be considered in making decisions pertaining to his or her safety and well-being. Cultural and religious differences (on the part of both the counselor and the client) regarding the status and treatment of the elderly must also be taken into account.

It is also important for rehabilitation counselors working with elderly clients to become familiar with the medical and psychosocial aspects of emerging age-related disabilities. They should consult the professional literature and seek online information regarding conditions such as stroke, cancer, dementia, diabetes, sensory impairments, arthritis, heart disease, and orthopedic impairments—especially how these conditions affect one's independence and the functioning of his or her family. Some helpful online resources to consult regarding age-related disabilities include MedlinePlus from the U.S. National Library of Medicine (www.nlm.nih.gov/medlineplus/seniorshealth.html), the National Council on Aging website (www.ncoa.org), and the American Society on Aging website (www.asaging.org).

Effective geriatric rehabilitation requires collaboration among an interdisciplinary team of professionals, so rehabilitation counselors must become familiar with medical and allied health specialists who serve elderly people. These include geriatric care physicians, geriatric nurses, rheumatologists, endocrinologists, oncologists, cardiologists, geropsychologists, psychiatrists, physiatrists, physical therapists, occupational therapists, and speech and language pathologists. Many elderly people with age-related disabilities will also seek services from accountants, financial planners, and attorneys who specialize in elder issues. Becoming knowledgeable about other professionals who serve people with age-related disabilities will enable rehabilitation counselors to function as informed members of service delivery teams.

Outreach and Eligibility Determination

Many individuals with age-related health conditions do not consider themselves people with disabilities even after the onset of their conditions, especially if they were in good health earlier in their lives. This behooves rehabilitation counselors to employ proactive outreach strategies with geriatric health care providers, Area Agencies on Aging, and other providers who serve people with conditions that increase in incidence with advancing age (e.g., diabetes, cardiovascular disease, stroke, cancer, arthritis, visual impairments, hearing impairments, dementia). Additionally, the fact that many people with one age-related disability often have other co-occurring medical conditions requires vigilance on the part of rehabilitation counselors to ensure that applications for services include a full accounting of the impact that the person's overall medical and psychological condition has on his or her functioning. This facilitates eligibility decisions that consider the individual's entire set of rehabilitation needs rather than focusing on one diagnosis. For example, a 70-year-old applicant for independent living services who had a stroke 2 years ago might also have diabetes, a respiratory condition, and/or hypertension, all of which must be taken into consideration when determining his or her need and eligibility for services.

It may also be necessary for rehabilitation agencies to reconsider their eligibility criteria to accommodate people with age-related disabilities. Suppose that a state vocational rehabilitation agency has a policy that it only provides services to clients who are seeking full-time employment. In that case, a 68-year-old retiree with RA who wishes to supplement his or her pension with part-time employment may not qualify for services on the basis of his or her part-time employment goal. If the agency allows for independent living services related to transportation and housing, for example, this individual could be considered eligible for services even though his or her health and life circumstances do not permit full-time employment.

It is also of utmost importance that rehabilitation counselors make appropriate referrals when seeking diagnostic testing, medical exams, and psychological evaluations to aid in making eligibility determinations. For example, older individuals who have psychiatric disabilities should be referred to mental health professionals. People with arthritis should be referred to rheumatologists. People with diabetes may need to be referred to endocrinologists. Geriatric care physicians may need to be consulted in the event that an elderly applicant is coping with two or more co-occurring health conditions.

Rehabilitation Assessment and Planning

In rehabilitation assessment and planning, the unique characteristics, needs, and developmental aspects of age-related disabilities must be thoroughly considered if successful rehabilitation outcomes are to be realized. In particular, issues such as the client's medical history and overall health status, social support network, need for health care, need for accessible housing and transportation, financial status, health insurance coverage, receipt of disability benefits (if applicable), and interest in paid employment or volunteer work must be assessed and addressed in the rehabilitation plan.

For example, the first step in rehabilitation assessment and planning with older clients who have limited economic means is to determine if their basic needs are being met. Do they have stable housing, enough food and clothing, natural supports, access to health care, and transportation? If these needs are not being met, rehabilitation counselors should work with the consumer to identify resources in his or her social support system or in the community for meeting these needs. Local governmental resources may be limited, especially in sparsely populated areas, so rehabilitation counselors will need to familiarize themselves with resources provided by other entities such as the federal or state government, nonprofit organizations, long-term care facilities, and religious institutions.

Because older individuals with age-related health conditions are especially vulnerable to severe weather, storms and floods, and extreme heat or cold, it is important to consider the potential impact of changes in weather on this emerging rehabilitation counseling clientele. In extreme weather circumstances, it is important that rehabilitation counselors assess elderly clients' physical and mental health status and make amendments to the rehabilitation plan if additional services (e.g., physical and mental restoration) or referrals to outside service providers are needed. During extreme weather events, rehabilitation counselors can work with their supervisors and coordinate with public health and other human services agencies to develop policies and procedures for ensuring the welfare and safety of elderly consumers who may be especially vulnerable to the negative health consequences of these events. For example, during extremely hot weather, if elderly consumers do not have air conditioning in their residences, procedures should be in place to ensure that they are provided temporary accommodations in air conditioned shelters because even spending a few hours a day in cool settings has been found to serve as a protective factor against detrimental health consequences (Bouchama, 2003). Here again, the importance of social supports and the resources of the person's family to provide needed climate-controlled shelter cannot be overstated. For aging clients who live alone and do not have any other place to go to avoid extreme heat, rehabilitation counselors can make referrals to community-independent living centers to install air conditioning units in the homes of consumers without these or, alternatively, purchase air conditioning units to be installed in their homes as a service within the rehabilitation plan.

Counseling and Guidance

In providing counseling and guidance services to individuals with age-related disabilities, the issue of chronicity is often of paramount concern. Not only are many age-related disabilities chronic, unpredictable, and sometimes progressive, they may be accompanied by several or many other health concerns. Important issues that may need to be addressed in counseling and guidance include adherence to treatment and medication regimens, wellness strategies to prevent secondary complications of illness or injury, fall prevention and safety in the home, transportation, diet and nutrition, exercise, stress management, family dynamics, planning for the future including estate planning, and managing needed eldercare (Wickert et al., 2013). If the person's disability was caused by or contributed to by lifestyle factors such as poor nutrition, obesity, physical inactivity, and/or smoking, counseling and guidance services may need to focus on the problem behavior that underlies the health condition—examining the motivations for the behavior, strategies for cessation or modification of the behavior, and the impact of behavioral change on the person's psychological and social functioning (Atherton & Toriello, 2012; Cole & Fiore, 2014; Koch, Conyers, & Rumrill, 2012).

Many older consumers will experience difficulties coping with the changes in their health status and functional capabilities that accompany advancing age. It is important for rehabilitation counselors to differentiate normal and natural grief responses to declining health from reactions that meet diagnostic criteria for psychiatric disorders (Smart, 2009). It is also important to recognize early signs of dementia such as forgetfulness, extreme moodiness, and decrements in short- and intermediate-term memory and then make referrals to geriatric neurologists for consultation. Case reviews and evaluations with psychological and medical consultants are recommended to determine if referrals for mental health services are warranted.

It is also important to identify the need for family counseling and make appropriate referrals if family members are exhibiting grief and mourning over the changes that their elderly loved one is going through. Older clients may also need to grieve and mourn the deaths of significant others, siblings, parents, and even children as part of their own adjustment to declining health and age-related disability (Wickert et al., 2013). For family members, the economic burden of eldercare can be staggering, frequently causing families to transfer the responsibility for caregiving from public social services to unpaid family members. Family members are not only adjusting to the acquisition of age-related disabilities and the chronic, sometimes progressive, nature of such disabilities, they must also contend with identity and role changes, stress, fatigue, anxiety, depression, and the economic implications of eldercare (McCurry & Hunter Revell, 2015). These issues should be considered in counseling families with age-related emerging disabilities.

For the elderly loved one, entrusting his or her personal care to a younger family member can be a difficult proposition. Conversely, it can be equally difficult for a younger family member to relate to his or her elderly loved one due to generational gaps in world views, value systems, and perspectives on the future (Kerson & Michelsen, 1995). Furthermore, deterioration of cognitive functioning in a family member can cause major shifts in the decision-making structure of a family. Overall, family relationships are a critical factor in the well-being of older clients, so it is important to consider family counseling interventions as a means to increase support and manage conflict within the family (Qualls, 2000).

In counseling and guidance with elderly consumers, rehabilitation counselors must not impose their own grief reactions and coping styles onto consumers. Nor should they make cross-consumer comparisons of responses to aging and declining health. There are no rules regarding how individuals should adjust to advancing age and changes in their health status, nor are there prescribed stages of emotional responses that must be "worked through" in order to achieve resolution. It is also important to note here that not all older consumers will experience grief as their health and lifestyles change over time; the individualized nature of rehabilitation planning and service delivery lends itself very well to the vast range of emotional responses that people with age-related disabilities present (Rubin et al., 2016).

Listening is perhaps the most helpful response that can be provided to these consumers. Wickert et al. (2013) pointed out that elderly people, especially those who live alone and who have few or no family members nearby, are often plagued by loneliness and a lack of social interactions. These individuals derive great psychological benefits from simply talking about "the old days," their current and future interests, their children and/or grandchildren, politics, religion, or any other topics of interest.

Enlisting the assistance of volunteers to provide companionship and social interaction may be necessary to help elderly clients combat loneliness. Joining clubs, community organizations, or travel groups may also provide senior citizens with much-needed human contact, not to mention an organized schedule of things to do. Part-time employment is an excellent reason to get out of the house, meet people, and earn extra money, and many employers report a strong affinity for hiring older workers because of their work ethic, reliability, and positive influence on younger coworkers (Strauser, 2013). Where paid employment is not an option, volunteer work can yield many of the same psychosocial benefits for older individuals looking for things to do to keep busy while contributing to the well-being of their communities. Identifying ways to keep busy while interacting with others in pro-social contexts is an important issue to address in counseling and guidance services with consumers who have age-related disabilities.

Like those with other kinds of emerging disabilities, clients with age-related health conditions may also need to process their feelings about the multitude of severe symptoms they experience, along with the impact that familial, medical, and societal biases regarding aging have on their ability to cope. Providing these consumers with a nonjudgmental and validating "listening ear" is an important service in and of itself. Additionally, counseling and guidance services should emphasize coping with the stress and stigma associated with their conditions, dealing with the lack of understanding and support from others if that is an issue in their social support networks, developing new or expanded support networks, facilitating the development of skills to manage stress and pain, determining the effects that paid employment may have on retirement and disability benefits they may be receiving, generalizing coping and self-management skills to work and other settings outside of the home, and making referrals to mental health professionals if individuals have co-occurring anxiety and/or depression that further impairs their functioning (Koch et al., 2012).

As a profession, rehabilitation counseling should also consider following the examples of nursing and public health (Falvo, 2014) in developing initiatives to mitigate the impact of aging on human health and functioning. Rehabilitation counselors have long partnered with people with disabilities to advocate for empowering disability-related public policy, and the considerable political power of senior advocacy organizations is well established (Wickert et al., 2013). Older people with disabilities are in the unique position to benefit from the advocacy and public policy successes of the disability community and the senior community, and those consumer advocacy efforts will be greatly enhanced if professionals who serve older people with disabilities in health care, allied health, and rehabilitation settings join these consumers in advancing their agenda.

Health Promotion Services

Research evidence is accumulating that documents positive health outcomes for people with disabilities who receive health promotion services, and rehabilitation researchers are advocating for these services to be more systematically incorporated into plans for employment as a means to improve VR outcomes (Crystal & Espinosa, 2012). Health promotion services may be especially beneficial to individuals with age-related disabilities who are particularly susceptible to secondary complications related to physical inactivity and developmental processes. Health promotion services can be provided in any residential setting regardless of the person's functional capabilities—there is always room for improvement in one's ability to manage one's health. Failure to deliver interventions that address the overall health of the growing population of older people with disabilities is likely to impair their ability to achieve desired employment, independent living, and quality of life goals. In addition to contracting with outside vendors to provide health promotion workshops, VR counselors, as well as rehabilitation counselors working in settings other than the state–federal VR program, can recommend health-promoting behaviors in counseling sessions, provide support and encouragement as older individuals make health-related changes, and include provision of health promotion interventions (e.g., weight management, dietary consultation, fitness programs, stress management, smoking cessation; Ipsen, Jensen, & Anderson, 2010) in individualized rehabilitation and employment plans.

Home modifications can also have a health promoting function. For example, installation of air conditioning units in the homes of older individuals with preexisting conditions who live in communities prone to extreme heat events can preclude exacerbation of symptoms and secondary medical complications. For older individuals with respiratory or pulmonary conditions or multiple chemical sensitivity, home modifications should be targeted at improving air quality. If consumers with these chronic illnesses do not have safe home environments with good air quality, their symptoms will persist and worsen. Other modifications should be considered to make older consumers' homes more visually and physically accessible, which can improve residential safety and prevent orthopedic injuries.

Mental Health Counseling

Rehabilitation counselors must be vigilant in identifying signs that older consumers with disabilities need mental health counseling services. Depression, for example, often goes unrecognized and untreated in older adults because it is assumed that depression is a natural reaction to aging, decline in functional capabilities, death of loved ones, and the onset of chronic illnesses and disabilities (American Psychological Association, 2014; NIMH, 2016). Although research indicates that the prevalence of depression is actually lower in older adults than it is in younger adults, depression can co-occur with chronic illnesses such as heart disease, stroke, diabetes, cancer, and Parkinson's disease (NIMH, 2016). If mental health conditions are left untreated, disabling symptoms from primary disorders can be exacerbated and the progression of chronic illnesses can be accelerated (American Psychological Association, 2014). Health care professionals, and older adults themselves, may assume that depressive symptoms are a normal reaction to changes associated with these conditions (NIMH, 2016). Older adults are less likely than middle-aged and younger adults to receive mental health counseling, and when they do receive treatment for co-occurring mental health conditions, it is most likely to be provided by their primary care physicians (American Psychological Association, 2014). This underutilization of mental health services by older adults has been attributed to a variety of factors including inadequate insurance coverage; a shortage of mental health professionals who specialize in geriatrics; lack of coordination among primary care, mental health, and aging providers; stigma; denial of problems; and lack of transportation to get to medical appointments. Rehabilitation counselors should assess these factors and determine how they can be ameliorated so that elders receive the mental health treatment needed for comorbid psychiatric conditions.

Referrals to mental health providers should be considered if the consumer exhibits evidence of physical or emotional abuse from caregivers or family members; disorientation; persistent feelings of hopelessness and despair; depression; anxiety; withdrawal from others; feeling constantly restless or on edge; obsessive fears of illness and/or death; hearing voices; seeing visions; delusional thinking; disengaging from self-care activities (e.g., not eating, bathing, changing clothes, brushing teeth); suicidal or homicidal thoughts or plans; problematic use of alcohol or drugs; fluctuations in weight; and/or a lack of interest in participating in financial, residential, or health care decisions (Wickert et al., 2013). Caution is advised, however, because some older consumers may interpret the mere mention of mental health services as invalidation of their medical conditions and evidence that the rehabilitation counselor, like some of their friends, family members, and other professionals they have encountered, thinks that their symptoms are psychosomatic (Koch et al., 2012). Therefore, when recommending mental health services for these consumers, rehabilitation counselors must take care to explain that the purpose of these services is not to diagnose and treat them for a psychosomatic condition, but rather to (a) support them in dealing with normal emotional responses to changes in health status; (b) help them to identify coping resources and supports; and (c) treat co-occurring mental health conditions they may be experiencing.

Peer and Social Supports

Peer and social supports are invaluable resources for individuals with age-related disabilities, both to combat the loneliness and social isolation that often accompanies old age and to acquaint them with community resources that can assist them in meeting their needs. Same-age peers who have been successful in managing their health and personal affairs can serve as role models and mentors who inspire hope in those who may be having difficulties. Peer-provided health promotion interventions can also increase the likelihood that those with age-related disabilities will engage in activities to improve their overall health and functioning. Rehabilitation counselors should research the availability of relevant peer support groups and peer-provided services in their local communities so they can share these resources with consumers (Kalb, 2012). These peer supports may include groups of senior citizens (see local Area Agencies on Aging for referrals) or groups that are specific to the particular illness or disabling condition that the person is dealing with (e.g., multiple sclerosis, diabetes, dementia, cancer).

Members of these support and self-advocacy groups share strategies and resources to cope with age-related changes in health and advocate for changes in societal attitudes and public policy to increase access to much needed health and rehabilitation services. It is also important to keep in mind that many of these groups welcome the person's friends and family members as participants. Finally, for those who do not live near in-person groups or whose functional limitations make it difficult for them to attend group meetings in person, online support and self-advocacy groups are an alternative that may be beneficial. Again, rehabilitation counselors should thoroughly investigate the availability of these resources and share this information with consumers.

Job Development and Placement

It is important to remember that traditional job development and placement strategies may not meet the needs of people with age-related disabilities for several reasons. First, many of these consumers will be seeking part-time employment to supplement their retirement pensions rather than full-time hours. Second, although many older people have long employment histories and were successful in their former careers, they may need to choose jobs based more on proximity to their homes, flexibility in their work schedules, and the availability of workplace accommodations than on their previous experience and vocational interests (Strauser, 2013; Wickert et al., 2013). It should also be noted that older workers seeking to remain in or re-enter the workforce while dealing with chronic health conditions or disabilities may not have up-to-date technology skills, which can create difficulties in the job application process because many employers require applicants to submit their candidacy and accompanying materials online. This lack of current technology skills can also be a problem for older workers who are learning new jobs and who must use computerized cash registers, smartphones, tablet computers, and other devices to perform their job tasks.

Older workers, particularly those whose health conditions limit their transportation options, may be interested in telecommuting or home-based employment opportunities as opposed to jobs in traditional worksites (Strauser, 2013). Fortunately, many employers provide these opportunities to their employees because of the cost-effectiveness of these options (Rubin et al., 2016). Rehabilitation counselors can educate employers who do not provide their employees with these alternatives about the ease and cost-effectiveness of telecommuting and working from home.

In the job development and placement process with older individuals with disabilities, rehabilitation counselors must communicate to employers the wealth of experience, career maturity, and positive influence on younger workers that these seasoned workers bring to the workplace. Studies repeatedly show that workers over the age of 55 consistently outperform their younger coworkers in terms of punctuality and attendance, reliability and dependability, loyalty to the agency or business, and positive interactions with other employees and customers (Wickert et al., 2013). In return for the important contributions they make, older workers deserve to work in environments where the attitudinal climate respects their elder status and protects the health and well-being of all employees. In addition to conducting job analyses to determine what accommodations may be required for older workers to perform their jobs, assessment of the organizational cultures of potential workplaces is necessary because individuals with age-related (and other) disabilities often encounter negative reactions from both employers and coworkers (e.g., ignoring their requests for accommodations, responding to requests with hostility or harassment, treating these workers with incivility) when they disclose their disabilities and make accommodation requests (Rumrill, Fraser, & Johnson, 2013). First, workplace policies and procedures should be examined to determine if these promote inclusion; healthy work environments; flexibility in how and where work is performed; teamwork; appreciation of diversity; and intolerance of harassment, workplace bullying, and incivility. Then, observation of interactions between coworkers and interviews with employers and employees about the workplace culture will provide the rehabilitation counselor with additional evidence of the setting's attitudinal accessibility.

In job development and placement, employers often need to be educated about commonly occurring age-related disabling conditions because they are likely to have biases and misunderstandings about their associated functional limitations and how accommodations (most of which are no cost or very inexpensive and can benefit all workers) can enable these older individuals to be productive, reliable, and competent employees (Rubin et al., 2016). Given the extensive work experience and vocational sophistication of many older people with disabilities, they may be able to take an active role in educating employers about their on-the-job needs. Or, if the person is uncomfortable doing this on his or her own, rehabilitation counselors can jointly educate employers with the consumer. Coworkers, especially those who will be working most closely with the individual, are also likely to be unaware of the individual's disability-related needs. This lack of awareness among coworkers can be a major impediment to job satisfaction, satisfactoriness, and longevity on the job (Strauser, 2013); thus, it may be necessary to educate them as well. Rehabilitation counselors can assist older consumers with identifying appropriate strategies and developing the necessary communication skills that will elicit support and understanding from coworkers. Here again, the long employment histories that older workers bring to the labor force may enable them to relate very effectively with coworkers of different ages and from diverse racial, ethnic, and cultural backgrounds.

Accommodation Planning

The accommodation planning process with older consumers with disabilities is likely to be a complex endeavor because of the multitude of functional limitations these individuals experience, compounded by the extent of negative stereotypes and stigma regarding aging promulgated by both the medical community and society at large. Steps that can be taken to better ensure that necessary accommodations will be implemented include (a) educating individuals about the employment protections afforded by the Americans with Disabilities Act (ADA) and other legislation (e.g., the Age Discrimination in Employment Act, the Civil Rights Act); (b) engaging in a collaborative process of identifying workplace barriers and accommodation needs; and (c) assisting individuals to develop the self-advocacy and communication skills to request, implement, and evaluate accommodations (Roessler & Rumrill, 2015).

Because individuals with age-related chronic health conditions, especially those who were generally healthy during their younger years, may not consider themselves to have disabilities, the first step in accommodations planning is to educate them how legislation such as the ADA defines disability and protects their rights related to securing and maintaining employment (Rubin et al., 2016). Additionally, because many of these individuals have hidden disabilities and have encountered negative reactions when disclosing their disabilities to others, rehabilitation counselors should carefully listen to their concerns about disclosure and past negative experiences related to disclosure. Rehabilitation counselors can then explore with them the advantages and disadvantages of disclosure, the circumstances under which disclosure may be advantageous, how and when to disclose, and to whom to disclose (Rumrill et al., 2013).

The next step is to identify workplace barriers and potential accommodations to ameliorate these barriers. Roessler's (1995) Work Experience Survey (WES) is a valid and reliable needs assessment tool that has been used with workers of all ages who have chronic illnesses to identify barriers and accommodations. This instrument can be used in a collaborative and empowering approach that focuses first on the consumer's elucidation of barriers and accommodation ideas and then on additional ideas provided by the rehabilitation counselor to supplement the consumer's ideas. Many older individuals with the conditions discussed in this chapter have functional limitations that change over time or experience changes to their work environments that may negatively impact their capacity to continue working unless accommodations are implemented (e.g., modification of installation of new equipment, structural renovations to physical facilities, personal assistance from readers or interpreters, assistance with transportation to and from work, scheduling modifications; Koch, Rumrill, Hennessey, Vierstra, & Roessler, 2007). The potential application of the WES for use with individuals with age-related disabilities is promising because it is a tool that can be used for periodic reassessment of their accommodation needs.

The Job Accommodation Network (JAN) is an excellent resource for identifying specific accommodation ideas. For example, JAN suggests potential accommodations for age-related respiratory and pulmonary diseases that include removal of chemical triggers from the work environment, relocation of the employee's workspace, adding air purifiers to the workspace, liberal attendance and leave policies, modifications of where work is performed so that individuals can work from home or other environments where they will not be exposed to environmental triggers, accessible parking and restrooms, modified or part-time work, and modifications to the scheduling of breaks (JAN, 2014).

For individuals with chronic illnesses that are increasing in prevalence among older people, accommodation ideas offered by JAN include reduced work schedules, periodic rest breaks, and flexible leave time to reduce fatigue; transfers to less stressful positions within the organization, flexible work schedules, and working from home to reduce stress; sensitivity training to coworkers, allowing telephone calls to health care and other providers for support, referral to employee assistance programs to accommodate depression; and protective clothing to avoid exposure to chemical hazards for those with skin sensitivities.

Workers with diabetes mellitus call in sick four times more often than nondisabled workers (American Diabetes Association, 2015), so scheduling modifications are an especially important accommodation strategy for older workers with the disease (JAN, 2014). JAN also emphasized the importance of allowing employees with diabetes to have periodic breaks during the workday so they can have snacks and take oral or intravenous insulin to regulate their blood sugar. Older workers with diabetes, cancer, stroke, cardiovascular disease, multiple sclerosis, and RA may need flexible personal and medical leave policies in the event that they require hospitalizations or surgery for some of the more severe effects of their illnesses.

For older workers with chronic conditions that impose physical restrictions, accommodations may include reducing the lifting or exertional requirements of one's job, making work stations and facilities accessible for wheelchairs and motorized scooters, and reducing the amount of standing or walking that is required for a particular job. Older individuals who experience visual impairments may benefit from readers, Braille or large-print computer displays, voice-activated computer software, voice-output screen-reading programs, glare guards for computer monitors, and drivers to assist with required work-related travel. Older individuals who have hearing impairments may need oral or sign language interpreters, closed captioning to help them understand video training materials, telephone relay services, and auxiliary hearing aids.

Because individuals with age-related disabilities, like people with other types of emerging disabilities, have so often experienced invalidation of their symptoms and negative responses from others to their self-disclosures, they may understandably lack the inclination or self-efficacy to advocate for workplace accommodations from their employers. Hence, there is a compelling need for self-advocacy training to equip older workers with disabilities with the necessary and current skills to effectively request reasonable accommodations, document their disability status, and make formal complaints of employer discrimination. More intensive interventions may directly involve the rehabilitation counselor in facilitating collaborative decision making between the employer and employee, ensuring effective communication among all parties, and establishing a shared commitment to worker productivity and success (Johnson, 2015).

CONCLUSIONS

Due to increased life expectancies and the continued aging of the baby boom gen-eration's 77 million members, the American workforce and American society in general are older than ever before. The number of older people in society will increase exponentially over the next 30 years, and the needs that older people have regarding employment, housing, transportation, and health care pose signif-icant economic and practical challenges for families, friends, and neighbors of our growing elder population.

Not only are people living longer than ever before, population aging has resulted in increases in the incidence and prevalence of disabling conditions such as dementia, diabetes, cancer, stroke, rheumatoid arthritis, heart disease, mobil-ity impairments, visual impairments, and hearing impairments. Beginning in early adulthood, the rate of disability in the American populace increases as a linear function of age, to the extent that nearly all of the growing population of Americans who are over the age of 90 have disabilities that substantially limit their functioning in major life activities.

Older workers with disabilities also face a retirement crisis, which finds them needing to continue working later in life because of financial necessity while at the same time facing chronic health conditions that make it difficult for them to maintain full-time participation in the labor force. Traditional full-time employment may not be an option for older people with disabilities, so they may come to rehabilitation counselors seeking assistance in managing their medical conditions, planning for their future financial and housing needs, accessing quality health care services, arranging formal and informal elder-care, developing effective social support networks, and aging in comfort and with dignity.

Rehabilitation counselors must become familiar with commonly occurring age-related disabilities; understand the interactions among aging, health, and disability and the impact that population aging will have on American society for many years to come; advocate on behalf of older consumers and refer them to elder advocacy and disability advocacy organizations for needed support and consultation; and expand their scope of practice to more thoroughly address the health, wellness, and community living concerns of older Americans. Our parents, grandparents, and great-grandparents have spent their lives supporting our fam-ilies, our communities, and our economy, and they must be able to count on those of us in the succeeding generations to provide the care, comfort, and companion-ship they need in their twilight years.

DISCUSSION QUESTIONS

1. What biases, negative stereotypes, or misconceptions do you have that may inter-fere with your ability to work effectively with consumers with age-related disabil-ities?
2. What do you think are the most critical medical, psychosocial, and/or vocational issues for individuals with age-related disabilities? In your future or current reha-bilitation counseling practice, what can you do to address these issues?

3. What do you need to learn more about to effectively serve consumers with age-related disabilities? What actions can you take to strengthen your knowledge?
4. Discuss and create a list of resources in your local community to address the multifaceted needs of elderly individuals with disabilities.
5. Review and discuss the case of Adaline presented at the beginning of the chapter. What barriers does she face in participating in rehabilitation counseling and achieving a successful outcome? In determining eligibility and service needs, what additional assessments (if any) are needed? How will you go about identifying geriatric specialists to provide these services or educate providers about such practices if none are located in your community? What are considerations for providing counseling and guidance to Adaline and facilitating the rehabilitation planning process? What are potential services you would include in her rehabilitation plan?

REFERENCES

Akushevich, I., Kravchenko, J., Ukraintseva, S., Arbeev, K., & Yashin, A. I. (2013). Age patterns of incidence of geriatric disease in the U.S. elderly population: Medicare-based analysis. *Journal of the American Geriatrics Society, 60*(2), 323–327. doi:10.1111/j.1532-5415.2011.03786.x

Allaire, S. H., Li, W., & LaValley, M. P. (2003). Work barriers experienced and job accommodations used by persons with arthritis and other rheumatic diseases. *Rehabilitation Counseling Bulletin, 46*(3), 147–156.

Alzheimer's Association. (2016). *Alzheimer's disease facts and figures.* Retrieved from http://www.alz.org/facts/overview.asp

American Diabetes Association. (2015). *Statistics about diabetes.* Retrieved from http://www.diabetes.org/diabetes-basics/statistics/?loc=db-slabnav

American Psychological Association. (2014). *Data on behavioral health in the United States.* Retrieved from http://www.apa.org/helpcenter/data-behavioral-health.aspx

American Stroke Association. (2016). *Impact of stroke.* Retrieved from http://www.strokeassociation.org/STROKEORG/AboutStroke/Impact-of-Stroke-Stroke-statistics_UCM_310728_Article.jsp#.Vvh_yPkrJhE

Anderson, G. F., & Hussey, P. S. (2000). Population aging: A comparison among industrialized countries. *Health Affairs, 19*, 191–203.

Arthritis Foundation. (2016). *Rheumatoid arthritis.* Retrieved from http://www.arthritis.org/about-arthritis/types/rheumatoid-arthritis

Atherton, W. L., & Toriello, P. J. (2012). Re-conceptualizing the treatment of substance use disorders: The impact on employment. In P. J. Toriello, M. L. Bishop, & P. D. Rumrill (Eds.), *New directions in rehabilitation counseling: Creative responses to professional, clinical, and educational challenges* (pp. 282–304). Linn Creek, MO: Aspen Professional Services.

Baldwin, D., Johnstone, B., Ge, B., Hewett, J., Smith, M., & Sharp, G. (2012). Randomized prospective study of a work place ergonomic intervention for individuals with rheumatoid arthritis and osteoarthritis. *Arthritis Care & Research, 64*(10), 1527–1535. doi:10.1002/acr.21699

Berlau, D. J., Corrada, M. M., & Kawas, C. (2009). The prevalence of disability in the oldest-old is high and continues to increase with age: Findings from The 90+ Study. *International Journal of Geriatric Psychiatry, 24*(11), 1217–1225. doi:10.1002/gps.2248

Bird, C. E., & Rieker, P. P. (2008). *Gender and health: The effects of constrained choices and social policies.* New York, NY: Cambridge University Press.

Birnbaum, H., Pike, C., Kaufman, R., Maynchenko, M., Kidolezi, Y., & Cifaldi, M. (2010). Societal cost of rheumatoid arthritis patients in the US. *Current Medical Research and Opinion, 26*(1), 77–90. doi:10.1185/03007990903422307

Bouchama, A. (2003). The 2003 European heat wave. *Intensive Care Medicine, 30*, 1–3.

Brown, S. L., & Lin, I. (2012). The gray divorce revolution: Rising divorce among middle-aged and older adults, 1990–2010. *Journals of Gerontology, Series B, 67,* 731–741.

Bujick, B., & Koopmans, R. (2014). Determinants of geriatrics patients' quality of life after stroke rehabilitation. *Aging & Mental Health, 18*(8), 980–985.

Centers for Disease Control and Prevention. (2016a). *Rheumatoid arthritis (RA).* Retrieved from http://www.cdc.gov/arthritis/basics/rheumatoid.htm

Centers for Disease Control and Prevention. (2016b). *Stroke.* Retrieved from http://www.cdc.gov/stroke

Chatterji, S., Byles, J., Cutler, D., Seeman, T., & Verdes, E. (2015). Health, functioning, and disability in older adults—Present status and future implications. *The Lancet, 385,* 563–575.

Cole, H. M., & Fiore, M. C. (2014). The war against tobacco. *JAMA, 311*(2), 131–132.

Coleman, M., Ganong, L. H., Hans, J. D., Sharp, E. A., & Rothrauff, T. C. (2005). Filial obligations in post-divorce stepfamilies. *Journal of Divorce & Remarriage, 43,* 1–27. doi:10.1300/J087v43n03_01

Conroy, B. E., Milani, F., Levine, M., & Stein, J. (2009). Vocational rehabilitation after stroke. In R. L. Harvey, R. F. Macko, J. Stein, C. Winstein, & R. D. Zarowitz (Eds.), *Stroke recovery and rehabilitation* (2nd ed., pp. 735–746). New York, NY: Demos Medical.

Crockatt, S. Y., Targett, P., Cifu, D., & Wehman, P. (2009). Return to work of individuals with arthritis: A review of job performance and retention. *Journal of Vocational Rehabilitation, 30*(2), 121–131.

Crystal, R., & Espinosa, C. T. (2012). Individuals with disabilities and the American healthcare system. In P. J. Toriello, M. L. Bishop, & P. D. Rumrill (Eds.), *New directions in rehabilitation counseling: Creative responses to professional, clinical, and educational challenges* (pp. 140–163). Linn Creek, MO: Aspen Professional Services.

Dominick, K. L., Ahern, F. M., Gold, C. H., & Heller, D. A. (2004). Health-related quality of life among older adults with arthritis. *Health and Quality of Life Outcomes, 25,* 326–331.

Dupre, M. E. (2007). Educational differences in age-related patterns of disease: Reconsidering the cumulative disadvantage and age-as-leveler hypothesis. *Journal of Health and Social Behavior, 48*(1), 1–15.

Falvo, D. R. (2014). *Medical and psychosocial aspects of chronic illness and disability* (5th ed.). Burlington, MA: Jones & Bartlett.

Federal Interagency Forum on Aging-Related Statistics. (2012). *Older Americans 2011: Key indicators of well-being.* Washington, DC: U.S. Government Printing Office.

Freedman, V. A., Aykan, H., Wolf, D. A., & Marcotte, J. E. (2004). Disability and home care dynamics among older unmarried Americans. *Journals of Gerontology, Series B, 59,* S25–33. doi:10.1093/geronb/59.1.S25

Gabriel, S. E., Crowson, C. S., Campion, M. E., & O'Fallon, W. M. (1997). Direct medical costs unique to people with arthritis. *Journal of Rheumatology, 24*(4), 719–725.

Geruso, M. (2012). Black-white disparities in life expectancy: How much can the standard SES variables explain? *Demography, 49*(2), 553–574.

Graffigna, G., Barello, S., Wiederhold, B. K., Bosio, A. C., & Riva, G. (2013). Positive technology as a driver for health engagement. *Annual Review of Cybertherapy and Telemedicine, 191,* 9–17.

Haas, S., & Rohlfsen, L. (2010). Life course determinants of racial and ethnic disparities in functional health trajectories. *Social Science & Medicine, 70,* 240–250.

Hamilton, B. E., Martin, J. A., & Ventura, S. J. (2013). *Births: Preliminary data for 2012.* National Vital Statistics Reports, 62(3). Washington, DC: U.S. Department of Health and Human Services.

Hayward, M. D., Miles T. P., Crimmins, E. M., & Yang, Y. (2000). The significance of socioeconomic status in explaining the racial gap in chronic health conditions. *American Sociological Review, 65*(6), 910–930.

He, W., Sengupta, M., Velkoff, V. A., & DeBarros, K. A. (2005). *65+ in the United States: 2005, Current Population Reports, P23–209.* U.S. Census Bureau and National Institute on Aging.

Hooyman, N. R., Kawamoto, K. Y., & Kiyak, H. A. (2015). *Aging matters: An introduction to social gerontology.* Upper Saddle River, NJ: Pearson.

Hughes, M. J., & Thomas, M. E. (1998). The continuing significance of race revisited: A study of race, class, and quality of life in America, 1972 to 1996. *Annual Sociological Review, 63*, 785–795.

Ipsen, C., Jensen, P. L., & Anderson, V. (2010). Prevention of work-related stress—A participatory approach. In P. Vink & J. Kantola (Eds.), *Advances in occupational, social and organizational ergonomics* (pp. 305–314). Boca Raton, FL: CRC Press.

Job Accommodation Network. (2014). *Workplace accommodations: Low cost, high impact.* Retrieved from http://AskJAN.org/media/lowcosthighimpact.html

Johnson, E. (2015). Perspectives on work for people with epilepsy. In I. Schultz & R. Gatchel (Eds.), *Handbook of return to work: From research to practice* (pp. 617–632). New York, NY: Springer.

Kalb, R. (2012). *Multiple sclerosis: The questions you have, the answers you need* (5th ed.). New York, NY: Demos Medical.

Kawatkar, A. A., Jacobsen, S. J., Levy, G. D., Medhekar, S. S., Venkatasubramaniam, K. V., & Herrinton, L. J. (2012). Direct medical expenditure associated with rheumatoid arthritis in a nationally representative sample from the Medical Expenditure Panel Survey. *Arthritis Care & Research, 64*(11), 1649–1656. doi:10.1002/acr.21755

Kerson, T. S., & Michelsen, R. W. (1995). Counseling homebound clients and their families. *Journal of Gerontological Social Work, 24*, 159–190.

Koch, L., Conyers, L., & Rumrill, P. (2012). The nature and needs of people with emerging disabilities. In P. J. Toriello, M. L. Bishop, & P. D. Rumrill (Eds.), *New directions in rehabilitation counseling: Creative responses to professional, clinical, and educational challenges* (pp. 116–139). Linn Creek, MO: Aspen Professional Services.

Koch, L., Rumrill, P., Hennessey, M., Vierstra, C., & Roessler, R. (2007). An ecological approach to facilitate successful employment outcomes among people with multiple chemical sensitivity. *Work: A Journal of Prevention, Assessment, and Rehabilitation, 29*(4), 341–349.

Levine, M. E., & Crimmins, E. M. (2014). Evidence of accelerated aging among African Americans and its implications for mortality. *Social Science & Medicine, 118*, 27–32. doi:10.1016/j.socscimed.2014.07.022

Liao, Y., Greenlund, K. J., Croft, J. B., Keenan, N. L., & Giles, W. H. (2009). Factors explaining excess stroke prevalence in the US Stroke Belt. *Stroke: A Journal of Cerebral Circulation, 40*(10), 3336–3341. doi:10.1161/STROKEAHA.109.561688

Lin, S., Beck, A. N., Finch, B. K., Hummer, R. A., & Master, R. K. (2012). Trends in US older adult disability: Exploring age, period, and cohort effects. *American Journal of Public Health, 102*(11), 2157–2162. doi:10.2105/AJPH.2011.300602

McCurry, M. K., & Hunter Revell, S. M. (2015). Partners in family caregiving: A conceptual framework. *Journal of Theory Construction & Testing, 19*(1), 21–25.

Min, K., & Min, J. (2015). Health-related quality of life is associated with stroke deficits in older adults. *Age and Ageing, 44*(4), 700–704. doi:10.1093/ageing/afv060

Muennig, P. A., & Glied, S. A. (2010). What changes in survival rates tell us about US health care. *Health Affairs, 29*(11), 2105–2113. doi:10.1377/hlthaff.2010.0073

Myasoedova, E., Crowson, C. S., Kremers, H. M., Therneau, T. M., & Gabriel, S. E. (2010). Is the incidence of rheumatoid arthritis rising? *Arthritis & Rheumatism, 62*(6), 1576–1582. doi:10.1002/art.27425

National Center for Health Statistics. (2015). *Health, United States, 2014: With special feature on adults aged 55–64.* Retrieved from http://www.cdc.gov/nchs/data/hus/hus14.pdf

National Institute of Arthritis and Musculoskeletal and Skin Diseases. (2014). *Fibromyalgia.* Retrieved from http://www.niams.nih.gov/Health_Info/Fibromyalgia/default.aspA

National Institute of Mental Health. (2016). *Depression.* Retrieved from https://www.nimh.nih.gov/health/topics/depression/index.shtml

National Institute on Aging. (2016). *Alzheimer's Disease Education and Referral Center.* Retrieved from https://www.nia.nih.gov/alzheimers

National Stroke Association. (2016). *What is stroke?* Retrieved from http://www.stroke.org/understand-stroke/what-stroke

Prince, M. J., Wu, F., Guo, Y., Gutierrez Robledo, L. M., O'Donnell, M., Sullivan, R., & Yusuf, S. (2015). The burden of disease in older people and its implications for health policy and practice. *The Lancet, 385,* 549–562.

Qualls, S. H. (2000). Therapy with aging families: Rationale, opportunities and challenges. *Aging & Mental Health, 4*(3), 191–199. doi:10.1080/13607860050128210

Read, J. G., & Gorman, B. K. (2010). Gender and health inequality. *Annual Review of Sociology, 36,* 371–386.

Roessler, R. T. (1995). *The Work Experience Survey.* Fayetteville, AR: Arkansas Research and Training Center in Vocational Rehabilitation.

Roessler, R. T., & Rumrill, P. (2015). *Enhancing productivity on your job: The "win-win" approach to reasonable accommodations.* New York, NY: National Multiple Sclerosis Society.

Rubin, S., Roessler, R., & Rumrill, P. (2016). *Foundations of the vocational rehabilitation process* (7th ed.). Austin, TX: Pro-Ed.

Ruderman, E., & Tambar, S. (2013). *Rheumatoid arthritis.* Retrieved from http://www.rheumatology.org/I-Am-A/Patient-Caregiver/Diseases-Conditions/Rheumatoid-Arthritis

Rumrill, P., Fraser, R., & Johnson, K. (2013). Employment and workplace accommodation outcomes among participants in a vocational consultation service for people with multiple sclerosis. *Journal of Vocational Rehabilitation, 39,* 85–90.

Ryan, L. H., Smith, J., Antonucci, T. C., & Jackson, J. J. (2012). Cohort differences in the availability of available caregivers: Are the boomers at risk? *The Gerontologist, 52,* 177–188.

Saeki, S. (2000). Disability management after stroke: Its medical aspects for workplace accommodation. *Disability & Rehabilitation, 22*(13), 578–582. doi:10.1080/09638280050138241

Silverstein, M., & Giarrusso, R. (2010). Aging and family life: A decade review. *Journal of Marriage and Family, 72,* 1039–1058. doi:10.1111/j.1741-3737.2010.00749.x

Simons, W. R., Rosenblatt, L. C., & Trivedi, D. N. (2012). The economic consequences of rheumatoid arthritis: Analysis of Medical Expenditure Panel Survey 2004, 2005, and 2006 data. *Journal of Occupational and Environmental Medicine, 54*(1), 48–55. doi:10.1097/JOM.0b013e31823c13e7

Sinn, J. (2011). *Bridging the longevity gap: Sociologist seeks to increase life expectancy for African Americans, Hispanics.* Austin: University of Texas.

Smart, J. (2009). *Disability, society, and the individual* (2nd ed.). Austin, TX: Pro-Ed.

Strauser, D. (2013). *Career development, employment, and disability in rehabilitation.* New York, NY: Springer Publishing Company.

Stulik, H., & Vollmer, S. (2015). The fertility transition around the world. *Journal of Population Economics, 28*(1), 31–44.

The Commonwealth Fund. (2011). *U.S. health care from a global perspective: Spending, use of services, prices, and health in 13 countries.* Retrieved from http://www.commonwealthfund.org/publications/issue-briefs/2015/oct/us-health-care-from-a-global-perspective

Thompson, H. S., & Ryan, A. (2008). The impact of stroke consequences on spousal relationships from the perspective of the person with stroke. *Journal of Clinical Nursing, 18*(12), 1803–1811. doi:10.1111/j.1365-2702.2008.02694.x

U.S. Census Bureau. (2011). *Statistical abstract of the United States.* Retrieved from https://www.census.gov/library/publications/2011/compendia/statab/131ed.html

Varekamp, I., Haafkens, J. A., Detaille, S. I., Tak, P. P., & van Dijk, F. H. (2005). Preventing work disability among employees with rheumatoid arthritis: What medical professionals can learn from the patients' perspective. *Arthritis and Rheumatism, 53*(6), 965–972.

Vincent, V., & Velkoff, V. (2010). *The next four decades: The older population in the United States: 2010 to 2050.* Washington, DC: U.S. Census Bureau, Current Populations Reports.

Wang, D. (2004). Service delivery and research considerations for the 85+ population. *Journal of Gerontological Social Work, 43*(1), 5–18. doi:10.1300/J083v43n01_02

Wang, Y., Kapellusch, J., & Garg, A. (2014). Important factors influencing the return to work after stroke. *Work: Journal of Prevention, Assessment & Rehabilitation, 47*(4), 553–559.

Wickert, K., Dresden, D., & Rumrill, P. (2013). *The sandwich generation's guide to eldercare.* New York, NY: Demos Health.

Williams, D. R. (2005). The health of U.S. racial and ethnic populations. *Journals of Gerontology, Series B, 60*, 53–62.

Williams, D. R., & Harris-Reid, M. (1999). Race and mental health: Emerging patterns and promising approaches. In A. Horwitz & T. Scheid (Eds.), *A handbook for the study of mental health* (pp. 295–314). Cambridge, MA: Cambridge University Press.

Williams, D. R., & Jackson, B. P. (2005). Social sources of racial disparities in health. *Health Affairs, 24*, 325–334.

Williams, D. R., & Mohammed, S. A. (2009). Discrimination and racial disparities in health: Evidence and needed research. *Journal of Behavioral Medicine, 32*, 20–47.

Wolff, J. L., & Kasper, J. D. (2006). Caregivers of frail elders: Updating a national profile. *The Gerontologist, 46*, 344–356. doi:10.1093/geront/46.3.344

Zhang, Y., Chapman, A., Plested, M., Jackson, D., & Purroy, F. (2012). The incidence, prevalence, and mortality of stroke in France, Germany, Italy, Spain, the UK, and the US: A literature review. *Stroke Research & Treatment, 24*, 1–11. doi:10.1155/2012/436125

FIVE

Emerging Populations and Issues in Psychiatric Rehabilitation

Coauthored by Stephanie L. Lusk

CHAPTER OBJECTIVES

■ *Examine the medical, psychosocial, and vocational characteristics, challenges, and rehabilitation needs of emerging populations of individuals with psychiatric disabilities*

■ *Introduce a recovery-oriented approach to providing responsive services to individuals with psychiatric disabilities*

■ *Explore integrated, evidence-based and emerging practices to facilitate better recovery and rehabilitation outcomes for these populations*

CASE ILLUSTRATION: MAYA

Maya is a 39-year-old biracial (African American/White) female with a history of anxiety, depression, alcohol abuse, and nicotine dependence that dates back to her early adolescence. Maya graduated from high school and entered college with hopes of completing a business degree and then going to graduate school to get an MBA. However, she spent her evenings partying instead of studying, stopped going to classes, and received poor grades. She was dismissed for poor academic performance after the first semester of her sophomore year. Since her dismissal from college, she has held sporadic minimum wage jobs, but none of these jobs lasted long because she either stopped showing up for work or was terminated due to poor attendance, coming to work intoxicated, or not getting along with coworkers.

Maya has spent the majority of her adult life on the streets, in and out of homeless shelters, or living with abusive boyfriends. She has been arrested on multiple occasions for misdemeanor charges (i.e., public intoxication, disorderly conduct, petty theft, driving under the influence) and one felony charge (i.e., burglary and assault) that was dropped. Although she has made numerous attempts to stop drinking on her own, she has never been able to maintain sobriety for an extended length of time either because her living situation was too unstable and/or because her symptoms of anxiety and depression resurfaced. All of her family members live out of state, and she has not kept in contact with any of them except for her mother who occasionally sends her money and pays bonds for her release from jail.

A little over a year ago, Maya left an abusive relationship and was back on the streets. She indicates that this was her "dropping off point," and feeling completely hopeless and suicidal, she admitted herself into a county hospital where she detoxed for 5 days and was then admitted into a 90-day integrated treatment program operated by a local community mental health center. In the treatment program, she was diagnosed and treated for generalized anxiety disorder, major depressive disorder, and alcoholism. While in the program, she also applied for and received health insurance through the county. After completing the program, she entered a transitional county-run shelter/treatment program for single women with substance use disorders (SUDs), psychiatric disabilities, and other issues that interfered with living independently in the community. She underwent a complete medical and psychological assessment in the transitional program and worked with a case manager to develop a plan for transitioning to independent living. Her plan included maintaining sobriety, attending daily AA meetings, adhering to psychotropic medications, and finding employment.

She has now been sober for a year, adheres to treatment for her anxiety and depression, attends daily AA meetings, and reports that she feels happier and healthier than she can ever remember. She still lives in the transitional shelter and has been employed part-time for the past 4 months at a convenience store, but she does not see herself continuing in this line of work on a long-term basis. She is saving money for deposit on an apartment and has reestablished communications with several family members. For the first time ever, she feels optimistic about her future. Her goals are to get her own apartment, quit smoking, and return to college to complete a degree that will prepare her for a professional occupation that provides medical benefits.

Mental illness represents one of the leading causes of disability in the world. In the United States alone, approximately 43.6 million adults (18.1% of the populace) experienced some form of mental illness in 2014 (Substance Abuse and Mental Health Services Administration [SAMHSA], 2015). Mental illness is the leading cause of disability in the United States for individuals ages 15 to 44, and nearly half of those with a psychiatric disability meet the criteria for two or more mental disorders (National Institute of Mental Health [NIMH], 2008). Depression is the leading cause of disability worldwide, with global estimates indicating that more than 350 million people of all ages have depression (WHO, 2012).

SAMHSA (2015) reported that in 2014 approximately 9.8 million adults (4.1%) in the United States had a serious mental illness (SMI). SMI is defined as "having, at any time during the past year, a diagnosable mental, behavior, or emotional disorder that causes serious functional impairment that substantially interferes with or limits one or more major life activities" (SAMHSA, 2015, para. 7). SMI results in significant impairment in role functioning, enormous loss of human productivity, and has been estimated to cost the nation $193 billion in lost earnings alone

(Kessler et al., 2008; Mojtabai, 2011). Because the onset of SMI typically occurs in adolescence and young adulthood, disruptions to the completion of normal developmental tasks such as graduating from high school, living independently in the community, obtaining postsecondary training, and establishing a career pathway often occur and can result in long-term unemployment, underemployment, and limited career prospects (Becker, Martin, Wajeeh, Ward, & Shern, 2002; Davis, 2015). In fact, it has been estimated that more than 80% of individuals with SMI are unemployed, despite the fact that they desire competitive employment (Cook, 2006).

Although many individuals with psychiatric disabilities do not receive treatment, over the past few decades, an increase has occurred in the numbers of individuals seeking mental health services (Mojtabai, 2011). Typically these individuals receive treatment in primary care settings as opposed to mental health settings. Likewise, between the years 1987 and 2007, a twofold increase occurred in the numbers of individuals receiving disability payments for psychiatric conditions. In 2009, Drake, Skinner, Bond, and Goldman reported that people with psychiatric disabilities were the largest and most rapidly growing subgroup of individuals receiving Social Security benefits. These percentages are anticipated to continue growing because people with psychiatric disabilities tend to be diagnosed at younger ages than other Social Security beneficiaries and remain on Social Security rolls longer.

Although the demand for public mental health services continues to increase, massive cuts in mental health funding have severely restricted the ability of individuals with SMI to access these services. Services have been, and continue to be, cut across the spectrum of supports needed by individuals with psychiatric disabilities including crisis intervention, case management, employment, peer support, prescription medications, housing, day services, clinic services, workforce development, state acute inpatient hospitalization, and state long-term hospitalization (National Alliance on Mental Illness [NAMI], 2011). These funding cuts have shifted responsibility for service provision to emergency departments, community hospitals, law enforcement agencies, correctional facilities, and homeless shelters—all of which are ill-equipped to adequately respond to the mental health and psychiatric rehabilitation needs of this growing consumer population. Subsequently, adverse consequences such as frequent visits to emergency departments, hospitalizations, homelessness, use of illicit substances to self-medicate, involvement in juvenile and criminal justice systems, loss of critical developmental years, shortened life spans, and suicide are all too common among individuals with SMI. Rehabilitation counselors across employment settings are also experiencing an increasing demand for services from consumers with psychiatric disabilities. Rosenthal, Dalton, and Gervey (2007) found that individuals with psychiatric disabilities represented 32.2% of the sample in the Rehabilitation Services Administration 2001 Case Service Report, making them the largest disability group served during that fiscal year. Despite the considerable demand for services, vocational rehabilitation (VR) consumers with psychiatric disabilities who do receive services are less likely to achieve competitive employment outcomes than those with other disabilities. Among consumers with psychiatric disabilities who do achieve competitive outcomes, these tend to be low-paying, entry-level jobs without opportunities for career advancement (Cook, 2006). Rosenthal et al. (2007, p. 358) observed that "rehabilitation professionals trained in traditional rehabilitation counseling programs may not be equipped with the skills necessary to meet the challenges" presented by individuals with psychiatric disabilities. Likewise, Lee, Chan, Chronister, Chan, and Romero (2009, p. 11), suggested that "the increasing demand and complexity for rehabilitation counselors in serving people with psychiatric disability may not reflect an adequate training in this area." Thus, there appears to be a considerable demand for more focused preparation of rehabilitation counselors to partner with consumers who have psychiatric disabilities to assist them to "establish and re-establish career pathways, to reduce exclusion from mainstream society, and to increase prospects for equitable social and economic participation" (Waghorn & Lloyd, 2005, p. 4).

Emerging developments in the field of rehabilitation counseling such as the merger of the Council on Rehabilitation Education (CORE) and the Council for Accreditation of Counseling and Related Educational Programs (CACREP) and the newly adopted Clinical Rehabilitation Counseling (CIRC) Standards will expand opportunities for rehabilitation counselors to provide services to individuals with psychiatric disabilities in nontraditional settings (Koch, Carey, & Lusk, 2016). Because of their unique set of knowledge and skills, rehabilitation counselors can play a pivotal role in improving recovery and employment outcomes for individuals with psychiatric disabilities. However, additional knowledge regarding emerging and underserved populations of individuals with psychiatric disabilities is needed, as are adjustments to traditional service delivery approaches to better serve these populations.

YOUTHS AND YOUNG ADULTS WITH PSYCHIATRIC DISABILITIES

The number of youths and young adults with psychiatric disabilities is growing, with estimates indicating that 13% to 20% of American children and youths have a serious emotional disturbance (SAMHSA, 2015). Serious emotional disturbance is defined by SAMHSA (2015, para. 8) as a term that refers to "children and youth who have had a diagnosable mental, behavioral, or emotional disorder in the past year, which resulted in functional impairment that substantially interferes with or limits the child's role or functioning in family, school, or community activities."

Davis (2015) reported that serious emotional disturbance is especially high among youths who reside in low-income households and who receive public services. Other vulnerabilities include homelessness with 45% to 65% of homeless youths and young adults estimated to have a psychiatric disability; foster care with 50% of youths and young adults with foster care involvement estimated to have a psychiatric disability; and juvenile justice or corrections involvement with 50% of youths and 60% of young adults involved in these systems estimated to have a psychiatric disability (Walker & Gowen, 2011). The onset of approximately half of all lifetime cases of mental illness occurs by age 14, and research findings indicate that bodily changes that lead to mental illness often occur long before symptoms first appear (NIMH, 2015). The rates of diagnosis of serious emotional disturbance in children and youths are on the rise (Perou et al., 2013). For example, although the onset of bipolar disorder typically occurs in late adolescence to early adulthood, recent research has documented sharp increases in the diagnosis of bipolar disorder in children (Birmaher, 2013).

Despite the trend toward earlier diagnosis and treatment to preclude the development of a more severe course of illness, many youths still go undiagnosed and untreated for years. In children, it is difficult to distinguish normal developmental changes from symptoms of early onset psychiatric disabilities (NIMH, 2015). Diagnosis can also be challenging because children often express symptoms of psychiatric disabilities differently than adults and adolescents. For example, whereas adults with depression often exhibit sadness, children are more likely to express irritability (Mayo Clinic, 2015). Children are also more likely to exhibit headaches and stomachaches rather than anxiety and sadness and are often unable to express their thoughts and feelings. Examples of potential warning signs of childhood-onset psychiatric disabilities include functional difficulties or severe mood swings that cause problems at home, school, and in interactions with peers; appetite or sleep disturbances; feelings of persistent sadness, tearfulness, and social withdrawal that last for more than 2 weeks; returning to earlier developmental behaviors such as bed wetting; overwhelming worries and fears that interfere with daily activities; trouble focusing that leads to poor performance in school; drastic behavioral changes such as frequent fighting, dangerous or out-of-control behavior, using weapons, and expressing a desire to harm others; self-injury or destructive behaviors such as head banging; recurrent thoughts of death, suicidal thoughts, or attempts; and using drugs or alcohol to cope with feelings (Mayo Clinic, 2015; NIMH, 2015). Parents may not know where to turn if their child exhibits unusual behaviors and symptoms or they may resist seeking help for their child because of the stigma attached to mental illness, concerns about medications, and the cost and logistical challenges of accessing treatment (Mayo Clinic, 2015). Consequently, young people living with psychiatric disabilities do not receive treatment, on average, until 8 to 10 years after the onset of symptoms (NAMI, 2011).

The onset of psychiatric disabilities occurs during critical years when major changes are occurring in the areas of identity formation and cognitive, psychosocial, psychosexual, and career development (Davis, 2015). Davis noted that during these years, youths and young adults are also in the process of engaging in important developmental tasks in preparation for functioning as mature adults. These tasks include completing schooling and training, obtaining and maintaining rewarding work, developing an adult social network, becoming financially self-sufficient, and starting families. Although these tasks are equally important for youths and young adults with psychiatric disabilities as they are for other youths, substantial functional impairments in family relations, social skills, peer relations, school, work, community engagement, and activities of daily living are often present. In addition, psychosocial, cognitive, moral, social, and identity formation development is often delayed for youths and young adults with psychiatric disabilities. Likewise, role functioning for these youths can be compromised. Youths with psychiatric disabilities experience a risk of dropping out of high school that is six times greater than it is for youths without psychiatric disabilities (Davis, 2015). These youths are also at a high risk for dropping out of college, unemployment, engaging in criminal activities, and becoming involved in the juvenile justice system (Davis, 2015; Walker & Gowen, 2011). They are more likely to become parents at a young age and to have had experiences in the child welfare system. Furthermore, in comparison to their peers without psychiatric disabilities, they are at greater risk for co-occurring SUDs, poverty, homelessness, and institutionalization (Davis, 2015). They are also less likely than youths with other disabilities to participate in individualized educational and transition planning processes to prevent these unfavorable outcomes. In fact, Davis (2015) noted that the majority of students with psychiatric disabilities do not receive special education services. Wagner and Davis (2006) reported that among those students who did have transition plans, 16% did not attend their last transition meeting and 27% attended meetings but did not participate at all.

Systems barriers in transitioning from child services to adult services are also problematic. In particular, lack of continuity between child and adult systems contributes to a decrease in service utilization among transition-age groups. Criteria for adult services are more restrictive than they are for child services. As a result, many youths with psychiatric disabilities discontinue treatment at the age of 18 and are disenrolled from Medicaid (Davis, 2015). They may not apply for VR services because of distrust of adults and prior negative experiences with service providers. Compounding their distrust, adult service providers are not always sufficiently trained in the developmental aspects of adolescence and emerging adulthood. Furthermore, the stigma of seeking treatment is pronounced among transition-aged youth. In addition, the receipt of SSI may act as a barrier to employment if they fail to participate in employment to maintain their cash benefits and Medicaid eligibility (Burke-Miller, Razzano, Grey, Blyler, & Cook, 2012). In recent years, growing attention has been focused on the failure of existing mental health and related services to effectively respond to the needs of youths and young adults with serious mental health conditions (Walker & Gowen, 2011). Areas in which supports and services are lacking for these youths include employment services, education, housing, community integration, mentoring, peer supports, and development of social supports.

COLLEGE STUDENTS WITH PSYCHIATRIC DISABILITIES

In the Association for University and College Counseling Center Directors 2011–2012 Annual Survey, 95% of college counseling center directors indicated that the number of students with significant psychological problems is a growing concern for centers that do not have adequate staff or resources to appropriately serve these students (Mistler, Reetz, Krylowicz, & Barr, 2013). In a 2008 survey, the vast majority of college counseling center directors who responded to the survey indicated greater usage of counseling services by college students and a need among these students for a longer duration of treatment. Additionally, 70% of survey respondents reported an increase within the past year of the numbers of students receiving counseling services who had severe psychological problems (Byrd & McKinney, 2012).

This population influx can be attributed to the increasing demand for a postsecondary degree as a prerequisite for employment and to the expansion of legislation that has empowered students with psychiatric disabilities to attend college (Boutin & Accordino, 2011). Other factors that may contribute to this growth in enrollment of college students with psychiatric disabilities include an increase in the number of individuals being diagnosed with a psychiatric disability in the general population, advances in pharmacological treatment procedures, the increased potential for rehabilitation and recovery of individuals with psychiatric disabilities, and changes in public and professional perceptions about mental illness (Eudaly, 2002; Hartley, 2013; Kiuhara & Huefner, 2008; Megivern, Pellerito, & Mowbray, 2003).

Despite increasing enrollments in postsecondary institutions, it has been esti-mated that as many as 86% of students with psychiatric disabilities drop out of college in comparison to 45% of students in the general population (Salzer, 2012). Students with psychiatric disabilities face unique challenges in succeeding in post-secondary institutions. Psychiatric symptoms can interfere with areas of function-ing (e.g., motivation, concentration, social interactions) that are fundamental to academic success; medication side effects can interfere with attention, concentra-tion, and stamina; and the episodic nature of psychiatric disabilities makes aca-demic planning difficult (Belch, 2011; Boutin & Accordino, 2011; Hartley, 2013). At larger universities, barriers may also include higher academic pressure, less academic support, possible social isolation, and long-term financial debt (Hartley, 2013).

Although academic accommodations and other postsecondary supports are available to facilitate their success, many students with psychiatric disabil-ities do not avail themselves of these services. They may be unaware of avail-able university resources or fail to request classroom accommodations because they do not self-identify as persons with disabilities (Koch, Mamiseishvili, & Higgins, 2014). Fears of being stigmatized by faculty and peers may further pre-vent students from disclosing their need for classroom accommodations (Boutin & Accordino, 2011; Kiuhara & Huefner, 2008; Rehfuss & Quillin, 2005; Weiner & Weiner, 1996). This lack of utilization of available services coupled with the unavailability of more intensive supports may, in part, account for the high rates of students with psychiatric disabilities who fail to complete their degrees (Collins & Mowbray, 2005). Limited participation of students with psychiatric disabilities in academic and social activities could serve as an additional fac-tor that negatively impacts persistence because research has demonstrated that students who feel actively engaged in the academic and social aspects of post-secondary education are more likely than those who do not to persist to degree completion (Koch et al., 2014).

INDIVIDUALS WITH PSYCHIATRIC DISABILITIES AND CO-OCCURRING MEDICAL CONDITIONS

In comparison to the general population, people with SMI have poorer overall physical health. They experience consistently elevated rates of obesity, cardiovas-cular and gastrointestinal disorders, osteoporosis, epilepsy, human immunodefi-ciency virus (HIV), and pulmonary diseases (Gill, Murphy, Zechner, Swarbrick, & Spagnolo, 2009; Jones et al., 2004). Individuals with SMI often have co-occurring SUDs that contribute to their overall poorer health. They are more than twice as likely as individuals without SMI to smoke cigarettes and to be obese (Insel, 2011). Additionally, because individuals with SMI tend to be heavy smokers, they are exposed to more toxins from cigarettes than the average smoker (Gill et al., 2009). It is also more challenging for individuals with SMI to quit smoking because doing so can exacerbate their psychiatric symptoms.

In 2004, Jones et al. examined Medicaid claim forms to determine prevalence, severity, and co-occurrence of chronic physical health problems in a sample of 147 individuals with SMI. An astonishing 75% of their sample had a Medicaid-documented chronic health condition, and 50% had two or more chronic health conditions. Pulmonary disease was the most prevalent chronic health condition, affecting 31% of the sample. Colton and Manderscheid (2006) examined mortality statistics from eight states and found that, in comparison to the general population, individuals with SMI died 14 to 32 years earlier. The average life expectancy for individuals with SMI ranged from 49 to 60 years of age in comparison to the average life expectancy of the general population of 77.9 years. With respect to the early mortality of individuals with psychiatric disabilities, Insel (2011, para. 1) commented that:

> It would appear that the increase in longevity experienced by the general U.S. population over the past half century has been lost on those with serious mental illness (SMI). In fact, this drop in life expectancy due to mental illness would surpass the health disparities reported for most racial or ethnic groups. Yet this population is rarely identified as an under-served or at-risk group in surveys of the social determinants of health.

A variety of risk factors have been identified as potential contributors to the poor health of individuals with SMI. Psychotropic medications that ameliorate the symptoms of mental illness, especially the atypical antipsychotics, can cause health problems for individuals taking these medications (Gill et al., 2009). A serious and potentially life-threatening condition associated with these medications is metabolic syndrome. Metabolic syndrome is "a cluster of conditions—increased blood pressure, a high blood sugar level, excess body fat around the waist and abnormal cholesterol levels—that occur together, increasing your risk for heart disease, stroke, and diabetes" (Mayo Clinic, 2014, para. 1). Both disease-related and non–disease-related factors increase risk for metabolic syndrome. Disease-related risk factors include adverse metabolic side effects of antipsychotic medications that can cause weight gain and result in adverse changes in the metabolism of glucose and lipids (Newcomer, 2007). Metabolic syndrome has been found to be highly prevalent in individuals with schizophrenia, especially women (McEvoy et al., 2005). Non–disease-related risk factors for metabolic syndrome include substance abuse, smoking, lack of exercise, and poor diet (Gill et al., 2009). Individuals with schizophrenia are more likely to be obese, and this obesity is often a side effect of antipsychotic medications. These individuals are also more likely to be poor, have poor nutrition, and to lack access to health care. Long-term use of psychotropic medications can also result in oral complications such as tooth decay, periodontal disease, and gum disease resulting from "dry mouth" (Gill et al., 2009). Major depressive disorder has been associated with increased risk for cardiovascular disease and stroke (Insel, 2011). Risk factors that are associated with increased rates of cardiovascular disease in individuals with major depressive disorder include poor diet, a sedentary lifestyle, low adherence to treatment, and elevated inflammatory factors.

Access to preventive health care and early intervention is a problematic issue for people with psychiatric disabilities and co-occurring chronic illnesses, many of whom do not have the resources to obtain this care. These individuals often do not have medical insurance and may lack transportation to get to appointments (Gill et al., 2009). They are less likely than the general population to receive primary care services, routine testing, dental care, and early screening for preventive illnesses such as cancer and cardiovascular disease. Additionally, the side effects of psychotropic medications often go untreated or inadequately treated. Many individuals with psychiatric disabilities receive their health care in emergency departments and intensive care units and not until their secondary conditions create medical crises. Conversely, when individuals seek medical treatment for physical symptoms from primary physicians, their symptoms may be dismissed and attributed to their psychiatric disability. Compounding this problem, individuals with psychiatric disabilities experience many barriers to patient self-advocacy that impair their ability to effectively communicate with health care providers about their health concerns. For example, they often have low health literacy (i.e., "the capacity to obtain, process, and understand basic health information and services needed to make appropriate health decisions" [Committee on Health Literacy, 2004, p. 32]) and lack the knowledge and the self-efficacy to lead a healthy lifestyle (Gill et al., 2009). Additional barriers include feelings of hopelessness, more severe symptoms, perceptions of a power imbalance between physicians and patients, and fears of challenging providers or wasting their time (Jonikas et al., 2013). Swarbrick and Nemec (2016) noted that poor health among individuals with psychiatric disabilities negatively impacts their ability to pursue education; participate in employment; become financially self-sufficient; and be productive, contributing members of their communities. Poor health also undermines their ability to actively participate in rehabilitation planning. Psychiatric symptoms can be exacerbated by untreated co-occurring medical conditions and prevent individuals from achieving successful rehabilitation outcomes. The risk factors and health care disparities experienced by people with psychiatric disabilities, in combination with "service fragmentation among the mental health and medical service delivery systems, are associated with increased barriers to goal attainment, significantly reduced quality of life, and early mortality" (Gill et al., 2009, p. 32).

INDIVIDUALS WITH PSYCHIATRIC DISABILITIES AND CO-OCCURRING SUBSTANCE USE DISORDERS

Substance use disorders (SUDs) often co-occur with psychiatric disabilities. SAMHSA (2015) reported that in 2014, 7.9 million individuals had both a mental illness and SUD. Co-occurring disorders (CODs) include "any combination of two or more SUDs and mental disorders identified in the *Diagnostic and Statistical Manual of Mental Disorders*, Fifth Edition (*DSM-5*)" (SAMHSA, 2015, para. 14). Because of the prevalence of CODs, professionals providing treatment and rehabilitation services to individuals with psychiatric disabilities are advised to treat CODs as the rule rather than the exception in this population (Lusk, Koch, & Paul, 2016). Failure to address both conditions simultaneously is highly likely to impede the ability of individuals with CODs to achieve their recovery and rehabilitation goals. However, it is often difficult to disentangle overlapping symptoms in order to make accurate diagnoses and treatment decisions (National Institute on Drug Abuse [NIDA], 2010). Symptoms of psychiatric disabilities and SUDs can overlap and mimic each other; therefore, the diagnosis of COD requires that all drug and alcohol use be ceased before any other disorder is diagnosed. Symptoms of mood, anxiety, and psychotic or personality disorders may cease when the substance has cleared the individual's system. If this occurs, a diagnosis of a psychiatric condition is not made, and treatment is provided for the SUD alone.

Among individuals who seek treatment for SUDs, research studies indicate that anywhere from 15% to 50% have experienced major depressive disorder at some point in their lives. Furthermore, estimates of alcohol abuse among people with bipolar disorder are as high as 98% (Goodwin & Jamison, 2007; McDonald & Meyer, 2011). Goodwin et al. (2002) reported that approximately 18% of individuals with SUDs have at least one anxiety disorder, and among those seeking treatment for alcohol use disorders, rates of co-occurring anxiety are as high as 69%. These researchers have also observed higher rates of cocaine, sedative, and opioid use among individuals with co-occurring mood and anxiety disorders. Among individuals with schizophrenia, an estimated 33.7% also have co-occurring alcohol use disorders and nearly half meet the criteria for any SUD. Estimates of the rate of nicotine use among individuals with schizophrenia indicate that it is three times higher than it is in the general population (Nunes, Selzer, Levounis, & Davies, 2010). High rates of SUDs are also found among individuals with posttraumatic stress disorder (PTSD), antisocial personality disorder, and borderline personality disorder.

In considering why SUDs so frequently co-occur with psychiatric disabilities, several potential explanations have been postulated by researchers (NIDA, 2010). First, the abuse of drugs and alcohol can result in symptoms of psychiatric disabilities. The increased risk of psychosis in some cannabis users is evidence for this explanation. Second, individuals with psychiatric disabilities may abuse drugs and alcohol as a form of self-medication for their psychiatric symptoms. This explanation is supported by the high rate of tobacco use among individuals with schizophrenia. Use of tobacco products is believed to lessen the symptoms of schizophrenia and improve cognition. Psychiatric disabilities and substance use disorders involve similar brain regions as well as overlapping genetic vulnerabilities. Finally, individuals with psychiatric disabilities often have lower thresholds for experiencing the harmful effects of substances (Lusk et al., 2016).

Risk factors for developing CODs are numerous and include earlier age at onset of psychiatric disabilities; childhood physical or sexual abuse (Norman, Byambaa, Butchart, Scott, & Vos, 2012); difficulties at school (Thompson, Connelly, Thomas-Jones, & Eggert, 2013); environmental and pharmacological factors (Lusk, 2013; Perreau-Lenz & Spanagel, 2015); increased risk for psychiatric symptoms during detoxification from substances (Johnson, Brems, Mills, & Fisher, 2007); poverty (Knight et al., 2014); unemployment or problems at work (Thomas & Fraser, 2009); isolation or lack of a social network; lack of decent housing (Knight et al., 2014); family dysfunction (Leslie, 2008; Lusk, 2013); family history of psychiatric disability, substance abuse, or CODs; and past or ongoing trauma or abuse (Lusk, 2013).

Individuals with CODs face multiple barriers to independent living, community integration, and employment. These barriers include a lack of training and employment history (Magura & Staines, 2004); lack of education (Frounfelker, Wilkniss, Bond, Devitt, & Drake, 2011); attendance inconsistencies and work rates at approximately 75% capacity (SAMHSA, 2000); legal problems that may have resulted from supporting the substance use habit, lack of transportation, and unmet child care needs (Zanis, Coviello, Alterman, & Appling, 2001); and medical and emotional barriers (Matthews, Harris, Jaworski, Alam, & Bozdag, 2013).

Despite the positive impact of employment on treatment retention, continued recovery success, and other outcomes (e.g., enhanced self-esteem, increased personal empowerment, reduced clinical symptoms, decreased social isolation, improved quality of life, financial gains, improved mental health; Lusk et al., 2016; Dunn, Wewiorski, & Rogers, 2008; Waghorn & Lloyd, 2005), VR services are not incorporated into treatment programs to the degree that they should be, and unemployment and underemployment remain high within this population. Those who are employed tend to work in positions that are temporary and provide very low pay and little to no benefits (Becker, Whitley, Bailey, & Drake, 2007). In addition to the challenges these individuals face in securing employment, they also face barriers to treatment because very few treatment programs exist that concurrently treat substance use disorders and mental health conditions (Lusk et al., 2016). Consequently, rates of relapse are high.

Individuals with CODs are also underrepresented in the VR system. In fact, in a 2009 study, Donnell, Mizelle, and Zheng found that only 3% of a sample of 8,818 VR consumers had CODs. In considering possible reasons for the low representation of these individuals in the VR system, the researchers offered two plausible explanations: (a) they are not being identified because of challenges the VR system faces in the screening and assessment of SUDs, and (b) they are not applying for and accessing services because of a lack of a "recovery-themed platform" (Donnell et al., 2009, p. 47) within the VR system. Two additional plausible explanations include (a) the widespread perception that individuals with CODs are unemployable, and (b) written or unwritten policies indicating that they must be able to demonstrate a period of abstinence before they can be determined eligible for services (Becker, Drake, & Naughton, 2005).

PSYCHIATRIC DISABILITIES AND CORRECTIONS INVOLVEMENT

In a report by NAMI (2010, p. 1), the authors indicated that,

> with the decrease in inpatient psychiatric beds and declines in the availability of community mental health services, people with serious mental illness frequently go without the treatment and services they need. When someone experiences a psychiatric crisis or acts out as a result of symptoms of their illness, often police are the first-line responders, and jails and prisons are increasingly used to house these individuals.

Relatedly, Osher, D'Amora, Plotkin, Jarrett, and Eggleston (2012, p. 1) noted that "large numbers of adults with mental health and substance use disorders are churning through the nation's criminal justice, behavioral health, and social supports systems, often with poor—even tragic—individual, public health, and community safety results."

Bernacchio and Burker (2016) cited estimates indicating that the U.S. criminal justice system annually places more than 300,000 people with SMI in prisons and jails that are neither equipped nor staffed to respond to the unique challenges of this population. Research on the federal corrections population suggests that about 15.2% of the entire federal offender population needs some level of mental health services and approximately 9.3% have a history of inpatient psychiatric care (Magaletta, Diamond, Faust, Daggett, & Camp, 2009). Approximately one third of offenders who have SMI are estimated to also have an SUD (Bernacchio & Burker, 2016).

Individuals with psychiatric disabilities are more likely to be arrested for minor, nonviolent offenses that are often displays of their psychiatric symptoms rather than true crimes. These offenses are usually misdemeanors (e.g., public vagrancy, trespassing) or drug offenses (Bernacchio & Burker, 2016). Individuals who are arrested are often homeless and are not receiving treatment for their psychiatric disabilities. In fact, it has been estimated that ten times as many people with psychiatric disabilities are incarcerated in American prisons and jails as are treated in mental health facilities (National Sheriffs' Association and Treatment Advocacy Center, 2014). Those most at risk for incarceration include individuals with psychiatric disabilities who were diagnosed at a young age, those who experienced dysfunction in their families, and individuals who experienced early childhood trauma. Additional risk factors include substance use disorders, homelessness, physical and/or sexual abuse histories, living in foster homes, and growing up with parents with substance use disorders and/or incarceration histories (James & Glaze, 2006). Rates of psychiatric disability are also higher for incarcerated women than they are for incarcerated men in both prisons and jails. Steadman, Osher, Robbins, Case, and Samuels (2009) found an SMI rate of 14.5% for male offenders and 31% for female offenders in two jails in Maryland and three jails in New York. Even more alarming, estimates have indicated that as many as 66% of boys and 74% of girls in the juvenile justice system meet criteria for at least one mental illness (NAMI, 2010).

Prisons and jails are highly stressful environments that can create or exacerbate psychiatric conditions. In comparison to those in the general corrections population, inmates with psychiatric disabilities are at increased risk of being victimized by other inmates, seeing others being victimized, and experiencing traumatic interactions with inmates or staff (Torrey et al., 2014). Jail and prison staffs are inadequately trained in mental health issues and may subject those with SMI to routine neglect, humiliation, and/or abuse. These inmates often experience a sense of social isolation and abandonment from family. Exacerbation of psychiatric symptoms is, in many cases, the result of this lack of social connection and can cause maladaptive behaviors that put these individuals at risk of rule violations that result in harsh disciplinary sanctions. Because of overcrowded facilities and the increasing numbers of individuals with psychiatric disabilities who are incarcerated, inmates with psychiatric disabilities are far too often housed in punitive segregation units where they are subjected to solitary confinement, and mental health services provided to these individuals while in solitary confinement are limited (Metzner & Fellner, 2010). Solitary confinement involves isolation, extensive use of surveillance and security controls, the absence of ordinary social interaction, abnormal stimuli, and unstructured days that can have serious psychological consequences. Inmates with psychiatric disabilities who are confined for prolonged periods can experience sleep and appetite disturbances, anxiety, panic, hopelessness, depression, rage, loss of control, paranoia, hallucinations, self-mutilation, and suicidal ideation (NAMI, 2016). Suicide rates are also higher in incarcerated populations of individuals with psychiatric disabilities than they are in the general population of incarcerated individuals.

Although correctional facilities are mandated to provide psychiatric treatment to individuals with psychiatric disabilities, this treatment is often inadequate because of overcrowding in jails and prisons and lack of sufficient funding to provide effective diagnosis, treatment, and monitoring of psychiatric conditions (Bernacchio & Burker, 2016). Likewise, educational and vocational training are not implemented in jails and prisons as widely as they should be (American Psychological Association, 2014). State and local governments face budget deficits that reduce community services, especially mental health. At the same time, corrections is grappling with growing jail populations, with increased substance use offenses among the adult psychiatric population (Bernacchio & Burker, 2016).

Going on probation and returning to their communities create additional stress and complex problems that are difficult to treat in traditional community-based mental health settings. People with psychiatric disabilities returning to their communities after release from jails confront a multitude of barriers that must be ameliorated to effectively manage their psychiatric disabilities, adhere to treatment, actively engage in mental health services, and pursue and secure meaningful employment. These barriers include lack of education; limited job skills; poor work history; employer reluctance to hire ex-offenders because of state statutes; legal issues; family problems; unstable housing; concerns about employee violence, theft, and other workplace issues; the stigma associated with being an ex-offender; substance abuse histories; co-occurring substance use disorders; history of emotional, physical, or sexual abuse; poor continuity of care; unstable housing; homelessness; and loss of medical and social entitlements (Bernacchio & Burker, 2016; Holzer, Raphael, & Stoll, 2003; Kethineni & Falcone, 2007; Shivy, Wu, Moon, Mann, Holland, & Eacho, 2007; Zelenev et al., 2013).

Once released, these individuals often experience difficulties with the cumbersome process of reestablishing Medicare, Medicaid, and Social Security benefits (Bernacchio & Burker, 2016). A high rate of discontinuation of the treatment provided in correctional settings is also problematic because individuals do not believe they need treatment or they cannot afford the costs of medication. Ex-offenders with psychiatric disabilities face double discrimination in obtaining low-income housing and securing employment (Rich et al., 2001). As a result, they have a high rate of recidivism. Additionally, Shivy et al. (2007) reported that about one third of offenders are unemployed prior to incarceration, and pre-incarceration unemployment has been identified as a major risk factor for both postrelease unemployment and recidivism. Among ex-offenders who do obtain employment after release from correctional facilities, most are employed in low-paid, low-skill positions (Holzer et al., 2003; Kethineni & Falcone, 2007). Barriers to employment and community integration are compounded when ex-offenders are individuals with psychiatric disabilities. Research has documented that the same factors (e.g., poverty, homelessness, unemployment, release into environments where illegal activity is the norm, SUDs) that contribute to recidivism in the general corrections population contribute to recidivism in the population of people with psychiatric disabilities. Additional risk factors for recidivism for people with psychiatric disabilities include nonadherence to treatment and subsequent behaviors associated with their disorders (Osher et al., 2012). To address the overrepresentation of people with psychiatric disabilities in American jails and prisons, efforts have been implemented to divert these individuals from jails and prisons into treatment programs (Bernacchio & Burker, 2016). Although these efforts have been somewhat successful at decriminalizing psychiatric disabilities, reducing recidivism rates, and improving outcomes for individuals with psychiatric disabilities, their rates of incarceration and recidivism remain high.

REHABILITATION COUNSELING IMPLICATIONS: A RECOVERY-ORIENTED APPROACH

In response to Donnell et al.'s (2009) recommendation for VR programs to adopt a recovery-themed platform to better address the multifaceted rehabilitation needs of consumers with psychiatric disabilities, we introduce a recovery-oriented model of rehabilitation assessment and planning. Recovery serves as the "cornerstone" of psychiatric rehabilitation practice (Pratt, Gill, Barrett, & Roberts, 2014). Deegan (1988) succinctly, yet aptly, described recovery as "the urge, the wrestle, and the resurrection" (p. 15). Anthony (1993, p. 15) provided one of the most oft-cited definitions of recovery as:

> a deeply personal unique process of changing one's attitudes, values, feelings, goals, skills, and/or roles. It is a way of living a satisfying, hopeful, and contributing life even with limitations caused by illness. Recovery involves the development of new meaning and purpose in one's life as one grows beyond the catastrophic effects of mental illness.

Anthony (1993) further noted that recovery does not necessarily mean that the individual is asymptomatic, but that despite experiencing episodic symptom exacerbation, people with psychiatric disabilities can still perform life tasks and roles, overcome opportunity barriers, and enjoy a high quality of life.

The recovery movement started in the United States by mental health consumers/survivors who acted as grassroots advocates who paved the way to a system-wide cultural shift in mental health services delivery (Zinman, Budd, & Bluebird, 2009). SAMHSA (2012, para. 5) has since adopted core principles of recovery and developed a working definition of recovery as "a process of change through which individuals improve their health and wellness, live a self-directed life, and strive to reach their full potential." The guiding principles of recovery, as proposed by SAMHSA, are that it emerges from hope; is person-driven; occurs via many pathways; is holistic; is supported by peers, allies, and strong networks; is culturally based and influenced; addresses trauma; involves individual, family, and community strengths; and is based on respect. The definition and guiding principles serve as a framework for providing integrated mental health and rehabilitation services to individuals with psychiatric disabilities.

In addition to SAMHSA's working definition and principles of recovery, the Boston University Center for Psychiatric Rehabilitation (2016) underscored the importance of vocational recovery. Vocational recovery is defined as "preserving, regaining, or acquiring competitive employment despite being affected by a disabling psychiatric condition" (para. 2). Preliminary research conducted by investigators from the Center for Psychiatric Rehabilitation has established that individuals who have successfully transitioned from severe work dysfunction and receipt of Social Security Income to full- or part-time sustained competitive employment have the capacity to experience vocational recovery. Vocational recovery is associated with a higher level of education, having a job that requires creativity, and having employment that involves doing a variety of tasks. The factors that individuals who experience vocational recovery report as contributing to the capacity to keep a high-level job include psychotropic medications and the support of spouses/partners, psychiatrists, therapists, bosses, supervisors, and coworkers.

The principles of recovery align with the core values and principles of rehabilitation counseling. Yet, the less than favorable outcomes of individuals with psychiatric disabilities who receive rehabilitation services suggest that these principles are not integrated as fully as they should be into the rehabilitation process. For this reason, we highlight recovery-oriented strategies and services to implement throughout the rehabilitation process, beginning with counselor self-reflection and extending through to job placement and follow-up.

Counselor Awareness and Self-Reflective Practice

As a prerequisite to providing recovery-oriented rehabilitation services, rehabilitation counselors must be willing to examine their own biases about mental illness and the capabilities of people with psychiatric disabilities to live independently in their communities, work in occupations that bring them personal fulfillment, and experience life satisfaction. Myths about mental illness are widely perpetuated by the media, and rehabilitation counselors are not exempt from being negatively influenced by these myths. Several strategies can be implemented to examine how these myths have influenced counselors' own perceptions of people with psychiatric disabilities and potential biases that can impede effective service delivery. Developing friendships with individuals or listening to the stories of already known family and friends in recovery is the best approach to challenging biases. Another strategy is to take an inventory of personal biases and misperceptions and to investigate the facts to replace the myths from which these biases arise. Reading recovery narratives and watching testimonial videos of individuals is a useful strategy for combatting myths. The National Empowerment Center has released a CD entitled *Voices of Hope and Recovery: Our Stories, Our Lives,* which includes the recovery stories of 12 individuals. The National Empowerment Center also has a page on their website and links to other websites with recovery stories. Likewise, NAMI includes recovery stories on their website, and a link to stories of hope and recovery can be found at mentalhealth.gov. Rehabilitation counselors must also set aside their biases regarding treatment approaches and adequately inform clients with psychiatric disabilities about all treatment options, as well as their potential risks and benefits, so that these individuals can make informed choices about which options to pursue on their own paths to recovery.

Outreach and Eligibility Determination

The pressing need for early outreach and intervention is a theme across the emerging populations of people with psychiatric disabilities discussed in this chapter. Rehabilitation counselors in many settings already provide outreach to secondary schools, primary medical care offices, mental health and substance abuse treatment facilities, and corrections facilities. However, systems barriers such as large caseloads and challenges in coordinating services with other agencies and service providers can serve as impediments to providing outreach on a larger scale. These impediments must be eradicated through policy changes and adjustments to service delivery approaches if rehabilitation services are to become more accessible to populations of people with psychiatric disabilities who are most in need of these services.

Because most youths with psychiatric disabilities do not receive special education services, rehabilitation counselors who partner with secondary schools to provide transition services to youths with disabilities should also conduct outreach to the general student populations in these settings. Similarly, outreach efforts should target college and university counseling centers because postsecondary students with psychiatric disabilities are most likely to receive services from these offices. Likewise, because individuals with psychiatric disabilities are often treated by general practitioners and may not seek out services from mental health providers due to stigma, Mojtabai (2011) identified the need for the provision of evidence-based, recovery-oriented psychiatric rehabilitation services in primary medical settings.

As previously discussed, individuals with psychiatric disabilities who are transitioning out of correctional facilities into their local communities represent a vastly underserved rehabilitation population with a multitude of internal and external barriers to employment, mental health services, health care, and community integration. Clearly, rehabilitation counselors can play a much more pivotal role in working collaboratively with correctional staff and mental health professionals to establish eligibility for rehabilitation services prior to their release and to develop prerelease plans to link these individuals to disability benefits, education, training, housing, and job placement services.

To increase access to rehabilitation counseling for individuals with psychiatric disabilities, including those with co-occurring SUDs and/or corrections involvement, eligibility criteria that exclude these individuals from receiving services must be changed. Most importantly, criteria that require individuals to be stabilized on psychiatric medications and/or to have achieved a certain period of sobriety before services can be initiated need to be reconsidered. Recovery from both psychiatric disabilities and addictions is not a linear process, and periods of symptom exacerbation and relapse are part of the recovery process. Therefore, rather than denying services or discontinuing services when individuals stop treatment, symptoms come out of remission, or relapses occur, it is important to modify eligibility criteria and requirements for continued service provision to reflect the reality of recovery as a nonlinear process. Rehabilitation services should be adapted so that premature ineligibility decisions are not made. Employment is an important part of the recovery process and failure to provide rehabilitation services in an early intervention format is problematic. Partnering early on with individuals with psychiatric disabilities to engage them in rehabilitation counseling and to provide services that are truly integrated with mental health and addictions services can instill hope and offer an incentive to treatment adherence and abstinence from substance use.

Sheehan and Lewicki (2016) identified collaborative documentation (CD) as a promising practice for actively engaging individuals with psychiatric disabilities in the entire rehabilitation process, beginning with the intake interview. In CD, the client and clinician jointly develop intake summaries, progress notes, treatment plans, and other documentation. The process is unique in that time is reserved at the end of each session for collaborative writing of notes and documents. The client and clinician jointly summarize issues discussed in the session, goals that were addressed, and plans for follow-up. Although research on CD is limited, preliminary evidence indicates positive outcomes for clients including empowerment, client satisfaction, adherence to treatment, engagement in treatment, transparency, strengthening of the therapeutic alliance, and overall client well-being. It is also beneficial to clinicians because it reduces the burden of paperwork, enables the clinician to focus more on the client, and increases job satisfaction. Sheehan and Lewicki discussed the potential applications of CD to the rehabilitation process, noting that this practice is coherent with both the philosophy and guiding principles of rehabilitation counseling and has the potential to empower clients with disabilities to take greater ownership of their rehabilitation plans.

Rehabilitation counselors working in all settings must be cognizant of the fact that because co-occurring health conditions are so prevalent in people with psychiatric disabilities, intake interviews should include inquiry into the overall health of these consumers as well as any physical symptoms they may be experiencing in addition to their psychiatric symptoms. Comprehensive medical evaluations are crucial because of the strong likelihood that these individuals have not had any recent medical care (Ziedonis et al., 2005). Additionally, Lusk et al. (2016) recommended that screening for SUDs in the intake interview and making appropriate referrals for further evaluation is imperative because of the high rate of co-occurrence of psychiatric disabilities with SUDs. The *Substance Abuse in Vocational Rehabilitation Screener* (SAVR-S) is a tool developed for use during the VR intake process, and its purpose is to identify consumers who may need further assessment. SAMHSA has also organized a listing of other screening instruments and issues pertinent to screening during the VR process. This information can be accessed via its websites at www.integration.samhsa.gov/clinical-practice/screening-tools and www.ncbi.nlm.nih.gov/books/NBK64281/respectively.

Rehabilitation Assessment and Planning

Again, a theme throughout this chapter has been the need for integrated services from professionals who partner with individuals with psychiatric disabilities in a team approach to identify and provide the supports and services they need to achieve their self-determined recovery and rehabilitation goals. Examples of such approaches include wraparound teams for youths with psychiatric disabilities, case management in one-stop on-campus mental health centers, primary care medical homes, integrated treatment for individuals with COD, and prerelease planning for individuals with psychiatric disabilities and corrections involvement.

WRAPAROUND

Because of the growing number of youths with psychiatric disabilities in the United States along with the poor adult outcomes they often experience, increased federal funding is being targeted toward developing, implementing, and evaluating interventions to improve the mental health, rehabilitation, and recovery outcomes for youths with psychiatric disabilities. One particular area of focus is how to better coordinate child and adult services to create seamless transitions and empower youths to become more actively engaged in interdisciplinary team planning. One such approach is wraparound, a strengths-based team process for planning and implementing "individualized community-based care for children and adolescents with serious mental health conditions and typically involved in multiple child- and family-serving systems" (Walker, Pullman, Moser, & Burns, 2012, p. 190).

In addition to youths and their parent(s) or guardians, wraparound team members include professionals from schools, mental health agencies, vocational rehabilitation programs, child welfare, peer-run programs, and juvenile justice systems (Walker et al., 2012). Wraparounds can be applied to any team-based approach to serving youths with psychiatric disabilities (e.g., individualized education program [IEP] teams, transition teams). Key features of wraparound include (a) full involvement of the youth and his or her family members or guardians, and (b) a prioritization of the youth's and family members'/guardians' perspectives in identifying needs to be addressed and services to include in the wraparound plan. In consultation with the youth and his or her family members/guardians, the wraparound plan is continuously evaluated to determine if services are effective at addressing the youth's most pressing issues and concerns, and additional services are added to the plan as needed.

A challenge confronted by wraparound teams is the youth's willingness to disclose personal information to family members/guardians and professionals who are viewed as authority figures (Walker et al., 2012). As a natural part of adolescent development, "young people gradually expand the boundaries of what they consider their private sphere and become more reluctant to disclose to parents information about, for example, their whereabouts and activities, their friends, and their romantic relationships" (Walker et al., 2012, p. 190). Secrecy and reluctance to disclose to adults can undermine the effectiveness of the wraparound team process. If youths are pressured by team members to disclose, they are likely to become more secretive and distrustful. Another challenge for wraparound teams is disagreements between youths and their parents/guardians regarding needed services and desired outcomes. These disagreements can result in conflicts and dissatisfaction with the wraparound team process.

To address these challenges, innovative approaches that focus on increasing youths' capacity to be self-determined and actively involved in wraparound teams have been developed (Davis, 2015). An example of a promising approach is *Achieve My Plan!* (AMP) developed by researchers at the Rehabilitation Research and Training Center for Pathways to Positive Futures. AMP is a team process that can be used in any intervention that involves youths and adults in planning for their care, treatment, education, employment, or other future goals (Walker & Gowen, 2011). The developmental skills that AMP reinforces in youths with psychiatric disabilities are: (a) a positive identity with an increased sense of purpose, self-efficacy, and self-determination; (b) motivation, self-control, confidence, and skills to make decisions and execute plans; (c) skills needed to assume adult roles and leverage resources; and (d) prosocial behaviors and capacities to develop supportive relationships.

AMP coaches work on an individual basis with youths to prepare them to take ownership of the wraparound process and to become actively engaged in team meetings (Walker & Gowen, 2011). AMP coaches assist youths in developing effective skills to communicate to caregivers about their needs and desires (prior to the team meeting) to elicit their support for the ideas and suggestions these youths plan to present to the team. The AMP coach also assists the youth to (a) identify potential conflicts that may arise in team meetings; (b) develop conflict management and resolution skills; and (c) manage and resolve unanticipated conflicts. In addition to working with the youth, the AMP coach also provides training and coaching to AMP team members to conduct and participate in team meetings in a manner that empowers youths to assert their needs and desires. AMP coaches also train team members to recognize and appropriately respond to team conflict so that the youths do not become disengaged from the AMP team process.

Research is currently underway to evaluate the effectiveness of AMP interventions in empowering youths to become active participants in wraparound teams. Preliminary pilot testing of AMP teams has demonstrated significant increases in segments of team meetings in which youths spoke without interruption from other team members, significant increases in youths' verbal contributions to planning, increased instances of adults agreeing to include youths' suggestions into the AMP plan, increases in youths' confidence in working with service providers on AMP teams, and increased youth and caregiver satisfaction with the AMP team (Walker et al., 2011).

CASE MANAGEMENT IN CAMPUS MENTAL HEALTH CENTERS

Hartley (2013) noted that to adequately address the mental health needs of growing numbers of college and university students with psychiatric disabilities and to improve their rates of persistence to degree completion, universities and colleges are shifting toward one-stop campus mental health offices where seamless coordination of the various mental health services, classroom accommodations, and academic supports needed by these students is available. Likewise, a growing trend in campus counseling and mental health centers is to provide case management for students with complex mental health needs (Baker & DeIrish, 2015). Koch et al. (2016) noted that rehabilitation counselors, perhaps more than any other human service professionals, possess the knowledge and skills to fill this role.

The case manager in campus mental health centers provides assessment and planning, counseling, crisis intervention, community outreach, and coordination of services (Baker & DeIrish, 2015). Assessment and planning focus on making arrangements for psychiatric evaluations, if needed, to determine students' support needs and to develop a plan to address the student's ongoing mental health needs for the length of their college stay along with follow-up after the student leaves college. The case manager provides counseling services on a short-term basis until linkages are made for more long-term counseling within the campus mental health center or in the community. In crisis intervention, the case manager collaborates with other university and community auspices to respond to the crisis and ensure follow-up after the crisis to assist the student to transition back into college. Community outreach is provided to establish partnerships with internal and external providers to ensure coordinated care and ongoing services for students while they are in college. Finally, the case manager coordinates all the students' service needs and acts as a liaison with internal and external providers. These case managers ensure student access to resources and supports that are provided in both postsecondary (e.g., offices for students with disabilities, financial aid offices, student affairs, student health centers, career services) and local community (e.g., mental health providers in private practice, community mental health centers, hospitals, state VR offices) settings. Additional responsibilities of case managers include conducting outreach to new incoming students, providing campus-wide outreach and training to reduce stigma and increase awareness of psychiatric disabilities, and facilitating successful exits and reentries into postsecondary programs for students who may need to temporarily withdraw from college to receive treatment for their psychiatric conditions (Koch et al., 2016).

Because students with psychiatric disabilities often fail to access and use classroom accommodations, case managers can also do more targeted outreach on university and college campuses to increase general awareness of the availability of these resources. To increase awareness, case managers can collaborate with disability service providers to conduct informational sessions at orientations for incoming first-year students and presentations in first-year experience seminars. They can also educate students about their rights and responsibilities related to academic accommodations and how to apply for and access these services; explore the advantages and disadvantages of disclosure; provide information regarding how and what to disclose to campus counselors, disability service providers, and classroom instructors; and assess students' specific accommodation and support needs. Finally, they can educate counseling center staff about the availability of classroom accommodations and how to apply for and access these services so that staff can pass this information along to students.

In addition to these services, the case manager can reinforce with students the importance of becoming engaged in academic and social activities outside of the classroom (e.g., study groups, meetings with instructors outside of the classroom, organized campus social events, campus clubs, sports) and how doing so is likely to facilitate a greater sense of inclusion on their campuses and increase the likelihood that they will complete their degree or certificate programs (Koch et al., 2014). These case managers can also advocate for services (e.g., transportation, child care) from state VR agencies to enable these students to participate in social and academic activities.

Because students with psychiatric disabilities may also have demographic characteristics (e.g., first-generation college students, single parents, veterans) that pose additional risk factors to successful completion of their postsecondary education, these factors must be taken into consideration in rehabilitation and disability service assessment and planning (Koch et al., 2014). Rehabilitation case managers and disability service providers should be knowledgeable about institutional programs and resources designed specifically for nontraditional and at-risk students. They can then inform students with psychiatric disabilities who possess these additional at-risk characteristics about these programs and encourage them to take advantage of the services they offer.

Bertram (2010) called attention to the need for institutional initiatives to be developed across U.S. postsecondary institutions to create more inclusive environments where students with psychiatric disabilities feel like valued members of the campus community who do not have to hide their conditions. Peer education and the creation of supportive communities both inside and outside of the classroom should be the goal of these initiatives. Supportive communities can be established in residence halls, fraternities, sororities, and student organizations. Bertram further recommended that advisors, student leaders, and residence hall staff can take on leadership roles in "destigmatizing the discussion of mental health issues [and ensuring that these discussions] can begin in safe spaces" (p. 32). This is another area in which the case manager can take on a leadership role.

PRIMARY CARE MEDICAL HOMES

To improve health outcomes for individuals with psychiatric disabilities, stake-holders have advocated for the provision of evidence-based mental health interventions in primary care settings, particularly because these are the settings where many individuals receive treatment for psychiatric conditions and because of the frequent co-occurrence of chronic health conditions. Insel (2011) indicated that the current movement in health care toward the development of medical homes could improve access to medical and health care services as well as overall quality of care for individuals with psychiatric disabilities and co-occurring chronic physical disorders. The Agency for Healthcare Research and Quality (AHRQ, 2012) defines primary care medical homes (PCMHs; also referred to as patient-centered medical homes) as "not simply a place but as a model of the organization of primary care that delivers the core functions of primary health care" (para. 1). PCMHs represent another area in which rehabilitation counselors can lend their expertise and incorporate consideration of employment into health plans.

The AHRQ (2012) has identified five functions and attributes of PCMHs: (a) comprehensive care; (b) patient-centered; (c) coordinated care; (d) accessible services; and (e) quality and safety. The PCMH is responsible for providing comprehensive care that includes physical and mental health services, prevention and wellness services, acute care, and chronic care. The PCMH comprises a team of care providers that could include physicians, psychiatrists, nurses, physician assistants, pharmacists, social workers, health educators, and care coordinators. An emphasis is placed on patient-centered care that is holistic and relationship-based. The PCMH team members partner with patients and their families in a manner that is respectful of patients' unique needs, culture, values, and preferences. Patients are active partners in their health care and are provided the education, resources, and tools to manage their care as they choose. The PCMH coordinates care across all settings where services are provided (e.g., hospitals, specialty care, home health care, community services). This coordination of services is especially critical when patients transition between levels of care and service delivery settings. The PCMH emphasizes easily accessible services that are responsive to patients' preferences and include shorter waiting times for urgent care, enhanced in-person hours, 24-hour telephone services and electronic access to a PCMH team member, and alternative modes of communication such as e-mail. Finally, the PCMH is committed to quality of services as well as ongoing quality improvement.

Evidence-based practices are used to guide patients in shared decision making about their treatment options. Performance and patient satisfaction are continuously measured, and performance and satisfaction data are shared with the public. A growing body of research evidence has demonstrated an array of positive outcomes associated with PCMHs. Among these outcomes are reduced health care expenditures; decreased emergency department visits and hospitalizations; reduced disparities in screening and management of chronic health conditions such as cancer, cardiovascular disease, and diabetes; improved patient access to care; and more engaging patient relationships with health care providers (National Committee for Quality Assurance, 2015).

INTEGRATED TREATMENT FOR CODs

Integrated treatment is an evidence-based practice that combines mental health and addictions treatment to simultaneously address both psychiatric disabilities and SUDs in the same location (Ziedonis et al., 2005). Ideally, this treatment approach involves a seamless integration of mental health, addictions, *and rehabilitation counseling services* that are provided by a single agency or treatment program (Wüsthoff et al., 2014). A wide variety of interventions along a continuum of care are tailored to the individual's unique needs. Continuum of care is defined as "an integrated system that guides and tracks patients through a comprehensive array of…services spanning all levels of intensity of care" (Evashwick, 1989, p. 30). Integrated treatment also involves follow-up or aftercare, which serves to continue the provision of support throughout the recovery process.

Assessment, the first step in the process of integrated treatment, typically involves screening for SUDs using client self-reports and other screening instruments such as urine or blood toxicology tests and breathalyzers (Ziedonis et al., 2005). The next step is to evaluate the severity of the SUD and establish if a substance use diagnosis is warranted. The treatment team also assesses clients' motivation for change to determine where they are in terms of readiness for change. Many individuals with SMI will be at early stages and may not see a need to stop using substances, and instead of screening them out of services, the team focuses on establishing rapport with them without pushing them to make an immediate commitment to change. Treatment team members sometimes use external motivators (e.g., family, legal system) to enhance low internal motivation. The next step often involves a comprehensive medical evaluation to determine the medical consequences of the psychiatric condition and SUD. Conducting a comprehensive medical exam is crucial because so many individuals with psychiatric disabilities and SUDs have additional chronic medical conditions. It is also extremely important because, as previously mentioned, many of these individuals have gone for extensive periods of time without a complete physical work-up.

These assessments guide the development of the treatment plan. The treatment plan is a working document that is reviewed and amended to reflect changes in the individual's level of motivation for change. Treatment planning focuses on the active involvement of the client, regardless of the state of readiness for change, and abstinence may not be an immediate treatment goal. Treatment plans include components such as the client's choice of medication and therapy options, ongoing assessment, monitoring of medication adherence, strategies for managing ongoing psychiatric symptoms, interactions between substance use and psychiatric conditions, and monitoring and treatment of co-occurring medical conditions (Ziedonis et al., 2005).

Treatment for mental health disorders generally requires psychotropic medications such as antidepressants, anxiolytics, and mood stabilizers along with psychosocial interventions (Lusk et al., 2016). Medication may also be prescribed to treat withdrawal symptoms and comorbid medical conditions. Pharmacological treatment for smoking cessation may be warranted as well. Prescribing medications to treat individuals with co-occurring SUDs is carefully considered as "their use might thus be, for at least some substance abusers, an extension of their addictive thinking, rather than an adjunct to treatment" (Doweiko, 2012, p. 419). Medications such as benzodiazepines, which are prescribed for some anxiety disorders, are associated with higher rates of abuse and dependence and should therefore be considered carefully when treating individuals with co-occurring SUDs (Lusk et al., 2016). Other problems associated with pharmacological treatment include nonadherence, negative side effects, and negative interactions with other drugs. If medications are prescribed, careful monitoring is conducted. Psychosocial interventions are also provided and include social skills training, motivational enhancement therapy (MET; i.e., an evidence-based practice for the treatment of CODs that expands on traditional motivational interviewing to include ongoing personal feedback to clients from baseline assessment to relapse prevention; Miller, Zweben, DiClemente, & Rychtarik, 1992), psychoeducation, and vocational services.

The continuation of care normally involves the implementation of relapse prevention services and continued participation in self-help groups. Ancillary services may be necessary such as individual, group, and family counseling; medical and dental care; legal assistance; financial services; and supportive housing. Successful completion of integrated treatment and having appropriate follow-up services in place to address social/family, legal, financial, and employment and any other issues helps to better position the individuals with CODs for long-term posttreatment success.

Research has demonstrated the overall effectiveness of utilizing an integrated approach in the treatment of CODs (e.g., Kelly & Daley, 2013; Morrissey et al., 2005). Additionally, according to McKay and Weiss (2001, p. 148) "better long-term substance abuse outcomes [are] associated with better performance while in treatment; more self-help involvement during and after treatment; lower psychiatric, social/family, and legal problem severities; and fewer treatment readmissions, lower life stress, and better coping responses after treatment." However, the availability of these programs is limited (Lusk & Koch, 2013), and many systemic obstacles must be overcome to make these programs more readily available. Among these obstacles are separate systems of care for mental health and addictions treatment, inflexible and mutually exclusive funding sources, disparate health insurance coverage, and a lack of providers who have the knowledge and competencies to simultaneously treat mental health conditions and SUDs (Ziedonis et al., 2005).

PRERELEASE PLANNING

Osher et al. (2012) suggested that the high recidivism rates of individuals with psychiatric disabilities who have been incarcerated are partially explained by the lack of coordination between the multiple systems (e.g., corrections, mental health, substance abuse treatment, VR) that serve these individuals. They proposed the need for an integrated framework for collaboration and pooling of limited resources that targets individuals who are at greatest risk for recidivism. In addition, Bernacchio and Burker (2016) underscored the importance of prerelease planning and the involvement of rehabilitation counselors as team members in the planning process to assist individuals with corrections involvement to address the many challenges they face in integrating back into their communities.

Prerelease planning involves an interdisciplinary team approach that integrates services from mental health agencies, substance abuse programs, vocational rehabilitation agencies, parole and probation, and other human services (Bernacchio & Burker, 2016). Team members recognize that treatment needs may be exacerbated by the stresses of community living, and a multitude of services are often needed to assist individuals to successfully integrate into their communities postincarceration. The demands to find paid work, reunite with family, secure and maintain stable housing, and refrain from criminal activity can exacerbate psychiatric symptoms and lead to recidivism if not proactively addressed. Consequently, community-based programs for mental health, substance use treatment, and rehabilitation counseling must be integrated to improve outcomes for this population. The receipt of integrated services while in custody, beginning with admissions screening, can subsequently ease transition to the community and can help inform and influence the work conducted by community-based providers (Lamberti, 2007).

Prerelease planning consists of assessing mental health, housing, health care, employment, and social support needs prior to release; developing a plan to address these needs; implementing the plan; and providing follow-along services. Evidence-based community reentry practices include medication and substance abuse monitoring, integrated mental health and substance abuse treatment, motivational interviewing, cognitive behavioral therapy, intensive case management, forensic assertive community treatment, and supportive housing (Osher et al., 2012). Employment-based reentry programs that focus on preparing detainees for employment and placing them in high-quality jobs that are consistent with their skills and interests have also been demonstrated to reduce recidivism (Kethineni & Falcone, 2007). Assistance with reinstating benefits such as Medicaid, Medicare, and Social Security income is also a critical service need. Bernnachio and Burker (2016) noted that rehabilitation counselors are an untapped resource in prerelease planning. With their training in counseling, psychiatric rehabilitation, case management, and vocational planning and placement, rehabilitation counselors have all the essential skills to be an integral part of helping individuals with psychiatric disabilities in the criminal justice system to successfully reenter and function in their communities.

Rehabilitation Services

Substantial research evidence documents the effectiveness of a variety of psychiatric rehabilitation interventions (e.g., Bond, 2004; Cook et al., 2005, 2011; Dixon et al., 2001; Farkas, Gagne, Anthony, & Chamberlin, 2005), and emerging interventions are being developed and evaluated to respond to the changing needs of individuals with psychiatric disabilities. Although each individual with a psychiatric disability will require a unique set of rehabilitation services, we provide a discussion of some of the evidence-based practices, emerging interventions, and rehabilitation considerations that have particular applications to individuals in the populations we have discussed.

COUNSELING AND GUIDANCE

Individuals with psychiatric disabilities who apply for rehabilitation services may not initially recognize the need to continue treatment for their psychiatric conditions, to receive treatment for co-occurring SUDs, to change behaviors to improve their overall health, or to engage in treatment and rehabilitation to prevent reincarceration. These individuals may also have ambivalence about going to work. In providing counseling and guidance to consumers with psychiatric disabilities, rehabilitation counselors can establish rapport, create strong working alliances, and help to facilitate needed changes to achieve rehabilitation and recovery goals by using techniques from MET (Miller et al., 1992). Rather than screening out individuals who do not express a predetermined level of motivation, these techniques focus on working with clients from where they are at in terms of their readiness for change. MET utilizes a nonconfrontational approach to counseling that is respectful of the individual's ambivalence and readiness for change. Using MET, counseling techniques and rehabilitation services focus on facilitating movement through the stages of readiness for change as identified by Prochaska, Norcross, and DiClemente (1994).

Ziedonis et al. (2005) provided definitions and targeted interventions for each stage of change that are applicable to the rehabilitation counseling process. For example, at the precontemplation stage, people typically do not view a behavior as problematic or have any intention to change, and the rehabilitation counselor can conduct a baseline assessment (e.g., intake interview, screening for co-occurring conditions, referral for comprehensive psychological and medical evaluations) and provide assessment information to increase consumers' awareness of the risks associated with their current behaviors. At the contemplation phase, the individual acknowledges that he or she has a problem and begins to think about what to do to solve the problem. An appropriate intervention at this stage would be to explore with the client what it would take to make a change and what the potential consequences of not changing might be. At the preparation stage, individuals are ready to make a change and committed to taking action to resolve the problem, but they are often in need of assistance to determine what steps and courses of action are necessary. An appropriate intervention at this stage would be to educate consumers about various options and assist them with identifying manageable steps as part of an action (i.e., rehabilitation) plan. In the action phase, consumers are ready to make a change and the plan for change is implemented. Consumers in the action phase are supported and encouraged as they take initial steps toward change, while corrective feedback is also provided. In the maintenance phase, individuals continue to carry out the changes made in the action phase over a prolonged period of time. Relapse prevention strategies are identified so that the change can be maintained. Finally, the relapse phase involves helping individuals to recycle through earlier phases (rather than terminating services) without becoming stuck or demoralized. Providing access to follow-up services is extremely important in maintaining recovery.

ILLNESS MANAGEMENT AND RECOVERY

Self-management of psychiatric disabilities and co-occurring physical conditions and SUDs is a critical component of recovery. Illness management and recovery (IMR) is an evidence-based practice for equipping individuals with the knowledge and skills they need to self-manage their disabilities (U.S. Department of Health and Human Services, 2015). IMR programs are based on the premise that if provided with the appropriate knowledge and skills, individuals with psychiatric disabilities are empowered to manage their symptoms, make informed choices about their treatment, and realize their self-determined recovery goals. Interventions typically involve 3 to 10 months of weekly individual or group sessions with practitioners trained in IMR. Interventions include psychoeducation about psychiatric diagnoses and treatment, coping skills training to manage stress and deal with psychiatric symptoms, information about medications and strategies to manage daily medication regimens, relapse prevention to identify triggers and early warning signs of pending relapse and to develop relapse prevention plans, and skills to effectively collaborate with mental health and other practitioners as well as significant others who can support them in their recovery.

Bartels et al. (2014) developed and evaluated the Integrated Illness Management and Recovery (I-IMR) program that was delivered to a total of 36 individuals aged 50 and older who had a psychiatric diagnosis and co-occurring health condition (e.g., diabetes, chronic obstructive pulmonary disease, congestive heart failure, ischemic heart disease, hypertension, hyperlipidemia, osteoarthritis). The intervention was individually tailored to the psychiatric and medical conditions of each client and was provided in 10 modules that were delivered in weekly sessions over a period of 8 months. A psychiatric component of the intervention addressed psychiatric disability and treatment, strategies to increase medication adherence, relapse prevention, coping skills to manage persistent symptoms, and social skills training. The medical component involved training in applying the skills learned in the psychiatric component to the self-management of general medical illness. Additionally, participants met twice a month with a nurse case manager to discuss their progress in meeting their general mental health and medical goals as well as obstacles to achieving these goals.

Results of the investigation demonstrated that in comparison to individuals who received usual care, participants in the I-IMR program demonstrated greater improvements in psychiatric illness self-management, greater diabetes self-management, greater preferences for detailed diagnosis and treatment information during encounters with primary care providers, and decreased hospitalization for psychiatric or general medical conditions. In considering the research results, Bartels et al. (2014) concluded that providing I-IMR training recognizes the interrelationship of recovery and wellness, treats the whole person, and recognizes that physical and mental health are both necessary in supporting optimal recovery and quality of life.

The Wellness Recovery Action Plan (WRAP; Copeland, 2011) is the most widely used IMR intervention in the United States. WRAP is supported by a significant body of research evidence demonstrating the positive impact that WRAPs have on multiple recovery outcomes including reductions in psychiatric symptoms, increased hopefulness about meeting recovery goals, improved quality of life, and increased engagement in self-advocacy with service providers (Cook et al., 2011; Fukui et al., 2011; Jonikas et al., 2013; Starnino et al., 2010). WRAPs are peer-led, self-management interventions that "are intended to help people manage a variety of long-term illnesses, whether or not they choose to receive formal services" (Cook et al., 2009, p. 246). WRAPs emphasize holistic health and wellness along with individual strengths and social support (Cook et al., 2009). In addition to peer-led groups, the WRAP process can be completed on one's own or with the assistance of a mental health provider or rehabilitation counselor who has obtained certification as a WRAP facilitator.

The key elements of WRAPs include: (a) a wellness toolbox; (b) a daily maintenance plan; (c) identifying triggers and an action plan; (d) identifying early warning signs and an action plan; (e) identifying when things are breaking down and an action plan; (f) crisis planning; and (g) postcrisis planning (Copeland, 2011).

The wellness toolbox includes a list of activities that individuals have used in the past or would like to use in the future to support their recovery and overall health and wellness. The daily maintenance plan includes a description of what the individual is like when he or she is feeling well, wellness tools that can be used on a daily basis, and wellness tools that can be used on any given day. Triggers are events or experiences that may precipitate feeling worse, and the action plan for dealing with triggers includes strategies for responding to triggers in a manner to prevent feeling worse. Early warning signs are subtle indicators (e.g., sleep difficulties, nervousness) that the individual is feeling worse, and the action plan includes wellness tools that can be used to respond to triggers and prevent a possible relapse. Signs that things are breaking down may include experiencing psychiatric symptoms such as hearing voices or persistent feelings of despair. Recognizing these signs enables the individual to then develop a powerful action plan to be immediately implemented to preclude the onset of even more severe symptomology. Because relapses can occur regardless of how well individuals implement their WRAPs, it is critical to include a crisis plan in the WRAP. The crisis plan is a proactive strategy that enables individuals to identify signs that they may need others to assume responsibility for their care and decision making until the crisis subsides. The crisis plan includes a list of individuals (both professionals and natural supports) who can provide assistance in getting through the crisis; important health care information such as preferred providers and facilities as well as providers and facilities to avoid, medications that the individual prefers and those that he or she does not want to be prescribed; a plan for recovering at home; and helpful strategies that others can use to support the individual to get through the crisis as well as strategies to avoid. The postcrisis plan is a description of how others can support the individual as she or he begins to recover, what the individual needs to do in order to resume typical daily activities (e.g., activities of daily living, employment, recreation, community participation), and strategies that can be implemented to prevent another crisis.

Even when not working directly with consumers with psychiatric disabilities to develop WRAPs, rehabilitation counselors can ensure that rehabilitation plans address the overall health of these consumers by including health-promoting services such as dietary consultation, gym memberships, smoking cessation programs designed specifically for individuals with psychiatric disabilities, and ongoing specialty treatment for secondary conditions. Rehabilitation counselors can also assist those without medical insurance to obtain coverage through Social Security programs or the Affordable Care Act.

PEER SUPPORT GROUPS AND PEER SERVICE PROVIDERS

Peer support groups focus on recovery and provide members with an experience of commonality (i.e., recognition that one is not alone in her or his struggles); a sense of belonging and community; and opportunities to share resources and ideas, develop and practice social skills, and receive constructive feedback (Pratt et al., 2014). When support groups are not available in one's community or for individuals who may have difficulties with face-to-face interactions, online support groups are an option. Many peer support groups also engage in advocacy initiatives to reduce stigma, increase mental health resources, and protect the civil rights of individuals with psychiatric disabilities. Involvement in these advocacy initiatives can be very empowering for individuals with psychiatric disabilities and give them a sense of purpose and pride in being agents of change.

Peer support has been identified as crucial to the recovery of youths and young adults with psychiatric disabilities because peer influence is so strong at this stage in their development (Davis, 2015). Many evidence-based service delivery and intervention models have subsequently been modified to incorporate peer supports and services for youths. For example, to make supported employment services more amenable to youths with psychiatric disabilities, the University of Massachusetts Medical School Transitions Research and Training Center in collaboration with the Thresholds Young Adult Program developed a model that integrates peer mentoring into vocational services/supported employment for youths with psychiatric disabilities (Klodnick, Sabella, Brenner, Kaiser, & Ellison, 2014). Peer mentors receive a 40-hour training on the individualized placement and supports (IPS) model of supported employment, the mentor's role in helping to facilitate the supported employee's achievement of his or her vocational goals, both group and individual techniques for engaging the supported employee in services, how to share his or her own stories in a way that empowers the supported employee, maintaining appropriate boundaries, and confidentiality. Additionally, peers receive weekly group supervision that focuses on issues such as managing relational boundaries, identifying when their own mental health issues arise and connecting them with supports, training on issues that arise over the course of their relationship with mentees, check-in about their own work-related struggles and successes, and empowering them to develop advocacy skills to use in team meetings.

Active Minds is a nonprofit organization with campus-based chapters at postsecondary institutions across the United States and Canada, the aim of which is to do exactly what Bertram recommended, that is, "to empower students to speak openly about mental health in order to educate others and encourage help-seeking" (Active Minds, 2016, para. 1). Active Minds chapters are open to all students interested in mental health issues. Members of chapters provide programming that includes advocacy training, education about mental health issues, connection of students to resources and supports, campus-wide stigma reduction, and creation of more inclusive campuses where mental health issues can be openly discussed. Rehabilitation counselors working on postsecondary campuses can play leading roles in partnering with students with psychiatric disabilities to establish chapters on campuses where these do not exist. Active Minds provides information on its website regarding how to go about developing new chapters. In postsecondary settings, peer mentors are also involved in integrated supported employment and education programs. These mentors are usually individuals with psychiatric disabilities who are further along in their education than mentees.

Peer support is often viewed as an integral component of treatment and recovery for individuals with psychiatric disabilities and SUDs as well. However, access to such programs can be problematic because the same stigma about psychiatric disabilities that is so widespread in the general population is often present among members of self-help groups (Lusk et al., 2016). In addition, some self-help groups may impede the individual's treatment by promoting abstinence from all substances including psychotropic medications. Because of these obstacles, self-help groups have been developed to specifically support the recovery of individuals with CODs. Two examples are Dual Diagnosis Anonymous and Double Trouble in

Recovery (NAADAC, 2010). Unfortunately, these groups are much fewer in number than traditional recovery groups.

In addition to peer support groups, an increasing emphasis has been placed on the delivery of peer-delivered services. These services are provided by individuals with psychiatric disabilities in both peer-designated roles and traditional professional roles. Peer providers now have the opportunity to become certified peer specialists (CPS), professionals who are viewed as essential members of mental health treatment teams. As Cook (2011, p. 87) noted,

> a growing body of evidence suggests that peer-provided, recovery-oriented mental health services produce outcomes as good as and, in some cases superior to, services from non-peer professionals. As evidence continues to mount, the stage has been set for a coordinated, national peer workforce development and maintenance initiative.

The CPS role is distinguished from other mental health positions in that in addition to traditional knowledge and competencies in providing support, the CPS has experiential knowledge about living with a psychiatric disability. CPSs work in a variety of capacities such as professional members of assertive community treatment teams and forensic assertive community treatment teams; trainers in WRAP interventions; vocational specialists in employment programs; case managers in residential programs; and service providers in drop-in centers, partial hospitalization programs, and community mental health centers (Salzer, Schwenk, & Brusilovskiy, 2010). CPSs have become such an invaluable resource in supporting the recovery of individuals with psychiatric disabilities that in many states, their services are Medicaid reimbursable (Salzer et al., 2010). Peers also function in professional roles in psychiatric rehabilitation such as rehabilitation counselors, psychiatrists, mental health counselors, nurses, and social workers.

INTEGRATED SUPPORTED EMPLOYMENT AND SUPPORTED EDUCATION

Carnevale, Smith, and Strohl (2010) estimated that by 2018, 63% of all job openings will require at least some college education. Additionally, Davis (2015) reported that the earnings gap between those with a baccalaureate degree and those with only a high school diploma has almost doubled since 1980, and the prospects for earning a livable wage are extremely limited for individuals without any postsecondary credentials. Thus, targeting postsecondary education as a rehabilitation service for individuals with psychiatric disabilities and providing the necessary supports that they need to achieve their educational goals are imperative (Boutin & Accordino, 2011). Also, as noted by Ellison et al. (2015), for young adults with psychiatric disabilities, engaging in typical activities of emerging adulthood such as attending college boosts self-esteem, provides a sense of agency, and decreases stigma. Researchers have indicated a need for greater dissemination and implementation of supported employment for youths. However, the emphasis of supported employment models on job retention is problematic because youths are at a stage in their career development in which a central task is to complete secondary and postsecondary schooling and begin adult careers. Frequent degree major and job changes are often part of the process of finding an appropriate match between their interests and skills and available job opportunities. Thus, supported employment services should be adapted to the developmental stage of youths and augmented with other services such as supported education, benefits counseling, and peer mentoring.

Both supported employment and supported education are upheld by a large body of research evidence demonstrating their positive effects on both the recovery process and the employment outcomes of individuals with psychiatric disabilities (e.g., Bond, 2004; Cook et al., 2005, 2011) The IPS model of supported employment, in particular, is an evidence-based approach with significant research evidence supporting its efficacy. Key components of IPS focus on placement in competitive employment in occupations of consumer choice, zero exclusion, use of a rapid job search approach, integration of vocational and clinical services, and indefinite provision of follow-along supports (Bond, 2004; Cook et al., 2006). Nuechterlein et al. (2008) underscored the importance of early intervention during the initial onset of a psychiatric disorder to prevent the development of chronic work disability. They further noted that many individuals are in postsecondary educational programs or starting their careers during the initial onset of psychiatric illness and want to return to school or work but need supports to manage their psychiatric symptoms and cope with stigma associated with mental illness. Subsequently, these researchers applied the principles of the IPS model of supported employment to a combined supported education and supported employment program offered in a treatment program to individuals with recent-onset schizophrenia (2008). Components of their model of integrated supported education and employment included zero exclusion; vocational and mental health treatment integration; benefits counseling; rapid placement in postsecondary education, employment, or both; and time-unlimited services based on individual preferences.

Rudnick et al. (2013) integrated the IPS model with a supported education component, both services of which were co-located at universities. The joint goal of the program was to assist students with completing their postsecondary programs and securing work experiences relevant to their studies through co-op or trial work experiences. Finally, Ellison et al. (2014) adapted the IPS model for youths ages 17 to 20, the majority of whom were African Americans, in custody of the state, and diagnosed with major mood disorders, to include near-age peer mentors, a supported education component, and a career development focus. Participants could enroll in employment services, education services, or both. Although preliminary feasibility studies suggest that integrated supported employment and supported education is a potentially promising service for youths and young adults with psychiatric disabilities, randomized controlled trials of these interventions are needed.

Job Development and Placement

One of the first considerations in job placement is the need to reduce stigma among employers to increase employment opportunities for individuals with psychiatric disabilities. Rehabilitation counselors can collaborate with advocacy organizations to offer informational workshops to employer organizations or consult with individual employers to address their concerns about hiring people with psychiatric disabilities. Education for co-workers should also take precedence because they are also prone to stereotypes and stigma and could mistreat employees with psychiatric disabilities; thus creating a hostile environment and undermining job stability.

Testimonials from employers who have hired workers with psychiatric disabilities who have turned out to be highly valued employees can also help to reduce stigma.

Low expectations regarding the ability of individuals with psychiatric disabilities, particularly those with SMI, to engage in competitive employment are still prominent in the general population, even among mental health and rehabilitation service providers. These can result in low expectations among individuals with psychiatric disabilities regarding their own employment potential. The consequence of these low expectations among service providers and individuals themselves has led to placement in low-skill, high-stress positions that are incompatible with the individual's employment desires and capabilities. Rehabilitation counselors must keep in mind that people with psychiatric disabilities are employed in all types of occupations, including high-level managerial and professional positions. In working with individuals with psychiatric disabilities, high, yet realistic expectations should be established that are consistent with the individual's career aspirations.

A common myth about psychiatric disabilities is that individuals with these conditions are incapable of handling stress on the job. The reality is that all individuals vary in their responses to stressors on the job. All jobs are stressful in some regard, and individuals with and without psychiatric disabilities are unique in terms of situations that they find stressful. Productivity is maximized when there is a good match between the employee's needs and his or her working conditions, whether or not the individual has a psychiatric disability. Furthermore, preliminary research has documented that for individuals with psychiatric disabilities, the capacity to experience vocational recovery and sustain employment is associated with a higher level of education and having a job that requires creativity and involves doing a variety of tasks (Boston University Center for Psychiatric Rehabilitation, 2011).

In providing job placement and follow-along services to individuals with psychiatric disabilities, principles of the IPS model of supported employment should be used. Likewise, placement in high demand jobs with livable wages and benefits that require postsecondary training should be targeted as rehabilitation outcomes for consumers who have the capacity to participate in postsecondary education. Job development, placement, and follow-along services should also be tailored to the unique concerns and developmental needs of consumers with psychiatric disabilities. Youths, for example, should be provided with opportunities to "try out" different occupations. Likewise, college students should be provided with assistance in securing work studies, co-op experiences, and internships to develop job skills related to their college majors.

Furthermore, employment services should be provided simultaneously with substance use and mental health treatment. Although it is often presumed that individuals who are actively using drugs or alcohol are not capable of participating in employment, research has demonstrated that this is not the case. In fact, studies have shown that current SUDs in samples of individuals with psychiatric disabilities had no association with employment status and did not affect participation in employment (Cook et al., 2007). In fact, Cook et al. cited one study in which participants with psychiatric disabilities and CODs actually had better work functioning, more involvement in vocational rehabilitation, and a greater likelihood of employment than participants with only a psychiatric disability.

Finally, consideration of the negative effects of having a history of incarceration on employment potential is indicated in providing employment assistance to consumers with psychiatric disabilities. For example, Bernacchio and Burker (2016) highlighted practices for serving consumers with criminal justice involvement including use of a strengths-based approach that emphasizes the individual's skills and capabilities, taking incremental steps to assist consumers with obtaining and maintaining employment as well as advancing in their careers, and targeting job searches at smaller businesses where background checks are less likely to be required and recruitment methods are less rigorous.

Long-term supports are a hallmark of the IPS model, and follow-along services should be available indefinitely on an as-needed basis to both employers and employees with psychiatric disabilities. The goal of supported employment is for individuals to establish natural supports on the job to assist them with maintaining employment without the need for outside assistance. However, due to the episodic nature of psychiatric disabilities, supports are often needed during stressful times such as periods of symptom exacerbation, when individuals must take extended time off from work to receive treatment, when changes are made to the work environment such as the introduction of new technologies or the hiring of new supervisors, and when individuals change jobs or advance in their careers.

Accommodation Planning

Because psychiatric disabilities are episodic and accompanied by functional limitations that vary by psychiatric condition, identifying classroom and workplace accommodations is not as straightforward as it is for people with physical and sensory disabilities. Accommodation planning with individuals with psychiatric disabilities will involve not only considerations for changes implemented in the classroom or workplace, but also illness self-management strategies as well as postsecondary, worksite, and community supports. Additionally, because individuals with psychiatric disabilities frequently have co-occurring medical conditions, SUDs, and/or criminal records, accommodation planning will need to target the functional limitations and employment barriers associated with these conditions and circumstances.

In a multisite, longitudinal study of 191 employees in 22 supported employment programs across three states, MacDonald-Wilson, Rogers, and Massaro (2003) found that the most frequently reported functional limitation was cognitive (e.g., learning the job, concentrating, following schedule/attending work, assessing own work performance, solving problems/organizing work, using basic language/literacy skills, initiating new tasks). This limitation was followed by social (e.g., interacting with others, interpreting work/social cues); physical (e.g., maintaining work stamina, bending, lifting heavy objects, preventing physical injury, maintaining safe driving standards, continuing Social Security/health insurance, availability of public transportation); and emotional (e.g., adjusting to work situations, managing symptoms/tolerating stress). Examples of additional functional limitations that may impede successful school and work performance include responding to negative feedback, memory problems, overstimulation, racing thoughts, difficulties with self-pacing, problems dealing with change, feeling paranoid or self-conscious, difficulties completing tasks on time, and hearing voices (Legere, Furlong-Norman, Gaylor, & St. Pierre, 2009).

In the study conducted by MacDonald-Wilson et al. (2003), the research participants reported that the reasonable accommodations they most frequently used were the presence of a job coach during the hiring process or on the job, extra or modified training or supervision, modified job duties, and flexible scheduling. Other potential workplace accommodations that may benefit students and employees with psychiatric disabilities include telecommuting, flexibility in scheduling breaks, flexible sick leave and vacation policies, removal of distractions in the work area, "white noise" or environmental sound machines, permitting beverages or foods at work stations to manage side effects of medication, and relevant training for coworkers and staff (Legere et al., 2009; U.S. Department of Labor Office of Disability Employment Policy, 2015).

Another important consideration in accommodation planning is the low rate at which youths with psychiatric disabilities disclose their disabilities to postsecondary school staff and employers so that they can receive supports and accommodations. This problem indicates the need for training in self-determination skills. Training in self-determination skills focuses on developing knowledge and self-awareness about psychiatric conditions and symptomology as well as communication and assertiveness skills to effectively self-advocate for needed supports and accommodations. Wagner and Newman (2012) pointed out the need for this training to begin with students with psychiatric disabilities in secondary educational settings. Training for secondary students should focus on the development of self-awareness regarding their disability and support needs and preparation for self-advocating for these supports in both postsecondary and employment settings.

Because stigma can be an issue that contributes to underuse of disability-related supports and workplace accommodations for individuals with psychiatric disabilities, issues related to disclosure are often pronounced and complicated. The potential internalization of stigma by the individual with a psychiatric disability and prior experiences with disclosure that may have resulted in negative consequences can create reluctance to disclose. Therefore, it is imperative that rehabilitation counselors and disability service professionals engage consumers in thoughtful discussions about their prior experiences with disclosure, the risks and benefits of disclosure, how and to whom to disclose, and their potential to benefit from on-campus disability or work supports such as mental health counseling, classroom and work accommodations, and employee assistance programs.

The starting point in identifying accommodations is to consider accommodations and supports that have worked for individuals in the past. For example, rehabilitation counselors can discuss with consumers how accommodations used in the classroom can be applied to the worksite. Then, rehabilitation counselors can explore with these consumers additional accommodations they have not used but could benefit from. Legere et al. (2009) developed a higher education supports toolkit that rehabilitation counselors can use with students to (a) clarify challenges that interfere with academic success and satisfaction; (b) identify potential solutions and strategies to respond to these challenges; and (c) determine possible courses of action and accommodations to request as well as campus resources and supports to utilize. The toolkit includes comprehensive lists of potential challenges, accommodation ideas, and resources. It could easily be modified for use in planning job accommodations.

CONCLUSIONS

Individuals with psychiatric disabilities represent a population of rehabilitation consumers who have significant internal and external barriers to achieving their rehabilitation goals. Despite the availability of evidence-based treatment, wellness, recovery, and employment interventions, people with psychiatric disabilities still experience poorer health in comparison to the general population, are more likely to be incarcerated, less likely to complete secondary education, less likely obtain postsecondary degrees to increase their employment potential, and more likely to be unemployed. Rehabilitation counselors can improve these outcomes by advocating for and delivering integrated, recovery-oriented services to these individuals.

Interventions with established and emerging evidence emphasize the rapid delivery of integrated services, the tailoring of services to the individual's developmental stage and level of readiness for change, holistic planning to respond to their overall health and wellness, co-occurring substance abuse and health conditions, and needs for ongoing follow-along supports. Providing rehabilitation services coupled with mental health, substance abuse, and health care services in an early intervention context can increase the likelihood that these individuals will experience a more manageable course of illness with reduced symptomology, increased employment stability, and improved health and wellness.

DISCUSSION QUESTIONS

1. What myths have influenced your perceptions of people with psychiatric disabilities? What information presented in this chapter has challenged you to reconsider your perceptions?
2. Describe the psychosocial and vocational challenges that you think present the greatest barriers to quality of life and employment for people with psychiatric disabilities.
3. What do you think are the most important considerations for forming strong working alliances with clients with psychiatric disabilities?
4. What are the most important implications for rehabilitation planning discussed in this chapter?
5. At the beginning of the chapter we described Maya's case. Discuss implications for determining Maya's eligibility for rehabilitation services; specific services you would include on her rehabilitation plan; and implications for job development, placement, follow-along, and reasonable accommodations.
6. If Maya had applied for rehabilitation services while she was still drinking and was not being treated for her anxiety and depression, how would you proceed with the rehabilitation assessment and planning process? Discuss the implications if Maya lived in a community that did not have the multitude of services that Maya was able to access in her community.

REFERENCES

Active Minds. (2016). *Active minds: Changing the conversation about mental health.* Retrieved from http://www.activeminds.org

Agency for Healthcare Research and Quality. (2012). *Migraine in adults: Preventative pharmacologic treatments.* Retrieved from https://www.effectivehealthcare.ahrq.gov/ehc/products/313/1453/migraine-report-130408.pdf

American Psychological Association. (2014). *Data on behavioral health in the United States.* Retrieved from http://www.apa.org/helpcenter/data-behavioral-health.aspx

Anthony, W. A. (1993). Recovery from mental illness: The guiding vision of the mental health system in the 1990's. *Psychosocial Rehabilitation Journal, 16*(4), 11–23.

Baker, K., & DeIrish, M. (2015). *Campus mental health partnerships: Case management toolkit.* Retrieved from http://campusmentalhealth.ca/resource/campus-mental-health-partnerships-case-management-toolkit

Bartels, S. J., Pratt, S. I., Mueser, K. T., Naslund, J. A., Wolfe, R. S., Santos, M.,…Riera, E. G. (2014). Integrated IMR for psychiatric and general medical illness for adults aged 50 or older with serious mental illness. *Psychiatric Services, 65*(3), 330–337.

Becker, D., Whitley, R., Bailey, E. L., & Drake, R. E. (2007). Long-term employment trajectories among participants with severe mental illness in supported employment. *Psychiatric Services, 58*(7), 922–928.

Becker, D. R., Drake, R. E., & Naughton, W. J. (2005). Supported employment for people with co-occurring disorders. *Psychiatric Rehabilitation Journal, 28*(4), 332–338.

Becker, M., Martin, L., Wajeeh, E., Ward, J., & Shern, D. (2002). Students with mental illnesses in a university setting: Faculty and student attitudes, beliefs, knowledge, and experiences. *Psychiatric Rehabilitation Journal, 25*(4), 359–368.

Belch, H. A. (2011). Understanding the experiences of students with psychiatric disabilities: A foundation for creating conditions of support and success. *New Directions for Student Services, 2011*(134), 73–94.

Bernacchio, C., & Burker, E. J. (2016). Psychiatric rehabilitation of persons with co-occurring disorders and corrections involvement. *Rehabilitation Research, Policy and Education, 30*(3), 230–242.

Bertram, M. (2010). Bottom line: Student mental health: Reframing the 'problem.' *About Campus, 15*(4), 30–32.

Birmaher, B. (2013). Bipolar disorder in children and adolescents. *Child and Adolescent Mental Health, 18*(3), 140–148.

Bond, G. R. (2004). Supported employment: Evidence for an evidence-based practice. *Psychiatric Rehabilitation Journal, 27*(4), 345–359.

Boston University Center for Psychiatric Rehabilitation. (2011). *Readings in psychiatric rehabilitation and recovery.* Retrieved from https://cpr.bu.edu/resources

Boston University Center for Psychiatric Rehabilitation. (2016). *Photovoice.* Retrieved from https://cpr.bu.edu/resources/photovoice

Boutin, D. L., & Accordino, M. P. (2011). Importance of collegiate training for vocational rehabilitation consumers with psychiatric disabilities. *American Journal of Psychiatric Rehabilitation, 14*(1), 76–95.

Burke-Miller, J., Razzano, L. A., Grey, D. D., Blyler, C. R., & Cook, J. A. (2012). Supported employment outcomes for transition age youth and young adults. *Psychiatric Rehabilitation Journal, 35*(3), 171–179.

Byrd, D. R., & McKinney, K. J. (2012). Individual, interpersonal, and institutional level factors associated with the mental health of college students. *Journal of American College Health, 60*(3), 185–193. doi:10.1080/07448481.2011.584334

Carnevale, A. P., Smith, N., & Strohl, J. (2010). *Help wanted: Projections of jobs and education requirements through 2018. Executive summary.* Washington, DC: Georgetown University Center on Education and the Workforce.

Collins, M. E., & Mowbray, C. T. (2005). Higher education and psychiatric disabilities: National survey of campus disability services. *American Journal of Orthopsychiatry, 75*, 304–315.

Colton, C. W., & Manderscheid, R. W. (2006). Congruencies in increased mortality rates, years of potential life lost, and causes of death among public mental health clients in eight states. *Preventing Chronic Disease, 3*(2), A42.

Committee on Health Literacy. (2004). *Health literacy: A prescription to end confusion.* Retrieved from http://www.ncbi.nlm.nih.gov/books/NBK216035

Cook, J. A. (2006). Employment barriers for person with psychiatric disabilities: Update of a report for the president's commission. *Psychiatric Services, 57*(10), 1391–1405.

Cook, J. A. (2011). Peer-delivered wellness recovery services: From evidence to widespread implementation. *Psychiatric Rehabilitation Journal, 35*(2), 87–89.

Cook, J. A., Copeland, M., Hamilton, M., Jonikas, J., Razzano, L., Floyd, C.,…Grey, D. (2009). Initial outcomes of a mental illness self-management program based on wellness recovery action planning. *Psychiatric Services, 60*(2), 246–249.

Cook, J. A., Copeland, M. E., Jonikas, J. A., Hamilton, M. M., Razzano, L. A., Grey, D. D.,…Boyd, S. (2011). Results of a randomized controlled trial of mental illness self-management using Wellness Recovery Action Planning. *Schizophrenia Bulletin, 38*(4), 881–891.

Cook, J. A., Lehman, A., Drake, R., McFarlane, W., Gold, P., Leff, H.,…Gray, D. D. (2005). Integration of psychiatric and vocational services: A multisite randomized, controlled trial of supported employment. *American Journal of Psychiatry, 162*, 1948–1956.

Cook, J. A., Mulkern, V., Grey, D. D., Burke-Miller, J., Blyler, C. R., Razzano, L. A.,…Steigman, P. A. (2006). Effects of local unemployment rate on vocational outcomes in a randomized trial of supported employment for individuals with psychiatric disabilities. *Journal of Vocational Rehabilitation, 25*(2), 71–84.

Cook, J. A., Razzano, L. A., Burke-Miller, J. K., Blyler, C. R., Leff, H. S., Mueser, K. T.,…Grey, D. D. (2007). Effects of co-occurring disorders on employment outcomes in a multisite randomized study of supported employment for people with severe mental illness. *Journal of Rehabilitation Research & Development, 44*(6), 837–850.

Copeland, M. A. (2011). *Wellness Recovery Action Plan* (5th ed.). Dummerston, VT: Peach Press.

Davis, M. (2015). *Research-based employment supports for youth with chronic mental health disorders* [Webcast]. Richmond: Virginia Commonwealth University Rehabilitation Research and Training Center on Work Supports.

Deegan, P. E. (1988). Recovery: The lived experience of rehabilitation. *Psychosocial Rehabilitation Journal, 11*, 11–19.

Dixon, L., McFarlane, W. R., Lefley, H., Lucksted, A., Cohen, M., Falloon, I.,…Sondheimer, D. (2001). Evidence-based practices for services to families of people with psychiatric disabilities. *Psychiatric Services, 52*(7), 903–910.

Donnell, C. M., Mizelle, N. D., & Zheng, Y. (2009). Consumers of vocational rehabilitation services diagnosed with psychiatric and substance use disorders. *Journal of Rehabilitation, 75*(3), 41–49.

Doweiko, H. E. (2012). *Concepts of chemical dependency* (8th ed.). Belmont, CA: Brooks/Cole.

Drake, R. E., Skinner, J. S., Bond, G. R., & Goldman, H. H. (2009). Social Security and mental illness: Reducing disability with supported employment. *Health Affairs, 28*(3), 761–770.

Dunn, E. C., Wewiorski, N. J., & Rogers, E. S. (2008). The meaning and importance of employment to people in recovery from serious mental illness: Results of a qualitative study. *Psychiatric Rehabilitation Journal, 32*(1), 59–62.

Ellison, M., Klodnick, V., Bond, G., Krzos, I., Kaiser, S., Fagan, M., & Davis, M. (2015). Adapting supported employment for emerging adults with serious mental health conditions. *Journal of Behavioral Health Services & Research, 42*(2), 206–222.

Eudaly, J. (2002). *A rising tide: Students with psychiatric disabilities seek services in record numbers.* Retrieved from https://heath.gwu.edu/files/downloads/psychiatric_disabilities.pdf

Evashwick, C. (1989). Creating the continuum of care. *Health Matrix, 7*(1), 30–39.

Farkas, M., Gagne, C., Anthony, W., & Chamberlin, J. (2005). Implementing recovery oriented evidence based programs: Identifying the critical dimensions. *Community Mental Health Journal, 41*(2), 141–158.

Frounfelker, R. L., Wilkniss, S. M., Bond, G. R., Devitt, T. S., & Drake, R. E. (2011). Enrollment in supported employment services for clients with a co-occurring disorder. *Psychiatric Services, 62*(5), 545–547.

Fukui, S., Starnino, V., Susana, M., Davidson, L., Cook, K., Rapp, C., & Gowdy, E. (2011). Effect of Wellness Recovery Action Plan (WRAP) participation on psychiatric symptoms, sense of hope, and recovery. *Psychiatric Rehabilitation Journal, 34*(3), 214–222.

Gill, K. J., Murphy, A. A., Zechner, M. R., Swarbrick, M., & Spagnolo, A. B. (2009). Co-morbid psychiatric and medical disorders: Challenges and strategies. *Journal of Rehabilitation, 75*(3), 32–40.

Goodwin, F. K., & Jamison, K. R. (2007). *Manic-depressive illness: Bipolar disorders and recurrent depression* (2nd ed.). New York, NY: Oxford University Press.

Goodwin, R. D., Stayner, D. A., Chinman, M. J., Wu, P., Tebes, J. K., & Davidson, L. (2002). The relationship between anxiety and substance use disorders among individuals with severe affective disorders. *Comprehensive Psychiatry, 43*(4), 245–252.

Hartley, M. T. (2013). Investigating the relationship of resilience to academic persistence in college students with mental health issues. *Rehabilitation Counseling Bulletin, 56*(4), 240–250. doi:10.1177/0034355213480527

Holzer, H. J., Raphael, S., & Stoll, M. A. (2003). *Employer demand for ex-offenders: Recent evidence from Los Angeles.* Retrieved from http://www.urban.org/research/publication/employer-demand-ex-offenders

Insel, T. R. (2011). *Director's blog: No health without mental health.* Retrieved from http://www.nimh.nih.gov/about/director/2011/no-health-without-mental-health.shtml

James, D. J., & Glaze, L. E. (2006). *Mental health problems of prison and jail inmates.* Retrieved from http://www.bjs.gov/content/pub/pdf/mhppji.pdf

Johnson, M. E., Brems, C., Mills, M. E., & Fisher, D. G. (2007). Psychiatric symptomatology among individuals in alcohol detoxification treatment. *Addictive Behaviors, 32*(8), 1745–1752.

Jones, D., Macias, C., Barreira, P., Fisher, W., Hargreaves, W., & Harding, C. (2004). Prevalence, severity, and co-occurrence of chronic physical health problems of persons with serious mental illness. *Psychiatric Services, 55*(11), 1250–1257.

Jonikas, J. A., Grey, D. D., Copeland, M. E., Razzano, L. A., Hamilton, M. M., Floyd, C. B., ... Cook, J. A. (2013). Improving propensity for patient self-advocacy through wellness recovery action planning: Results of a randomized controlled trial. *Community Mental Health Journal, 49*(3), 260–269.

Kelly, T. M., & Daley, D. C. (2013). Integrated treatment of substance use and psychiatric disorders. *Social Work in Public Health, 28*(3/4), 388–406.

Kessler, R. C., Heeringa, S., Lakoma, M. D., Petukhova, M., Rupp, A. E., Schoenbaum, M., ... Zaslavsky, A. M. (2008). Individual and societal effects of mental disorders on earnings in the United States: Results from the National Comorbidity Survey Replication. *American Journal of Psychiatry, 165*(6), 703–711.

Kethineni, S., & Falcone, D. N. (2007). Employment and ex-offenders in the United States: Effects of legal and extra legal factors. *Probation Journal, 54*(1), 36–51.

Kiuhara, S. A., & Huefner, D. S. (2008). Students with psychiatric disabilities in higher education settings. *Journal of Disability Policy Studies, 19*(2), 103–113.

Klodnick, V. V., Sabella, K., Krzos, I. M., Brenner, C., Kaiser, S. M., Ellison, M. L., ... Fagan, M. A. (2014). Perspectives of early emerging adults with serious mental health conditions on vocational peer mentors. *Journal of Emotional & Behavioral Disorders, 1–12.* doi: 10.1177/1063426614565052

Knight, K. R., Lopez, A. M., Comfort, M., Shumway, M., Cohen, J., & Riley, E. D. (2014). Single room occupancy (SRO) hotels as mental health risk environments among impoverished women: The intersection of policy, drug use, trauma, and urban space. *International Journal of Drug Policy, 25*(3), 556–561.

Koch, L. C., Carey, C., & Lusk, S. L. (2016). Introduction to the special issue on psychiatric rehabilitation. *Rehabilitation Research, Policy, and Education, 30*(3), 198–203.

Koch, L. C., Mamiseishvili, K., & Higgins, K. (2014). Persistence to degree completion: A profile of students with psychiatric disabilities in higher education. *Journal of Vocational Rehabilitation, 40*(1), 73–82.

Lamberti, J. (2007). Understanding and preventing criminal recidivism among adults with psychotic disorders. *Psychiatric Services, 58*(6), 773–781.

Lee, E., Chan, F., Chronister, J., Chan, J. Y., & Romero, M. (2009). Models, research, and treatment of coexisting depression for people with chronic illness and disability. In F. Chan, E. Da Silva Cardoso, & J. A. Chronister (Eds.), *Understanding psychosocial adjustment to chronic illness and disability: A handbook for evidence-based practitioners in rehabilitation* (pp. 75–107). New York, NY: Springer Publishing Company.

Legere, L., Furlong-Norman, K., Gayler, C., & St. Pierre, C. (2009). *Student self-assessment checklist.* Boston, MA: Boston University Centre for Psychiatric Rehabilitation.

Leslie, K. (2008). Youth substance use and abuse: Challenges and strategies for identification and intervention. *Canadian Medical Association Journal, 178*(2), 145–148.

Lusk, S. (Ed.). (2013). *Counseling the addicted family: Implications for practitioners.* Linn Creek, MO: Aspen.

Lusk, S., & Koch, L. (2013). *Psychiatric disabilities and co-occurring substance use disorders: Rehabilitation implications.* 2013 Arkansas Rehabilitation Association Annual Training Conference. Little Rock, AR.

Lusk, S., Koch, L., & Paul, T. (2016). Recovery-oriented VR services for individuals with co-occurring psychiatric disabilities and substance use disorders. *Rehabilitation Research, Policy, and Education, 30*(3), 243–258.

MacDonald-Wilson, K. L., Rogers, E. S., & Massaro, J. (2003). Identifying relationships between functional limitations, job accommodations, and demographic characteristics of persons with psychiatric disabilities. *Journal of Vocational Rehabilitation, 18*(1), 15–24.

Magaletta, P. R., Diamond, P. M., Faust, E., Daggett, D. M., & Camp, S. D. (2009). Estimating the mental illness component of service need in corrections: Results from the Mental Health Prevalence Project. *Criminal Justice and Behavior, 36*(3), 229–244.

Magura, S., & Staines, G. L. (2004). Introduction: New directions for vocational rehabilitation in substance user treatment: Rebuilding damaged lives. *Substance Use & Misuse, 39*(13–14), 2157–2164.

Matthews, L. R., Harris, L. M., Jaworski, A., Alam, A., & Bozdag, G. (2013). Function in job seekers with mental illness and drug and alcohol problems who access community based disability employment services. *Disability & Rehabilitation, 35*(6), 460–467.

Mayo Clinic. (2014). *Metabolic syndrome.* Retrieved from http://www.mayoclinic.org/diseases-conditions/metabolic-syndrome/home/ovc-20197517

Mayo Clinic. (2015). *Mental illness in children: Know the signs.* Retrieved from http://www.mayoclinic.org/healthy-lifestyle/childrens-health/in-depth/mental-illness-in-children/art-20046577

McDonald, J. L., & Meyer, T. D. (2011). Self-report reasons for alcohol use in bipolar disorders: Why drink despite the potential risks? *Clinical Psychology & Psychotherapy, 18*(5), 418–425.

McEvoy, J. P., Meyer, J. M., Goff, D. C., Nasrallah, H. A., Davis, S. M., Sullivan, L., ... Lieberman, J. A. (2005). Prevalence of the metabolic syndrome in patients with schizophrenia: Baseline results from the Clinical Antipsychotic Trials of Intervention Effectiveness (CATIE) schizophrenia trial and comparison with national estimates from NHANES III. *Schizophrenia Research, 80*(1), 19–32.

McKay, J. R., & Weiss, R. V. (2001). A review of temporal effects and outcome predictors in substance abuse treatment studies with long-term follow-ups: Preliminary results and methodological issues. *Evaluation Review, 25*(2), 113–161.

Megivern, D., Pellerito, S., & Mowbray, C. (2003). Barriers to higher education for individuals with psychiatric disabilities. *Psychiatric Rehabilitation Journal, 26*(3), 217–231.

Metzner, J., & Fellner, J. (2010). Solitary confinement and mental illness in U.S. prisons: A challenge for medical ethics. *Journal of the American Academy of Psychiatry Law, 38*, 104–108.

Miller, W. R., Zweben, A., DiClemente, C. C., & Rychtarik, R. G. (1992). Motivational enhancement therapy manual: A clinical research guide for therapists treating individuals with alcohol abuse and dependence. *NIAAA Project MATCH Monograph Series, Volume 2.* DHHS Publication No. (ADM) 92–1894. Rockville, MD: National Institute on Alcohol Abuse and Alcoholism.

Mistler, B., Reetz, D. R., Krylowicz, B., & Barr, V. (2013). *The 2012 Association for University and College Counseling Center Directors Annual Survey.* Indianapolis, IN: AUCCCD.

Mojtabai, R. (2011). National trends in mental health disability, 1997–2009. *American Journal of Public Health, 10*(11), 2156–2163.

Morrissey, J. P., Ellis, A. R., Gatz, M., Amaro, H., Reed, B. G., Savage, A., ... Banks, S. (2005). Outcomes for women with co-occurring disorders and trauma: Program and person-level effects. *Journal of Substance Abuse Treatment, 28*(2), 121–133.

National Alliance on Mental Illness. (2010). *What is mental illness: Mental illness facts.* Retrieved from http://www.nami.org/Content/NavigationMenu/Inform_Yourself/About_Mental_Illness About_Mental_Illness.htm

National Alliance on Mental Illness. (2011). *State mental health cuts: A national crisis.* Retrieved from http://www2.nami.org/ContentManagement/ContentDisplay.cfm?ContentFileID=126233

National Alliance on Mental Illness. (2016). *Solitary confinement fact sheet.* Retrieved from https://www.prisonlegalnews.org/media/publications/Solitary%20Confinement%20Fact%20Sheat%20NAMI%202012.pdf

National Association for Alcoholism and Drug Abuse Counselors. (2010). *Integrating treatment for co-occurring disorders: An introduction to what every addiction counselor needs to know.* Retrieved from http://www.naadac.org/assets/1959/cod_manual_peek.pdf

National Committee on Quality Assurance. (2015). *Latest evidence: Benefits of the patient-centered medical care home.* Retrieved from http://www.ncqa.org/Portals/0/Programs/Recognition/NCQA%20PCMH%20Evidence%20Report,%20June%202015.pdf

National Institute of Mental Health. (2008). *The numbers count: Mental disorders in America.* Retrieved from http://www.naminys.org/images/uploads/pdfs/The%20Numbers%20Count%20Mental%20Disorders%20in%20America%20.doc

National Institute of Mental Health. (2015). *Treatment of children with mental illness.* Retrieved from http://www.nimh.nih.gov/health/publications/treatment-of-children-with-mental-illness-fact-sheet/index.shtml

National Institute on Drug Abuse. (2010). *Comorbidity: Addiction and other mental illnesses.* Retrieved from https://www.drugabuse.gov/sites/default/files/rrcomorbidity.pdf

National Sheriffs' Association and Treatment Advocacy Center. (2014). *The treatment of persons with mental illness in prisons and jails.* Retrieved from http://nicic.gov/library/028094

Newcomer, J. W. (2007). Metabolic syndrome and mental illness. *American Journal of Managed Care, 13*(7S), S170–S177.

Norman, R. E., Byambaa, M., De, R., Butchart, A., Scott, J., & Vos, T. (2012). The long-term health consequences of child physical abuse, emotional abuse, and neglect: A systematic review and meta-analysis. *PLOS Medicine, 9*(11), 1–32.

Nuechterlein, K. H., Subotnik, K. L., Turner, L. R., Ventura, J., Becker, D. R., & Drake, R. E. (2008). Individual placement and support for individuals with recent-onset schizophrenia: Integrating supported education and supported employment. *Psychiatric Rehabilitation Journal, 31*(4), 340–349.

Nunes, E. V., Selzer, J., Levounis, P., & Davies, C. A. (2010). *Substance dependence and co-occurring psychiatric disorders: Best practices for diagnosis and treatment.* Kingston, NJ: Civic Research Institute.

Osher, F., D'Amora, D. A., Plotkin, M., Jarrett, N., & Eggleston, A. (2012). *Adults with behavioral health needs under correctional supervision: A shared framework for reducing recidivism and promoting recovery.* New York, NY: Council of State Governments Justice Center.

Perou, R., Bitsko, R. H., Blumberg, S. J., Pastor, P., Ghandour, R. M., Gfroerer, J. C., ... Huang, L. N. (2013). Mental health surveillance among children—United States, 2005–2011. *Morbidity & Mortality Weekly Report, 62*(Suppl. 2), 1–35.

Perreau-Lenz, S., & Spanagel, R. (2015). Clock genes x stress x reward interactions in alcohol and substance use disorders. *Alcohol, 49,* 351–357.

Pratt, C. W., Gill, K. J., Barrett, N. M., & Roberts, M. M. (2014). *Psychiatric rehabilitation* (3rd ed.). London, UK: Elsevier.

Prochaska, J. O., Norcross, J. C., & DiClemente, C. C. (1994). *Changing for good: A revolutionary six-stage program for overcoming bad habits and moving your life positively forward.* New York, NY: Avon.

Rehfuss, M. C., & Quillin, A. B. (2005). Connecting students with hidden disabilities to resources. *National Academic Advising Association Journal, 25*(1), 47–50.

Rich, J., Holmes, L., Salas, C., Macalino, G., Davis, D., Ryczek, J., & Flanigan, T. (2001). Successful linkage of medical care and community services for HIV-positive offenders being released from prison. *Journal of Urban Health, 78*(2), 279–289.

Rosenthal, D., Dalton, J., & Gervey, R. (2007). Analyzing vocational outcomes of individuals with psychiatric disabilities who received state vocational rehabilitation services: A data mining approach. *International Journal of Social Psychiatry, 53*(4), 357–368.

Rudnick, A., McEwan, R. C., Pallaveshi, L., Wey, L., Lau, W., Alia, L., & Van Volkenburg, L. (2013). Integrating supported education and supported employment for people with mental illness: A pilot study. *International Journal of Psychosocial Rehabilitation, 18*(1), 5–25.

Salzer, M. S. (2012). A comparative study of campus experiences of college students with mental illnesses versus a general college sample. *Journal of American College Health, 60*(1), 1–7.

Salzer, M. S., Schwenk, E., & Brusilovskiy, E. (2010). Certified peer specialist roles and activities: Results from a national survey. *Psychiatric Services, 61*(5), 520–523.

Sheehan, L., & Lewicki, T. (2016). Collaborative documentation in mental health: Applications to rehabilitation counseling. *Rehabilitation Research, Policy, and Education, 30*(3), 305–320.

Shivy, V. A., Wu, J. J., Moon, A. E., Mann, S. C., Holland, J. G., & Eacho, C. (2007). Ex-offenders reentering the workforce. *Journal of Counseling Psychology, 54*(4), 466–473.

Starnino, V., Mariscal, S., Holter, M., Davidson, L., Cook, K., Fukui, S., & Rapp, C. (2010). Outcomes of an illness self-management group using wellness recovery action planning. *Psychiatric Rehabilitation Journal, 34*(1), 57–60.

Steadman, H., Osher, F., Robbins, P., Case, B., & Samuels, S. (2009). Prevalence of serious mental illness among jail inmates. *Psychiatric Services, 60*(6), 761–765.

Substance Abuse and Mental Health Services Administration. (2000). *Integrating substance abuse treatment and vocational services*. Retrieved from https://store.samhsa.gov/shin/content/QGCT38/QGCT38.pdf

Substance Abuse and Mental Health Services Administration. (2012). *SAMHSA's working definition of recovery*. Retrieved from http://store.samhsa.gov/product/SAMHSA-s-Working-Definition-of-Recovery/PEP12-RECDEF

Substance Abuse and Mental Health Services Administration. (2015). *Mental and substance use disorders*. Retrieved from http://www.samhsa.gov/disorders

Swarbrick, M., & Nemec, P. (2016). Supporting the health and wellness of individuals with psychiatric disabilities. *Rehabilitation Research, Policy, and Education, 30*(3), 321–333.

Thomas, J. R., & Fraser, W. (2009). Implementing evidence-based supported employment in a recovery-oriented mental health agency. *American Journal of Psychiatric Rehabilitation, 12*(2), 143–160.

Thompson, E. A., Connelly, C. D., Thomas-Jones, D., & Eggert, L. L. (2013). School difficulties and co-occurring health risk factors: Substance use, aggression, depression, and suicidal behaviors. *Journal of Child and Adolescent Psychiatric Nursing, 26*(1), 74–84.

Torrey, E. F., Zdanowicz, M. T., Kennard, A. D., Lamb, H. R., Eslinger, D. F., Biasotti, M. C., & Fuller, D. (2014). *The treatment of persons with mental illness in prisons and jails: A state survey*. Retrieved from http://www.tacreports.org/storage/documents/treatment-behind-bars/treatment-behind-bars.pdf

U.S. Department of Health and Human Services. (2015). *Practitioner guides and handouts: Illness management and recovery*. Retrieved from https://store.samhsa.gov/shin/content/SMA09-4463/PractitionerGuidesandHandouts.pdf

U.S. Department of Labor Office of Disability Employment Policy. (2015). *Maximizing productivity: Accommodations for employees with psychiatric disabilities*. Retrieved from https://www.dol.gov/odep/pubs/fact/psychiatric.htm

Waghorn, G., & Lloyd, C. (2005). *The employment of people with mental illness: A discussion document prepared for the Mental Illness Fellowship of Australia*. The University of Queensland, Australia.

Wagner, M., & Davis, M. A. (2006). How are we preparing students with emotional disturbances for the transition to young adulthood? Findings from the National Longitudinal Transition Study-2. *Journal of Emotional & Behavioral Disorders, 14*(2), 86–98.

Wagner, M., & Newman, L. (2012). Longitudinal transition outcomes of youth with emotional disturbances. *Psychiatric Rehabilitation Journal, 35*(3), 199–208.

Walker, J. S., & Gowen, L. K. (2011). *Community-based approaches for supporting positive development in youth and young adults with serious mental health condition*s. Portland, OR: Research and Training Center for Pathways to Positive Futures, Portland State University.

Walker, J. S., Pullman, M. D., Moser, C. L., & Burns, E. J. (2012). Does team-based planning "work" for adolescents? Findings from studies of wraparound. *Psychiatric Rehabilitation Journal, 35*(3), 189–198. doi:10.2975/35.3.2012.189.198

Weiner, E., & Weiner, J. (1996). Concerns and needs of university students with psychiatric disabilities. *Journal of Postsecondary Education and Disability, 12*(1), 2–9.

World Health Organization. (2012). *Depression*. Retrieved from http://www.who.int/mediacentre/factsheets/fs369/en

Wüsthoff, L. E., Waal, H., & Gråwe, R. W. (2014). The effectiveness of integrated treatment in patients with substance use disorders co-occurring with anxiety and/or depression: A group randomized trial. *BioMed Central Psychiatry, 14*(1), 1–26.

Zanis, D. A., Coviello, D., Alterman, A. I., & Appling, S. E. (2001). A community-based trial of vocational problem-solving to increase employment among methadone patients. *Journal of Substance Abuse Treatment, 21*(1), 19–26.

Zelenev, A., Marcus, R., Kopelev, A., Cruzado-Quinones, J., Spaulding, A., Desabrais, M.,… Altice, F. (2013). Patterns of homelessness and implications for HIV health after release from jail. *AIDS & Behavior, 17*, 181–194.

Ziedonis, D. M., Smelson, D., Rosenthal, R. N., Batki, S. L., Green, A. I., Henry, R. J.,… Weiss, R. D. (2005). Improving the care of individuals with schizophrenia and substance use disorders: Consensus recommendations. *Journal of Psychiatric Practice, 11*(5), 315–339.

Zinman, S., Budd, S., & Bluebird, G. (2009). *The history of the mental health consumer/survivor movement.* Presentation sponsored by SAMHSA's Resource Center to Promote Acceptance, Dignity and Social Inclusion Associated with Mental Health. Retrieved from http://www.mindlink.org/dwnld_docs/samhsa_history_consumer_movement.pdf

Emerging Disabilities Associated With Lifestyle and Climate Change

SIX

With Contributions by Rachel Timblin

CHAPTER OBJECTIVES

- *Examine the roles that lifestyle factors and climate change play in the onset and exacerbation of emerging disabilities*
- *Provide examples of chronic illnesses and disabilities linked to lifestyle and climate change that are increasing in the population*
- *Consider the medical, psychosocial, and vocational characteristics of emerging disabilities associated with lifestyle and climate change*
- *Explore characteristics of populations at risk of acquiring disabilities and chronic illnesses associated with lifestyle and climate change*
- *Recommend strategies that can be implemented in each phase of the rehabilitation process to respond to the needs of the populations discussed in this chapter*

CASE ILLUSTRATION: DAVID

David is a 46-year-old African American male who works as a Certified Financial Planner with a large investment firm in the southwestern United States. He works with clients in person, over the telephone, and online to help them establish long-term financial objectives; save for college tuition and retirement; manage household debt; purchase stocks, bonds, and mutual funds; and prepare their estates for succeeding generations of family members. David works full-time, up to 60 hours per week, on a 12-month basis. His job requires frequent automobile travel to meetings and conferences in the community and airplane travel to conferences once or twice per year.

David was diagnosed with type 2 diabetes at the age of 37. He regulates his blood sugar through diet, regular exercise, and orally ingested insulin pills. Symptoms of David's diabetes include fatigue, numbness in his hands and feet due to circulatory problems, occasional blurred vision, excessive bruising, and memory deficits when he experiences fatigue. David takes accrued sick leave when he is unable to work, and he uses a handheld electronic planner to combat his problems with memory. In fact, he has taken to using the handheld device at all times. David will also ask his employer to make minor scheduling modifications on days when he is working and experiencing fatigue. One such scheduling modification involves David holding his client meetings in the morning and early afternoon so he can go home early and rest. Because all of the Certified Financial Planners in David's firm schedule their own client meetings, this is an easy and no-cost accommodation for David to implement.

David has disclosed his diabetes to his employer, and the scheduling modification and the handheld planner are the only accommodations he requires to do his job at this time. Several of David's friends at work know about his diabetes. David is doing well in his job and managing his symptoms fairly effectively, but he sometimes worries about the future and whether his health will decline.

Throughout this textbook, we examine the multitude of environmental factors (e.g., violence, health care disparities, stigma, discrimination) that are associated with emerging disabilities. The focus of this chapter is on emerging disabilities that are linked to two additional environmental factors—lifestyle and climate change. During the 21st century, both of these factors have received increasing attention from health care providers, researchers, and policymakers because of growing evidence of their adverse effects on human health and functioning (Cha et al., 2015; Yang et al., 2014). Lifestyle and climate change have a reciprocal impact on the onset of chronic illnesses and disabilities as well as the exacerbation of preexisting conditions because it is primarily lifestyle choices (e.g., unsustainable consumption patterns, overreliance on use of personal vehicles for transportation) that have contributed both to dramatic increases in chronic illnesses and disabilities as well as more frequently occurring and severe weather patterns. Conversely, lifestyle changes that can improve people's health (e.g., eating less red meat and dairy food, eating more healthy foods that are locally grown and produced, walking, bicycling) can also mitigate the negative effects of climate change and further improve human health and functioning.

Lifestyle factors related to nutrition, exercise, organized athletics, smoking, use of alcohol and other drugs, access (or lack thereof) to prenatal and preventive care, and sexual behavior have contributed greatly to the increased incidence of a number of emerging disabilities. The widespread problem of obesity in the United States, caused by a combination of poor nutrition and inadequate exercise, has been marked by significant increases in diagnoses of diabetes (especially among children), hypertension and other circulatory diseases, sleep disorders, heart disease, stroke, and orthopedic impairments (Cha et al., 2015). Concussions and traumatic brain injuries among children and young adults who participate in organized athletics (especially football) have increased exponentially in recent years (Rose, Weber, Collen, & Heyer, 2015). Smoking, which is still on the rise in several segments of the American populace, increases a person's risk of various forms of cancer (especially lung cancer), heart disease, and pulmonary disease (Cole & Fiore, 2014). Poor prenatal care often results in premature or complicated births and accompanying heightened risks of autism and other developmental disabilities, asthma, allergies, intellectual disabilities, and blindness among children (Partridge, Balayla, Holcroft, & Abenhaim, 2012). HIV/AIDS remains a lifelong threat to health and wellness for intravenous drug users and those who engage in unprotected sexual activity (Adil Mansoor, Muazzam, & Hasan Imam, 2014).

Although climate change and the role of humans as causal agents are often debated in the media, the general consensus among scientists is that climate change is occurring primarily as a result of anthropogenic (human caused) factors such as the production of greenhouse gases and not merely as a result of the natural cycle of warming and cooling of the Earth (Barna, Goodman, & Mortimer, 2012; Costello et al., 2009). According to the U.S. Interagency Working Group on Climate Change and Human Health (2010, p. 38):

> Scientific evidence indicates that global warming will be accompanied by changes in the intensity, duration, and geographic extent of weather and climate extreme events; therefore, the threat to human health and well-being from events such as hurricanes, wildfires, flooding, and tornadoes is likely to continue, and perhaps worsen.

Detecting the human health effects of climate change is somewhat speculative because the long-term effects of this phenomenon are yet to be observed. Studying the effects of climate change on human health and functioning is further complicated by additional contributing factors (e.g., other social, economic, behavioral, and environmental factors) that make attribution of cause difficult (McMichael, Woodruff, & Hales, 2006). However, researchers have begun to investigate the health effects of recent severe weather events and have discovered that these events do, indeed, have a negative impact on both physical and mental health.

EMERGING DISABILITIES LINKED TO LIFESTYLE

A number of emerging disabilities have been attributed to lifestyle factors such as diet and exercise; sports and recreation; high-risk behavior; violence; and use of tobacco, alcohol, and other addictive substances (Koch, Conyers, & Rumrill, 2012). In particular, the respective incidences of diabetes, asthma, and heart disease have reached epidemic proportions in the United States. As can be seen in the paragraphs to follow, the emergence of these and other lifestyle-related conditions has placed a tremendous burden on the American systems of health care and rehabilitation, not to mention the impact they have on individuals and families.

Diabetes

Diabetes is the leading cause of adventitious blindness, amputations, and death by disease in the United States (American Diabetes Association, 2015). Diabetes is a metabolic disorder in which the pancreas' inability to regulate insulin results in high levels of unprocessed sugar in the blood, thereby causing a myriad of circulatory problems and secondary complications. With its wide-ranging symptoms and dramatically increasing incidence, diabetes has been a growing public health concern since the 1980s (Kiefer, Silverman, Young, & Nelson, 2015). According to the American Diabetes Association (2015), 29.1 million Americans or 9.3% of the population had diabetes in 2012. Approximately 1.25 million American children and adults have type 1 diabetes, which is characterized by the inability of the pancreas to produce any insulin on its own (Centers for Disease Control and Prevention [CDC], 2014b). Globally, the prevalence of diabetes among people between the ages of 20 and 79 has been estimated at 387 million, and by 2035 that worldwide prevalence figure is projected to exceed 592 million (International Diabetes Federation, 2014).

Although diabetes is an equal-opportunity disease that can affect any person of any age, rates of diabetes are on the rise among children and the elderly (American Diabetes Association, 2015). According to the National Diabetes Statistics Report of 2014, American Indian/Alaska Native, non-Hispanic Black, and Hispanic adults in the United States are twice as likely to be diagnosed with diabetes as non-Hispanic White Americans (CDC, 2014b). Lifestyle factors such as physical inactivity, poor nutrition, and obesity are strongly linked to type 2 diabetes, especially among children (World Health Organization [WHO], 2015a). Experts have pointed out that the risk of acquiring type 2 diabetes can be dramatically reduced by maintaining a healthy diet, participating in regular physical activity, and avoiding tobacco use (Milligan et al., 2014).

On the other hand, the cause of type 1 diabetes is not known, and this form of the disease is not preventable. It is usually diagnosed during early childhood, and those affected by type 1 diabetes are dependent on exogenous insulin for the rest of their lives. People who live in poverty and who have limited access to quality health care have much shorter life expectancies following the onset of type 1 diabetes than do people who have the means to obtain treatment, especially insulin that must be injected into their bodies to metabolize blood sugar (International Diabetes Federation, 2015).

The inability of the pancreas to produce sufficient insulin to process blood sugar brings with it a number of comorbidities and secondary complications for people coping with diabetes. Diabetes can cause damage to the heart, eyes, blood vessels, nerves, and kidneys (WHO, 2015a). Heart problems and stroke often co-occur with diabetes; 50% of people with diabetes die of cardiovascular disease. Neuropathy often causes pain and numbness in the extremities. Decreased blood flow stemming from high blood sugar levels results in skin ulcers, especially in the feet, that do not heal effectively. These unhealed ulcers often necessitate amputations of the toes, feet, and legs. Blindness and visual impairments are also common among people with diabetes due to damage to the small blood vessels in the retina (American Diabetes Association, 2015). Given the chronic nature of diabetes and its multiple and severe medical accompaniments, it is not surprising that people with this disease frequently experience psychosocial problems such as depression, anxiety, feelings of hopelessness, family role strain, and extreme psychological stress (American Diabetes Association, 2015; Falvo, 2014).

Diabetes has become relatively easy to diagnose in recent years. The first and most common diagnostic approach involves testing the person's hemoglobin A1C level. Diabetes is observed if the individual's A1C level measures 6.5% or greater. The second method is to test an individual's fasting plasma blood glucose level. Diabetes is diagnosed when the fasting plasma glucose level is at 126 mg/dL or higher. The third common testing method is an oral glucose tolerance test, which checks blood glucose before and after the person consumes a sweet drink. If blood glucose levels are 200 mg/dL or higher using this method, diabetes is diagnosed (American Diabetes Association, 2015).

Once a diabetes diagnosis is officiated, the treatment and care plan are unique to each person's circumstances and lifestyle. Information and education about the disease and its effects are often among the first steps in disease management. For people with type 1 diabetes, insulin injections are usually prescribed due to the pancreas' inability to generate or utilize insulin on its own (American Diabetes Association, 2015). Treatment for type 2 diabetes typically starts with managing diet, exercise, and weight loss, but when these measures are not sufficient, oral insulin is prescribed to help the person regulate his or her blood glucose level (American Diabetes Association, 2015). Insulin injections are prescribed for type 2 diabetes if the person cannot regulate his or her blood sugar through lifestyle changes or oral insulin. Diabetes treatment also involves medications and other interventions to address secondary complications of the disease (e.g., skin ulcers, pain, fatigue, circulatory problems).

Asthma

Asthma is an emerging and increasing public health problem across the globe. It is usually a lifelong disease that affects the airways of the lungs and restricts breathing. Individuals with asthma experience symptoms such as wheezing, labored breathing, tightness in the chest, and coughing (CDC, 2011). Common triggers of asthma attacks include upper respiratory infections; the common cold; high-exertion activities; and exposure to secondhand smoke, dust mites, mold, animal dander, and strong odors or sprays (Global Asthma Network [GAN], 2015). Diagnosis of asthma usually involves a family health history assessment, a physical examination conducted by a primary care physician, and assessment of air flow obstructions in the lungs using spirometry and/or bronchodilator reversibility tests (Galloway, 2015; National Heart, Lung, & Blood Institute [NHLBI], 2014). The multistep diagnostic process is necessary because many of the symptoms of asthma are also symptoms of other conditions such as allergies, respiratory infections, and pneumonia (Galloway, 2015).

Asthma incidence rates have risen steadily in the United States over the past several decades. According to the Environmental Protection Agency (EPA, 2015a), 23 million Americans are currently living with asthma, including 6 million children. Eleven million Americans reported having at least one asthma attack in 2015 (EPA, 2015a). Global prevalence estimates run as high as 334 million cases worldwide (GAN, 2015). Scientists have been unable to fully explain why the incidence and prevalence of asthma have increased so dramatically in recent decades, but it is clear that living in poverty and being exposed to air pollution and other environmental toxins significantly increase one's risk of acquiring this intrusive disease (GAN, 2015).

African Americans with asthma are 300% more likely than their Caucasian counterparts to receive treatment for asthma in the emergency department and 225% more likely to be hospitalized by the disease. Nearly 3 million Hispanics/ Latinos in the United States and its territories have asthma, with the incidence among Puerto Ricans 113% higher than non-Hispanic Whites and 50% higher than non-Hispanic Blacks (EPA, 2015a). Worldwide, the GAN reported that 14 million children regularly experience asthmatic symptoms, and asthma is the third leading cause of hospitalizations for Americans 15 years of age or younger (EPA, 2015a).

Treatments for asthma vary from individual to individual, but the disease has become increasingly manageable in recent decades thanks to advances in respiratory medicine. Asthma is treated with two different types of medication, one for long-term control and one for quick relief control (NHLBI, 2014). The long-term control medication, usually in the form of an inhaler or nasal spray, is used to reduce airway inflammation, thereby decreasing overall symptoms. Quick relief sprays and inhalers are used when the person suffers an acute attack of severe asthma symptoms that compromise his or her ability to breathe (NHLBI, 2014). Childhood asthma often decreases in intensity as the person reaches adolescence and young adulthood, and long-term prognoses for people with asthma continue to improve with the availability of long-term and quick relief medications.

Heart Disease

Heart disease, also known as cardiovascular disease, is a serious health condition that has reached epidemic proportions in the United States and abroad. Today, heart disease is the leading cause of death for both men and women in America. Heart disease can be caused by a variety of hereditary, congenital, and lifestyle factors, but its link to smoking, poor nutrition, lack of exercise, and obesity is generally attributed as the main reason for its dramatic increase in incidence and prevalence across the globe over the past several decades (Falvo, 2014).

Heart disease is a broad classifying term that encompasses numerous conditions such as coronary heart disease, stroke, and heart failure. Heart disease occurs most often when the heart and blood vessel system are damaged due to the buildup of plaque, which causes a narrowing of the arteries, thus reducing blood flow to the heart (American Heart Association, 2014).

The most common type of heart disease is coronary heart disease, which results in a heart attack caused by a blockage in the vessels or arteries of the heart. Numerous tests can be conducted to diagnose coronary heart disease, including chest x-rays, angiograms, electrocardiograms, and stress tests. Unfortunately, many individuals do not experience symptoms of heart disease until they have a heart attack or stroke, which often causes death or lifelong functional impairments (WHO, 2015b). Indeed, according to the American Heart Association (2014), nearly 787,000 Americans died of heart attacks in 2011, and some 85.6 million Americans are currently living with some type of heart disease or with the residual effects of stroke. Globally, heart disease is the number one cause of death for all people, with an estimated 17.5 million deaths worldwide being attributed to heart disease (7.4 million of which were related to coronary heart disease and 6.7 million of which were related to stroke) in 2012 (WHO, 2015b).

Heart disease is on the rise worldwide for both men and women and for people in virtually every age bracket. In the United States, minority populations such as Alaska Natives, Pacific Islanders, Hispanics/Latinos, and African Americans are especially vulnerable to heart disease. African Americans have the highest rates of high blood pressure among all identifiable racial and ethnic groups in the United States, and they are more than twice as likely as European Americans to develop heart disease (Million Hearts, 2015). Regardless of race or ethnicity, the risk of heart disease increases dramatically in old age (Wickert, Dresden, & Rumrill, 2013).

There are a number of controllable risk factors that have been chiefly blamed for the heart disease epidemic. Notable among these are the use of tobacco, alcohol abuse, high blood pressure, high cholesterol, diabetes, obesity, physical inactivity, and a high-fat/low-fiber diet (National Heart, Lung, & Blood Institute, 2014). It is also well established that heart disease disproportionally affects people living in poverty (American Heart Association, 2014). In the United States, those who live in the South have the highest death rates due to heart disease and those in the West have the lowest (CDC, 2014a).

As mentioned earlier, heart disease is diagnosed through a variety of measures, but it is usually first detected following a significant health complication. Treatment is oriented toward preventing further damage to the cardiovascular system and includes monitoring and reducing cholesterol levels through diet and medication, regulating blood pressure through lifestyle changes and medication, physical activity, healthy dietary regimens, stress management, smoking cessation, avoiding alcohol and other drugs, and surgical procedures—all depending upon the individual's specific heart condition and his or her personal circumstances (CDC, 2014a). People with heart disease also receive treatment for secondary complications such as fatigue, sexual dysfunction, headaches and other pain experiences, depression, and anxiety disorders (Falvo, 2014).

EMERGING DISABILITIES LINKED TO CLIMATE CHANGE

In 2003, the World Health Organization (WHO) reported that worldwide, climate change has resulted in 150,000 deaths per year since 1961 and 920,300 disability-adjusted life years (DALYs; Barna et al., 2012). DALYs are defined by WHO as "the sum of years of potential life lost due to premature mortality and the years of productive life lost due to disability." Scientists posit that climate change represents the greatest global threat to human health and functioning in the 21st century and will impact the lives, health, and well-being of billions of individuals (Costello et al., 2009). Climate change is defined by the Intergovernmental Panel on Climate Change (2007, p. 871) as "any change in climate over time, whether due to natural variability or as a result of human activity."

The EPA (2014) provides an overview of climate change and its impact on the earth, natural resources, and human health and functioning. First, the EPA has noted that although natural causes (e.g., changes in the sun's energy, shifts in ocean currents) contribute to climate change, the dramatic changes we have seen in recent years are primarily attributed to human activities such as annually releasing billions of tons of greenhouse gases into the atmosphere. Greenhouse gases (e.g., carbon dioxide, methane, nitrous oxide, fluorinated gases) come from burning fossil fuels for heat and energy, clearing forests, fertilizing crops, storing waste in landfills, raising livestock, and producing industrial waste. The build-up of greenhouse gases and other pollutants in the atmosphere has resulted in the warming of the planet. Over the last century, the average global temperature has increased by more than 1.3 degrees Fahrenheit, and the average arctic temperature has increased by more than twice that amount. Global warming has caused changing patterns of precipitation, increased ocean temperatures, increased sea level and acidity, and melting glaciers. According to Anderko, Davies-Cole, and Strunk (2014), these changes are happening at a rate that surpasses climate changes that have occurred over the past 650,000 years. Indeed, in recent years, we have seen a dramatic increase in severe weather-related events and natural disasters caused by climate change both across the United States and throughout the world.

Although the long-term health consequences of climate change and recent weather-related disasters associated with climate change are not fully understood, entities such as the CDC and the WHO are tracking the health of individuals who experience these disasters. Preliminary findings from this research indicate that climate change can exacerbate preexisting chronic health conditions and, in some instances, cause permanent disability and functional limitations in those without preexisting conditions. Although it is beyond the scope of this chapter to examine all of the health-related consequences of climate change, we provide an overview in the following sections of the health impacts of (a) extreme heat; (b) extreme weather events; (c) air pollution; and (d) vector-borne diseases.

Extreme Heat

Extreme heat events are extended periods of heat, usually lasting several days or more, during which temperatures and/or humidity are substantially higher than what is typical in a given location at a particular time of year (Luber & McGeehin, 2008). Whereas some regions of the United States are experiencing heavier rainfalls and more flooding, others such as the West and Southwest are experiencing extreme droughts and wildfires. Warmer temperatures have increased the frequency, intensity, and duration of extreme heat events (EPA, 2014). Research suggests that extreme heat events will continue to become more intense and more humid in the foreseeable future (Guirgulis, Gershunov, Tardy, & Basu, 2014).

Attempting to cope with prolonged heat can be both physically and psychologically stressful. During extreme heat events, hospital admissions increase for a variety of chronic illnesses such as respiratory diseases, cardiovascular diseases, and asthma (Guirgulis et al., 2014). In the United States, extreme heat events are responsible for more deaths each year than hurricanes, lightning, tornadoes, floods, and earthquakes combined (Luber & McGeehin, 2008). Recent heat waves in the United States and across the world (e.g., the 2006 California heat wave, the 2003 European heat wave, the 2010 Russian heat wave) have resulted in tens of thousands of deaths. The European heat wave of 2003 resulted in an unprecedented loss of human life. France was the hardest hit with 14,800 deaths attributed to the 9 days of extreme summer heat (Bouchama, 2003). Environmental factors that have been postulated to contribute to the extensive casualties that occurred during the European heat wave include the unparalleled intensity and prolonged length of the heat wave, the extreme nighttime temperatures that did not allow for a recovery period from severe daytime heat, and the exceedingly high level of ozone.

Exposure to heat, ozone, and increased particulate emissions from power plants to support greater demands for air conditioner usage during extreme heat events can exacerbate preexisting conditions such as cardiovascular and respiratory diseases (Hess, Malilay, & Parkinson, 2008). Likewise, ground level ozone pollution created by warmer temperatures exacerbates asthma and has contributed to the dramatic increase in asthma rates that have more than doubled over the past 30 years (White House, 2014). Ground level air pollution can cause breathing difficulties even for those who do not have respiratory conditions (EPA, 2011). In addition to exacerbating preexisting conditions, extreme heat can cause severe heat strokes that can lead to permanent neurological damage (U.S. Interagency Working Group on Climate Change and Health, 2010).

Extreme heat can also result in mental health conditions or exacerbate symptoms of preexisting mental health conditions. Suicide rates tend to increase with high temperatures (Dixon et al., 2014) indicating that heat waves may have a negative impact on those with depression and other psychiatric disabilities. Also of concern, one side effect of some psychotropic medications is their negative effect on the body's ability to regulate temperature; thus, individuals taking these medications may be at risk of developing heat-related illnesses during extreme heat events (Luber & McGeehin, 2008; SAMHSA, 2012).

Extreme Weather Events

Extreme weather events are especially severe and unseasonable and, in addition to heat waves, include severe thunderstorms, ice storms, blizzards, flooding, hurricanes, high winds, and tornadoes. The U.S. National Oceanic and Atmospheric Administration (NOAA, 2016) reported that from 1980 to 2015, 196 extreme weather events with damages or losses that exceeded $1 billion per event occurred in the United States. The total cost of these 196 events exceeded $1.1 trillion. In 2015 alone, 10 weather events occurred that resulted in losses exceeding $1 billion each. The NOAA reported that among these events were a drought, two floods, five severe storms, a wildfire, and a severe winter storm. The 1980–2015 average number of annual severe weather events was 5.2. However, for the past 5 years the average annual number increased to 10.8.

In addition to causing extensive damage to property and community infrastructure, these extreme weather events can cause personal injury, chronic illness, and mental health disorders in affected populations. Hess et al. (2008) described the injuries and illnesses that can result from these events. They noted that physical injuries (e.g., traumatic brain injuries, fractures, burns, amputations) can be incurred from such weather-related occurrences as wind strewn debris or collapsing building structures in tornadoes and hurricanes, near drowning in floods, injuries from snow removal and slipping on ice, and motor vehicle accidents caused by poor driving conditions. Individuals may also injure themselves in their recovery efforts after the extreme weather event has ceased. Injuries and deaths can result from electrocution and carbon monoxide poisoning from generator use. Respiratory illnesses from living in extremely damp environments caused by flooding can also occur. Individuals with fibromyalgia may have difficulty with thermoregulation in extreme cold weather, thus increasing their pain, stiffness, and fatigue (Larson, Pardo, & Pasley, 2014). Repeated episodes of acute psychological stress or chronic stress associated with extreme weather events can also increase the risk for cardiovascular disease. Disruption of public health services and health care infrastructures further increases the likelihood of negative health effects for members of communities affected by these disasters. Finally, for those who have to evacuate their homes and live in overcrowded evacuation centers without good sanitation, risks for acquiring contagious diseases increase (Hess et al., 2008).

After landfall of Hurricane Katrina, the CDC (2006) collaborated with state and local health departments in Arkansas, Louisiana, Mississippi, and Texas to collect daily aggregate morbidity surveillance data from evacuation centers and health care facilities. Data were collected from September 1st through September 21st. Chronic illness (e.g., diabetes, asthma, emphysema, cardiovascular disease) was the most commonly reported category of health conditions reported by evacuation centers, followed by gastrointestinal illness, respiratory illness, rash illnesses, injuries, and mental illness. Injury was the category most frequently reported by health care facilities followed by respiratory illness, rash, chronic illness, and mental illness. In another study, Sastray and Gregory (2013) analyzed data from the American Community Survey to compare pre- and post-Katrina disability-related measures of health among adults from New Orleans. Results of their analyses revealed that 1 year after Hurricane Katrina, disability rates increased from 20.6% to 24.6% with the highest increase in mental health impairment and, to a lesser degree, physical impairment.

The mental health effects of extreme weather events can range from mild stress responses to chronic stress and mental health disorders (Interagency Working Group on Climate Change and Health, 2010). In addition to the substantial losses that people can experience in extreme weather events (e.g., loss of homes and valued possessions, unemployment, death of loved ones), these events can lead to increased anxiety and worries about the future, especially among individuals living in communities that are likely to experience repeated occurrences of these events. Compounding these issues, immediately following extreme weather events, communities may lack the resources to provide early response to the psychological distress experienced by survivors. Geographic displacement is also associated with negative mental health effects. Extreme weather events can force individuals to relocate to new areas because their homes and communities have been destroyed, and they lack the resources to rebuild. Climate change researchers have estimated that by the year 2050, the number of individuals worldwide who will have to migrate because of climate change will reach 50 million or more (National Geographic, 2016). As noted by Hess et al. (2008), "disruption of place attachment and identity are traumatic for the individual and collective psyche, and rupture of the strong bonds humans have with place has detrimental health effects at the individual and community levels" (p. 475). Indirect health effects can result when individuals and families must contend with the stressors of acculturating to new communities, unemployment, reemployment, and the absence of the social supports they had before being displaced. These stressors can exacerbate preexisting mental health conditions and precipitate depression, anxiety, substance use disorders, and suicidality (Interagency Working Group on Climate Change and Human Health, 2010). Additional stressors occur for people with preexisting disabilities and chronic illnesses or serious injuries sustained during the weather event who have to relocate and establish new relationships with health care and service providers in their new communities. Beck and Franke (1996, p. 28) highlighted the multitude of losses that can occur as well as typical grief-related responses to these losses, noting that individuals who have lived through these experiences are often "thrown into situations where they must lodge themselves in temporary shelters, without restrooms or cooking arrangements, and with poor sleeping conditions."

Air Pollution

Warmer air and ocean temperatures, increased rainfall, and more frequent droughts result in the accumulation of greenhouse gases such as carbon dioxide and methane in the atmosphere (EPA, 2011). Greenhouse gas emissions result from electricity generation, motor vehicles, and industries such as power plants, petroleum refineries, landfills, and suppliers of certain fossil fuels. Additionally, the stagnant air that often accompanies heat waves can result in increased levels of air pollution and negative human health consequences.

The American Lung Association (2015) reported that in 2008, 127 million Americans lived in counties with unhealthy levels of ozone or particle pollution. Poor outdoor air quality is associated with chronic illnesses such as cancer, respiratory diseases, and cardiovascular diseases. Although a variety of factors contribute to the onset of asthma, environmental risk factors resulting from climate change such as exposure to allergens, air pollutants, tobacco smoke, and workplace pollutants have been identified as contributing factors in the recent increase in asthma diagnoses (GAN, 2015). Particle pollution from dust, dirt, soot, smoke, and chemicals such as sulfur dioxides and nitrogen oxides emitted from power plants increases the risk for damage to the lungs, lung cancer, and hospitalization for asthma (EPA, 2015a, 2015b). In extreme heat events and droughts, wildfires can occur, producing extensive wildfire smoke that contains pollutants such as particulate matter, carbon monoxide, and nitrogen oxides that can significantly reduce air quality in both the area where the wildfire has occurred as well as areas that are downwind from the wildfire (Kinney, 2008). Given the increased frequency and severity of wildfires in the United States, public officials and health researchers express concern about the likelihood of increased respiratory and cardiovascular diseases (White House, 2014). Relatedly, in 2008, the EPA reported that 160 tons of pollution is emitted into the atmosphere each year, and in the past 50 years 80,000 new chemicals were released into the environment. Finally, droughts can reduce food yields and lead to increased food prices as well as food insecurity and diseases associated with malnutrition, particularly for those living in poverty who already struggle with affording food costs (Interagency Working Group on Climate Change and Human Health, 2010).

In considering the effects of air pollution on human health and functioning, indoor air pollution is as much a concern as outdoor air pollution. Because most people spend the majority of their time indoors, they are exposed to many pollutants such as mold and pollen; tobacco smoke; cleaning and office products with harsh chemicals; synthetic perfumes and colognes used in personal products; pesticides; and radon and carbon monoxide from the use of building materials such as asbestos, formaldehyde, and lead (EPA, 2015b). Exacerbating the problem, structures in which people spend a significant amount of time (e.g., homes, offices, schools) are often built with poor ventilation, less exchange of outdoor air, and restricted air distribution. Many acute and chronic illnesses have been linked to poor indoor air quality. Among those that can result in long-term or permanent disability are asthma, respiratory diseases, and cancer. Multiple chemical sensitivity (MCS; to be discussed later in this chapter) is another chronic medical condition that is triggered by exposure to chemicals in both indoor and outdoor environments and results in a multitude of debilitating symptoms.

Vector-Borne Diseases

Temperature increases, changing precipitation patterns, and extreme weather events have resulted in the increased spread of vector-borne diseases (EPA, 2014). Vectors are:

> living organisms that can transmit infectious disease between humans or from animals to humans. Many of these vectors are blood-sucking insects that ingest disease-producing microorganisms during a blood meal from an infected host (human or animal) and later inject it into a new host during their subsequent blood meal. (WHO, 2014, para. 2)

Mosquitoes, ticks, flies, sandflies, and fleas are common vectors that can spread diseases like the Zika virus to humans. Examples of recent vector-borne disease outbreaks in the United States include dengue fever and West Nile virus. Lyme disease, the most commonly reported form of vector-borne illness in the United States, is transmitted to humans by infected ticks (EPA, 2014; Ogden et al., 2014). According to Ogden et al. (2014), Lyme disease emerged, or likely reemerged, in the U.S. population in the late 1970s due to decades of land use changes that resulted in reforestation and growth in the population of deer that are hosts for the ticks carrying the disease. Also, longer, warmer summers have resulted in increased numbers of ticks and tick bites as well as the spread of ticks into areas that were previously uninhabitable. We discuss Lyme disease in greater detail later in this chapter.

Multiple Chemical Sensitivity

Over the past several decades, increasing numbers of individuals have reported that they experience extreme allergic reactions or hypersensitivity to chemicals in the environment. In fact, Martini, Iavicoli, and Corso (2013) reported that chemical sensitivities are becoming so prevalent that the numbers of individuals with these conditions are growing daily. This upward trend is not surprising given the vast number of complex chemical compounds in our natural environment as well as the building of highly insulated houses and other buildings that reduce indoor air exchange and negatively affect indoor air quality (EPA, 2016).

Although some individuals are only mildly affected by these environmental chemicals, others develop a severely debilitating chronic condition called multiple chemical sensitivity (MCS). MCS is triggered by exposure to low-level chemicals in the environment. Although these chemicals are well tolerated by most individuals, individuals with MCS experience adverse reactions affecting multiple organ systems (Lamielle, 2003). Ongoing exposure can result in adverse reactions to even lower level exposures to the chemical trigger and to other chemicals as well. In some cases, MCS is developed in response to a sudden exposure to an environmental trigger. In other cases, MCS develops from an accumulation of repeated exposures to various triggers (Gibson, 2006; Gibson, Cheavens, & Warren, 1996; Koch & Eaton, 2005; Koch, Vierstra, & Penix, 2006; Lamielle, 2003). Thus, some individuals with MCS can identify the initial exposure event whereas others report prolonged, repetitive, or cumulative low-level exposures to chemical triggers, and some cannot identify a specific chemical exposure (Lamielle, 2003). Numerous chemicals can trigger MCS symptoms, and individuals vary in terms of the specific chemicals that cause them to experience adverse reactions. Table 6.1 provides a list of common chemicals that can trigger MCS.

TABLE 6.1 Common Chemical Triggers of Multiple Chemical Sensitivity

- Pesticides
- Paint
- Perfumes and colognes
- Hairspray
- Tobacco smoke
- Scented soaps, lotions, and deodorant
- Dry-cleaning residues
- Air fresheners
- Scented laundry detergents and fabric softeners
- New carpet or flooring
- Solvents
- Chlorine
- Formaldehyde
- Mold
- Newsprint
- Printer and photocopier ink
- Natural gas
- Cleaning products
- Disinfectants
- Automobile and diesel exhaust fumes

Source: Gibson (2006); Gibson, Cheavens, and Warren (1996); Koch and Eaton (2005);
Koch, Vierstra, and Penix (2006); Lamielle (2003); Victor and Cullen (1987).

MCS affects multiple organs and results in numerous symptoms. Symptoms vary across individuals, and, whereas some initially experience mild symptoms, continued exposure to the triggering chemical can result in multiple and severely debilitating symptoms that cause significant functional limitations, reduced work productivity, job loss, financial difficulties, and major disruptions to social and family functioning (Gibson, 2006; Gibson et al., 1996; Koch et al., 2006). Examples of the organ systems affected and their associated MCS symptoms are listed in Table 6.2.

In addition to these symptoms, other effects of MCS may include skin rashes, food and medication intolerances, irritability, and sensitivities to electromagnetic fields (Gibson, 2006; Koch & Eaton, 2005).

MCS is a controversial condition with many physicians questioning its legitimacy and others treating it as a psychological problem. Conversely, specialists in environmental medicine and clinical ecology diagnose and treat MCS as a legitimate chronic health condition caused by environmental factors, and they work with individuals with MCS to manage their symptoms primarily through prevention/avoidance (Koch & Eaton, 2005) and other strategies such as detoxification and emotional self-care (Gibson, Elms, & Ruding, 2003; Koch et al., 2006;

TABLE 6.2 Multiple Chemical Sensitivity Symptoms

Organ System	Symptoms
Neurological	Headaches (migraines, sinus)
	Dizziness/vertigo
	Nausea
	Short-term memory difficulties
	Difficulty concentrating
	Brain fog (i.e., clouded thinking)
Respiratory	Asthma
	Sinusitis
Gastrointestinal	Acute gastrointestinal pain
	Bloating and indigestion
	Diarrhea
	Food intolerances
	Constipation
Musculoskeletal	Joint pain
	Muscle pain and weakness
	Muscle spasms
	Tingling, twitching, and numbness in extremities
Immune	Frequent infections
Sensory	Sensitivity to light, sound, scents, heat, and/or cold
	Pain or irritation of eyes, ears, and/or nasal tract
	Tinnitus
Cardiovascular	Irregular heartbeat

Adapted from Koch and Eaton (2005, p. 25). Copyright © 2005. Reprinted by permission of the National Rehabilitation Counseling Association.

Lipson, 2001). Unfortunately, the number of specialists in environmental medicine and clinical ecology is limited, and many individuals with MCS are consequently unable to receive an appropriate diagnosis and treatment for their condition.

The 1990s, a consensus document listing criteria for establishing the presence of MCS was developed by a panel of international experts including allergologists; occupational physicians; clinical ecologists; specialists in internal medicine; and ear, nose, and throat specialists. These criteria are listed in Table 6.3.

In 2005, Lacour, Zunder, Schmidtke, Vaith, and Scheidt (2005) proposed extensions to the original criteria (see Table 6.4).

Incidence and prevalence rates in the general U.S. population are difficult to obtain because of the controversy surrounding MCS and the underdiagnosis and treatment of the condition. American prevalence estimates range anywhere from 3% to 16% of the general population (Caress & Steinemann, 2009; Gibson et al., 1996). However, due to the increase in extreme weather events that can expose individuals to high levels of environmental contamination, it is likely that the number of cases is much higher than these estimates (Vierstra, Rumrill, Koch, and McMahon, 2007). Although MCS can be acquired by males and females of all races and ages, the typical demographic profile in MCS studies is of White, middle-aged females between the ages of 40 and 50 who are in the prime of their careers at the onset of MCS symptoms.

TABLE 6.3 Consensus Criteria for Recognition of Multiple Chemical Sensitivity

1. Symptoms are reproducible with repeated (chemical) exposure.

2. Condition is chronic.

3. Low levels of exposure (lower than previously or commonly tolerated).

4. Symptoms improve or resolve when the incitant is removed.

5. Responses occur to multiple chemically unrelated substances.

6. Symptoms involve multiple organ systems.

Source: "Multiple Chemical Sensitivity" (1999). May 1, 1999, Taylor & Francis. Reprinted by permission of the publisher Taylor & Francis Ltd, http://www.tandfonline.com and http://www.informaworld.com.

TABLE 6.4 2005 Extended Criteria for Recognition of Multiple Chemical Sensitivity

1. Chronic condition lasting more than 6 months and causing deterioration of lifestyle and body functions.

2. Symptoms recur reproducibly and affect the nervous system, with a characteristic hypersensitivity to odors.

3. Continuous involvement of the central nervous system and of at least one other apparatus.

4. Responses induced after low levels of exposure.

5. Responses to multiple unrelated chemicals.

6. Improvement or resolution after removal of exposure.

Source: Lacour et al. (2005, p. 145).

Chronic Lyme Disease

Lyme disease is a vector-borne bacterial infection that is transmitted to humans by bites from ticks that carry the pathogen *Borrelia burgdorferi*. The CDC (2015a) reported a prevalence rate of 8.6% of the U.S. population in 2013. However, it is speculated that this is a gross underestimate of the true number of cases because some individuals go undiagnosed for many years and thus do not have their cases reported to health officials. Also according to the CDC, the incidence of Lyme disease in the United States has almost doubled in the past two decades from 3.74 reported cases per 100,000 people in 1991 to 7.01 reported cases per 100,000 people in 2012. Currently, it is estimated that 300,000 people are diagnosed with Lyme disease each year.

Lyme disease in humans is on the rise because of temperature increases and changing rainfall patterns resulting in longer and warmer summers that have expanded the length of time that ticks are active. Warming temperatures have also contributed to the expansion of the range of ticks to areas where they previously were unable to survive because temperatures were not warm enough. New Hampshire and Delaware have experienced the largest increases in reported case rates since 1991. These states are followed by Maine, Vermont, and Massachusetts. These five states now report an average of 50 to 90 more cases of Lyme disease per 100,000 people than they did in 1991. However, Lyme disease is not limited to the East Coast; cases have been reported in all 50 states (CDC, 2015a). Lyme disease is now surpassing HIV and breast cancer in new cases, making it the fastest growing epidemic in the United States (CDC, 2015a; Johnson, Wilcox, Mankoff, & Stricker, 2014). CDC surveillance data indicate that cases of Lyme disease are most prevalent in the northeastern United States among children ages 5 to 9 and adult males ages 55 to 59.

Lyme disease is difficult to diagnose. The classic bull's eye rash that occurs with Lyme disease is the primary symptom by which it is diagnosed, but this rash is absent in many patients (CDC, 2015a; Stricker, 2007). Because of the small size of ticks, many individuals may not even be aware that they have been bitten. Laboratory blood work is used to diagnose Lyme disease, but these tests often fail to rule out the infection, and they are often so insensitive that most cases are missed (Ali, Vitulano, Lee, & Colson, 2014; Stricker, 2007). Short-course antibiotic therapy can cure the infection, but it is not always effective (Institute of Medicine [IOM], 2011). Additionally, it is not uncommon for individuals with Lyme disease to see multiple specialists over a period of years before being accurately diagnosed. Lyme disease can mimic other chronic health conditions such as chronic fatigue syndrome, fibromyalgia, rheumatoid arthritis, lupus, multiple sclerosis, Parkinson's disease, amyotrophic lateral sclerosis (ALS), stroke, brain tumors, attention deficit hyperactivity disorder (ADHD), and mental illness (CDC, 2015a). Finding a physician who is knowledgeable about Lyme disease is difficult, and more than half of respondents to one Lyme disease survey reported traveling over 100 miles and even to other states to obtain care from a knowledgeable physician (CDC, 2015a). Because most people with Lyme disease also have at least one other tick-borne infection, and multiple infections suppress the immune system (IOM, 2011; Stricker, 2007), it can be even more difficult to find a physician who is also knowledgeable about these other infections.

The symptoms of Lyme disease occur in stages and become progressively worse over time. Table 6.5 lists both early signs and symptoms and those that occur at a later stage.

Other symptoms may include fatigue, night sweats, abdominal pain, nausea, sleep disturbance, and irritability (Ali et al., 2014; Aucott, Rebman, Crowder, & Korttee, 2013). In the absence of early diagnosis and treatment or even following short course antibiotic therapy, as many as 36% of patients with Lyme disease experience lingering and debilitating later stage symptoms (Johnson et al., 2014). These symptoms can persist for months to years and substantially restrict individuals' ability to perform activities of daily living, work, attend school, and engage in social activities. This condition is referred to as chronic Lyme disease (CLD) or as posttreatment Lyme disease. The exact cause of CLD is unknown, but some medical experts report that there is no credible scientific evidence for persistent infection (Stricker, 2007). Others believe that lingering symptoms are the result of residual damage to tissue and the immune system, whereas others believe ongoing symptoms represent persistent infection with *Borrelia burgdorferi*. Still others

TABLE 6.5 Early and Later Signs and Symptoms of Lyme Disease

Early Signs and Symptoms (3–30 days after tick bite)

● Fever, chills, headache, fatigue, muscle and joint aches, and swollen lymph nodes

● Erythema migrans (EM) rash
  – Occurs in approximately 70%–80% of infected persons
  – Begins at the site of a tick bite after a delay of 3–30 days (average is about 7 days)
  – Expands gradually over a period of days reaching up to 12 inches or more (30 cm) across
  – May feel warm to the touch but is rarely itchy or painful
  – Sometimes clears as it enlarges, resulting in a target or "bull's-eye" appearance
  – May appear on any area of the body

Later Signs and Symptoms (days to months after tick bite)

● Severe headaches and neck stiffness

● Additional EM rashes on other areas of the body

● Arthritis with severe joint pain and swelling, particularly the knees and other large joints

● Facial or Bell's palsy (loss of muscle tone or droop on one or both sides of the face)

● Intermittent pain in tendons, muscles, joints, and bones

● Heart palpitations or an irregular heartbeat

● Episodes of dizziness or shortness of breath

● Inflammation of the brain and spinal cord

● Nerve pain

● Shooting pains, numbness, or tingling in the hands or feet

● Problems with short-term memory

Source: CDC (2015b).

believe that reported symptoms are psychological or that symptoms are attributable to other conditions such as fibromyalgia (Ali et al., 2014; Hasett, Radvanski, Buyske, Savage, & Sigal, 2009; IOM, 2011). Despite these varying medical perspectives, individuals with CLD report impairments that are similar to those associated with congestive heart failure or osteoarthritis (IOM, 2011). Additionally, the pain they report experiencing is equivalent to postsurgical pain, and their fatigue is reported to be as severe as the fatigue experienced by people with multiple sclerosis.

Significant controversy also exists regarding the treatment of CLD. Although some physicians treat CLD with long-term antibiotics as per treatment guidelines from the International Lyme and Associated Diseases Society (Burrascano, 2008), and Lyme advocacy groups support long-term antibiotic treatment (Ali et al., 2014; Stricker, 2007), entities such as the American Lyme Disease Association, the CDC, and the National Institutes of Health (NIH) do not recommend periods of antibiotic therapy for more than a few weeks, even if no treatment was provided in early stages of the disease. These organizations also indicate that long-term antibiotic treatment has not been demonstrated in clinical trials to be more effective than placebos, and it can be associated with serious complications (Hasett et al., 2009). Finally, the CDC recommends treatment for CLD similar to that which is used to treat chronic fatigue syndrome and fibromyalgia. Patients with Lyme disease report that they also use complementary and alternative medicine (CAM) approaches such as vitamins and minerals, herbal medications, natural products, and other CAMs (e.g., acupuncture, Reiki [i.e., an approach in which practitioners use light touch or placement of their hands just above a person to facilitate healing; National Center for Complementary and Integrative Health, 2016], Vega machines [a form of electrodermal testing for allergies, Ali et al., 2014; Lewith, Hyland, & Gray, 2001]). However, the efficacy of CAMs in treating CLD has not been solidly established and some may even be harmful.

PSYCHOSOCIAL ASPECTS

Individuals with disabilities associated with lifestyle and climate change must often contend with a multitude of psychosocial challenges such as the management of multiple symptoms, significant functional impairments, co-occurring physical and psychiatric conditions, trauma, diagnostic uncertainties, medical invalidation, and societal stigma. Additionally, individuals who acquire disabilities or develop chronic illnesses as a result of severe weather events are often confronted with the challenges of not only adapting to changes in their functional abilities but also coping with a multitude of other losses (e.g., homes, valued possessions, jobs, death of family and friends) at the same time.

Because disabilities associated with lifestyle factors and climate change are often chronic, episodic, and sometimes life-threatening, these conditions can be accompanied by significant psychological distress. For example, individuals with MCS encounter numerous psychosocial challenges in the "overwhelming effort needed to survive" (Gibson, Sledd, McEnroe, & Vos, 2011, p. 223) in a world where chemical exposures are encountered everywhere. Likewise, the struggle to cope with severely disabling symptoms of CLD can sometimes seem insurmountable (Ali et al., 2014). Individuals with conditions associated with lifestyle and climate change may also have fears and anxieties about their personal safety and impending death. During asthma attacks, for example, individuals may feel like they are dying, and fears of dying may persist even when the individual is not having an asthma attack (Andrews, Jones, & Mullen, 2013). Individuals with CLD may experience fears of dying or even suicidality due to the lack of a clear and predictable disease course (Ali et al., 2014). People with emerging disabilities that are thought to be attributed to their lifestyle choices or behavior (e.g., diabetes, HIV/AIDS, cardiovascular disease, cancer, traumatic brain injuries) may experience shame, guilt, and blame and ostracism from family members and friends as part of their psychosocial response to disability (Smart, 2009). Those who have survived extreme weather events may experience persistent anxiety and feelings of unsafety, especially if they live in areas that are prone to recurrent weather-related disasters (Balbus & Malina, 2009). Likewise, individuals with MCS and CLD often experience worsening of their symptoms and fears that they have a life-threatening illness, especially when their conditions are undiagnosed or diagnosed as unexplained medical symptoms (Ali et al., 2014; Koch et al., 2012). These same issues are prominent concerns for people living with lifestyle-related conditions such as diabetes, cancer, and cardiovascular disease (Rubin, Roessler, & Rumrill, 2016)—all of which are also life-threatening and bring with them concerns regarding death and dying.

In addition, individuals with MCS and those with CLD must contend with diagnostic uncertainties and invalidation of their conditions, misdiagnoses, contradictory diagnoses, treatment that exacerbates their conditions, and/or consultation with multiple specialists over a period of years before they are diagnosed (Ali et al., 2014). The uncertainty and prolonged period of seeking out a diagnosis and ruling out other conditions can take a tremendous emotional and financial toll on the individual. These individuals often encounter medical skepticism, dismissal of their complaints, and are treated as if they are malingerers and hypochondriacs. As Weintraub, author of the book *Cure Unknown: Inside the Lyme Epidemic*, describes her experience with medical providers,

> Being sick is hard enough, but being so sick for so long and also being a suspect, having your physical pain, your integrity, and your very sanity called into question as you travel the medical landscape begging for help: That is a crushing course of events. (Institute of Medicine, 2011, p. 35)

Lack of consensus on the part of medical providers can cause individuals themselves to question if they have a legitimate disability or if their symptoms are "all in their heads." Accompanying these self-doubts, they may also experience feelings of hopelessness and distrust of their medical and health care providers. Likewise, families, friends, employers, and coworkers who also doubt the legitimacy of their symptoms often refuse to provide the emotional support and/or accommodations that individuals with these conditions request. These reactions can trigger feelings of alienation, abandonment, and isolation that can further undermine their health and functional capacities (Ali et al., 2014; Koch et al., 2006).

The difficulty that individuals with MCS experience in accessing safe spaces substantially limits their social interactions (Gibson et al., 2011). For many individuals with MCS, even their homes are unsafe. In addition to psychosocial isolation and pervasive feelings of unsafety, individuals with MCS must often contend with a loss of identity associated with their impaired capacity to function in valued roles and activities (Gibson et al., 2011). Financial struggles can lead to additional stress and anxiety. Similarly, individuals with CLD struggle with isolation because of symptoms such as pain and fatigue that impair their ability to interact with others, loss of identity related to their inability to continue to participate in meaningful life activities, and financial struggles related to unemployment and health care expenses (Ali et al., 2014). In fact, in a survey of the health-related quality of life (HRQoL) of a sample of 3,090 individuals with CLD, Johnson et al. (2014) found that in comparison to a sample of individuals with other chronic health conditions (i.e., chronic low back pain, asthma, diabetes, cancer, depression, cardiovascular disease), those with CLD reported significantly lower HRQoL, greater health care utilization, more days when they felt physically or mentally impaired, more activity limitations, greater impairment in their ability to work, and higher out-of-pocket medical expenses. Individuals with lifestyle disabilities and disabilities associated with climate change often have comorbid conditions that further complicate the psychosocial challenges they confront. The sheer chronicity, unpredictability, and (often) progressive nature of diabetes, HIV/AIDS, cancer, heart disease, and other lifestyle-related disabilities cause tremendous psychological uncertainty, which can manifest in depression, anxiety, bipolar disorders, and other adjustmental problems (Falvo, 2014). Survivors of weather-related disasters may incur both physical and mental health conditions. Individuals with MCS often have co-occurring depression and anxiety because of the combination of factors such as disruptive symptoms, pervasiveness of chemicals in the environment, medical and societal invalidation of their illness experiences, failure of others to provide accommodations that will prevent chemical exposures, psychosocial isolation, unemployment, and financial struggles (Gibson et al., 2011; Koch, Rumrill, Hennessey, Vierstra, & Roessler, 2007). Also, according to the National Fibromyalgia and Chronic Pain Association (2015) as many as 16% of people with fibromyalgia and 40% of people with chronic fatigue syndrome have MCS. Individuals with CLD can have additional tick-borne illnesses that complicate diagnosis and treatment and result in comorbid anxiety and depression (Stricker, 2007).

Stigma is associated with both lifestyle diseases and diseases related to climate change. Individuals with lifestyle disabilities are prone to stigma and discrimination because of societal perceptions that they are responsible for causing their disability and should also be solely responsible for the treatment and management of the disability (Smart, 2009). Smart noted that, especially in our health conscious society, individuals with disabilities (e.g., respiratory diseases, some cancers, obesity, type 2 diabetes) that may be attributed to unhealthy behaviors (e.g., smoking, eating unhealthy foods, alcohol consumption, failure to exercise) are often viewed by others as weak, lazy, or irresponsible. Resentment toward these individuals is also encountered, and they are blamed for raising health care premiums, using up scarce medical and health care resources, and raising costs of disability that are incurred by taxpayers. The stigma associated with these disabilities has negative psychosocial consequences such as lack of empathy and emotional social support from family members, friends, and health care providers. Individuals with these conditions may also engage in self-blame that undermines their willingness to participate in activities to manage their illnesses.

As another example, asthma was historically viewed as a symptom of nervousness, hysteria, and psychoneurosis (Andrews et al., 2013). Although this characterization has long been medically disclaimed, many in the general population still view people with asthma in this negative way. Movies often portray characters with asthma as "wimps" or "social outcasts," which further increases the stigma associated with asthma. In response to this stigma, individuals with asthma may deny that they have a disability or attempt to hide their condition to appear "normal." These responses can be detrimental to employment outcomes, self-efficacy, and ability to manage one's asthma. For example, failure to disclose precludes individuals from receiving social support as well as classroom and workplace accommodations. Embarrassment over use of medications in public can lead to poor asthma control and increase one's risk of advanced disease. Indeed, Andrews et al. (2013) found that poor asthma control was significantly associated with feelings of stigma. Likewise, people with MCS and CLD are often perceived by others as hypochondriacs or as "faking" their conditions to get attention or to be relieved from unpleasant activities. This is also true for people with diabetes, HIV/AIDS, heart disease, and some forms of cancer whose symptoms may not be readily apparent to friends and family members. In these cases, much-needed emotional support is often absent.

VOCATIONAL ASPECTS

Individuals with lifestyle- and climate-change–related disabilities can experience a wide range of functional limitations that can substantially interfere with their ability to work. The symptoms of diabetes, cancer, and heart disease can necessitate prolonged absences from work or flexibility in scheduling so that the person can attend doctor's appointments or otherwise manage his or her illness (Falvo, 2014). Individuals who have incurred injuries from extreme weather events (e.g., traumatic brain injuries, orthopedic impairments) can experience cognitive and/or physical limitations that may preclude them from working in certain occupations without reasonable accommodations. CLD can result in chronic pain that is caused by arthritic-type symptoms as well as migraine headaches (Ali et al., 2014). Fatigue is also a common symptom of CLD, and both pain and fatigue can be exacerbated by on-the-job stressors. The cognitive and memory deficits associated with both MCS and CLD can create additional impediments to performing essential job functions. Co-occurring depression can interfere with work attendance and create difficulties with concentration. Some individuals with CLD also experience impaired vision and hearing loss from damaged nerves.

Premature disengagement from the workforce is also an issue of concern. In the Johnson (2015) study that was previously cited, the researchers found that of the participants with CLD, 43% reported that they had stopped working as a result of their illness, and those who continued to work reported missing an average of 15 days of work during the preceding 240-day work year and an inability to concentrate at work during 42 days of the preceding work year. In an investigation of the impact of MCS on employment, Gibson et al. (1996) found that in a sample of 268 participants with MCS, 205 had been terminated from employment or forced to quit their jobs because of their inability to tolerate the chemicals in their workplace. People with MCS encounter numerous barriers to employment, in addition to the functional limitations resulting from their conditions, that can contribute to premature disengagement from the workforce. Prominent among these workplace problems are harassment (i.e., coworkers increasing their use of perfumes and colognes after being requested by the individual with MCS to refrain from the use of these products) and being denied requested workplace accommodations (Gibson et al., 2011; Koch et al., 2006; Vierstra et al., 2007).

Because of medical controversies regarding the legitimacy of conditions such as MCS and CLD, employers may also question the legitimacy of these conditions and may refuse to provide requested reasonable accommodations to workers with these conditions. For example, Vierstra et al. (2007) investigated the employment discrimination experiences of people with MCS and found that they were proportionately more likely than a general disability comparison group to allege discrimination under Title I of the Americans with Disabilities Act (ADA) related to reasonable accommodations. They were also more likely than the comparison group to receive nonmeritorious resolutions as a result of the Equal Employment Opportunity Commission's (EEOC) investigatory process.

CHARACTERISTICS OF INDIVIDUALS AT RISK FOR LIFESTYLE DISABILITIES AND DISABILITIES LINKED TO CLIMATE CHANGE

A variety of demographic factors have been identified that can increase the risk of acquiring disabilities linked to lifestyle and climate change. Foremost among these factors is poverty. People living in poverty are at greater risk for obesity than the general population, which makes them vulnerable to emerging disabilities such as asthma, diabetes, heart disease, and orthopedic impairments (Cha et al., 2015; Strauser, 2013).Those who live in poverty are also at the greatest risk of experiencing the negative health-related consequences of extreme weather events (Balbus & Malina, 2009). They often have inadequate shelter and lack the resources to find alternative shelter. They are at an increased risk for heat-related morbidity and mortality because of lack of air conditioning and small living spaces. The financial burden of unaffordable utility bills compounds these risks. Individuals living in poverty are also at risk of experiencing the negative health effects of air pollution as well as food insecurity that results from reduced crop yields caused by climate change. Increases in the costs of food that results from reduced crop yields can create a substantial burden for those who already have difficulties affording food costs. Finally, the severity of the mental health impact on individuals who have experienced extreme weather events is likely to be even higher in poorer communities that have fewer resources and supports to aid individuals in coping and recovery both during and following the event.

Both pregnant women and children represent vulnerable populations as well (Balbus & Malina, 2009). Gestational diabetes is a well-documented precursor to delivery complications and health problems for mothers and infants (Falvo, 2014). Pregnancy increases susceptibility to vector- and food-borne diseases, and pregnant women who are exposed to environmental toxins during extreme weather events often experience limited access to safe food and water, psychological stressors, and disrupted health care in the aftermath of these events (Balbus & Malina, 2009). Women with debated conditions such as MCS and CLD are also more likely than men to have their conditions dismissed by physicians or diagnosed as medically unexplained symptoms (Vierstra et al., 2007). Children experience an increased risk of acquiring lifestyle and environmentally related disabilities because of factors such as their small body mass, increased breathing rates, greater time spent outdoors, and developing respiratory tracts that increase their sensitivity to the negative health impacts of ozone air pollution (Balbus & Malina, 2009). In the 2012 National Health Interview Survey, results indicated that more than 10 million children in the United States under the age of 18 had been diagnosed with asthma at some time in their lives, and 6.8 million still had asthma (Bloom, Cohen, & Freeman, 2012). Children are also more vulnerable to infectious diseases and have an increased risk of developing serious complications from water- and food-borne diseases (Balbus & Malina, 2009). The fastest-growing segments of the population of Americans with diabetes are (a) children under the age of 18 who live in poverty and who are morbidly obese, and (b) people over the age of 80 (CDC, 2014b; Cha et al., 2015). Finally, children are at an increased risk of experiencing the mental health effects of climate change.

Race is also a risk factor for experiencing lifestyle disabilities and the negative impact of climate change. For example, non-Hispanic Black children experience higher rates of asthma than non-Hispanic White children (Balbus & Malina, 2009). Those most at risk live in urban areas, and boys have higher risk rates than girls. Lewis and Burris (2012) identified a number of health disparities between African Americans and European Americans, noting that African Americans across the United States, especially those living in poverty with limited access to preventive health care, are significantly more likely than European Americans to incur lifestyle-related disabilities such as stroke, cardiovascular disease, diabetes, and substance use disorders. Atherton and Toriello (2012) described the epidemic of substance use disorders among Latinos and African Americans. The prevalence rates of diabetes and alcoholism among Native Americans are two to four times the rates of those conditions reported for the general population (CDC, 2014b; Lewis & Burris, 2012).

In their examination of pre- and post-Katrina disability-related measures of health, Sastray and Gregory (2013) found that declines in health and increases in disability were most prominent among young and middle-aged Black females. For young Black females, significant increases occurred in physical impairment, mobility restrictions, and work restrictions. For middle-aged Black females, significant increases occurred in sensory impairment and mental impairment. The researchers pointed to a variety of stress-related factors that could explain why young and middle-aged Black women fared the worst in terms of health outcomes. These factors include living in houses and neighborhoods that experienced the most damage from the hurricane, displacement, property losses, unemployment, loss of community and neighborhood, death or injury of family members, breakup of households, stressors experienced by their children, and increased vulnerability due to their sex.

People with chronic health conditions and preexisting disabilities and older adults represent other vulnerable populations (Balbus & Malina, 2009). As we have discussed, symptoms of many conditions can be exacerbated by the stressors of extreme weather events and reduced access to medical care and medications during and shortly after these events. In addition to being more vulnerable than younger people to disabilities in general and lifestyle-related disabilities in particular (e.g., diabetes, stroke, heart disease; Wickert et al., 2013), older adults are also particularly vulnerable to the negative effects of climate change, especially extreme heat. In the European heat wave of 2003, for example, the highest death rates were among the elderly (Bouchama, 2003). Risk factors that contributed to these high mortality rates included social isolation; the absence of air condition-ing; co-occurring conditions such as psychiatric disabilities, pulmonary diseases, and cardiovascular conditions; and use of medications that interfere with ther-moregulation (i.e., the body's process of maintaining a consistent internal tem-perature that is independent of the environmental temperature). Because of their increased likelihood of having preexisting medical conditions (e.g., cardiovascular and respiratory illnesses) and mobility impairments, the elderly are at risk of hav-ing these conditions exacerbated by extreme weather.

Outdoor workers, especially those whose jobs require heavy exertion, are at increased risk of the negative consequences of exposure to ozone air pollution and heat stress (Balbus & Malina, 2009). Outdoor workers (e.g., electricity and pipeline utility workers) who provide services in rural and suburban areas can experience an increased risk of infection with Lyme disease. Finally, popula-tions residing in certain regions of the United States that are prone to recurrent extreme weather events may experience increased risks of acquiring disabilities and chronic illnesses or exacerbation of preexisting conditions during or shortly after these events. The risks for specific health-related outcomes depend on the "regions' baseline climate, abundance of natural resources such as fertile soil and fresh water supplies, dependence on private wells for drinking water, and/or vul-nerability to coastal surges or riverine folding" (Balbus & Malina, 2009, p. 34).

REHABILITATION COUNSELING IMPLICATIONS

Counselor Awareness and Self-Reflective Practice

Rehabilitation counselors are subject to the same biases and misperceptions about disabilities linked to lifestyle and climate change as the general public. Therefore, it is crucial that they examine their perceptions of individuals with disabilities that may have been incurred from poor health habits (e.g., smoking, substance abuse, sedentary lifestyle, poor eating habits) and disabilities related to climate change (e.g., MCS, CLD) that are medically debated. If rehabilitation counselors identify biases, they will then need to determine how they can suspend these biases. One strategy they can use is to take an inventory of their own unhealthy behaviors because as Smart (2009, p. 179) noted "almost everybody engages in some types of behaviors, or, more accurately, does not engage in other behavior, that put them at risk for a disability, injury, or illness." Awareness of counselors' own unhealthy behaviors can increase empathy for consumers who have chronic illnesses and dis-abilities linked to lifestyle choices. Another strategy is for counselors to reflect on their attitudes about the legitimacy and severity of conditions such as MCS and CLD as well as their beliefs about whether these individuals should be eligible to receive rehabilitation counseling services. They can then turn to the professional lit-erature and consult with knowledgeable experts and advocates for these conditions about the severity and functional limitations associated with MCS and CLD so that they do not make hasty ineligibility decisions.

Rehabilitation counselors living in communities that have experienced extreme weather events may also experience negative physical and mental health conse-quences. They may have sustained extensive, and in some cases irreparable, dam-age to their homes; acquired injuries that could result in permanent disabilities;

and/or lost loved ones. Thus, they may be experiencing some of the same stress reactions as consumers. Therefore, engaging in their own self-care is extremely important. Self-care activities to counter the negative physical and psychological effects of weather-related disasters include maintaining a healthy diet, exercising, participating in valued leisure activities, getting enough sleep, keeping in contact with social support systems, engaging in civic activities, meditation, prayer, fellowship, and volunteerism (CDC, 2016). Additionally, these rehabilitation counselors have an ethical obligation to (a) recognize when their own psychological response to their disaster experience is interfering with their effectiveness in working with clients, and (b) take an appropriate course of action (e.g., seek mental health counseling, take a temporary leave from work to attend to their own mental health issues). Supervisors should provide ample opportunities for debriefing sessions that allow office staff to talk with each other about their emotions and reactions to weather-related disasters and hear about the devastating losses that some of their consumers may have experienced. Resources such as employee assistance programs or outside psychological consultants should be utilized to facilitate staff debriefings and individual counseling sessions.

Outreach and Eligibility Determination

Many individuals whose disabilities are related to lifestyle factors do not consider themselves to be people with disabilities even after the onset of their conditions, which behooves rehabilitation counselors to employ proactive outreach strategies with health care providers that serve people with diabetes, cardiovascular disease, asthma, and other lifestyle-related disabilities. Additionally, the fact that many people with one lifestyle-related disability often have other co-occurring lifestyle-related conditions requires vigilance on the part of rehabilitation counselors to ensure that applications for services include a full account of the impact that the person's overall medical and psychological condition has on his or her functioning. This facilitates eligibility decisions that consider the individual's entire set of rehabilitation needs rather than focusing on one diagnosis. For example, an applicant for services who has type 2 diabetes due to obesity may also have hypertension and therefore be at risk for heart attacks or stroke, respiratory problems, and orthopedic impairments, all of which must be taken into consideration when determining his or her need and eligibility for services. Likewise, outreach and rapid eligibility determination for those who have sustained injuries and/or lost their jobs as a result of natural disasters can prevent more severe disabilities and other long-term adverse consequences. To provide these services, rehabilitation counselors can coordinate with organizations providing disaster relief to set up stations in the field for recruitment and rapid eligibility determination.

Because environmentally linked chronic illnesses such as MCS and CLD are medically debated, fraught with diagnostic uncertainty, and characterized by long periods of time between symptom onset and appropriate diagnosis, rehabilitation counselors should be aware that individuals with these conditions may, understandably, be distrustful upon initially meeting with them. As noted by Koch et al. (2012), it is, therefore, imperative that rehabilitation counselors interact with these individuals in a manner that "communicate[s] respect and validation rather than judgment and skepticism" (p. 131).

It is also of utmost importance that rehabilitation counselors make appropriate referrals when seeking diagnostic testing, medical exams, and psychological evaluations to aid in making eligibility determinations. For example, individuals who have psychiatric disabilities linked to extreme weather events or exacerbated by these events should be referred to mental health professionals who specialize in treating trauma-related disorders. According to the American Counseling Association (2016), a new specialty in counseling is emerging that focuses on disaster mental health. For more information, readers are referred to www.counseling.org/knowledge-center/trauma-disaster. Another useful resource is the American Psychological Association's Psychologist Locator. This tool allows individuals to conduct geographic searches of psychologists and areas of specialization (including trauma). The Psychologist Locator can be accessed at locator.apa.org.

When working with individuals who have emerging disabilities such as MCS and CLD that are not generally understood and recognized, it is equally important to make referrals to appropriate specialists. The American Academy of Environmental Medicine has a physician referral link on their website that provides a state-by-state list of specialists in environmental medicine. This link can be accessed at wwwaaemonline.org/referral. In areas where these specialists are not available, rehabilitation counselors should consult with MCS self-help and advocacy organizations such as the Chemical Sensitivity Foundation or Multiple Chemical Sensitivity Referral and Resources to identify practitioners in their own or nearby communities who are knowledgeable about MCS and have experience treating individuals with this condition. Likewise, finding practitioners who are knowledgeable and experienced in treating CLD may be difficult, and peer and self-advocacy support groups as well as organizations such as Lymedisease.org can be consulted, keeping in mind that those who are consulted may have divergent opinions regarding the best course of treatment.

Because rehabilitation counselors can be expected to serve growing numbers of consumers with disabilities that can be linked to air pollution (e.g., asthma, other respiratory diseases, MCS), and because control of exposure to pollutants, allergens, and inciting chemicals can significantly improve their health and functioning, practitioners must consider what their role is in advocating for measures (e.g., federal and state legislation) to reduce emissions of air pollutants into the atmosphere, construct safer buildings, and improve both indoor and outdoor air quality. Relatedly, they should conduct an assessment of their own personal work spaces and office buildings to ensure that these are environmentally accessible. One important step they can take is to implement a fragrance-free office policy. Likewise, rehabilitation counselors should advocate for their agencies to contract with vendors who provide nontoxic office supplies or use eco-friendly and chemical-free products to clean office spaces.

Alternatively, rehabilitation counselors should be flexible in where they meet with consumers and willing to accommodate those with chemical sensitivities and respiratory diseases by avoiding the use of scented personal and office products that could trigger a symptomatic response. In some cases, in-person meetings with the consumer could trigger symptomatic responses, and appointments may need to be conducted via telephone or through use of other communication technologies. Eligibility criteria for services may need to be changed, as well, to ensure that disability is defined as a product of the interaction between individual characteristics (i.e., functional limitations as opposed to definitive medical diagnosis, services preferences, and individual goals) and environmental characteristics (i.e., as both a cause of disability and a substantial contributor to impairment; Fox & Kim, 2004). Eligibility criteria that rely heavily on medical diagnoses will likely exclude individuals with medically debated conditions from receiving services despite the fact that they often have significant disabilities that substantially interfere with their ability to actively participate in employment and other life activities (Koch et al., 2012).

Rehabilitation Assessment and Planning

In rehabilitation assessment and planning, the unique characteristics, needs, and environmental determinants of disabilities linked to lifestyle and climate change must be thoroughly considered if successful rehabilitation outcomes are to be realized. In particular, issues such as overall health and well-being, environmental trauma, stigma, medical invalidation, and how others in consumers' lives respond to their conditions must be assessed and addressed in the rehabilitation plan.

For example, the first step in rehabilitation assessment and planning with individuals who have experienced natural disasters may be to determine if their basic needs are being met. Do they have stable housing, enough food and clothing, natural supports, access to health care, and transportation? If these needs are not being met, rehabilitation counselors should work with the consumer to identify resources in the community for meeting these needs. Local resources may be limited because of damage to community infrastructures, so rehabilitation counselors will need to familiarize themselves with resources provided by other entities such as the federal or state government, nonprofit organizations, and religious institutions. Likewise, because individuals with MCS often do not have adequate health care or safe housing, addressing these issues through appropriate referrals to health care providers and housing assistance programs will be a prerequisite to rehabilitation planning (Gibson, Placek, Lane, Brohimer, & Lovelace, 2005).

Because individuals on rehabilitation counselors' caseloads may experience secondary complications or exacerbation of their symptoms as a result of severe weather events, it is important that, under these circumstances, rehabilitation counselors assess their physical and mental status and make amendments to the rehabilitation plan if additional services (e.g., physical and mental restoration) or referrals to outside service providers are needed. Likewise, during extreme heat and other severe weather events, rehabilitation counselors can work with their supervisors and coordinate with public health and other human services agencies to develop policies and procedures for ensuring the welfare and safety of consumers who may be especially vulnerable to the negative health consequences of these events. For example, during extreme heat events, if consumers do not have air conditioning in their dwellings, procedures should be in place to ensure that they are provided temporary accommodations in air-conditioned shelters because even spending a few hours a day in cool settings has been found to serve as a protective factor against detrimental health consequences (Bouchama, 2003). Additionally, rehabilitation counselors can make referrals to community independent living centers to install air-conditioning units in the homes of consumers without these or, alternatively, purchase air-conditioning units to be installed in their homes as a service on rehabilitation plans.

Rehabilitation Counseling Services

COUNSELING AND GUIDANCE

In providing counseling and guidance services to individuals with lifestyle disabilities, the issue of chronicity is often of paramount concern. Not only are many lifestyle disabilities chronic, unpredictable, and sometimes progressive, they may be accompanied by several or many other health concerns. Important issues that may need to be addressed in counseling and guidance include adherence to treatment and medication regimens, wellness strategies to prevent secondary complications of illness or injury, diet and nutrition, exercise, and stress management (Falvo, 2014). If the person's lifestyle disability was caused by addictive, compulsive, or high-risk behavior such as smoking, overeating, substance abuse, or unprotected sex, counseling and guidance services may need to focus on the problem behavior that underlies the lifestyle disability—examining the motivations for the behavior, strategies for cessation or modification of the behavior, and the impact of behavioral change on the person's psychological and social functioning (Atherton & Toriello, 2012; Cole & Fiore, 2014; Koch et al., 2012).

For those who have acquired disabilities or who developed chronic illnesses related to extreme weather events, rehabilitation counselors are challenged with the difficult task of distinguishing normal grief reactions from mental health conditions. Case reviews and evaluations with psychological and medical consultants are recommended to determine if referrals for mental health services are warranted. Furthermore, the CDC (2016) has provided guidance for understanding and responding to the needs of individuals who have experienced losses as a consequence of these events. First and foremost, the CDC noted that grief is a "normal response to an abnormal situation" (para. 1). Common reactions described by the CDC include survivor guilt, concerns for basic survival, feelings of vulnerability and insecurity, fear and anxiety, sleep disturbances, nightmares consisting of imagery from the disaster, anger directed toward public officials and rescuers for not responding quickly enough to the disaster and toward insurance companies for denying claims or processing claims too slowly, worries and concerns about relocation and related isolation, a need to talk (often incessantly) about events and feelings associated with the disaster, and the need to feel that one is part of his or her community and its recovery efforts.

In counseling and guidance, rehabilitation counselors must not impose their own grief reactions onto consumers. Nor should they make cross-consumer comparisons of responses to severe weather events. There are no rules regarding how individuals should grieve catastrophic losses due to lifestyle and the environment, nor are there prescribed stages of emotional responses that must be "worked through" in order to achieve resolution. Contemporary grief and bereavement experts have abandoned the stage model because of its lack of empirical support and now regard grief as a fluid and highly individualized process, taking into consideration an individual's coping resources and constraints as well as social support systems that can mediate the grief process (Shallcross, 2009).

Listening is perhaps the most helpful response that can be provided to these consumers (CDC, 2016). Individuals who have experienced natural disasters can substantially benefit from simply talking about their experiences while the counselor listens with genuine interest and concern. These consumers may also have a need to vent their feelings of frustration, anger, and helplessness related to federal, state, and nonprofit agencies disaster assistance programs and their slowness in responding to disaster recovery needs. Reassuring these consumers that their reactions are normal, in a manner that does not invalidate the seriousness of their situations, can also be helpful. Rushing to problem solving, without giving these individuals an opportunity to express their feelings and concerns about the losses they have incurred can undermine rapport and potentially result in their withdrawal from services. This is also true for individuals whose chronic illnesses are related to their lifestyles.

Like those who have acquired disabilities and chronic illnesses from extreme weather events, individuals with conditions such as MCS and CLD may also need to process their feelings about the multitude of severe symptoms they experience along with the impact that medical and societal invalidation has on their ability to cope. Providing these consumers with a nonjudgmental and validating "listening ear" is an important service. Additionally, counseling and guidance should emphasize coping with the stress and stigma associated with their conditions, dealing with the lack of understanding and support from others, developing new support networks, facilitating the development of skills to manage stress and pain, generalizing these skills to work settings, and making referrals to mental health professionals if individuals have co-occurring anxiety and/or depression that further impairs their functioning (Koch et al., 2012).

As a profession, rehabilitation counseling should also consider following the examples of nursing and public health (Barna et al., 2012) in developing initiatives to mitigate the impact of climate change on human health and functioning. Rehabilitation counselors have long partnered with people with disabilities to advocate for empowering disability-related public policy. Because individuals with disabilities are a large at-risk group for experiencing the negative health consequences of climate change, we must consider ways to expand our advocacy role in reducing air pollution and constructing healthier buildings. This expanded role might involve joining forces with disability advocacy organizations and environmentalists to promote strategies for creating healthier communities.

HEALTH PROMOTION SERVICES

Research evidence is accumulating that documents positive health outcomes for people with disabilities who receive health promotion services, and rehabilitation researchers are advocating for these services to be more systematically incorporated into plans for employment as a means to improve vocational rehabilitation (VR) outcomes (Crystal & Espinosa, 2012). For example, in comparing health-related outcomes of VR clients (N = 162) to those of individuals with disabilities who participated in a Living Well with a Disability health promotion workshop (N = 188), Ipsen, Jensen, and Anderson (2010) found that the Living Well sample experienced significantly greater (a) reductions in reported limitations from secondary health conditions, and (b) improvements in health promoting behaviors that were maintained over time. Based on these results, the researchers recommended that VR counselors contract with community independent living centers and community rehabilitation programs to provide health promotion interventions such as the Living Well workshop to VR clients. They also recommended exploring the benefits of delivering health promotion interventions through the state–federal VR system.

Health promotions services may be especially beneficial to individuals with lifestyle disabilities to assist them with changing health-related behaviors. Health promotion services can also be beneficial for individuals with chronic illnesses linked to climate change such as asthma, MCS, and Lyme disease for better management of their disabilities and prevention of secondary complications. Failure to respond to the overall health needs of the populations discussed in this chapter is likely to impede their ability to achieve their desired educational, employment, independent living, and community integration outcomes. In addition to contracting with outside vendors to provide health promotion workshops, VR counselors, as well as rehabilitation counselors working in settings other than the state–federal VR program, can recommend health promoting behaviors in counseling sessions, provide support and encouragement as individuals make health-related changes, and include provision of health promotion interventions (e.g., weight management, dietary consultation, fitness programs, stress management, smoking cessation; Ipsen et al., 2010) in individualized rehabilitation and employment plans.

Home modifications can also have a health promoting function. For example, installation of air-conditioning units in the homes of individuals with preexisting conditions who live in communities prone to extreme heat events can preclude exacerbation of symptoms and secondary medical complications. For individuals with asthma, other respiratory conditions, and MCS, home modifications should be targeted at improving air quality. If consumers with these chronic illnesses do not have safe home environments with good air quality, their symptoms will persist and worsen, and it is unlikely that they will be able to actively participate in employment. In some instances, they may need assistance with finding safe housing.

MENTAL HEALTH COUNSELING

The CDC has identified "red flags" indicating that referral to mental health specialists with expertise and experience in treating individuals who have survived disaster-related events may be warranted. These "red flags" include disorientation; persistent feelings of hopelessness and despair; withdrawal from others; feeling constantly restless or on edge; obsessive fears of another disaster; hearing voices; seeing visions; delusional thinking; disengaging from self-care activities (e.g., not eating, bathing, changing clothes, brushing teeth); suicidal or homicidal thoughts or plans; problematic use of alcohol or drugs; and domestic violence, child abuse, or elder abuse.

For individuals with medically contested conditions such as MCS and CLD, the mere mention of mental health services may be interpreted by these consumers as invalidation of their medical condition and evidence that the rehabilitation counselor, like so many other professionals they have encountered, thinks their symptoms are psychosomatic (Koch et al., 2012). Therefore, when recommending mental health services for these consumers, rehabilitation counselors must be cautious to communicate that the purpose of these services is not to diagnose and treat them for a psychosomatic condition, but rather to (a) support them in dealing with normal emotional responses that anyone with a medically invalidated condition would have; (b) help them to identify coping resources and supports; and (c) treat co-occurring mental health conditions that may arise from living with a chronic condition that is invalidated by others.

PEER AND SOCIAL SUPPORTS

Peer and social supports are invaluable resources for individuals with disabilities who are attempting to make significant lifestyle changes to improve their health and for those who have experienced changes in their health and functional status resulting from severe weather events. Peers who have been successful at making lifestyle changes to reduce the symptoms associated with their conditions and improve their overall health can serve as role models and mentors who inspire hope in those who are contemplating or just beginning to make changes. Peer-provided health promotion interventions can also increase the likelihood that those with lifestyle disabilities will engage in activities to improve their overall health and functioning. Rehabilitation counselors should research the availability of relevant peer support groups and peer-provided services in their local communities so they can share these resources with consumers (Kalb, 2012).

Peer support and self-advocacy groups can serve to diminish the sense of isolation and hopelessness experienced by people with medically invalidated and socially unaccepted conditions. These groups offer an opportunity for consumers with these conditions to connect with others who share their experiences and understand what they are going through. Members of these support and self-advocacy groups also share strategies and resources to cope with these conditions and advocate for changes in societal attitudes and public policy to increase access to much needed health and rehabilitation services. However, interacting with others in peer support groups who have more severely disabling symptoms could be disheartening for some. Thus, both the risks and benefits of peer support groups should be explored with consumers before rehabilitation counselors make referrals. If in-person meetings are not available in the consumers' communities or if individuals experience symptoms that could be exacerbated from participating in in-person meetings, online support and self-advocacy groups are an alternative that may be beneficial. Again, rehabilitation counselors should thoroughly investigate the availability of these resources and share this information with consumers.

Mental health experts have indicated that participating in community recovery efforts can help to facilitate personal recovery from the devastating consequences of weather-related events (CDC, 2016). By working with others who have experienced the negative consequences of these events to rebuild their communities, individuals can experience a sense of connectedness and empowerment as well as hope that they will recover from these events. Rehabilitation counselors working with individuals who have been forced to relocate because of extreme weather events must also take into consideration the additional stressor of living in a new community where social supports may be lacking; thus, it may be important to help these individuals to establish new social support networks through employment, recreational and leisure activities, volunteer work, and involvement with religious institutions.

Job Development and Placement

Traditional full-time placement at an established job site could exacerbate symptoms, worsen conditions, or impair the overall health and functioning of some individuals with the conditions we have discussed in this chapter. In these cases, alternatives such as telecommuting and home-based employment may need to be considered (Strauser, 2013). Fortunately, many employers are beginning to provide these opportunities to their employees because of the cost-effectiveness of these options (Rubin et al., 2016). Rehabilitation counselors can educate employers who do not provide their employees with these alternatives about the ease and cost-effectiveness of telecommuting and working from home.

In the job development and placement process with individuals who have stigmatized and/or medically invalidated disabilities linked to lifestyle and/or climate change, workplaces that are attitudinally accessible and promote the health and well-being of their employees should be targeted. In addition to conducting job analyses, assessment of the organizational cultures of potential workplaces is necessary because individuals with these conditions often encounter negative reactions from both employers and coworkers (e.g., ignoring their requests for accommodations, responding to requests with hostility or harassment, treating these workers with incivility) when they disclose their disabilities and make accommodation requests (Rumrill, Fraser, & Johnson, 2013). First, workplace policies and procedures should be examined to determine if these promote inclusion; healthy work environments; flexibility in how and where work is performed; teamwork; appreciation of diversity; and intolerance of harassment, workplace bullying, and incivility. Then, observation of interactions between coworkers and interviews with employers and employees about the workplace culture will provide the rehabilitation counselor with additional evidence of the setting's attitudinal accessibility.

In job development and placement, employers often need to be educated about these disabling conditions because they are likely to have biases and misunderstandings about their associated functional limitations and how accommodations (most of which are no cost or very inexpensive and can benefit all workers) can enable these individuals to be productive, reliable, and competent employees (Rubin et al., 2016). Individuals with these conditions themselves can be coached about how to educate employers, or rehabilitation counselors can jointly educate employers with the consumer. Coworkers, especially those who will be working most closely with the individual, are also likely to be unaware of the individuals' disability-related needs. This lack of awareness among coworkers can be a major impediment to job satisfaction, satisfactoriness, and longevity on the job (Strauser, 2013); thus, it may be necessary to educate them as well. Rehabilitation counselors can assist consumers with identifying appropriate strategies and developing the necessary communication skills that will elicit support and understanding from coworkers.

Potential job sites should also be assessed to determine if they have fragrance-free office policies. These policies should go beyond prohibiting the use of colognes and perfumes to ensuring the absence of all fragranced products in the workplace. For example, the CDC fragrance-free office policy requires employees to refrain from using perfumes; colognes; aftershave; scented personal care products including deodorants, shampoos, hair products, cosmetics, soaps, hand creams, laundry-scented detergents, and fabric softeners (Martini et al., 2013). The CDC policy also requires workers to air smoke-laden and dry-cleaned clothing before entering the workplace. Additionally, incense, candles, reed diffusers, potpourri, plug-in or spray air fresheners, and urinal or toilet blocks cannot be used in workspaces.

Accommodation Planning

The accommodation planning process with disability populations discussed in this chapter is likely to be a complex endeavor because of the multitude of functional limitations these individuals experience, compounded by the extent of negative stereotypes and stigma promulgated by both the medical community and society at large. Steps that can be taken to better ensure that necessary accommodations will be implemented include (a) educating individuals about the employment protections afforded by the ADA and other legislation; (b) engaging in a collaborative process of identifying workplace barriers and accommodation needs; and (c) assisting individuals to develop the self-advocacy and communication skills to request, implement, and evaluate accommodations (Roessler & Rumrill, 2015).

Because individuals with conditions such as asthma, diabetes, MCS, and CLD may not consider themselves to have disabilities, the first step in accommodation planning is to educate them how legislation such as the ADA defines disability and protects their rights related to securing and maintaining employment (Rubin et al., 2016). Additionally, because many of these individuals have hidden disabilities and have encountered negative reactions when disclosing their disabilities to others, rehabilitation counselors should carefully listen to their concerns about disclosure and past negative experiences related to disclosure. Rehabilitation counselors can then explore with them the advantages and disadvantages of disclosure, the circumstances under which disclosure may be advantageous, how and when to disclose, and to whom to disclose (Rumrill et al., 2013).

The next step is to identify workplace barriers and potential accommodations to ameliorate these barriers. Roessler's (1995) Work Experience Survey (WES) is a valid and reliable needs assessment tool that has been used with populations of workers with chronic illnesses to identify barriers and accommodations. This instrument can be used in a collaborative and empowering approach that focuses first on the consumer's elucidation of barriers and accommodation ideas and then on additional ideas provided by the rehabilitation counselor to supplement the consumer's ideas. Many individuals with the conditions discussed in this chapter have functional limitations that change over time or experience changes to their work environments that may negatively impact their capacity to continue working without accommodations put in place (i.e., the addition of new equipment, the hiring of new workers, remodeling of workplaces that could introduce new chemical exposures which could impair the ability of workers with MCS to maintain their employment; Koch et al., 2007). The potential application of the WES for use with individuals with lifestyle- and climate-change–related disabilities is promising because it is a tool that can be used for periodic reassessment of their accommodation needs.

The Job Accommodation Network (JAN) is an excellent resource for identifying specific accommodation ideas. For example, JAN suggests potential accommodations for respiratory diseases such as asthma and MCS that include removal of chemical triggers from the work environment, relocation of the employee's workspace, adding air purifiers to the workspace, liberal attendance and leave policies, modifications of where work is performed so that individuals can work from home or other environments where they will not be exposed to environmental triggers, accessible parking and restrooms, modified or part-time work, and modifications to the scheduling of breaks (JAN, 2014).

Perhaps one of the most effective accommodations for these workers is fragrance-free office policies. In employment sites where these do not exist, rehabilitation counselors can assist employers in developing comprehensive policies, using the CDC's fragrance-free policy as a guidepost. Vierstra et al. (2007) recommended that the most effective way to advocate for fragrance-free policies with employers is to emphasize that clean air in the work environment is healthier for *all* employees. Employers' willingness to establish fragrance-free office policies is more likely using this strategy rather than approaching employers regarding how to accommodate a single employee.

For individuals with CLD, accommodation ideas offered by JAN include reduced work schedules, periodic rest breaks, and flexible leave time to reduce fatigue; transfers to less stressful positions within the organization, flexible work schedules, and working from home to reduce stress; sensitivity training to coworkers; allowing telephone calls to health care and other providers for support; referral to employee assistance programs to accommodate depression; and protective clothing to avoid exposure to chemical hazards for those with skin sensitivities. JAN suggests that individuals with CLD may also benefit from accommodations used by individuals with chronic pain, arthritis, and vision loss (JAN, 2014).

Workers with diabetes call in sick four times more often than nondisabled workers (American Diabetes Association, 2015), so scheduling modifications are an important accommodation strategy for these individuals (JAN, 2014). JAN also emphasized the importance of allowing employees with diabetes to have periodic breaks during the workday so they can have snacks and take oral or intravenous insulin to regulate their blood sugar. Workers with diabetes, cancer, cardiovascular disease, and HIV/AIDS may need flexible personal and medical leave policies in the event that they require hospitalizations or surgery for some of the more severe effects of their illnesses. Because individuals with emerging disabilities associated with lifestyle factors and/or climate change have so often experienced invalidation of their symptoms and negative responses from others to their self-disclosures, they may lack the self-efficacy to advocate for workplace accommodations from their employers. Hence, there is a compelling need for self-advocacy training to equip these individuals with the necessary skills to effectively request reasonable accommodations, document their disability status, and make formal complaints of employer discrimination. More intensive interventions may directly involve the rehabilitation counselor in facilitating collaborative decision making between the employer and employee, ensuring effective communication among all parties, and establishing a shared commitment to worker productivity and success (Johnson, 2015).

CONCLUSIONS

Lifestyle factors and the environment have had a profound impact on health and wellness in contemporary society. A number of emerging disabilities such as diabetes, heart disease, asthma, cancer, and HIV/AIDS trace their incidence to poor nutrition, physical inactivity, poor preventive and prenatal care, tobacco use, intravenous drug use, and high-risk sexual behavior. Climate change, air pollution, and natural disasters have been linked to rising rates of Lyme disease, MCS, asthma, allergies, certain types of cancer, and psychological disorders related to stress and trauma.

Emerging disabilities linked to lifestyle and the environment disproportionally affect people living in poverty and people from traditionally underrepresented racial and ethnic groups. Most of these disabling conditions discussed in this chapter are chronic, some are progressive, and many bring with them a wide range of symptoms and secondary complications. These facts make lifestyle-related and environmentally related disabilities exceedingly difficult to adjust to and cope with for people diagnosed with these conditions and their significant others.

Rehabilitation counselors working with people who have emerging disabilities related to lifestyle and the environment must attend to the negative stereotypes and stigma that accompany these poorly understood, sometimes underreported, and often invisible disabilities—including counselors' own biases about people with these conditions. Responsive, client-centered, and holistic rehabilitation services that validate clients' medical and psychological experiences are the keys to improving the disappointing health and vocational outcomes that are too frequently reported by people with emerging disabilities related to lifestyle and the environment.

DISCUSSION QUESTIONS

1. What are lifestyle disabilities that are prominent in your community? Are individuals with these disabilities accessing rehabilitation services? If not, what can be done to increase their access to services?
2. Discuss recent severe weather events and their potential implications for the onset of chronic illnesses and disabilities and the exacerbation of preexisting conditions.
3. What do you think the most important rehabilitation considerations are for individuals with lifestyle disabilities?
4. What do you think the most important rehabilitation considerations are for people with disabilities resulting from climate change?
5. What are your personal biases that may interfere with your ability to work with individuals with the disabilities and chronic illnesses discussed in this chapter? What can you do to challenge those biases?
6. In considering David's case, what did you learn about his experiences that could be applied to rehabilitation assessment and planning with individuals whose diabetes is not well managed?

REFERENCES

Adil Mansoor, S., Muazzam, M., & Hasan Imam, H. S. (2014). HIV infection: Prevalence among intravenous drug users. *Professional Medical Journal, 21*(5), 975–979.

Ali, A., Vitulano, L., Lee, R., Weiss, T. R., & Colson, E. R. (2014). Experiences of patients identifying with chronic Lyme disease in the healthcare system: A qualitative study. *BMC Family Practice, 15*(1), 1.

American Chronic Pain Association. (2015). *ACPA resource guide to chronic pain medication & treatment.* Retrieved from https://theacpa.org/uploads/documents/ACPA_Resource_Guide_2015_Final%20edited%20(3).pdf

American Counseling Association. (2016). *Disaster mental health.* Retrieved from https://www.counseling.org/knowledge-center/trauma-disaster

American Diabetes Association. (2015). *Statistics about diabetes.* Retrieved from http://www.diabetes.org/diabetes-basics/statistics/?loc=db-slabnav

American Heart Association. (2014). *Heart disease and stroke statistics: At a glance.* Retrieved from https://www.heart.org/idc/groups/ahamah-public/@wcm/@sop/@smd/documents/downloadable/ucm_470704.pdf

American Lung Association. (2015). *State of the air 2015: Key findings for 2011–2013.* Retrieved from http://www.stateoftheair.org/2015/key-findings

Anderko, L., Davies-Cole, J., & Strunk, A. (2014). Identifying populations at risk: Interdisciplinary environmental climate change tracking. *Public Health Nursing, 31*(6), 484–491.

Andrews, K. L., Jones, S. C., & Mullen, J. (2013). Stigma: Still an important issue for adults with asthma. *Journal of Asthma and Allergy Educators, 4*(4), 165–171.

Atherton, W. L., & Toriello, P. J. (2012). Re-conceptualizing the treatment of substance use disorders: The impact on employment. In P. J. Toriello, M. L. Bishop, & P. D. Rumrill (Eds.), *New directions in rehabilitation counseling: Creative responses to professional, clinical, and educational challenges* (pp. 282–304). Linn Creek, MO: Aspen Professional Services.

Aucott, J. N., Rebman, A. W., Crowder, L. A., & Kortte, K. B. (2013). Post-treatment Lyme disease syndrome symptomatology and the impact on life functioning: Is there something here? *Quality of Life Research, 22*(1), 75–84.

Balbus, J. M., & Malina, C. (2009). Identifying vulnerable subpopulations for climate change health effects in the United States. *Journal of Occupational and Environmental Medicine, 51*, 33–37.

Barna, S., Goodman, B., & Mortimer, F. (2012). The health effects of climate change: What does a nurse need to know? *Nurse Education Today, 32*(7), 765–771.

Beck, R. J., & Franke, D. L. (1996). Rehabilitation of victims of natural disasters. *Journal of Rehabilitation, 62*(4), 28.

Bloom, B., Cohen, R. A., & Freeman, G. (2012). *Summary health statistics for U.S. children: National Health Interview Survey, 2011.* Vital and Health Statistics. Series 10, Number 254, Data from the National Health Survey, pp. 1–88.

Bouchama, A. (2003). The 2003 European heat wave. *Intensive Care Medicine, 30*, 1–3.

Burrascano, J. J., Jr. (2008). Advanced topics in Lyme disease. *Diagnostic Hints and Treatment Guidelines for Lyme and Other Tick Borne Illnesses, 15.*

Caress, S. M., & Steinemann, A. C. (2009). Asthma and chemical hypersensitivity: Prevalence, etiology, and age of onset. *Toxicology and Industrial Health, 25*(1), 71–78.

Centers for Disease Control and Prevention. (2006). Morbidity surveillance after Hurricane Katrina—Arkansas, Louisiana, Mississippi, and Texas, September 2005. *Morbidity and Mortality Weekly Report, 55*(26), 727–731.

Centers for Disease Control and Prevention. (2011). *Asthma in the US.* Retrieved from http://www.cdc.gov/vitalsigns/asthma

Centers for Disease Control and Prevention. (2014a). *Heart disease and stroke statistics—At-a-glance.* Retrieved from https://www.heart.org/idc/groups/ahamah-public/@wcm/@sop/@smd/documents/downloadable/ucm_470704.pdf

Centers for Disease Control and Prevention. (2014b). *National Diabetes Statistics Report, 2014.* Retrieved from http://www.cdc.gov/diabetes/pubs/statsreport14/national-diabetes-report-web.pdf

Centers for Disease Control and Prevention. (2015a). *Lyme disease data tables.* Retrieved from http://www.cdc.gov/lyme/stats/tables.html

Centers for Disease Control and Prevention. (2015b). *Signs and symptoms of untreated Lyme disease.* Retrieved from www.cdc.gov/lyme/signs_symptoms/index.html

Centers for Disease Control and Prevention. (2016). *Coping with a disaster or traumatic event.* Retrieved from https://emergency.cdc.gov/coping/families.asp

Cha, E., Akazawa, M. K., Kim, K. H., Dawkins, C. R., Lerner, H. M., Umpierrez, G., & Dunbar, S. B. (2015). Lifestyle habits and obesity progression in overweight and obese American young adults: Lessons for promoting cardiometabolic health. *Nursing & Health Sciences, 17*(4), 467–475. doi:10.1111/nhs.12218

Cole, H. M., & Fiore, M. C. (2014). The war against tobacco. *JAMA, 311*(2), 131–132.

Costello, A., Abbas, M., Allen, A., Ball, S., Bell, S., Bellamy, R., & Patterson, C. (2009). Managing the health effects of climate change: Lancet and University College London Institute for Global Health Commission. *The Lancet, 373*(9676), 1693–1733.

Crystal, R., & Espinosa, C. T. (2012). Individuals with disabilities and the American healthcare system. In P. J. Toriello, M. L. Bishop, & P. D. Rumrill (Eds.), *New directions in rehabilitation counseling: Creative responses to professional, clinical, and educational challenges* (pp. 140–163). Linn Creek, MO: Aspen Professional Services.

Dixon, P. G., Sinyor, M., Schaffer, A., Levitt, A., Haney, C. R., Ellis, K. N., & Sheridan, S. C. (2014). Association of weekly suicide rates with temperature anomalies in two different climate types. *International Journal of Environmental Research and Public Health, 11*(11), 11627–11644.

Falvo, D. R. (2014). *Medical and psychosocial aspects of chronic illness and disability* (5th ed.). Burlington, MA: Jones & Bartlett.

Fox, M. H., & Kim, K. (2004). Understanding emerging disabilities. *Disability and Society, 19*, 323–337.

Galloway, M. (2015). Asthma: What the guideline says. *Practice Nurse, 45*(4), 12–17.

Gibson, B. E. (2006). Disability, connectivity and transgressing the autonomous body. *Journal of Medical Humanities, 27*(3), 187–196.

Gibson, P. R., Cheavens, J., & Warren, M. L. (1996). Chemical sensitivity/chemical injury and life disruption. *Women & Therapy, 19*(2), 63–79.

Gibson, P. R., Elms, A. N. M., & Ruding, L. A. (2003). Perceived treatment efficacy for conventional and alternative therapies reported by persons with multiple chemical sensitivity. *Environmental Health Perspectives, 111*(12), 1498.

Gibson, P. R., Placek, E., Lane, J., Brohimer, S. O., & Lovelace, A. C. E. (2005). Disability-induced identity changes in persons with multiple chemical sensitivity. *Qualitative Health Research, 15*(4), 502–524.

Gibson, P. R., Sledd, L. G., McEnroe, W. H., & Vos, A. P. (2011). Isolation and lack of access in multiple chemical sensitivity: A qualitative study. *Nursing & Health Sciences, 13*(3), 232–237.

Global Asthma Network. (2015). *The Global Asthma Report, 2014*. Retrieved from http://www.globalasthmanetwork.org/publications/Global_Asthma_Report_2014.pdf

Guirguis, K., Gershunov, A., Tardy, A., & Basu, R. (2014). The impact of recent heat waves on human health in California. *Journal of Applied Meteorology and Climatology, 53*(1), 3–19.

Hassett, A. L., Radvanski, D. C., Buyske, S., Savage, S. V., & Sigal, L. H. (2009). Psychiatric comorbidity and other psychological factors in patients with "chronic Lyme disease." *American Journal of Medicine, 122*(9), 843–850.

Hess, J. J., Malilay, J. N., & Parkinson, A. J. (2008). Climate change: The importance of place. *American Journal of Preventive Medicine, 35*(5), 468–478.

Institute of Medicine. (2011). *Relieving pain in America*. Washington, DC: National Academies Press.

Interagency Working Group on Climate Change and Human Health. (2010). *A human health perspective on climate change: A report outlining the research needs on the human health effects of climate change*. Retrieved from https://www.niehs.nih.gov/health/assets/docs_p_z/interagency_climate_508.pdf

Intergovernmental Panel on Climate Change. (2007). *Climate change 2007: Impacts, adaptation and vulnerability*. Retrieved from https://www.ipcc.ch/pdf/assessment-report/ar4/wg2/ar4_wg2_full_report.pdf

International Diabetes Federation. (2014). *Annual report 2014*. Retrieved from https://www.idf.org/sites/default/files/IDF-2014-Annual-Report-final.pdf

Ipsen, C., Jensen, P. L., & Anderson, V. (2010). Prevention of work-related stress—A participatory approach. In P. Vink & J. Kantola (Eds.), *Advances in occupational, social and organizational ergonomics* (pp. 305–314). Boca Raton, FL: CRC Press.

Job Accommodation Network. (2014). *Workplace accommodations: Low cost, high impact*. Retrieved from http://AskJAN.org/media/lowcosthighimpact.html

Johnson, E. (2015). Perspectives on work for people with epilepsy. In I. Schultz & R. Gatchel (Eds.), *Handbook of return to work: From research to practice* (pp. 617–632). New York, NY: Springer.

Johnson, L., Wilcox, S., Mankoff, J., & Stricker, R. B. (2014). Severity of chronic Lyme disease compared to other chronic conditions: A quality of life survey. *PeerJ, 2*, e322.

Kalb, R. (2012). *Multiple sclerosis: The questions you have, the answers you need* (5th ed.). New York, NY: Demos Medical.

Kiefer, M., Silverman, J., Young, B., & Nelson, K. (2015). National patterns in diabetes screening: Data from the National Health and Nutrition Examination Survey (NHANES) 2005–2012. *Journal of General Internal Medicine, 30*(5), 612–618. doi:10.1007/s11606-014-3147-8

Kinney, P. L. (2008). Climate change, air quality, and human health. *American Journal of Preventive Medicine, 35*(5), 459–467.

Koch, L., Conyers, L., & Rumrill, P. (2012). The nature and needs of people with emerging disabilities. In P. J. Toriello, M. L. Bishop, & P. D. Rumrill (Eds.), *New directions in rehabilitation counseling: Creative responses to professional, clinical, and educational challenges* (pp. 116–139). Linn Creek, MO: Aspen Professional Services.

Koch, L., & Eaton, B. (2005). Multiple chemical sensitivity and rehabilitation planning implications. *Journal of Applied Rehabilitation Counseling, 36*(1), 24–29.

Koch, L., Rumrill, P., Hennessey, M., Vierstra, C., & Roessler, R. (2007). An ecological approach to facilitate successful employment outcomes among people with multiple chemical sensitivity. *Work: A Journal of Prevention, Assessment, and Rehabilitation, 29*(4), 341–349.

Koch, L., Vierstra, C., & Penix, K. (2006). A qualitative investigation of the psychosocial impact of multiple chemical sensitivity. *Journal of Applied Rehabilitation Counseling, 37*(3), 33–40.

Lacour, M., Zunder, T., Schmidtke, K., Vaith, P., & Scheidt, C. (2005). Multiple chemical sensitivity syndrome (MCS): Suggestions for an extension of the US MCS-case definition. *International Journal of Hygiene and Environmental Health, 208*(3), 141–151.

Lamielle, M. (2003). *Multiple chemical sensitivity and the workplace*. Voorhees, NJ: National Center for Environmental Health Strategies, Inc.

Lewis, A.N., & Burris, J. L. (2012). The multicultural rehabilitation counseling imperative in the 21st century. In P. J. Toriello, M. L. Bishop, & P. D. Rumrill (Eds.), *New directions in rehabilitation counseling: Creative responses to professional, clinical, and educational challenges* (pp. 164–208). Linn Creek, MO: Aspen Professional Services.

Lewith, G. T., Hyland, M., & Gray, S. F. (2001). Attitudes to and use of complementary medicine among physicians in the United Kingdom. *Complementary Therapies in Medicine, 9*(3), 167–172.

Lipson, J. G. (2001). We are the canaries: Self-care in multiple chemical sensitivity sufferers. *Qualitative Health Research, 11*(1), 103–116.

Luber, G., & McGeehin, M. (2008). Climate change and extreme heat events. *American Journal of Preventive Medicine, 35*(5), 429–435.

Martini, A., Iavicoli, S., & Corso, L. (2013). Multiple chemical sensitivity and the workplace: Current position and need for an occupational health surveillance protocol. *Oxidative Medicine and Cellular Longevity, 6*, 1–13.

McMichael, A. J., Woodruff, R. E., & Hales, S. (2006). Climate change and human health: Present and future risks. *The Lancet, 367*(9513), 859–886.

Milligan, L. P., France, J., Niroshan Appuhamy, J. R., Kebreab, E., Simon, M., & Yada, R. (2014). Effects of diet and exercise interventions on diabetes risk factors in adults without diabetes: Metaanalyses of controlled trials. *Diabetology & Metabolic Syndrome, 6*(1), 1–28. doi:10.1186/1758-5996-6-127

Million Hearts. (2015). *Risks for heart disease and stroke*. Retrieved from http://millionhearts.hhs.gov/learn-prevent/risks.html

Multiple chemical sensitivity: A 1999 consensus. (1999). *Archives of Environmental & Occupational Health, 54*(3), 147–149.

National Center for Complementary and Integrative Health. (2016). *Complementary, alternative, or integrative health: What's in a name?* Retrieved from https://nccih.nih.gov/health/integrative-health

National Geographic Society. (2016). *Climate refugee*. Retrieved from http://nationalgeographic.org/encyclopedia/climate-refugee

National Heart, Lung, and Blood Institute. (2014). *Who is at risk for heart disease?* Retrieved from http://www.nhlbi.nih.gov/health/health-topics/topics/hdw/atrisk

Ogden, N. H., Radojevic, M., Wu, X., Duvvuri, V. R., Leighton, P. A., & Wu, J. (2014). Estimated effects of projected climate change on the basic reproductive number of the Lyme disease vector Ixodesscapularis. *Environmental Health Perspectives (Online)*, *122*(6), 631.

Partridge, S., Balayla, J., Holcroft, C. A., & Abenhaim, H. A. (2012). Inadequate prenatal care utilization and risks of infant mortality and poor birth outcome: A retrospective analysis of 28,729,765 U.S. deliveries over 8 years. *American Journal of Perinatology, 29*(10), 787--793. doi:10.1055/s-0032-1316439

Roessler, R. T. (1995). *The Work Experience Survey.* Fayetteville, AR: Arkansas Research and Training Center in Vocational Rehabilitation.

Roessler, R. T., & Rumrill, P. (2015). *Enhancing productivity on your job: The "win-win" approach to reasonable accommodations.* New York, NY: National Multiple Sclerosis Society.

Rose, S. C., Weber, K. D., Collen, J. B., & Heyer, G. L. (2015). The diagnosis and management of concussion in children and adolescents. *Pediatric Neurology, 53*(2), 108–118. doi:10.1016/j.pediatrneurol.2015.04.003

Rubin, S., Roessler, R., & Rumrill, P. (2016). *Foundations of the vocational rehabilitation process* (7th ed.). Austin, TX: Pro-Ed.

Rumrill, P., Fraser, R., & Johnson, K. (2013). Employment and workplace accommodation outcomes among participants in a vocational consultation service for people with multiple sclerosis. *Journal of Vocational Rehabilitation, 39*, 85–90.

Sastry, N., & Gregory, J. (2013). The effect of Hurricane Katrina on the prevalence of health impairments and disability among adults in New Orleans: Differences by age, race, and sex. *Social Science & Medicine, 80*, 121–129.

Shallcross, L. (2009). Rewriting the "rules" of grief. *Counseling Today, 52*(3), 28–33.

Smart, J. (2009). *Disability, society, and the individual* (2nd ed.). Austin, TX: Pro-Ed.

Strauser, D. (2013). *Career development, employment, and disability in rehabilitation.* New York, NY: Springer Publishing Company.

Stricker, R. B. (2007). Counterpoint: Long-term antibiotic therapy improves persistent symptoms associated with Lyme disease. *Clinical Infectious Diseases, 45*(2), 149–157.

Substance Abuse and Mental Health Services Administration. (2012). *Excessive heat exposure can pose higher risks for those on psychotropic medication or other substances.* Retrieved from http://blog.samhsa.gov/2012/06/29/excessive-heat-exposure-can-pose-higher -risks-for-those-on-psychotropic-medication-or-other-substances/#.V6EDVaKrErg

U.S. Environmental Protection Agency. (2011). *Climate change and air quality.* Retrieved from http://www.epa.gov/airquality/airtrends/2011/report/climatechange.pdf

U.S. Environmental Protection Agency. (2014). *Climate change indicators in the United States: Lyme disease.* Retrieved from http://www.epa.gov/climatechange/science/indicators/ health-society/lyme.html

U.S. Environmental Protection Agency. (2015a). *Asthma facts.* Retrieved from https:// www.epa.gov/sites/production/files/2015-10/documents/asthma_fact_sheet_eng_ july_30_2015_v2.pdf

U.S. Environmental Protection Agency. (2015b). *Particulate matter (PM): Basic information.* Retrieved from http://www.epa.gov/pm/basic.html

U.S. Environmental Protection Agency. (2016). *Chemicals and toxics resources.* Retrieved from https://www.epa.gov/learn-issues/chemicals-and-toxics-resources#common-chemicals

U.S. National Oceanic and Atmospheric Administration. (2016). *Billion-dollar weather and climate disasters: Overview.* Retrieved from https://www.ncdc.noaa.gov/billions/overview

Victor, B., & Cullen, J. (1987). A theory and measure of ethical climate in organizations. In W. C. Fredrick & L. Preston (Eds.), *Research in Corporate Social Performance and Policy* (pp. 51–71). London, UK: JAI.

Vierstra, C. V., Rumrill, P. D., Koch, L. C., & McMahon, B. T. (2007). Multiple chemical sensitivity and workplace discrimination: The national EEOC ADA research project. *Work, 28*(4), 391–402.

White House. (2014). *The health impacts of climate change on Americans.* Retrieved from https://www.whitehouse.gov/sites/default/files/docs/the_health_impacts_of_climate_change_on_americans_final.pdf

Wickert, K., Dresden, D., & Rumrill, P. (2013). *The sandwich generation's guide to eldercare.* New York, NY: Demos Health.

World Health Organization. (2014). *Injuries and violence: The facts 2014.* Retrieved from http://www.who.int/iris/handle/10665/149798#sthash.orTUv3TT.dpuf

World Health Organization. (2015a). *Cardiovascular diseases: Key facts.* Retrieved from http://www.who.int/mediacentre/factsheets/fs317/en

World Health Organization. (2015b). *Diabetes.* Retrieved from http://www.who.int/mediacentre/factsheets/fs312/en

Yang, H. J., Lee, S. Y., Suh, D. I., Shin, Y. H., Kim, B. J., Seo, J. H.,… Lee, K. S. (2014). The Cohort for Childhood Origin of Asthma and Allergic Diseases (COCOA) study: Design, rationale and methods. *BMC Pulmonary Medicine, 14*(1), 109.

Disabilities Caused by Violence

Coauthored by Melissa D. Wilkins

CHAPTER OBJECTIVES

- *Understand various types of violence and their impact on human health, functioning, and onset of physical and psychiatric disabilities*
- *Identify approaches and programs for treating individuals who have sustained disabilities from violent acts*
- *Examine populations that are most vulnerable to violence*
- *Explore trauma-informed approaches to providing services to these clients in all phases of the rehabilitation counseling process*

CASE ILLUSTRATION: AMALIA

Amalia is a 20-year-old Mexican American woman who was referred for vocational rehabilitation (VR) services by a social worker at a local women's shelter. In conducting the intake interview, the VR counselor learned that Amalia has a long history of physical, emotional, and sexual abuse that began at the age of 10 when she was repeatedly sexually abused by an uncle until the age of 15. She became pregnant with her daughter in the 11th grade and dropped out of high school. She then moved into a small apartment with her daughter's father, Paul. Money was very tight because Paul was only working odd jobs and Amalia did not work so she could take care of her daughter. Over time, Paul became increasingly overwhelmed and physically and emotionally abusive, especially when he was drinking. One night he came after Amalia with a knife. She was able to escape with her daughter to a neighbor's apartment. The neighbor called the police, and Paul was taken into custody. Despite Amalia's reluctance to press charges, Paul was charged with aggravated assault with a deadly weapon and received a sentence of 5 years in state prison.

Amalia ended up taking her daughter to a women's shelter where she spent approximately a week before she moved in with an aunt. While at the shelter, the social worker helped her fill out an application for VR services. Amalia was already receiving benefits from the Special Supplemental Nutrition Program for Women, Infants, and Children (WIC), food stamps, Transitional Employment Assistance

(TEA) program benefits, and Medicaid for her daughter. The social worker also helped Amalia register for general equivalency diploma (GED) classes at the local adult education program. Currently, Amalia's aunt is providing free childcare for Amalia while she attends GED classes, but Amalia would like to eventually find a full-time job, get her own place, and pay her aunt, who lives on a modest fixed income, for childcare.

The VR counselor asked Amalia if she had any disabilities, and Amalia responded that she has a hearing loss and "nerve problems." Her hearing loss is especially pronounced in crowded, noisy rooms and sometimes on the phone. Amalia does not remember when her last hearing test was, but she believes that she had one in school when she was a child. When asked what she means by "nerve problems," Amalia stated that she often has nightmares about past abuse and cannot get back to sleep when she awakens from these nightmares. She also describes feeling panic (e.g., tight chest, rapid heart rate, fast breathing, sweating) when in a physical space that she cannot easily escape (e.g., a small classroom or a crowded store), constantly worrying about her daughter's safety, feeling anxious when her daughter is not with her, and experiencing persistent fears about both their safety when Paul is released from prison.

Amalia's only reported work experience is 6 months at McDonalds while she was pregnant with her daughter. She reports that she had a lot of difficulty at this job, both emotionally and with being able to hear when it was very crowded. Her current goals are to get her GED and to receive additional training for a job that pays above minimum wage and provides health benefits for both her daughter and herself. However, when asked about her vocational interests, Amalia stated that she could not think of any, and she also reported self-doubts about her ability to be successful and to achieve her goals.

Even though the rate of violent victimization has declined from previous years, violence continues to result in considerable physical, emotional, social, and economic adversities for individuals who have experienced violence at the hands of other people (Truman & Langton, 2014). Living through traumatic violent events can change the way individuals view themselves and the world around them. In the United States in 2013, aggravated assaults accounted for 62.3% of violent crimes, robbery offenses accounted for 29.7%, rape accounted for 6.9%, and murder accounted for 1.2% (U.S. Department of Justice, 2014). Furthermore, violent crime victimization is now one of the leading causes of disability in the world (Hoffman et al., 2014), with estimates indicating that as many as one quarter of disabilities worldwide are the product of violence (World Health Organization [WHO], 2014).

Although many individuals survive violent acts without negative long-term consequences, others do not. An individual's ability to cope with violence is moderated by individual and contextual factors, including social support, cognitive functioning, personality variables, behavioral capacities, preexisting psychological conditions, and the duration and intensity of the traumatic experience (Coursol, Lewis, & Garrity, 2001; Strauser, Lustig, Cogdal & Uruk, 2006). Regardless of individuals' coping abilities, violent acts have caused millions of people across the world to acquire chronic illnesses and injuries that result in long-term disabilities.

Trauma from violence can be physical or psychological, sudden or gradual, and result from a single occurrence or ongoing events. Psychological trauma, a common consequence of violence, results from direct or indirect exposure to an overwhelming event or experience that poses a threat to a person's physical, emotional, or psychological safety (Ramirez, 2014). Individuals with trauma- and stressor-related disorders can experience symptoms such as anxiety, fear, anhedonia (i.e., the inability to experience pleasure), dysphoria (i.e., feelings of unhappiness), externalizing and aggressive symptoms, dissociative symptoms, unpredictable emotions, flashbacks, strained relationships, and physical symptoms such as headaches or nausea (American Psychiatric Association [APA], 2013). Even more subtle forms of interpersonal mistreatment such as microaggressions and workplace incivilities can have a detrimental impact on physical and emotional well-being.

TYPES OF VIOLENCE AND RESULTING DISABILITIES

Military Combat

The need for rehabilitation services for injured combat veterans has never been greater than it is at present. In 2014, Fischer reported estimates from the U.S. Department of Defense (DoD) indicating that 51,986 service members had been wounded in action during Operation Iraqi Freedom (OIF) and Operation Enduring Freedom (OEF). This represents the largest burden of casualties for veterans since the Vietnam War. The trauma of war and the high survival rate of injured military personnel have resulted in a large number of veterans who have a wide range of physical and mental health issues as a result of their exposure to combat and blast injuries (Gean, 2014; Lawhorne & Philpott, 2011; Meyer et al., 2011). The survival rate for injured military personnel is more than 90% due to advances in battlefield medical treatment and protective gear (Hyer, 2006). However, many of these survivors will have lasting disabilities such as polytrauma, traumatic brain injuries (TBI), physical wounds, depression, and posttraumatic stress disorder (PTSD; Capehart & Bass, 2012; Wolf, Strom, Kehle, & Eftekhari, 2012).

With the primary cause of injuries from Iraq being from the use of high-energy explosives with shrapnel, which often causes fragmentation injuries to the head and extremities, polytrauma is an emerging disability acquired by numerous military personnel (DePalma, Cross, Buckley, & Gunnar, 2014; Pugh et al., 2014). Polytrauma is defined by the U.S. Department of Veterans Affairs (VA; 2015b, para. 13) as "two or more injuries to physical regions or organ systems, one of which may be life-threatening, resulting in physical, cognitive, psychological, or psychosocial impairments and functional disability." Common conditions associated with polytrauma include TBI; PTSD; fractures; amputations; chronic pain, including musculoskeletal and headache pain; hearing loss; spinal cord injury; loss of vision; and burns (DePalma et al., 2014; Pugh et al., 2014). Blast-related polytrauma from high-energy explosives leads to an average of five surgeries per survivor (Hyer, 2006).

In 2004, the VHA developed the polytrauma system of care to respond to the multiple and complex injuries sustained by veterans in recent and current conflicts in Afghanistan and Iraq (Eapen, Jaramillo, Tapia, Johnson, & Cifu, 2013).

Treatment for polytrauma may vary significantly based on the severity and number of injuries, time since injury, and the current needs and goals of the veteran. The VHA's polytrauma system of care is composed of four components: polytrauma rehabilitation centers (PRCs), polytrauma network sites (PNSs), polytrauma support clinic teams (PSCTs), and polytrauma point of contact (PPOC; Eapen et al., 2013).

PRCs provide acute, comprehensive, inpatient rehabilitation. Veterans with moderate to severe polytrauma are typically referred for admission to one of five of the VHA's PRCs (Goodrich et al., 2013). These are located in Tampa, Florida; Richmond, Virginia; Minneapolis, Minnesota; San Antonio, Texas; and Palo Alto, and California (Zadov, Eapen, & Cifu, n.d.). Advanced medical technologies and assistive devices are available at these centers to provide the best assessment and treatment for veterans with polytrauma (Goodrich et al., 2013; Zadov, Eapen, & Cifu, n.d.).

Following discharge from a PRC, the next step is often referral to a PNS (Eapen et al., 2013). Currently, there are 23 specialized rehabilitation programs located throughout the United States (Eapen et al., 2013). Depending on the veteran's needs and distance from home, these services may be provided on an inpatient or outpatient basis (VA, 2010). These offer continued medical care and rehabilitation services for veterans who are transitioning closer to home. PNS programs may also be the entry point for rehabilitation services for veterans who have experienced a mild to moderate polytraumatic injury (VA, 2010).

After completing their treatment at a PNS, veterans are then referred for specialized outpatient care at one of 87 PSCTs located in VA medical centers across the country (Eapen et al., 2013). PSCTs provide continued medical and rehabilitation care and support closer to the veteran's home community (Andrews, 2013; McNamee, Howe, Nakase-Richardson, & Peterson, 2012; VA, 2010). Finally, for those Veterans Administration Medical Centers (VAMCs) without specialized rehabilitation teams, PPOC are available at 39 VAMCs (Andrews, 2013; Eapen et al., 2013). These were established in 2007 and have staff members available who are knowledgeable about the VA polytrauma/TBI system of care and can coordinate case management and referrals throughout the system or provide a more limited range of rehabilitation services (Andrews, 2013; McNamee et al., 2012; VA, 2010).

Another common injury acquired by current military personnel is TBI. TBI has now been coined the "signature wound" of these conflicts (Joyner, 2014). It has been estimated that as of 2014, approximately 307,282 veterans had been diagnosed with a service-connected TBI (Fischer, 2014). This figure includes injuries that occurred anywhere U.S. forces were or are located, including the continental United States. TBI results from "severe or moderate force to the head, where physical portions of the brain are damaged and functioning is impaired" (U.S. Department of Veterans Affairs, 2015b, para. 16).

Compared to previous wars, the degree to which service members are being diagnosed with TBI from OEF and OIF is unprecedented (Fulton et al., 2015). For military service members, wartime TBI is often the result of blast injuries (Bagalman, 2011). In a blast injury, the detonation of an explosive device changes the air pressure around the blast site causing a shock wave that crashes into the body (Bass et al., 2012). These detonations can also be accompanied by fragments from the device itself. Service members are now surviving injuries that at one time would have been fatal because of advances in protective equipment, combat medicine, and air evacuation (Gawande, 2004). Additionally, health care professionals are more alert to the possibility of TBI and may therefore be more likely to detect and diagnose TBI (Ling, Bandak, & Rocco Armonda, 2009).

The DoD (2016) categorizes TBI cases as mild, moderate, severe, or penetrating. Mild TBI is characterized by a loss of consciousness lasting less than 30 minutes, memory loss or a disoriented state for less than 24 hours, and normal structural brain imaging results. Moderate TBI is characterized by a loss of consciousness from 30 minutes to 24 hours, memory loss lasting from 24 hours to 7 days, and normal to abnormal structural brain imaging results. Severe TBI is characterized by a loss of consciousness that lasts more than 24 hours, memory loss lasting more than 7 days, and normal to abnormal structural brain imaging results. Finally, penetrating TBI, or an open head injury, is a head injury in which the outer layer of the system of membranes, the dura mater, which envelops the central nervous system, is penetrated. Penetrating injuries can be caused by high-velocity projectiles or objects of lower velocity, such as knives, or bone fragments from a skull fracture that are driven into the brain.

Effects of TBI can include impaired thinking and memory, movement, sensation, and emotional functioning. These effects can be temporary or permanent. Memory loss is the most common cognitive impairment, usually resulting in an inability to remember certain past events and trouble remembering new information and events (Solovieva & Walls, 2014). Depending upon the areas of the brain affected by the TBI, people may exhibit psychological symptoms such as depression, anxiety, emotional lability, irritability, irrational anger, hypersexuality, disinhibition, and poor interpersonal judgment (Fabian et al., 2014). People with TBI also experience speech disorders, sleep disorders, chronic pain, diminished strength and coordination, sexual dysfunction, and bowel and bladder dysfunction.

The current emergency response protocol for TBIs includes immediate care in the field, transport to combat support hospitals with brain imaging equipment, and prompt evaluation by neurosurgeons (Morrison & Casper, 2012). Treatment for TBI depends on the severity of the injury and should be provided in the least restrictive setting possible. For veterans with a mild TBI, recovery occurs in a relatively short period of time (days to weeks). Treatment for a mild TBI includes counseling, education, a period of rest and observation, and pharmacological and nonpharmacological interventions for any persistent symptoms (e.g., headache, sleep issues; Johnson, Hawley, & Theeler, 2014; Petraglia, Maroon, & Bailes, 2012). Meeting with a therapist or counselor who can validate symptoms and educate veterans with mild TBIs about their symptoms and treatment can help to alleviate stress (VA, 2010). Mittenberg and colleagues (1996) found that individuals with a mild TBI who met with a therapist who reviewed expected symptoms with them experienced significantly fewer symptoms, less symptom duration, and lower average symptom severity levels at 6 months follow-up.

For a veteran with a moderate to severe TBI, the initial focus of treatment is to stabilize the individual in order to minimize secondary complications (DePalma et al., 2014; Johnson et al., 2014; VA, 2010). Inpatient rehabilitation at an established interdisciplinary brain injury program is the best alternative for comprehensive evaluation and medical stabilization (McNamee et al., 2012). As a veteran enters a care facility, initial medical treatment goals include stabilizing vitals (e.g., oxygen, blood pressure, blood flow to the brain) and treating any problems or conditions affecting other parts of the body that have arisen because of the injury (McNamee et al., 2012). Interdisciplinary brain injury programs are staffed with TBI-trained specialists and physiatrists (i.e., physicians specially trained in physical medicine and rehabilitation; VA, 2010). An interdisciplinary team approach that includes the patient, family members, physicians, nurses, therapists, social workers, rehabilitation counselors, and psychologists has been demonstrated to result in the best patient outcomes (DePalma et al., 2014; Johnson et al., 2014; VA, 2010).

During the initial several months (acute phase) of recovery from a moderate to severe TBI, rehabilitation professionals frequently use the Rancho Los Amigos Level of Cognitive Function Scale to characterize the veteran's level of functioning and track the course of recovery. Ratings range from Level I (no response/comatose) to a Level VIII (while possibly not at preinjury levels, behavior is purposeful and appropriate; VA, 2010). During this stage of treatment, the person with a TBI requires frequent physician checkups to monitor new or ongoing complications of the brain injury. After veterans with a TBI have been stabilized, the treatment plan generally involves rehabilitation efforts to teach patients how to cope with symptoms and to restore function (DePalma et al., 2014; Johnson et al., 2014; VA, 2010).

For veterans who do not require inpatient rehabilitation, or for those who have progressed to needing less intensive medical services, transitioning to services in their home community is the next step. Community-based services include outpatient therapy, transitional rehabilitation, and VR. As a general rule, patients with a TBI gradually improve and stabilize over time (VA, 2010). While in the healing stages, it is helpful for veterans with a TBI to get plenty of rest and sleep; increase activity slowly; carry and use a notebook, calendar, or smartphone to write down important things; establish a regular daily routine to structure activities; focus on one task at a time to avoid distractions (e.g., turn off the television or radio while working); and designate someone with whom to discuss important decisions (Cozza, Holmes, & Van Ost, 2013; Drescher & Foy, 2012; VA, 2010).

In addition to polytrauma and TBI, another common disability acquired by service members is PTSD. PTSD can occur along with these other disorders or in the absence of polytrauma and TBI. In a given year, approximately 11% to 20% of veterans who served in OIF or OEF have PTSD (U.S. Department of Veterans Affairs, 2015a). Events such as ongoing exposure to horrible and life-threatening situations, being shot at, seeing a fellow soldier get shot at, and witnessing death can predispose military personnel to PTSD. Although PTSD was previously considered an anxiety disorder, the *Diagnostic and Statistical Manual of Mental Disorders*, Fifth Edition (*DSM-5*; APA, 2013) made multiple changes to the diagnoses of PTSD. Disorders such as PTSD that are precipitated by specific stressful and potentially traumatic events are now included in a new diagnostic category, "Trauma and Stress-Related Disorders." Symptoms associated with PTSD, as outlined in the *DSM-5*, include intrusive, distressing memories of the traumatic event; nightmares; flashbacks; marked psychological distress and physiological reactions to internal or external cues that resemble aspects of the event; attempts to avoid distressing memories or external reminders (e.g., people, places, conversations) of the event; exaggerated negative beliefs about self and others (e.g., "the world is a very dangerous place"; "no one can be trusted," "I am permanently damaged"); persistent feelings of horror, anger, guilt, or shame; disinterest in or disengagement from participation in valued activities; feelings of detachment from others; negative alterations in cognitions and mood; loss of pleasure; irritability and angry outbursts; self-destructive behaviors; hypervigilance; exaggerated startle responses; concentration problems; and sleep disturbances. Some individuals may also have dissociative symptoms, and others may have delayed responses.

Treatment for PTSD is offered for military personnel by all VA medical centers and some have specific PTSD programs. Evidence-based treatments for PTSD include cognitive processing therapy (CPT), prolonged exposure therapy (PE), eye movement desensitization and processing therapy (EMDR), and selective serotonin reuptake inhibitors (SSRIs; National Center for PTSD, 2013). CPT is a cognitive behavioral intervention that consists of four components: (a) psychoeducation about PTSD symptomology and benefits of treatment; (b) increasing awareness of one's thoughts and feelings; (c) cognitive restructuring to challenge thoughts and feelings; and (d) understanding typical changes in thoughts and feelings that occur from trauma. PE, like CPT, includes psychoeducation about PTSD and treatment, and couples it with education about breathing techniques to manage distressful thoughts and feelings. Breathing techniques are then practiced with in vivo exposure to reduce distress in safe situations that the individual is avoiding. Imaginal exposure is also used to talk through the traumatic experience in order to better manage accompanying distressful thoughts and feelings. EMDR involves focusing on hand movements while talking about traumatic experiences and is based on the notion that rapid eye movements make it easier for the brain to process traumatic memories. In this practice, the therapist instructs the individual to focus on mental images while doing eye movements (i.e., following therapist's hands that move back and forth). Then, when traumatic memories and images are resolved, the individual is taught to replace those with positive ones.

Another potential disability-related consequence of the current military experience is military sexual trauma (MST). The U.S. Department of Veterans Affairs (n.d., para. 1) defines MST as "sexual assault or repeated threatening sexual harassment that occurred while the veteran was in the military." MST includes physical force, sexual activity during which the individual is unable to consent (e.g., when intoxicated), and pressure to engage in sexual activity by threatening negative consequences or implying that it will result in positive benefits such as faster promotions. It also includes unwanted sexual touching or grabbing, threatening or offensive sexual remarks, and unwelcome sexual advances.

Unfortunately, even with the implementation of the DoD's Sexual Assault Prevention and Response (SAPR) program in 2005, the rate of service-connected sexual abuse continues to increase (Farrell et al., 2013; Ogilvie & Tamlyn, 2012). According to the 2012 Workplace and Gender Relations Survey of Active Duty Members, 6.1% of active duty women and 1.2% of active duty men indicated they experienced some kind of unwanted sexual contact (USC) in the previous year. This was a 4.4% increase for women and an unchanged rate for males from the USC rate in 2010.

MST has been associated with problems with readjustment following military service (Cater & Leach, 2011; Kimerling et al., 2010). It has been linked to depression, anxiety, relationship issues, and substance abuse (Cater & Leach, 2011; Himmelfarb, Yaeger, & Mintz, 2006; Kimerling et al., 2010). MST is heavily confounded by military culture, making the decision to report sexual trauma extremely difficult. In fact, very few military personnel actually report MST because reporting the abuse can increase the chances of further abuse and even end the victim's military career (Corbett, 2007; U.S. Commission on Civil Rights, 2013). Perpetrators are typically other military personnel, and abuse often occurs in a setting where the person who is assaulted must continue living and working with the assailant on a daily basis, which increases the risk for distress and for subsequent victimization (Cater & Leach, 2011). MST is associated with numerous negative physical and mental health consequences including increased risk for suicide, PTSD, major depressive disorder, alcohol and drug abuse, dissociative disorders, eating disorders, personality disorders, sexual dysfunction, employment difficulties, and physical illness (Cater & Koch, 2010).

Although MST is more common in women, men can also experience MST during their service but may be even less likely to report it due to gender role stereotypes. It is now common practice that all veterans seen at VHA facilities, regardless of gender, are asked about experiences of sexual trauma (VA, n.d.). It has been recognized that this type of trauma can affect a person's physical and mental health even many years later (Surís & Lind, 2008; Valdez et al., 2011). Treatment for MST often involves addressing any immediate health and safety concerns, followed by counseling to help cope with the effects of trauma (VA, n.d.). Veterans do not need to have a service-connected disability rating or to have reported the incident when it occurred in order to receive MST counseling services through the VA (VA, n.d.). Many VA health care facilities have specialized outpatient mental health services focusing on sexual trauma. Another option for those who need more services than can be provided in an outpatient setting is a residential or inpatient treatment setting.

Domestic Violence

The U.S. Office on Violence Against Women (OVW; 2014, para. 4) defines domestic violence as "a pattern of abusive behavior in any relationship that is used by one partner to gain or maintain power and control over another intimate partner." Domestic violence can occur in any type of relationship, even platonic care-giving relationships. It also takes on many different forms including physical abuse, sexual abuse, emotional abuse, social isolation, threats against loved ones, economic deprivation, and intimidation (Warshaw, Sullivan, & Rivera, 2013). One characteristic that is constant across incidences of domestic violence is the inequality of power in a relationship. In the United States, a woman is assaulted every 9 seconds, and at least three women are killed every day by their partners (OVW, 2014). The World Health Organization (WHO, 2014) estimated that between 10% and 50% of women worldwide report having been assaulted physically or sexually by an intimate partner at some time in their lives. Many recover relatively quickly from domestic violence, especially if the abuse is shorter in duration, less severe, and they have a strong support system and access to resources (Warshaw, Sullivan, & Rivera, 2013). Others, especially those who experience more frequent and severe abuse, can develop symptoms such as reliving the traumatic event(s), hyperarousal, avoiding reminders of the trauma, depression, anxiety, PTSD, and sleep disturbances (Crofford, 2007; Green, McLaughlin, & Kessler, 2010; Saxe, Ellis, & Kaplow, 2009; Warshaw et al., 2013). Domestic violence can also cause injuries (e.g., head trauma, orthopedic impairments) that can result in permanent physical disabilities.

The earlier, more severe, and more chronic the abuse, the more likely it will be for the individual to show a range of symptoms into adulthood. Adults with a history of child abuse may experience depression, anxiety, substance abuse, eating disorders, suicidal ideation, and PTSD (Briere & Scott, 2006). The lasting effects of abuse not only continue into adulthood, but have been shown to persist for generations. Even without experiencing direct abuse, children of trauma survivors can show effects of their parent's trauma (Hesse, Main, Abrams, & Rifkin, 2003). This is believed to be the result of higher levels of dissociative behavior in interactions between parents with unresolved trauma and their children.

Research has also demonstrated that women who were abused as children are more likely to be involved in a violent relationship as adults (Briere & Scott, 2006). Victims of early abuse may come to expect it as a normal way of life and put themselves in abusive relationships as an adult, not because they want to be further abused but because they may be seeking a different outcome. The theory of complex trauma also posits that severe, chronic childhood abuse is associated with an increased vulnerability to future victimization and a more complex symptom presentation (Briere et al., 2008; van der Kolk, 2003). Complex trauma is described as a type of trauma that occurs repeatedly and cumulatively, originating in the formative years of childhood. Complex trauma is often associated with a more complicated symptom presentation than is seen in noninterpersonal or one-time traumas, such as a natural disaster or car accident (van der Kolk et al., 2005). Many adult survivors of physical, sexual, or severe emotional abuse show symptoms of PTSD. Generally, domestic violence occurs over an extended time period. Coping with the effects of domestic violence can be overwhelming due to the victim's lack of control over the situation. This abuse can have a serious impact on an individual's ability to cope in the short term and long term. The chronic nature of domestic violence can cause not only immediate physical injury, but also lasting mental health issues as a person attempts to process the trauma.

Commonly reported symptoms associated with PTSD resulting from domestic violence include flashbacks, nightmares, severe anxiety, and uncontrollable thoughts about the trauma. The severity of the violence, duration of exposure, age of onset and perceived degree of threat exacerbate symptoms. In addition to physical injuries that result in permanent disability and trauma-related psychiatric disabilities, ongoing exposure to abuse may act as an environmental trigger to developing stress-related chronic illnesses (Crofford, 2007). Additionally, physical injury acquired from domestic violence may act as a pain generator that leads to altered pain processing and development of conditions such as fibromyalgia, chronic fatigue syndrome, and irritable bowel syndrome.

The most urgent need in treatment of PTSD is to ensure the physical and emotional safety of the individual who has experienced domestic violence. Often, women find themselves going to a shelter for safety and access to resources. There are approximately 2,000 community-based domestic violence programs across the United States, and 1,200 of these programs have shelter facilities providing emergency housing to victims (National Coalition Against Domestic Violence, 2015). Shelter programs offer multiple services including counseling, social service referrals, transitional housing, legal resources, and resources for children. Unfortunately, many shelters are not accessible to women with disabilities, and an urgent need exists for advocacy to make the necessary modifications so that these shelters are accessible.

Treatment and support are critical for survivors of domestic violence. Trauma-informed treatment approaches address safety as a priority; treat symptoms as potential coping strategies rather than maladaptive behaviors; and underscore the importance of respectful, collaborative working alliances to support individuals in their healing and recovery (Warshaw, Sullivan, & Rivera, 2013). Treatment approaches may also include cognitive behavioral therapy (CBT) to help individuals change the thought patterns and behaviors that keep them from overcoming their anxiety and fears. Exposure therapy, as previously discussed, allows an individual to work with a therapist while confronting the memories and situations that can trigger psychiatric conditions such as PTSD, anxiety, and depression. Family therapy may also help family members cope with the impact of domestic violence on family functioning. Along with nonpharmacological interventions, medications such as SSRIs can be used to treat the symptoms of PTSD, anxiety, and depression. Antianxiety medication and sedatives for sleep problems may be utilized as well.

Warshaw et al. (2013) cautioned that trauma-based therapies were originally designed to address single events (e.g., nonpartner sexual assault) or events that took place in the past and were unlikely to recur. CBT approaches may not be desired or effective for all individuals who have experienced or continue to experience domestic violence. Nor do these approaches address all the domains affected by long-standing trauma such as the multitude of pressing concerns these women have (e.g., protecting their children, dealing with the legal system, becoming financially stable). In addition, frequently used techniques in trauma-based therapy such as reliving the abuse through some form of exposure therapy could actually escalate, rather than decrease, some women's distress. Exposure therapy is most likely to result in re-traumatization when individuals are still experiencing traumatic events. In their review of treatment approaches, Warshaw et al. (2013) concluded that effective approaches to treating trauma include (a) brief interventions that provide psychoeducation about intimate partner violence and its potentially traumatic effects on the individual; (b) ongoing attention to and prioritization of safety needs; (c) cognitive re-framing and skill enhancement to address trauma-related symptoms, life goals, and other issues; (d) cultural competencies to identify not only individual survivor strengths but also cultural strengths to draw upon in facilitating recovery; (e) social connection; and (f) individualization of techniques and interventions to survivors' needs. Likewise, the focus of interventions should be on women's empowerment, raising self-esteem, improving problem-solving skills for independent living, developing skills to set and reach goals, teaching women to manage PTSD symptoms and triggers, and treating co-occurring substance use disorders. Relatedly, in a meta-analysis of 152 clinical trials, Erford et al. (2016) found that trauma-focused (i.e., narrative therapy, in vivo exposure, PET, and EMDR) and nontrauma-focused (i.e., supportive therapy, interpersonal psychotherapy, meditation, and dialectical behavior therapy) counseling approaches were equally effective in treating PTSD. This research underscores the importance of tailoring therapeutic approaches to the individualized characteristics and needs of each client.

School Bullying

Bullying is defined as acts of aggression that are repeated over time and involve a power imbalance between perpetrators and their targets who are perceived as weak (Copeland, Wolke, Angold, & Costello, 2013; Dooley, Pyżalski, & Cross, 2009; Kowalski & Limber 2013; Salmivalli & Peets, 2009). Bullying is not limited to physical assaults. It also includes threats, rumor spreading, teasing, and exclusion (Copeland et al., 2013; Kumpulainen, 2008). In 2008, Sansone and Sansone reported that approximately 10% of school-aged children in the United States experience frequent bullying. School bullying is highest among sixth through eighth graders with males being more likely to be both perpetrators and victims (Nansel et al., 2001). Victims of bullying can develop a variety of symptoms, some even lasting into adulthood, including depression, suicidal ideation, eating disorders, and substance use disorders (Klomek, Marrocco, Kleinman, Schonfeld, & Gould, 2007; Sansone & Sansone, 2008).

In the past, most bullying occurred at school or in face-to-face encounters. This form of bullying has now been labeled as "traditional" or "schoolyard" bullying. With the advances in technology, a new form of bullying, coined "cyberbullying" has become disturbingly common among children and even adults (Hinduja & Patchin, 2014; Patchin & Hinduja, 2006). The National Crime Prevention Council (NCPC, 2015, para. 2) defines cyberbullying as "the process of using the Internet, cell phones or other devices to send or post text or images intended to hurt or embarrass another person." With social media outlets ever increasing, modes used for cyberbullying include text messages, e-mails, phone calls, photo or video clips, instant messages, websites, and chat rooms. According to a study conducted by researchers at the University of British Columbia (2012), cyberbullying is more common than traditional bullying, with about 25% to 30% of the young people surveyed admitting experiencing or taking part in cyberbullying.

Several distinctions make cyberbullying unique from traditional bullying (Reed, Cooper, Nugent, & Russell, 2016). One noted difference between traditional bullying and cyberbullying is that cyberbullying is often done impulsively. Also, because of the anonymity of cyberbullying, individuals may lose empathy for the person they are bullying, and their anonymity leads to increased aggression in comparison to traditional bullying. Because they are not face to face with their victim, bullies do not physically see the damage they are causing. This leads people to say or do things online that they would not do in person. The anonymity of cyberbullying may also lead individuals to believe that they cannot be caught or experience negative consequences for their actions. Finally, for individuals who are bullied, there is no safe haven (such as their homes) or escape from the bullying because instances of bullying can be continuously viewed on social media outlets and quickly distributed to large numbers of individuals to witness. For this reason, students who have been cyberbullied are at an even greater risk of depression and suicidality than those who have experienced traditional bullying.

A strong link has been established between bullying and a variety of negative psychosocial outcomes such as decreased academic achievement, increased isolation, feelings of alienation, impairment in abilities to interact with peers, questioning of one's self-worth, lowered self-esteem, anxiety, high rates of school absenteeism, and physical symptoms of illness (Kshirsagar, Agarwal, & Bavdekar, 2007; Swearer, Song, Cary, Eagle, & Mickelson, 2001; Wolke, Woods, Bloomfield, & Karstadt, 2001). Of the utmost concern is the link between being bullied and both depression and suicidality (Carlyle & Steinman, 2007; Kaltiala-Heino, Rimpelä, Marttunen, Rimpelä, & Rantanen, 1999; Klomek et al., 2007; Reed et al., 2016). Furthermore, both victims and bullies are more likely to experience depression than youth who are not involved in bullying (Reed et al., 2016). This connection can have long-lasting effects even into adulthood, and the worst adult outcomes are experienced by bully victims. Moreover, in addition to disabling conditions that are directly caused by bullying, strong evidence suggests that people with disabilities are considerably more likely than nondisabled people to be the victims of cyberbullying and traditional bullying in school and in the workplace (Strauser, 2013).

Schools are increasingly beginning to adopt approaches to address bullying that encompass everyone from students to parents, teachers, and administrators. Strategies used emphasize parental involvement, teaching students about the consequences of bullying, peer-led interventions to reduce bullying, and teaching coping skills to those who have been the victims of bullying (Reed et al., 2016). In considering antibullying interventions, Paterson (2011) recommended the development of system-wide policies with descriptions of acceptable and unacceptable behaviors. These policies should include clear consequences for unacceptable behaviors and should be distributed to and discussed with all students and parents. Having students sign antibullying pledges can also be helpful. Paterson further recommended that parents take responsibility for children's appropriate use of electronic media by establishing and discussing with their children rules for appropriate and inappropriate use and content along with consequences for violating agreed upon rules. Finally, bystanders should be educated about both how they contribute to the problem when they fail to intervene and how to recognize when they should step forward.

Although the most successful bullying prevention approaches involve the entire school, sometimes children who have been victimized and develop signs of depression and/or suicidality need individual attention with a mental health professional (e.g., school-based mental health counselor) to develop strategies to cope with the effects of bullying. In these cases, a combination of medication and mental health counseling may be necessary. One of the most common therapies in addressing the emotional distress caused by bullying is CBT (Cohen & Mannarino, 2008; Kuipers et al., 2006). CBT teaches individuals to better understand their thoughts and feelings in relation to the situation. Furthermore, it teaches individuals how their thoughts and feelings influence their actions and ultimately their behavior and equips them with coping skills.

Interventions should also be targeted at bullies. Paterson (2011) pointed out that bullies have often been bullied themselves, and traditional punitive approaches do nothing more than drive the bullying underground and make it harsher. CBT interventions for bullies focus on correcting errors in their thinking and hostile distribution bias in which bullies think others are acting against them instead of the reverse. Some schools have developed support groups that include the target, the target's supporters, and the bully or bullies. Because bullies often do not understand the impact of their bullying, this type of intervention provides an opportunity for them to learn about the damage it causes, become repentant, make amends, and help to rectify the problem. Then together, with the support of administration, the bully, the target, and supporters can identify strategies to prevent bullying. In this respect, they all become empowered to take the lead in solving the problem on a broader (e.g., school-wide) scale. Despite the availability of these various interventions, Reed et al. (2016) noted the need for more research to determine their effectiveness.

Workplace Microaggressions and Incivilities

Workplace violence is another topic that has received increasing attention in the media in recent years. Although the media perpetuates misunderstandings about workplace violence by focusing exclusively on the disgruntled employee who commits mass workplace shootings (Denenberg & Denenberg, 2011; Dillon, 2012), the majority of workplace violence is nonlethal and more insidious. Although shootings in the workplace are undoubtedly traumatic, this type of violence is much rarer than more low-level types of workplace aggression (e.g., microaggressions, workplace incivility, bullying, harassment, intimidation, sexual harassment) that can undermine workers' productivity, job satisfaction, mental health, and physical well-being (Dillon, 2012). Workplace mistreatment is so prominent that Dillon (2012) cited harassment as the reason for one third of employees leaving their jobs.

Microaggression, one of the more unnoticed but prevalent forms of workplace mistreatment, includes subtle, stereotypical, and insensitive behavior or comments about a person's identity, background, ethnicity, or disability (Thomas & Schwarzbaum, 2010). In microaggression, the perpetrator may unconsciously say or do something that creates a hostile environment for another individual. Many times this is only realized in retrospect by the victim. Whereas a single microaggression may be brushed off as harmless, the cumulative effect of multiple incidents over a person's life can contribute to physical illness and affect a person's self-confidence. Sue (2010, p. 66) compared microaggressions to carbon monoxide, "invisible, but potentially lethal," with continuous exposure being like "a sort of death by a thousand cuts to the victim." Microaggressions include subtle insults about the worker's race, ethnicity, age, gender, sexual orientation, religion, sexual identity, and/or disability as well as invalidation of the employee's expertise and contributions. Microaggressions can also occur as unconscious verbal, nonverbal, and environmental communications that subtly convey rudeness and insensitivity that demean a person's heritage or identity. Additionally, microaggressions can include conscious and intentional discriminatory actions based on an employee's identity. Finally, microaggressions include communications that subtly exclude, negate, or nullify the thoughts, feelings, or experiential reality of a person's identity.

Workplace incivility, like microaggressions, is another subtle form of interpersonal mistreatment that has become quite prevalent in the modern workplace (Cortina, Magley, Williams, & Langhout, 2001). Cortina et al. (2001, p. 64) described workplace incivilities as "milder forms of psychological mistreatment in which intentionality is less apparent." Workplace incivility is more ambiguous than other, more overt workplace aggressions (e.g., bullying), but the intent is still to harm the target. It also differs from other forms of workplace aggression in that intentionality is less apparent and may result from ignorance. Workplace incivility typically involves rude, discourteous behaviors that violate social norms regarding mutual respect and civility. Examples of workplace incivility include "disrespectful, condescending behaviors from superiors or coworkers, devaluation of an employee's work, insulting remarks, social exclusion, ignoring or excluding the target from professional camaraderie, showing little interest in the targeted employee's opinions, and doubting the employee's judgment on matters over which the employee has authoritative expertise" (Cortina et al., 2001, p. 70). These incivilities can be perpetrated by employees at all organizational levels as well as by customers or contractors. Those with greater social power are more likely to be the instigators whereas those with lower social power are typically the targets. If allowed to escalate over time, workplace incivilities can result in major organizational conflict.

These types of subtle aggressions can have a negative impact on the physical and mental health of the target. Targets can develop chronic illnesses and other health problems such as insomnia, high blood pressure, gastrointestinal symptoms, weight loss, depression, increased use of alcohol, and suicide (Dillon, 2012). Cortina et al. (2001) cited evidence of workplace incivilities as being linked to poorer psychological well-being and higher levels of anxiety and depression in workers who are targets. Workplace incivilities can also have negative effects on job satisfaction and result in job withdrawal.

Coworkers who witness incidents of workplace incivilities can also experience negative health consequences as a result of observing these events. Furthermore, Cortina et al. (2001) noted that the accumulated effect of dealing with daily incivilities can be more detrimental to one's physical and emotional functioning than the occurrence of a single traumatic event for which control and coping strategies are more readily apparent. In fact, these authors indicated that "ordinary daily hassles considerably 'outstrip' major life stressors in predicting damaged morale, impaired social and work functioning, and psychosomatic symptoms" (Cortina et al., 2001, p. 75).

The most appropriate response to individuals who have experienced workplace microaggressions and incivilities is for employers to develop, implement, and enforce policies that cease these behaviors and prevent further incidents from occurring. Individuals who have experienced these types of subtle transgressions should also (a) be informed that harassment, in the form of microaggressions or incivilities on the basis of disability or membership in other protected classes, is illegal, and (b) receive education about courses of action to take to protect their rights. In addition to addressing these transgressions at an organizational level, some individuals may benefit from counseling if they are experiencing subsequent stress, anxiety, depression, and/or impaired work performance as a result of these transgressions. In these cases, referrals to employee assistance programs or community mental health providers may be warranted.

PSYCHOSOCIAL IMPLICATIONS

The psychosocial implications of acquiring disabilities from violent acts are vast. In addition to coping with the psychological trauma of surviving these events, individuals must often adapt to co-occurring physical disabilities and chronic illnesses (e.g., TBI, spinal cord injury, amputations, chronic pain). Ramirez (2014, p. 25) explained the psychological and physiological effects of trauma-related psychiatric conditions as follows:

> Trauma survivors experience psychological and physiological repercussions following a traumatic event. When the human body successfully responds to a stressful event, the brain and body work together to respond to the threat (e.g., heart rate increases, muscles tense, senses go on high alert). Once the stressor or threat is no longer present, the body is able to "rest and digest" or come back to equilibrium. For individuals who have experienced one or more extremely negative—or traumatic—events, their brains and bodies become overwhelmed and their nervous systems are unable to return to equilibrium after the threat has passed. Instead, they continue to live day to day in this stress response mode, unable to relax or achieve a sense of safety. Left untreated, trauma survivors are perpetually scanning their environments for a threat or interpreting various events and interactions as potentially unsafe.

Other people often do not understand why the individual who has experienced violence is behaving in these ways, and their lack of understanding in combination with the individual's expression of unusual symptoms can take a tremendous toll on relationships. To cope with their continuous heightened sense of stress, these individuals may engage in substance use, self-harm, bullying, withdrawal from certain activities, self-nurturing with food, and eating disorders. Intrusive trauma memories in daily life can cause problems with information processing and memory.

For military service members, readjustment to civilian life is often complicated by disabilities acquired while in the service. In many cases, these individuals must adapt to severely disabling conditions and, often, chronic pain. Additionally, the functional limitations associated with polytrauma and TBI often require them to make significant adjustments to performing activities of daily living. Symptoms associated with PTSD from war can have a substantially negative impact on functioning in multiple domains as well. PTSD symptoms can result in unpredictable behaviors, reduced stress tolerance, impaired ability to interact with others, difficulties adjusting to change, memory and concentration impairments, irritability, becoming easily angered, and substance use disorders (Cater & Leach, 2011; Strauser & Lustig, 2001). These veterans experience high rates of homelessness, unemployment, and poverty. They may behave differently than they did prior to their deployment, and their changed behaviors can cause secondary traumatization of the veterans' partners and spouses. Behaviors that can impair family functioning include isolating themselves or limiting their interactions with family, unpredictable moods, verbal and physical aggression, excessive drinking, or substance use.

MST also has a negative impact on readjustment to civilian life and is associated with an increased risk of physical illness, self-harm, relationship issues, and substance abuse (Cater & Leach, 2011). Additional psychosocial issues include anxiety and depression; PTSD; poor self-esteem; negative beliefs about self and others; difficulties regulating emotions; hyperarousal; and feelings of self-blame, guilt, loss, and social isolation. Cater and Leach also noted that MST can have a negative impact on physical functioning and contribute to the onset of illnesses such as chronic fatigue syndrome, chronic pain, gastrointestinal problems, hypertension, and gynecological conditions. The military culture can further undermine the psychosocial adaptation and reintegration into civilian life for injured veterans (Griffin & Stein, 2015). The military culture downplays, ignores, and/or perceives disability as a sign of weakness. This negative view of disability results in low acknowledgment of service-related disabilities among those who have acquired disabilities in war and delays in seeking disability benefits and rehabilitation services.

Individuals who endure ongoing abuse and violence, as is often the case in domestic violence, often experience reactions such as shock, disbelief, terror, and isolation that undermine their sense of self (Warshaw et al., 2013). They may be wary of others, lack trust, and experience paranoia—all of which are manifestations of the abuse they endured (or continue to endure). These reactions can make it difficult for them to establish relationships with others and to pursue activities (e.g., education, employment) that can enhance their self-esteem. Individuals who remain in abusive relationships may also encounter negative reactions (e.g., lack of empathy, impatience, withdrawal of support) from others who do not understand why they do not leave the perpetrator. Others may not understand that choosing to stay in a relationship is based on an analysis of safety and risks and is influenced by cultural and religious beliefs as well as the hope that the abuser will change. Individuals who experience domestic violence may not have the financial resources to leave relationships, they may have nowhere to go, and/or they may fear retaliation from the perpetrator if they leave. If they do leave the relationship, they may live in constant fear of being re-victimized, and if they have children, they may be constantly fearful for their safety as well. Children and youths who experience domestic violence and/or bullying can also experience significant psychosocial challenges that endure into adulthood. These include depression, suicidal ideation, eating disorders, and substance use disorders (Klomek et al., 2007; Sansone & Sansone, 2008).

Individuals who experience workplace microagressions and incivilities may also experience negative psychosocial outcomes, especially if these transgressions occur with high frequency, extend over a long period of time, and vary in form (Cortina & Magley, 2009). These outcomes can undermine personal well-being, increase stress, and impair the individual's emotional and cognitive capacities to manage the situation. As we have previously discussed, exposure to ongoing stress, even in subtle forms, can have serious psychological and physical consequences. Because most individuals do not make formal complaints when they experience recurring workplace incivilities, they are also likely to respond to this mistreatment by leaving their positions; unemployment can then further exacerbate their stress.

VOCATIONAL IMPLICATIONS

The functional limitations associated with disabilities acquired through violence can substantially impair survivors' ability to achieve and maintain competitive employment. For example, polytrauma can result in multiple functional limitations that affect the ability to perform a variety of job tasks. PTSD can negatively impact memory and concentration, and these deficits can make it difficult to complete job tasks requiring sustained attention and focus (Cater & Leach, 2011). Irritability, suspiciousness, and becoming easily angered in relationships with coworkers can also result in employment difficulties. Women and transgender individuals who have acquired disabilities from violent acts committed by men may have difficulties working for male supervisors. Additionally, violence-related physical disabilities can result in numerous functional limitations in performing the essential functions of jobs. Likewise, for individuals who have endured prolonged psychological abuse that undermines their self-esteem, career self-efficacy may also be diminished.

According to Griffen and Stein (2015), labor force participation is the quickest means for veterans with disabilities to secure both financial stability and participate in their communities. However, Ben-Shalom, Tennant, and Stapleton (2016) examined 2002–2013 data from the Current Population Survey and discovered that veteran self-reports of receiving disability benefits increased substantially over this time period, with the most notable growth occurring among younger veterans (ages 18–29) and older veterans (ages 50–64). These researchers also observed that self-reported cognitive disabilities substantially increased among younger veterans, likely owing to the dramatic increase in the incidence of TBI among veterans of the Iraq and Afghanistan theaters. Among other veterans, low disability self-identification hampers access to training and rehabilitation programs, job development and placement assistance, and workplace accommodations (Griffen & Stein, 2015). Younger veterans may also have limited work experience prior to their military service and are often in need of assistance in transferring the skills they learned in the military into the civilian labor market.

In addition to the previously mentioned employment barriers, employers may be reluctant to hire individuals with psychiatric disabilities associated with surviving violent acts. Because many of these individuals also frequently have co-occurring physical disabilities and/or chronic illnesses, employers may question their ability to work, have concerns about attendance, worry that hiring these individuals will increase health insurance premiums, and have concerns that workplace accommodations will be expensive and time-consuming.

Transgender individuals with disabilities acquired through violence confront additional barriers to securing and maintaining employment. They face discrimination because of both their gender identity and gender expression (Movement Advancement Project, National Center for Transgender Equality, Transgender Law Center, 2015). Additionally, they may face discrimination because of their sexual orientation or perceived sexual orientation. Transgender individuals of color face the highest rates of employment discrimination. In a study completed by the National Coalition of Anti-Violence Programs (2015), 26% of transgender respondents indicated that they had lost a job due to being transgender or gender nonconfirming, and they were four times as likely as the general population to live in poverty. In another study, between 13% and 47% of the participants reported being unfairly denied a job, and 78% reported being mistreated, harassed, or discriminated against at work. Specific forms of discrimination in employment that are faced by transgender employees include:

> unfairly firing or refusing to hire someone because they are transgender; prohibiting a transgender employee from dressing or appearing in accordance with their gender identity; limiting a transgender employee's interactions with customers; denying access to restrooms consistent with the employee's gender identity; using the wrong name or pronouns; outing a transgender employee to others or asking inappropriate questions; requiring a transgender employee to have updated identification documents or certain medical procedures in order to work or be hired as their

self-identified gender. Employers also frequently only offer discriminatory health plans that exclude coverage for transition-related care. (Movement Advancement Project, National Center for Transgender Equality,
Transgender Law Center, 2015, p. 2)

Unfortunately, only 18 states have laws that prohibit employment discrimination
based on gender identity or expression.

DEMOGRAPHIC CHARACTERISTICS OF PEOPLE AT RISK OF EXPERIENCING DISABILITIES RELATED TO VIOLENCE

Vulnerability to different types of violent victimization is higher in select populations. Research has consistently reported that women and children, individuals
with disabilities, people of color, those living in poverty, and elderly individuals
are at a much greater risk of violent crime victimization and overall physical, sexual, and emotional abuse (Hines, Malley-Morrison, & Dutton, 2013; Jones et al.,
2012; Plummer & Findley, 2012; Stalker & McArthur, 2012).

Evidence suggests that younger, unemployed women with a higher number
of children and low levels of social support are more at risk of experiencing PTSD
symptoms (Hughes & Jones, 2000). Other factors such as having a traditional sex
role orientation, poor health, and witnessing the destruction of personal property
also increase PTSD symptoms. In addition, female service members experience
MST at a rate that is 14 times higher than it is for male service members (Cater
& Leach, 2011). Women in correctional facilities are more likely than men in correctional facilities and women in the general population to have trauma histories
(e.g., sexual victimization, intimate partner violence, other maltreatment) with
some studies documenting rates as high as 90% (Ramirez, 2014). Women with trauma-related issues pose disciplinary challenges (e.g., not following rules, confron-
tations with staff and other inmates, displaying violent behaviors) and responses
from staff such as restraint and solitary confinement can result in re-traumatization. Untreated trauma may require ongoing attention from medical and mental
health staff that is often not adequately provided in correctional facilities, thus
making transitions back to their communities more difficult. Problems associated
with transition are further compounded when women have to return to environments where perpetrators are present.

The U.S. Department of Health and Human Services Administration for
Children and Families (2013) reported that the rate of child abuse declined
from 9.3 per 1,000 children in 2009 to 9.1 per 1,000 children in 2013. The majority (79.5%) of abused children were neglected, 18% were physically abused,
9% were sexually abused, and 8.7% were psychologically abused. Abuse and
neglect in childhood have been linked to increased risks for anxiety, affective,
regulatory, and attachment disorders that may continue and manifest into
more severe disorders in adulthood (Dube et al., 2009). For children, experiencing polyvictimization, or multiple forms of victimization, appears to be
of particular concern. Risk factors for polyvictimization include residing in
a dangerous community, living in a chaotic or dangerous family environment
or with a violent family member, and having a disability that compromises
the ability to protect oneself (Finkelhor et al., 2009). Studies have also shown

that exposure to community and family violence in childhood is associated with the risk of re-victimization (Margolin & Vickerman, 2007; Tolan, Gorman-Smith, & Henry, 2006). Children are more vulnerable to the long-term negative effects of trauma because it becomes the "organizing experience" of the child's life (Millar, 2013, p. 254). Additionally, it has been reported that individuals with developmental disabilities are four to 10 times more likely to become victims of crime than individuals without a disability (Tyiska, n.d.). Research conducted by the National Center on Child Abuse and Neglect (NCCAN) found that children with any kind of disability were more than twice as likely as children without a disability to be physically or sexually abused (Crosse, Kaye, & Ratnofsky, 1993).

Although individuals with disabilities cannot be viewed as a monolithic group, this population in general may have characteristics that lead to increased victimization from domestic abuse such as dependency on others for caregiving, limited mobility or communication, and possible social isolation (Blake, Banks, Patience, & Lund, 2014; Hines et al., 2013; Jones et al., 2012; Plummer & Findley, 2012; Stalker & McArthur, 2012). Unfortunately, many advocates report that crimes against people with disabilities often go unreported (Frohmader & Didi, 2015; Office for Victims of Crime, n.d). Many reasons could explain this underreporting: mobility or communication barriers, feelings of shame and self-blame, ignorance of the justice system, and the fact that the perpetrator is often a family member or primary caregiver. The high incidence of abuse by caregivers has prompted some researchers to promote the expansion of the definition of domestic violence to include paid caregivers (Lightfoot & Williams, 2009).

Children and youths with disabilities are at an increased risk of school bullying in comparison to their peers without disabilities (Blake, Lund, Zhou, Kwok, & Benz, 2012; U.S. Department of Education Office for Civil Rights, 2014; Young, Ne'eman, & Gesler, 2016). Research has clearly established that children and youths with all types of disabling conditions—visible and invisible, physical, developmental, emotional, and sensory—experience more bullying than their peers without disabilities. Social skills challenges, either as a characteristic of their disability or as a result of social isolation due to segregation and/or peer rejection, put these youths at an increased risk of being bullied (Young et al., 2016).

The Office for Civil Rights in the U.S. Department of Education (2014) has received an increasing number of complaints pertaining to the bullying of primary and secondary school students with disabilities and the negative impact of bullying on their education, special education, and services to which these students are entitled. Bullying can interfere with students' receipt of appropriate educational services, thus preventing them from receiving a free and appropriate education and civil rights protection under the Individuals with Disabilities in Education Act (IDEA), Section 504 of the Rehabilitation Act, and Title II of the Americans with Disabilities Act (ADA). For example, bullying may result in adverse changes in students' academic performance or behavior (e.g., increased numbers of missed classes to avoid bullying, sudden declines in grades, the onset of emotional outbursts, increased occurrences of behavioral disruptions) as responses to the experience of being bullied. Furthermore, the onus is on the school *not* students and parents to safeguard them against bullying.

Males disproportionately commit criminal offenses, particularly violent crimes (e.g., homicide) and certain crimes that are predominantly committed by males against females (e.g., stalking, intimate partner violence, sexual violence; Bureau of

Justice Statistics [BJS], 2015; Truman & Langton, 2014). Young people (ages 16–24) experience the most crime both in terms of being victims and being offenders as compared to other age groups (BJS, 2015; Truman & Langton, 2014). Young Black males are at a higher risk to be victims of violent crimes such as robbery, assault, and gang violence (Harrell, 2007). The increased exposure has led to higher rates of spinal cord injuries, TBI, and trauma-related mental health difficulties such as PTSD, depression, and generalized anxiety disorder in this population (Alim, Charney, & Mellman, 2006). The increased rate of mental health issues may be the result of disparities in mental health service use among urban, disadvantaged, and trauma-exposed individuals (Elhai, Patrick, Anderson, Simons, & Frueh, 2006; Elhai & Simons, 2007). Transgender and gender nonconforming children and youths experience substantial bullying and harassment in elementary, secondary, and postsecondary school (Movement Advancement Project, National Center for Transgender Equality, Transgender Law Center, 2015). These youths tend to miss school more often than children who have not been bullied, have lower GPAs, are more likely not to plan to attend college, have higher levels of depression, and report lower self-esteem.

For transgender individuals, the psychosocial consequences of violence are compounded by stigmatization, transphobia, and discrimination as well as a lack of knowledge on the part of medical and human service providers regarding their experiences. Of the respondents to the National Transgender Discrimination Survey, 41% reported attempting suicide (Grant, Flynn, Odlaug, & Schreiber, 2011). They face discrimination in all domains of life including health care, housing, public services, and employment. For example, even in health care, they encounter discriminatory health care exclusions that deny coverage for medically necessary care (e.g., hormone therapy, counseling, other medical care). Transgender individuals, particularly transgender women and transgender people of color, experience poorer health and well-being and higher rates of discrimination and violence than the general population. One in four Black transgender individuals in the United States is living with HIV. They are also more likely to live in poverty and are more vulnerable to violence, particularly police violence. Most arrests of transgender individuals are for "quality of life crimes" (i.e., loitering or sleeping outside due to homelessness) or "survival crimes" (i.e., sex work or drug use due to lack of employment). Among Black transgender people, nearly half have been incarcerated at some point in their lives. In sum, these experiences subject transgender individuals to ongoing trauma and diminished quality of life. Violence against transgender women of color occurs at an alarmingly high rate. In a report by the National Coalition of Anti-Violence Programs (2015), the researchers found that in comparison to lesbian, gay, bisexual, queer (LGBTQ) and HIV-affected individuals, transgender women of color experienced disproportionately higher rates of violence and more severe violence. They were also more likely to experience hate violence, police violence, physical violence, discrimination, harassment, sexual violence, threats, and intimidation. Over the years, the numbers of transgender women who survive hate crimes has increased. Yet many of these women are likely to survive with permanent psychiatric and physical disabilities. Transgender women of color are frequently targeted by police and subjected to traumatizing violence in the form of excessive force, entrapment, unjustified arrest, and other forms of police misconduct.

Research on microaggressions and workplace incivilities has demonstrated higher rates of reported incidents by women and members of racial and ethnic minority groups (Cortina et al., 2001). Adults with disabilities may also be at increased risk of experiencing microaggressions and workplace incivilities. As discussed in other chapters, in various qualitative research studies with individuals with emerging disabilities such as multiple chemical sensitivity, research participants have described numerous experiences of workplace microaggressions and incivilities. Furthermore, Shaw, Chan, McMahon, and Kim (2012) discovered that, in comparison to White males, women and members of racial and ethnic minority groups were more likely to file disability harassment charges under Title I of the ADA. The researchers also found that, in comparison to other disability groups, individuals with behavioral disorders such as anxiety, depression, PTSD, and TBI—prominent disabilities associated with violence—filed proportionally more harassment charges than did people with other disabilities.

People living in poverty also experience a higher risk of violent crime victimization than people not living in poverty. From 2008 to 2012, people living at or below the federal poverty level (FPL) experienced more than twice the rate of violent victimization than those in high-income households (Harrel, Langton, Berzosky, Couzens, & Smiley-McDonald, 2014). During this timeframe, people living at or below the FPL also experienced a higher rate of violence involving a firearm than people living above the FPL. The rate of violence experienced by people living at or below the FPL was consistent for both Blacks and Whites, but the rate for Hispanics did not vary across poverty levels. Furthermore, the rates of violence were similar for poor people living in rural and urban areas.

Older individuals are at an increased risk of experiencing violent crime victimization. Elder abuse is defined by the Centers for Disease Control and Prevention (CDC, 2016) as violence against individuals 60 and older. In 2008, one in 10 senior citizens reported emotional, physical, or sexual abuse in the previous year (CDC, 2016). The CDC describes six types of violence that are committed against elders: (a) physical (e.g., hitting, kicking, pushing, slapping, burning; (b) sexual (i.e., forcing the older person to engage in a sexual act when he or she does not or cannot consent); (c) emotional (e.g., name calling, scaring, embarrassing, isolating the individual from family or friends); (d) neglect (i.e., failure to meet the individual's basic needs for food, shelter, clothing, and medical care); (e) abandonment (e.g., when the caregiver leaves the older person alone and no longer provides necessary care for his or her health and safety); and (f) financial (i.e., taking advantage of the person by illegally using his or her money, property, or assets. Most violence against elders is perpetrated by a caregiver or someone whom the elder knows and trusts (CDC, 2016). Elder abuse may result in minor injuries such as cuts, scratches, or bruises. In more severe cases, it can result in physical injuries (e.g., head injuries, broken bones, chronic pain) that can become permanent disabilities or exacerbate preexisting disabilities and chronic illnesses. Elder abuse frequently goes unreported because elders often rely on the perpetrators for care or they may fear retribution.

REHABILITATION COUNSELING IMPLICATIONS

Counselor Self-Awareness and Reflective Practice

When providing rehabilitation counseling services to individuals who have acquired disabilities associated with violence, self-reflective practice is vital to maintaining a nonjudgmental attitude toward survivors of these acts and understanding the social structural stressors associated with violence. Rehabilitation counselor self-awareness may help eliminate issues such as "victim blaming" as can occur when attitudes toward individuals who experience domestic violence reflect judgment or lack of empathy for those who remain in abusive relationships. Rehabilitation counselors must keep in mind all of the factors involved in decisions to remain in or leave these relationships. They must also consider the role that culture plays in decision making (e.g., cultural beliefs about women's and men's roles in relationships and how divorce is perceived).

Because transgender individuals encounter high rates of stigmatization and discrimination, it is also important that rehabilitation counselors reflect on their attitudes toward individuals who are nongender conforming. Negative attitudes and transphobia on the part of the rehabilitation counselor can lead to failure to provide a space where these individuals feel safe, accepted, respected, and connected. Relatedly, rehabilitation counselors should also reflect on areas in which they may have knowledge deficits related to emerging consumer populations such as veterans with disabilities, survivors of domestic violence, and transgender individuals. For example, Posey (2016) noted that not all rehabilitation counselors are inadequately prepared to serve survivors of domestic violence and require additional training in this area. Frain, Bethel, and Bishop (2010) emphasized the growing need for those preparing for careers in rehabilitation counseling to expand their knowledge of issues affecting veterans because veterans represent an emerging disability population that has not been extensively served by rehabilitation counselors in recent years. Specifically, they recommended that entering and practicing rehabilitation counselors expand their knowledge about (a) screening for and identifying co-occuring invisible disabilities that often go unrecognized long after military discharge; (b) psychological and psychosocial consequences and symptoms of commonly experienced disabilities; (c) the multiple systems (e.g., military, medical, psychological, rehabilitation) that provide services to veterans with disabilities; and (d) veteran rights and laws. Cater and Koch (2010) and Cater and Leach (2011) recommended that rehabilitation counselors also advance their knowledge about military terminology, the impact of military culture on the disability experiences of veterans, and unique issues (e.g., MST) that affect female military personnel with disabilities.

Similarly, because contemporary youths and young adults are expressing their gender identity in more complex ways than youths and young adults from prior generations, rehabilitation counselors should advance their knowledge in areas such as (a) the diverse experiences and effects of discrimination, transphobia, and stigma on the lives of individuals who are gender nonconforming; (b) transgender and gender-nonconforming inclusive language; (c) how to change agency policies and practices that discriminate against gender-nonconforming and transgender individuals (e.g., forms and documents that only provide two options for identifying one's sex [male/female], failure to provide unisex bathrooms, failure to use the client's preferred name and gender pronoun); and (d) advocating for safe and inclusive school, work, and community environments (GLAAD, 2015).

Rehabilitation counselors who have experienced violence must be aware of the potential impact of their own trauma experiences on working effectively with clients who have acquired violence-related disabilities. Hearing about the trauma-related experiences of clients could trigger disturbing memories and thoughts about the rehabilitation counselor's own experiences, and these could contribute to secondary traumatization or counselor compassion fatigue, both of which could undermine the rehabilitation counselor's effectiveness in working with clients. Rehabilitation counselors must, therefore, attend to rather than ignore their own triggers and seek mental health counseling as needed for self-care.

Reflective practice also includes considerations of agency policies and procedures that could lead to re-traumatization of individuals with disabilities acquired from violence. For example, medical evaluations should be conducted by providers who are knowledgeable about trauma, how invasive medical procedures may re-traumatize individuals, and how explaining to the individual step-by-step what is being done can help prevent re-traumatization. It should also be taken into consideration when making referrals to medical providers that women who have experienced MST or domestic violence may prefer to see a female physician. Furthermore, loud office environments may need to be accommodated to ensure that counseling sessions take place in quiet settings with limited raised voices among staff (Ramirez, 2014). Likewise, rehabilitation consumers should be given the choice to work with a male, female, or transgender rehabilitation counselor, or a rehabilitation counselor who is a transgender ally. Rehabilitation counselors may also want to consider designing group interventions (e.g., career development workshops, job clubs) specifically for women to address the unique employment issues they face as well as to create a sense of safety for women who have been victimized by men. Rehabilitation counselors can advocate for staff training (including front office staff) to better understand trauma, how it impacts individuals who have survived traumatic experiences resulting from violent crime, and how trauma-informed strategies such as grounding techniques can be implemented to create safe, welcoming environments (Ramirez, 2014). Likewise, office spaces should be designed to reinforce a sense of safety and acceptance (e.g., providing gender-neutral bathrooms, designing waiting and reception areas to be warm and inviting, providing games and toys for children who accompany parents to appointments).

Outreach and Eligibility Determination

Outreach may be particularly necessary to inform individuals with violence-related disabilities about rehabilitation services. In many instances, these individuals may not self-identify as individuals with disabilities or they may be unaware of rehabilitation counseling programs and agencies. Outreach and education efforts should be targeted at homeless shelters, women's shelters, schools, public health agencies, courts, jails, prisons, and other organizations that provide services to individuals who have survived violent acts. Conducting outreach allows the rehabilitation counselor to both provide information about eligibility criteria and services offered by their own agency and receive the same information from other agencies. Outreach efforts can also familiarize rehabilitation counselors with referral sources in their communities such as physicians, psychiatrists, and psychologists who have expertise in trauma-informed care.

One of the first steps in the intake interview is to determine if the individual's basic needs (e.g., food, safety, sufficient social supports, accommodations) are met (Substance Abuse and Mental Health Services Administration [SAMHSA], 2014). If appropriate, referrals to food banks, women's shelters, support groups, and other community agencies should be made. Rehabilitation counselors should also consider the issue of safety and avoidance of re-traumatization in conducting intake interviews. Specifically, some individuals may not be ready to describe their experiences until they get to know and feel safe with the rehabilitation counselor. Others may prefer to avoid discussing their experiences altogether. Rehabilitation counselors should be sure to respect clients' privacy and adjust their interviewing techniques accordingly. Individuals who have survived violent acts have a need for respect, information, connectedness, and hopefulness (SAMHSA, 2014). The intake interview should be structured to respond to these needs. Rehabilitation counselors may also want to consider conducting intake interviews and follow-up appointments with individuals in environments where they feel safe (e.g., women's shelter, family member's home).

It is crucial that rehabilitation counselors screen for co-occurring disorders because many individuals will have both physical and psychiatric disabilities that go unidentified and will require additional medical or psychiatric evaluations to establish eligibility and service needs. For example, Frain et al. (2010) observed that veterans often have disabilities such as TBI, PTSD, and depression that go unrecognized for years after discharge from service. These authors provided examples of screening questions that can be incorporated into intake interviews with military veterans. These same questions can be adapted for use with survivors of other violent acts. In many cases, the trauma experienced as a result of violence may manifest as medically unexplained physical symptoms; therefore, thorough medical evaluations with trauma-informed physicians may also be warranted.

It is also important that, when individuals who have experienced violence are in need of psychotherapy or other mental health interventions, they are referred to mental health providers who specialize in trauma and can make an accurate assessment of the individual's needs for psychotherapy or mental health counseling and the most effective approaches to use in treating these individuals. The American Psychological Association has a psychologist locator that can be used by rehabilitation counselors and clients to identify local specialists in areas such as trauma/PTSD, gender identity, sexual abuse/rape, and domestic violence that can be accessed at locator.apa.org/index.cfm?event=search.map&id. Likewise, the VA has a locator for therapists and organizations that treat PTSD that can be accessed at www.va.gov/directory/guide/ptsd_flsh.asp. However, these specialists may not practice in smaller communities and alternatives such as tele-therapy may be necessary.

For members of transition teams, knowledge that a student is being bullied needs to be immediately addressed so that the bullying ceases. Under the IDEA, children and youths with disabilities must be provided a free and appropriate education in the least restrictive environment. If bullying interferes with their ability to participate in their education, it is the team's responsibility to immediately remedy the problem or else the school could be held liable for failure to comply with IDEA statutory regulations (Young et al., 2016).

Rehabilitation Assessment and Planning

Rehabilitation assessment and planning should be implemented using a trauma-informed approach to assist individuals to build on their resilience, gain or regain a sense of empowerment by focusing on individual strengths, and move toward self-management to identify triggers and strategies for preventing these from interfering with life goals (SAMHSA, 2014). SAMHSA has listed key principles of a trauma-informed service delivery: safety; trustworthiness and transparency; peer support; collaboration and mutuality; empowerment; voice and choice; and cultural, historical, and gender issues. These principles, all of which are directly aligned with rehabilitation principles and practices, provide a foundation for assessment and planning with clients who have acquired disabilities from violence.

Several considerations warrant attention with respect to a trauma-informed rehabilitation assessment and planning process. First, because the individuals who are most vulnerable to acquiring disabilities from violence are also among the most marginalized members of American society, rehabilitation counselors must address the intersectionality of multiple disadvantages (e.g., race, gender, gender identity, disability) in plan development. Second, the underlying effects of the trauma (e.g., psychological and behavioral issues that have resulted from the trauma) should be clearly understood by the rehabilitation counselor. Rehabilitation counselors should be aware of how clients' past experiences with trauma can interfere with the way they experience everyday life. The counselor can then ensure a better rehabilitation experience by exploring the lingering effects of trauma and ways to provide targeted services and accommodations. Third, individuals who have survived violent events often have multiple disabilities that all need to be addressed in the rehabilitation plan. Relatedly, they may have disabilities that have yet to be identified and diagnosed that could present the greatest barriers to goal achievement. Fourth, the rehabilitation planning process is likely to involve a multitude of services, service providers, and agencies (e.g., community mental health centers, the VA, shelters for women and children, homeless shelters, the criminal justice system). Therefore, being knowledgeable about community resources and having the ability to establish strong working alliances and ongoing communication with other service providers to ensure coordination of services are paramount. The rehabilitation counselor should be prepared to make appropriate referrals to fully address the client's needs. For example, when working with a client who has experienced domestic violence, it may be important for a counselor to know what agencies are able to help with shelter, food, medical care, clothing, and all the other basic needs that would need to be met first. Finally, when working with survivors of violent victimization, rehabilitation counselors need to meet the client's needs in a safe, collaborative, and compassionate manner. Important considerations for rehabilitation counselors working with these individuals include addressing safety issues, avoiding practices that can result in re-traumatization, building on the strengths and resources of clients in the context of their environments, and endorsing trauma-informed principles in agency policies.

REHABILITATION SERVICES

Counseling and Guidance

As safety is a primary concern in trauma-informed rehabilitation counseling practice, ethical issues such as privacy, confidentiality, informed consent for release of records, the limits of confidentiality, and mandated reporting of child abuse must be clearly communicated and understood by clients who have acquired disabilities from violent acts. Although discussing these issues up front is an ethical practice employed when providing services to all clients, it can be particularly important when working with clients who have survived violent crimes and can enhance their sense of trust and safety.

Also with regard to safety, Rubin, Roessler, and Rumrill (2016) discussed the role that rehabilitation counselors can play in assisting consumers, particularly those who have experienced domestic violence and may still be involved with their perpetrators or concerned about re-victimization by perpetrators. These authors identified key components to include in safety plans such as (a) important contact numbers (e.g., friends, police, hotlines, the local shelter); (b) safe places to go in case of an emergency (e.g., friend's house, shelter); (c) ways to leave home safely and get to a safe location (e.g., taxi, ride from friend); and (d) a list of important items that need to be brought (e.g., cash, legal documents, items for children, medications).

In providing counseling and guidance to individuals who have acquired disabilities from violent acts, Millar (2013) highlighted the importance of viewing and treating the client, not as a helpless victim, but as a person with a considerable capacity for adaptation, survival, and resiliency. This focus can be obtained by providing (or referring clients for) psychoeducation about typical reactions to and symptoms of traumatic stress as well as treatment options. Symptoms (e.g., dissociation, hypervigilance, exaggerated startle responses) should be reframed as safeguarding behaviors (i.e., creative responses to avoid further harm) rather than pathology (Millar, 2013; Warshaw et al., 2014). This approach normalizes the trauma experience and enables survivors to move forward in developing new coping strategies once they are no longer in danger (SAMHSA, 2014).

Because women who experience domestic violence may be fearful about leaving their children alone, it is important that the rehabilitation counselor reassure them that they can bring their children to appointments. Keeping games, toys, and activities for children to engage in during appointments can also serve as an indicator that children are welcome. It is also important to keep in mind that individuals may choose not to disclose their experiences of trauma; therefore, rehabilitation counselors should be alert to potential signs of violence-related trauma, consult with supervisors and mental health providers about how to sensitively bring up these issues with clients, and make referrals for mental health services when indicated.

In providing counseling and guidance to these clients, rehabilitation counselors should understand that trust is likely to be an issue, and the process of establishing rapport may take time. Belonging and social connectedness are important to individuals with trauma-related disabilities acquired from violence (Ramirez, 2012), and rehabilitation counselors who demonstrate patience, compassion, and encouragement can help these individuals to build trust and develop a sense of belonging and connectedness. Likewise, individuals should be given the opportunity to go at their own pace and not be rushed to share information or participate in services for which they are not ready. Structure and consistency are also important in trust building (SAMHSA, 2014). Finally, experiencing ongoing violence, whether it be physical, psychological, sexual or all of these, can seriously undermine one's self-esteem and confidence in decision making. Providing choices and enhancing the client's ability to establish self-determination can assist these consumers to develop a sense of self-empowerment and control over their own lives (Ramirez, 2014).

Language is also important when working with survivors of violent acts. For example, military service members often do not identify as individuals with disabilities. Instead, they identify themselves using terminology such as wounded warriors or injured service members. Cater and Koch (2010) recommended that rehabilitation counselors become familiar with military terminology when working with these individuals. A useful resource is the DoD Dictionary of Military and Associated Terms (2016) that can be accessed at www.dtic.mil/doctrine/dod_dictionary. Likewise, appropriate language use when working with transgender individuals is important in building cohesive relationships. GLAAD (2015) provided a tip sheet for transgender allies that addresses language issues and can be accessed at www.glaad.org/transgender/allies. In addition, the Association of Lesbian, Gay, Bisexual, and Transgender Issues in Counseling (2009) has developed competencies for counseling transgender clients that can be retrieved from https://www.counseling.org/docs/default-source/competencies/algbtic_competencies.pdf?sfvrsn=12.

Rehabilitation counselors should also learn how to use grounding strategies when individuals experience flashbacks, sudden panic, or dissociative states (Ramirez, 2014). These strategies confirm that where the clients are in the present moment is safe and that they will not be harmed. Rehabilitation counselors can verbally reassure them they are in a safe place or use other grounding techniques such as helping them to create an image of a safe space that can be retrieved during difficult times or making referrals for psychiatric service dogs. Finally, rehabilitation counselors can advocate for making shelters accessible to women with disabilities and transgender individuals with disabilities.

Self-Management Techniques

Throughout this book, we have underscored the importance of assisting individuals with emerging disabilities to self-manage their conditions, which are often chronic, episodic, and sometimes progressive. Survivors of violence with disabilities such as TBI, PTSD, depression, and substance use disorders can benefit from these strategies to ensure that they take care of themselves on a daily basis, actively engage in treatment to manage their symptoms, recognize triggers that could result in symptom exacerbation, and develop plans to respond to triggers.

Frain et al. (2010) emphasized the importance of training in self-management techniques for veterans because they tend to have poor self-management skills. Frain et al. (2010) identified two factors in particular that contribute to poor self-management. First, they noted that disabilities acquired from war such as PTSD inhibit veterans' ability to initiate self-care, resulting in maladaptive responses such as self-medicating with alcohol or other substances that can result in secondary medical health problems. Second, these authors noted that military veterans, as a group, are less likely to seek mental health services due to the stigma and perceived threat of having their military careers ended if their military records document mental health visits. They also noted that unmanaged secondary disabilities can be more problematic than primary disabilities and recommended that rehabilitation counselors use self-management scales developed by two of the authors to identify shortcomings in self-management and initiate strategies to assist veterans to improve their skills in areas where shortcomings are identified.

Individuals who have acquired catastrophic injuries (e.g., polytrauma) may require more intensive services to manage their disabilities. Life care planning in particular can ensure that their life-long medical and rehabilitation needs are addressed. The life care plan is:

> a dynamic document based upon published standards of practice, comprehensive assessment, data analysis and research, which provides an organized, concise plan for current and future needs with associated cost, for individuals who have experienced catastrophic injuries or have chronic health care needs. (Sutton, Deutsh, Weed, & Berens, 2002, p. 187)

Interested rehabilitation counselors can obtain additional training and supervision to become certified life care planners (CLCPs).

Trauma-Informed Peer Supports

Surviving the trauma of violence can be an isolating experience that consumes the survivor's thoughts, beliefs, feelings, and actions. Survivors are often left with beliefs that they are different, alone, and damaged. Receiving treatment and specialized services such as rehabilitation can reinforce these self-attributions; therefore, SAMHSA (2014) recommended that treatment and rehabilitation be coupled with peer support to enhance recovery. According to SAMHSA, trauma-informed peer supports should be focused on four main tasks: (a) building connections; (b) developing an understanding of one's worldview; (c) developing a sense of connection and mutual understanding of each other's experiences; and (d) helping each other to set and achieve goals for recovery. Trauma-informed peer supports provide opportunities for survivors to "form mutual relationships; to learn how one's history shapes perspectives of self, others, and the future; to move beyond trauma; and to mirror and learn alternate coping strategies" (SAMHSA, 2014, p. 116). Examples of consumer(peer)-run services include support groups, drop-in centers, consumer-run organizations, warm lines (peer-run telephone services that provide support and information) and Internet support and message boards (National Council on Disability [NCD], 2009).

Support groups can also be beneficial for individuals who have survived domestic violence. Talking to other survivors of domestic violence can be a helpful step in recovery. The group setting allows individuals to share their thoughts, resolve feelings, and gain confidence in communicating with the support of other people who can relate. Ramirez (2014) also noted that trained peers may be even more effective than mental health professionals at responding to crises because of the mutuality they share with those who have experienced violence. Acknowledging the valuable role that peers play in the recovery process, the VA employs peer specialists who are veterans actively engaged in their own recovery and who assist their fellow veterans to transition to civilian life. These peer specialists receive specialized training and certification to assist others in areas such as coping with physical and mental health challenges, navigating the VA system, and addressing employment issues. Consumers have also been hired as employees in mental health agencies, and, like peer service providers who work with military veterans, consumers as employees function in a variety of positions such as peer companions, peer advocates, consumer case managers, peer specialists, and peer counselors (National Council on Disability, 2009). Outcomes of peer supports and peer-provided services include increased social networks, improved coping skills, greater acceptance of one's mental health condition, improved medication adherence, lower levels of worry, higher satisfaction with health, and improved quality of life.

Employer Services

Another important service that rehabilitation counselors can provide on behalf of or in collaboration with individuals with violence-related disabilities is consultation with employers to develop policies and procedures to ensure safe, inclusive work environments for all employees. Dillion (2012) recommended a variety of relevant strategies that can be incorporated into policies and procedures and implemented by employers at the job site. First, employers should develop and implement policies and procedures that emphasize the organization's commitment to creating and sustaining an inclusive workplace culture in which *all* employees are treated with respect by management, immediate supervisors, and coworkers. These policies and procedures should include a commitment to zero tolerance of microaggressions, incivility, bullying, and other forms of aggression. Along these same lines, all employees should be informed that harassment is an illegal form of discrimination under the ADA and other civil rights legislation, and ignoring complaints by employees who are protected under these acts could result in serious repercussions for the business and offending employees.

Policies and procedures should be clearly written and regularly reviewed with employees (Dillon, 2012). For example, these policies should be provided in writing and discussed with employees in the hiring process and in new employee orientations. Ongoing monitoring and training of all employees and periodically testing their awareness of policies and procedures can help to reinforce their importance. It is also of the utmost importance that these policies and procedures are modeled by management and consistently reinforced (Dillon, 2012). When complaints about employees' behaviors are brought to management or supervisors, they should be addressed with offending employees in a respectful, nonpunitive manner that provides an opportunity for them to explain reasons for the behaviors as well as an opportunity for management or supervisors to educate these employees about why their behaviors cannot be tolerated. Implementing antiworkplace violence and mistreatment policies and procedures may require a transformation in the organizational culture, and periodic assessment of how the policies and procedures are changing the culture and individual employee behaviors may be warranted.

Employers should also be educated that disability harassment is illegal under the ADA, and failure on the part of employers to redress harassment reported by people with disabilities could result in harassment lawsuits against the employer. The American Diabetes Association (ADA, 1990) defines disability harassment as "bothering, tormenting, troubling, ridiculing, or coercing a person because of a disability." In research conducted by Shaw, Chan, McMahon, and Kim (2012) to examine the characteristics of employees and employers with elevated risks of filing harassment charges under Title I of the ADA, the researchers discovered that women, minorities, and people with behavioral disabilities were more likely to file harassment charges. Harassment lawsuits were more likely to be filed against employers in the educational services and public administration industries. Because survivors of violent victimization are more likely to be women from minority groups with behavioral disabilities (e.g., anxiety, depression, PTSD, TBI), these research findings bring up questions regarding the increased vulnerability that survivors of violence may have to workplace harassment. These findings have important implications for employer training about trauma and establishing trauma-informed policies and procedures, especially in the industries of educational services and public administration.

Job Development and Placement

Successful employment is valuable to individuals who have acquired disabilities or developed chronic illnesses associated with violence. In addition to the monetary rewards of employment, work can increase self-esteem, which can be an especially strong therapeutic tool because it provides a means of structuring and occupying time, creates opportunities for social interaction, and can result in a sense of personal achievement (Tschopp, Bishop, & Mulvihill, 2001; Waghorn et al., 2012). Many individuals with psychiatric disabilities cite employment as critical in their recovery process (Waghorn et al., 2012). Bond et al. (2001) found that individuals with psychiatric disabilities who worked in competitive employment showed a reduction in psychiatric symptoms, an increase in self-esteem, and heightened satisfaction in leisure and finances. When providing placement assistance to clients with violence-related disabilities, rehabilitation counselors are likely to provide the same services to these clients as are provided to all clients (e.g., active job search assistance, technical assistance in completing job applications, developing resumes, improving interview skills). In the job search process, it is important to take into consideration the abilities and limitations of each client when making a proper jobfit. While working with individuals with violence-related disabilities, this means addressing all aspects of the effects that the trauma has had on clients and ensuring that they have the proper accommodations to be successful in competitive employment.

Employed individuals who acquire injuries from violent acts can benefit from the assistance of a rehabilitation counselor to ensure return to work after they have healed from their injuries. These individuals should be educated about the Family and Medical Leave Act (FMLA) and their right under this Act to receive up to 12 weeks of unpaid leave (McMahon & Domer, 1997). Likewise, family members can receive unpaid leave to care for those who were injured. Because of the multiple identities of these clients, education about other laws that provide employment protections may be beneficial to both the employer and the employee. Also, although employers may be open to hiring, accommodating, and creating inclusive workplace policies, coworkers may react differently and require education regarding violence-related disabling conditions. Ongoing follow-up and support is as important to these clients as it is for all clients. This support is especially important in the initial stages of employment. As individuals increase their self-esteem and belief in their ability to achieve high occupational goals, support may be needed to assist these individuals to advance in their careers or to pursue different occupations that are more compatible with their newly recognized skills and abilities.

Accommodation Planning

Accommodation planning with rehabilitation clients who have acquired disabilities from violent acts follows the same format as it does for all clients. Resources discussed in other chapters can be used to guide this exploration of barriers, accommodations, and selection of specific accommodations to implement at the job site. In considering reasonable accommodations for individuals with disabilities acquired from violent acts, accessibility issues center on the removal of both attitudinal and physical barriers. Additionally, because safety and trust are often issues for these clients, disclosure is likely to be a major concern that will require exploration. In many contexts, disclosure has resulted in negative outcomes that further undermine clients' psychological and physical well-being, so rehabilitation counselors should be prepared to devote adequate time to this issue. They should thoroughly explore with clients both the risks and benefits of disclosure so that these clients can make informed decisions about whether, how, and to whom they should disclose. For those who choose to disclose, rehabilitation counselors can provide them with opportunities to role play and receive constructive feedback.

Because disabilities caused by violence can include a wide range of psychiatric and physical functional limitations, rehabilitation counselors, clients, and employers can use JAN as a resource for identifying accommodations specific to the disabling conditions of individual clients. Perhaps the most important accommodation for individuals whose disabilities are the result of violence is workplace policies that promote and ensure safe, inclusive environments for *all* employees. As we discussed, rehabilitation counselors can assess workplace climates and provide consultation to employers to develop policies, practices, and procedures for creating inclusive environments with zero-tolerance for any form of mistreatment of coworkers and supervisees.

CONCLUSIONS

In providing rehabilitation services to clients with histories of violent victimization, understanding the nature of the violence and its effects on functioning in multiple life domains is a prerequisite to establishing a strong counselor–client relationship and facilitating successful goal achievement. In this chapter, we have discussed common types of disabilities caused by trauma due to violence, the groups of people who are at an increased risk of victimization, treatments for each type of violence-related disability, and considerations that rehabilitation counselors must make when providing services to individuals with these disabling conditions.

Although we have discussed treatment approaches and rehabilitation interventions that target change at the individual level, one of the most striking implications for practice that we have discovered in our review of the literature for this chapter is the broad-based need for trauma-informed practices to be implemented in all settings where individuals spend their time (e.g., communities, schools, postsecondary institutions, rehabilitation agencies, workplaces). We encourage readers to consider the role that they can play in facilitating changes to create safer, more inclusive environments in which individuals feel accepted and connected to those around them.

DISCUSSION QUESTIONS

1. What biases, negative stereotypes, or misconceptions do you have that may interfere with your ability to work effectively with populations discussed in this chapter? What actions can you take to change your perceptions?
2. What do you think are the most critical medical, psychosocial, and/or vocational issues for individuals with disabilities acquired through violence? In your future or current rehabilitation counseling practice, what can you do to address these issues?
3. What do you need to learn more about to effective serve populations discussed in this chapter? What actions can you take to strengthen your knowledge? Discuss and create a list of resources in your local community to address the multifaceted needs of individuals who have acquired disabilities from violent acts.
4. Review and discuss the case of Amalia presented at the beginning of the chapter. What barriers does she face in participating in rehabilitation counseling and achieving a successful outcome? In determining eligibility and service needs, what additional assessments (if any) are needed? How will you go about identifying trauma-informed specialists to provide these services or educate providers about such practices if none are located in your community? What are considerations for providing counseling and guidance and facilitating the rehabilitation planning process? What are potential services you would include in her rehabilitation plan? What are issues you need to take into consideration in job development, placement, and follow-up?

REFERENCES

Alim, T. N., Charney, D. S., & Mellman, T. A. (2006). An overview of posttraumatic stress disorder in African Americans. *Journal of Clinical Psychology, 62*(7), 801–813.

American Diabetes Association. (2015). *Statistics about diabetes*. Retrieved from http://www.diabetes.org/diabetes-basics/statistics/?loc=db-slabnav

American Psychiatric Association. (2013). *Diagnostic and statistical manual of mental disorders* (5th ed.). Washington, DC: Author.

Andrews, E. (2013). *The VA polytrauma system of care: Serving those who served with multiple disabilities*. Spotlight on Disability Newsletter. American Psychological Association. Retrieved from http://www.apa.org/pi/disability/resources/publications/newsletter/2013/11/polytrauma-system.aspx

Association of Lesbian, Gay, Bisexual, and Transgender Issues in Counseling. (2009). *Competencies for counseling transgender clients*. Alexandria, VA: Author.

Bagalman, E. (2011). *Traumatic brain injury among veterans*. Washington, DC: Congressional Research Service, Library of Congress.

Bass, C. R., Panzer, M. B., Rafaels, K. A., Wood, G., Shridharani, J., & Capehart, B. (2012). Brain injuries from blast. *Annals of Biomedical Engineering, 40*(1), 185–202. doi:10.1007/s10439-011-0424-0

Ben-Shalom, Y., Tennant, J. R., & Stapleton, D. C. (2016). Trends in disability and program participation among U.S. veterans. *Disability and Health Journal, 9*(3), 449–456. doi: 10.1016/j.dhjo.2015.12.008

Blake, J. J., Banks, C. S., Patience, B. A., & Lund, E. M. (2014). School-based mental health professionals' bullying assessment practices: A call for evidence-based bullying assessment guidelines. *Professional School Counseling, 18*(1), 136.

Blake, J. J., Lund, E. M., Zhou, Q., Kwok, O., & Benz, M. R. (2012). National prevalence rates of bully victimization among students with disabilities in the United States. *School Psychology Quarterly: The Official Journal of the Division of School Psychology, American Psychological Association, 27*(4), 210–222.

Bond, G. R., Resnick, S. G., Drake, R. E., Xie, H., McHugo, G. J., & Bebout, R. R. (2001). Does competitive employment improve nonvocational outcomes for people with severe mental illness? *Journal of Consulting and Clinical Psychology, 69*(3), 489–501.

Briere, J., Kaltman, S., & Green, B. (2008). Accumulated childhood trauma and symptom complexity. *Journal of Traumatic Stress, 21*(2), 223–226.

Briere, J., & Scott, C. (2006). *Principles of trauma therapy: A guide to symptoms, evaluation, and treatment.* Thousand Oaks, CA: Sage.

Bureau of Justice Statistics. (2015). *Data collection: National Crime Victimization Survey (NCVS).* Retrieved from http://www.bjs.gov/index.cfm?ty=dcdetail&iid=245

Capehart, B., & Bass, D. (2012). Review: Managing posttraumatic stress disorder in combat veterans with comorbid traumatic brain injury. *Journal of Rehabilitation Research and Develpment, 49*(5), 789–812.

Carlyle, K., & Steinman, K. (2007). Demographic differences in the prevalence, co-occurrence and correlates of adolescent bullying at school. *Journal of School Health, 77*(9), 623–629.

Cater, J. K., & Koch, L. C. (2010). Women veterans with polytrauma: Rehabilitation planning implications. *Journal of Applied Rehabilitation Counseling, 41*(3), 9–17.

Cater, J. K., & Leach, J. (2011). Veterans, military sexual trauma and PTSD: Rehabilitation planning implications. *Journal of Applied Rehabilitation Counseling, 42*(2), 33–40.

Centers for Disease Control and Prevention. (2016). *Understanding elder abuse: Fact sheet.* Retrieved from https://www.cdc.gov/violenceprevention/pdf/em-factsheet-a.pdf

Cohen, J. A., & Mannarino, A. P. (2008). Trauma-focused cognitive behavioural therapy for children and parents. *Child and Adolescent Mental Health, 13*(4), 158–162.

Copeland, W., Wolke, D., Angold, A., & Costello, E. (2013). Adult psychiatric outcomes of bullying and being bullied by peers in childhood and adolescence. *JAMA Psychiatry, 70*(4), 419–426.

Corbett, S. (2007). The women's war. *New York Times Magazine, 156,* 40–72.

Cortina, L. M., Magley, V. J., Williams, J. H., & Langhout, R. D. (2001). Incivility in the workplace: Incidence and impact. *Journal of Occupational Health Psychology, 6*(1), 64.

Cozza, S. J., Holmes, A. K., & Van Ost, S. L. (2013). Family-centered care for military and veteran families affected by combat injury. *Clinical Child and Family Psychology Review, 16*(3), 311–321.

Crofford, L. (2007). Violence, stress, and somatic syndromes. *Trauma, Violence & Abuse, 8*(3), 299–313.

Crosse, S., Kaye, E., & Ratnofsky, A. (1993). *A report on the maltreatment of children with disabilities.* Washington, DC: National Clearinghouse on Child Abuse and Neglect Information.

Denenberg, R. V., & Denenberg, T. S. (2012). Workplace violence and the media: The myth of the disgruntled employee. *Work, 42*(1), 5–7.

DePalma, R., Cross, G., Buckley, C., & Gunnar, W. (2014). Blast related traumatic brain injury: Pathophysiology, comorbidities, and neurobehavioral outcomes. *Understanding Traumatic Brain Injury: Current Research and Future Directions,* 413–429.

Department of Defense. (2016). *Department of Defense dictionary of military and associated terms.* Retrieved from http://www.dtic.mil/doctrine/new_pubs/jp1_02.pdf

Dillon, B. L. (2012). Workplace violence: Impact, causes, and prevention. *Work: A Journal of Prevention, Assessment, and Rehabilitation, 42*(1), 15–20.

Dooley, J. J., Pyżalski, J., & Cross, D. (2009). Cyberbullying versus face-to-face bullying. *Journal of Psychology, 217*(4), 182–188.

Drescher, K. D., & Foy, D. W. (2012). When they come home: Posttraumatic stress, moral injury, and spiritual consequences for veterans. *Reflective Practice: Formation and Supervision in Ministry, 28.*

Dube, S., Fairweather, D., Pearson, W., Felitti, V., Anda, R., & Croft, J. (2009). Cumulative childhood stress and autoimmune diseases in adults. *Psychosomatic Medicine, 71*(2), 243–250. doi:10.1097/PSY.0b013e3181907888

Eapen, B. C., Jaramillo, C. A., Tapia, R. N., Johnson, E. J., & Cifu, D. X. (2013). Rehabilitation care of combat related TBI: Veterans Health Administration polytrauma system of care. *Current Physical Medicine and Rehabilitation Reports, 1*(3), 151–158.

Elhai, J. D., Patrick, S., Anderson, S., Simons, J., & Frueh, B. (2006). Gender- and trauma-related predictors of use of mental health treatment services among primary care patients. *Psychiatric Services, 57*(10), 1505–1509.

Elhai, J. D., & Simons, J. S. (2007). Trauma exposure and posttraumatic stress disorder predictors of mental health treatment use in college students. *Psychological Services, 4*(1), 38–45. doi:10.1037/1541–1559.4.1.38

Erford, B. T., Gunther, C., Duncan, K., Bardhoshi, G., Dummett, B., Kraft, J., … Ross, M. (2016). Meta-analysis of counseling outcomes for the treatment of posttraumatic stress disorder. *Journal of Counseling & Development, 94*(1), 13–30. doi:10.1002/jcad.12058

Fabian, L. A., Thygerson, S. M., & Merrill, R. M. (2014). Boarding injuries: The long and the short of it. *Emergency Medicine International, 2014*, 1–7. doi:10.1155/2014/924381

Farrell, B. S., Moser, D. E., Johnson, W. A., Lake, R. L., Mayo, K., Miller, A., …Willems, K. N. (2013). *Military personnel: DOD has taken steps to meet the health needs of deployed service-women, but actions are needed to enhance care for sexual assault victims* (No. GAO-13–182). Washington, DC: U.S. Government Accountability Office.

Finkelhor, D., Ormrod, R., Turner, H., & Holt, M. (2009). Pathways to poly-victimization. *Child Maltreatment, 14*(4), 316–329. doi:10.1177/1077559509347012

Fischer, H. (2014). *A guide to U.S. military casualty statistics: Operation New Dawn, Operation Iraqi Freedom, and Operation Enduring Freedom.* Washington, DC: Congressional Research Service.

Frain, M. P., Malachy, B., & Bethel, M. (2010). A roadmap for rehabilitation counseling to serve military veterans with disabilities. *Journal of Rehabilitation, 76*(1), 13–21.

Frohmader, C., & Didi, A. (2015). *Preventing violence against women and girls with disabilities: Integrating a human rights perspective.* Women With Disabilities Australia. Retrieved from http://wwda.org.au/wp-content/uploads/2013/12/Think-Piece_WWD.pdf

Fulton, J. J., Calhoun, P. S., Wagner, H. R., Schry, A. R., Hair, L. P., Feeling, N., … Beckham, J. C. (2015). The prevalence of posttraumatic stress disorder in Operation Enduring Freedom/Operation Iraqi Freedom (OEF/OIF) veterans: A meta-analysis. *Journal of Anxiety Disorders, 31*, 98–107.

Gawande, A. (2004). Casualties of war—Military care for the wounded from Iraq and Afghanistan. *New England Journal of Medicine, 351*(2), 2471–2475.

Gay and Lesbian Alliance Against Defamation (GLAAD). (2015). *Transgender FAQ.* Retrieved from http://www.glaad.org/transgender/transfaq

Gean, A. D. (2014). *Brain injury: Applications from war and terrorism.* Philadelphia, PA: Lippincott, Williams, & Wilkins.

Goodrich, G. L., Martinsen, G. L., Flyg, H. M., Kirby, J., Asch, S. M., Brahm, K. D., … Shea, J. E. (2013). Development of a mild traumatic brain injury-specific vision screening protocol: A Delphi study. *Journal of Rehabilitation Research and Development, 50*(6), 757–768.

Grant, J., Flynn, M., Odlaug, B., & Schreiber, L. (2011). Personality disorders in gay, lesbian, bisexual, and transgender chemically dependent patients. *American Journal on Addictions, 20*(5), 405–411. doi:10.1111/j.1521–0391.2011.00155.x

Griffin, C. L., Jr., & Stein, M. A. (2015). Self-perception of disability and prospects for employment among US veterans. *Work, 50*(1), 49–58.

Harrell, E. (2007). *Black victims of violent crime.* U.S. Department of Justice. Office of Justice Programs. Retrieved from http://www.bjs.gov/content/pub/pdf/bvvc.pdf

Harrell, E., Langton, L., Berzofsky, M., Couzens, L., & Smiley-McDonald, H. (2014). *Household poverty and nonfatal violent victimization, 2008–2012* (NCJ 248384). Washington, DC: U.S. Department of Justice, Office of Justice Programs, Bureau of Justice Statistics.

Himmelfarb, N., Yaeger, D., & Mintz, J. (2006). Posttraumatic stress disorder in female veterans with military and civilian sexual trauma. *Journal of Traumatic Stress, 19*(6), 837–846.

Hinduja, S., & Patchin, J. W. (2014). *Bullying beyond the schoolyard: Preventing and responding to cyberbullying.* Thousand Oaks, CA: Corwin Press.

Hines, D. A., Malley-Morrison, K., & Dutton, L. B. (2013). *Family violence in the United States: Defining, understanding, and combating abuse* (2nd ed.). Thousand Oaks, CA: Sage.

Hoffman, K., Cole, E., Playford, E. D., Grill, E., Soberg, H. L., & Brohi, K. (2014). Health outcome after major trauma: What are we measuring? *PLOS ONE, 9*(7). doi:10.1371/journal.pone.0103082

Hughes, M. J., & Jones, L. (2000). Women, domestic violence, and posttraumatic stress disorder (PTSD). *Family Therapy, 27*(3), 125–139.

Hyer, R. (2006). *Iraq and Afghanistan producing new pattern of extremity war injuries.* Retrieved from http://www.medscape.com/viewarticle/528624

Johnson, M. A., Hawley, J. S., & Theeler, B. J. (2014). Management of acute concussion in a deployed military setting. *Current Treatment Options in Neurology, 16*(9), 1–16.

Jones, L., Bellis, M. A., Wood, S., Hughes, K., McCoy, E., Eckley, L.,…Officer, A. (2012). Prevalence and risk of violence against children with disabilities: A systematic review and meta-analysis of observational studies. *The Lancet, 380*(9845), 899–907.

Joyner, J. R. (2014). *Co-occurring mild traumatic brain injury and posttraumatic stress disorder in the military* (Doctoral dissertation, Tennessee State University).

Kaltiala-Heino, R., Rimpelä, M., Marttunen, M., Rimpelä, A., & Rantanen, P. (1999). Bullying, depression, and suicidal ideation in Finnish adolescents: School survey. *British Medical Journal, 319*, 348–351.

Kimerling, R., Street, A. E., Pavao, J., Smith, M. W., Cronkite, R. C., Holmes, T. H., & Frayne, S. M. (2010). Military-related sexual trauma among Veterans Health Administration patients returning from Afghanistan and Iraq. *American Journal of Public Health, 100*(8), 1409.

Kowalski, R. M., & Limber, S. P. (2013). Psychological, physical, and academic correlates of cyberbullying and traditional bullying. *Journal of Adolescent Health, 53*(1), S13–S20.

Kshirsagar, V. Y., Agarwal, R., & Bavdekar, S. B. (2007). Bullying in schools: Prevalence and short-term impact. *Indian Pediatrics, 44*(1), 25–28.

Kuipers, E., Garety, P., Fowler, D., Freeman, D., Dunn, G., & Bebbington, P. (2006). Cognitive, emotional, and social processes in psychosis: Refining cognitive behavioral therapy for persistent positive symptoms. *Schizophrenia Bulletin, 32*(Suppl. 1), S24–S31.

Kumpulainen, K. (2008). Psychiatric conditions associated with bullying. *International Journal of Adolescent Medicine and Health, 20*(2), 121–132.

Lawhorne, C., & Philpott, D. (2011). *Combat-related traumatic brain injury and PTSD: A resource and recovery guide* (Vol. 3). Lanham, MD: Government Institutes.

Lightfoot, E., & Williams, O. (2009). The intersection of disability, diversity, and domestic violence: Results of national focus groups. *Journal of Aggression, Maltreatment & Trauma, 18*(2), 133–152.

Ling, G., Bandak, F., & Rocco Armonda, R. (2009). Explosive blast neurotrauma. *Journal of Neutrotrauma, 26*, 815–825.

Margolin, G., & Vickerman, K. A. (2007). Posttraumatic stress in children and adolescents exposed to family violence: I. Overview and issues. *Professional Psychology: Research and Practice, 38*(6), 613–619. doi:10.1037/0735-7028.38.6.613

McMahon, B. T., & Domer, T. M. (1997). Twenty questions surrounding unpaid medical leave: Navigating the Bermuda Triangle of employment law. *Work, 9*(2), 129–145.

Meyer, K., Ivins, B., Doncevic, S., Lew, H., Trudel, T., & Jaffee, M. S. (2011). Traumatic brain injury in the context of war. In J. M. Silver, T. W. McAllister, & S. C. Yudofsky (Eds.), *Textbook of traumatic brain injury* (2nd ed., pp. 415–426). Washington, DC: American Psychiatric Publishing.

Millar, A. (2013). Trauma therapy: An Adlerian perspective. *Journal of Individual Psychology, 69*(3), 245–261.

Morrison, D. R., & Casper, M. J. (2012). Intersections of disability studies and critical trauma studies: A provocation. *Disability Studies Quarterly, 32*(2), 8.

McNamee, S., Howe, L., Nakase-Richardson, R., & Peterson, M. (2012). Treatment of disorders of consciousness in the Veterans Health Administration polytrauma centers. *Journal of Head Trauma Rehabilitation, 27*(4), 244–252.

Mittenberg, W., Rotholc, A., Russell, E., & Heilbronner, R. (1996). Identification of malingered head injury on the Halstead-Reitan Battery. *Archives of Clinical Neuropsychology, 11*(4), 271–281. doi:10.1016/0887-6177(95)00040-2

Movement Advancement Project, National Center for Transgender Equality, Transgender Law Center. (2015). *Understanding issues facing transgender Americans.* Retrieved from http://www.lgbtmap.org/file/understanding-issues-facing-transgender-americans.pdf

Nansel, T. R., Overpeck, M., Pilla, R. S., Ruan, W. J., Simons-Morton, B., & Scheidt, P. (2001). Bullying behaviors among US youth: Prevalence and association with psychosocial adjustment. *Journal of the American Medical Association, 285*(16), 2094–2100.

National Center for PTSD. (2013). *Understanding PTSD treatment.* Retrieved from http://www.ptsd.va.gov/public/understanding_TX/booklet.pdf

National Coalition of Anti-Violence Programs. (2015). *Anti-violence project.* Retrieved from http://www.avp.org/about-avp/coalitions-a-collaborations/82-national-coalition-of-anti-violence-programs

National Council on Disability. (2009*). Invisible wounds: Serving service members and veterans with PTSD and TBI.* Retrieved from https://www.ncd.gov/publications/2009/March042009

National Crime Prevention Council. (2015). *Cyberbullying.* Retrieved from http://www.ncpc.org/topics/cyberbullying

Office for Victims of Crime. (n.d.). *Crime victims with disabilities.* Office for Victims of Crime. Retrieved from http://ovc.ncjrs.gov/topic.aspx?topicid=62

Ogilvie, B., & Tamlyn, E. (2012). Coming full circle: How VBA can complement recent changes in DoD and VHA policy regarding military sexual trauma. *Veterans Law Review, 4*, 1.

Patchin, J. W., & Hinduja, S. (2006). Bullies move beyond the schoolyard: A preliminary look at cyberbullying. *Youth Violence and Juvenile Justice, 4*(2), 148–169.

Paterson, J. (2011). Bullies with byte. *Counseling Today, 53*(12), 44.

Petraglia, A. L., Maroon, J. C., & Bailes, J. E. (2012). From the field of play to the field of combat: A review of the pharmacological management of concussion. *Neurosurgery, 70*(6), 1520–1533.

Plummer, S. B., & Findley, P. A. (2012). Women with disabilities' experience with physical and sexual abuse review of the literature and implications for the field. *Trauma, Violence, & Abuse, 13*(1), 15–29.

Posey, D. (in progress). *A grounded theory investigation of the experiences of rehabilitation administrators, counselors, and supervisors providing services to women with disabilities experiencing intimate partner violence* (Unpublished doctoral dissertation). University of Arkansas, Fayetteville, AR.

Pugh, M. J. V., Finley, E. P., Copeland, L. A., Wang, C. P., Noel, P. H., Amuan, M. E., … Pugh, J. A. (2014). Complex comorbidity clusters in OEF/OIF veterans: The polytrauma clinical triad and beyond. *Medical Care, 52*(2), 172–181.

Ramirez, D. A., Lyman, D., Jobe-Shields, L., George, P., Dougherty, R., Daniels, A.,… Delhin-Rittmon, M. (2014). Trauma-focused cognitive-behavioral therapy for children and adolescents: Assessing the evidence. *Psychiatric Services, 65*(5), 591–602.

Ramirez, R. (2014). Becoming more trauma-informed. *American Jails, 27*(6), 25.

Reed, K. P., Cooper, R. L., Nugent, W. R., & Russell, K. (2016). Cyberbullying: A literature review of its relationship to adolescent depression and current intervention strategies. *Journal of Human Behavior in the Social Environment, 26*(1), 37–45.

Rubin, S., Roessler, R., & Rumrill, P. (2016). *Foundations of the vocational rehabilitation process* (7th ed.). Austin, TX: Pro-Ed.

Salmivalli, C., & Peets, K. (2009). Bullies, victims, and bully–victim relationships in middle childhood and early adolescence. In K. H. Rubin, W. M. Bukowski, & B. Laursen (Eds.), *Handbook of peer interactions, relationships, and groups* (pp. 322–340). New York, NY: Guilford Press.

Sansone, R. A., & Sansone, L. A. (2008). Bully victims: Psychological and somatic aftermaths. *Psychiatry, 5*(6), 62–64.

Saxe, G. N., Ellis, B. H., & Kaplow, J. B. (2007). *Collaborative treatment of traumatized children and teens: The trauma systems therapy approach.* New York, NY: Guilford Press.

Shaw, L., Chan, F., McMahon, B. T., & Kim, J. H. (2012). Employee and employer characteristics associated with elevated risk of filing disability harassment charges. *Journal of Vocational Rehabilitation, 36*(3), 187–197.

Shaw, W. S., Tveito, T. H., Geehern-Lavoie, M., Huang, Y. H., Nicholas, M. K., Reme, S. E., … Pransky, G. (2012). Adapting principles of chronic pain self-management to the workplace. *Disability and Rehabilitation, 34*(8), 694–703.

Solovieva, T. I., & Walls, R. T. (2014). Barriers to traumatic brain injury services and supports in rural setting. *Journal of Rehabilitation, 80*(4), 10–18.

Stalker, K., & McArthur, K. (2012). Child abuse, child protection and disabled children: A review of recent research. *Child Abuse Review, 21*(1), 24–40.

Strauser, D. (2013). *Career development, employment, and disability in rehabilitation.* New York, NY: Springer Publishing Company.

Strauser, D. R., & Lustig, D. C. (2001). The implications of posttraumatic stress disorder on vocational behavior and rehabilitation planning. *Journal of Rehabilitation, 67*(4), 26–30.

Strauser, D. R., Lustig, D. C., Cogdal, P. A., & Uruk, A. Ç. (2006). Trauma symptoms: Relationship with career thoughts, vocational identity, and developmental work personality. *The Career Development Quarterly, 54*(4), 346–360.

Substance Abuse and Mental Health Services Administration. (2014). *Trauma-informed care in behavioral health services.* Treatment Improvement Protocol (TIP) Series 57. HHS Publication No. (SMA) 13–4801. Rockville, MD: Author.

Sue, D. W. (2010). *Microaggressions in everyday life: Race, gender, and sexual orientation.* Hoboken, NJ: Wiley.

Surís, A., & Lind, L. (2008). Military sexual trauma: A review of prevalence and associated health consequences in veterans. *Trauma, Violence, & Abuse, 9*(4), 250–269.

Sutton, A. M., Deutsh, P. M., Weed, R. O., & Berens, D. E. (2002). Reliability of life care plans: A comparison of original and updated plans. *Journal of Life Care Planning, 1*(3), 187–194.

Swearer, S. M., Song, S. Y., Cary, P. T., Eagle, J. W., & Mickelson, W. T. (2001). Psychosocial correlates in bullying and victimization: The relationship between depression, anxiety, and bully/victim status. *Journal of Emotional Abuse, 2*(2–3), 95–121.

Thomas, A. J., & Schwarzbaum, S.E. (2010). *Culture and identity: Life stories for counselors and therapists.* Thousand Oaks, CA: Sage.

Tolan, P., Gorman-Smith, D., & Henry, D. (2006). Family violence. *Annual Review of Psychology, 57*, 557–583.

Truman, J. L., & Langton, L. (2014). *Criminal victimization, 2013.* Washington, DC: U.S. Department of Justice. Retrieved from http://www.bjs.gov/content/pub/pdf/cv13.pdf

Truman, J. L., & Planty, M. (2014). *Criminal victimization, 2011.* Washington, DC: U.S. Department of Justice. Retrieved from http://www.bjs.gov/content/pub/pdf/cv11.pdf

Tschopp, M. K., Bishop, M., & Mulvihill, M. (2001). Career development of individuals with psychiatric disabilities: An ecological perspective of barriers and interventions. *Journal of Applied Rehabilitation Counseling, 32*(3), 25–30.

Tyiska, C. G. (n.d.). *Working with victims of crime with disabilities.* National Organization for Victim Assistance. Retrieved from https://www.ncjrs.gov/ovc_archives/factsheets/disable.htm

U.S. Commission on Civil Rights. (2013). *Sexual assault in the military.* U.S. Commission on Civil Rights. 2013 Statutory Enforcement Report. Retrieved from http://www.usccr.gov/pubs/09242013_Statutory_Enforcement_Report_Sexual_Assault_in_the_Military.pdf

U.S. Department of Education Office for Civil Rights. (2014). *Responding to bullying of students with disabilities.* Retrieved from http://www2.ed.gov/about/offices/list/ocr/letters/colleague-bullying-201410.pdf

U.S. Department of Health and Human Services. (2013). *Child maltreatment 2013.* Retrieved from https://www.acf.hhs.gov/sites/default/files/cb/cm2013.pdf

U.S. Department of Justice. (2014). *Crime in the United States, 2013*. Uniform Crime Report. U.S. Department of Justice–Federal Bureau of Investigation. Retrieved from http://www .fbi.gov/about-us/cjis/ucr/crime-in-the-u.s/2013/crime-in-the-u.s.-2013/violent -crime/violent-crime-topic-page/violentcrimemain_final.pdf

U.S. Department of Veterans Affairs. (n.d.). *Military sexual trauma*. Retrieved from http:// www.mentalhealth.va.gov/msthome.asp

U.S. Department of Veterans Affairs. (2010). *Traumatic brain injury*. Department of Veterans Affairs. Employee Education System. Retrieved from http://www.publichealth .va.gov/docs/vhi/traumatic-brain-injury-vhi.pdf

U.S. Department of Veterans Affairs. (2015a). *How common is PTSD?* Retrieved from http:// www.ptsd.va.gov/public/PTSD-overview/basics/how-common-is-ptsd.asp

U.S. Department of Veterans Affairs. (2015b). *Polytrauma/TBI system of care*. Retrieved from http://www.polytrauma.va.gov/news-and-resources/terminology-and-definitions .asp

U.S. Office on Violence Against Women. (2014). *Domestic violence*. Retrieved from http:// www.justice.gov/ovw/domestic-violence

Valdez, C., Kimerling, R., Hyun, J. K., Mark, H. F., Saweikis, M., & Pavao, J. (2011). Veterans Health Administration mental health treatment settings of patients who report military sexual trauma. *Journal of Trauma & Dissociation, 12*(3), 232–243.

van der Kolk, B. A. (2003). The neurobiology of childhood trauma and abuse. *Child and Adolescent Psychiatric Clinics of North America, 12*(2), 293–317.

van der Kolk, B. A., Roth, S., Pelcovitz, D., Sunday, S., Spinazzola, J., & Kilpatrick, D. (2005). Disorders of extreme stress: The empirical foundation of a complex adaptation to trauma. *Journal of Traumatic Stress, 18*(5), 389–399.

Waghorn, G., Saha, S., Harvey, C., Morgan, V., Waterreus, A., Bush, R.,... Porter, R. (2012). "Earning and learning" in those with psychotic disorders: The second Australian national survey of psychosis. *Australian and New Zealand Journal of Psychiatry, 46*(8), 774–785.

Warshaw, C., Sullivan, C. M., & Rivera, E. A. (2013). *A systematic review of trauma-focused interventions for domestic violence survivors*. National Center on Domestic Violence, Trauma & Mental Health. Retrieved from http://www.nationalcenterdvtraumamh .org/wp-content/uploads/2013/03/NCDVTMH_EBPLitReview2013.pdf

Wolf, G. K., Strom, T. Q., Kehle, S. M., & Eftekhari, A. (2012). A preliminary examination of prolonged exposure therapy with Iraq and Afghanistan veterans with a diagnosis of posttraumatic stress disorder and mild to moderate traumatic brain injury. *Journal of Head Trauma Rehabilitation, 27*(1), 26–32.

Wolke, D., Woods, S., Bloomfield, L., & Karstadt, L. (2001). Bullying involvement in primary school and common health problems. *Archives of Disease in Childhood, 85*(3), 197–201.

World Health Organization. (2014). *Injuries and violence: The facts 2014*. Retrieved from http://www.who.int/iris/handle/10665/149798#sthash.orTUv3TT.dpuf

Young, J., Ne'eman, A., & Gesler, S. (2016). *Brief paper: Bullying and students with disabilities*. Retrieved from https://www.ncd.gov/policy/briefing-paper-bullying-and-students -disabilities

Zadov, Y., Eapen, B., & Cifu, D. (n.d.). *The Polytrauma Transitional Rehabilitation Programs: A novel approach to community reintegration and return to work for America's heroes in the Veterans Health Administration*. Alexandria, VA: International Brain Injury Association. Retrieved from http://www.internationalbrain.org/the-polytrauma-transitional- rehabilitation-programs-veterans

EIGHT

Rehabilitation Counseling Implications

CHAPTER OBJECTIVES

- *Identify medical, psychosocial, and vocational issues across emerging disability populations that should be addressed in the rehabilitation process*
- *Discuss the application of the ecological model developed by Szymanski, Hershenson, Ettinger, and Enright (1998) as a framework for assessment and planning with consumers who have emerging disabilities*
- *Examine the role that rehabilitation counselors can play in responding to issues affecting the lives of people with emerging disabilities in each phase of the rehabilitation process*

As noted in Chapter 1, individuals with emerging disabilities are an underserved rehabilitation counseling population who stand to substantially benefit from rehabilitation services to achieve their independent living, community integration, educational, and employment goals. Although rapidly growing in number, individuals with emerging disabilities encounter numerous internal and external barriers to overall quality of life. The purpose of this chapter is to synthesize information from the preceding chapters into a framework for providing more responsive and effective rehabilitation services to these individuals. Key issues garnered from the research on emerging disabilities that should be addressed in the rehabilitation process include the following:

- The chronicity of emerging disabilities and multitude of symptoms and functional limitations resulting from these conditions
- The frequent co-occurrence of additional disabilities that often go unrecognized and untreated
- The disproportionate rate of emerging disabilities in socially and economically disadvantaged populations
- The diagnostic uncertainties and medical invalidation that adversely affect physical functioning and psychosocial and vocational adjustment
- The hidden and episodic nature of many emerging disabilities
- The stigma, myths, and prejudices associated with emerging disabilities and their impact on health and well-being

- The isolation experienced by many individuals with emerging disabilities
- The need to consider the individuals' responses to the causes of their emerging disabilities
- The importance of considering the developmental stage of the individual at onset of disability
- The emphasis on integrated treatment and rehabilitation to support individuals in achieving their rehabilitation goals
- The need for individuals to learn and practice illness self-management strategies and apply these strategies to work
- The role that peer supports play in the psychosocial and vocational adjustment of people with emerging disabilities
- The importance of inclusive educational, community, and workplace environments to the rehabilitation of these individuals
- The unique considerations in accommodation planning with individuals with emerging disabilities
- The pressing need for follow-along services after initial job placement to support these individuals in maintaining employment and advancing in their careers

The following sections address the role of rehabilitation counselors in responding to these issues, beginning with their own engagement in active self-reflection, and continuing through each phase of the rehabilitation process including (a) outreach and eligibility determination; (b) assessment and planning; (c) service delivery; (d) job placement and follow-up; and (e) accommodation planning.

SELF-REFLECTIVE PRACTICE

Throughout this book, we have addressed the need for rehabilitation counselors to engage in active and ongoing reflection about their professional practices. This step is imperative in providing responsive services to individuals with emerging disabilities because they have had so many encounters with stigmatization, invalidation, and marginalization. The concept of reflective practice, as originated by Schön (1983), has been explored in depth in fields as diverse as medicine, education, counseling, and social work (Shaw & Gould, 2001; White, 2001). Skovholt and Rønnestad (1992) identified continuous reflection about one's practices as the most important factor in the ongoing professional development of counselors and therapists. The term "reflective practice" (Schön, 1983) refers to the ability of counselors to work beyond the mere technical knowledge of their field and bring creativity and insight into their work. Reflective practice has been taught in counselor education as the practice of realizing one's own strengths and capitalizing on those strengths while also realizing one's limitations and acknowledging areas of potential growth. The ability of rehabilitation counselors to truly know themselves and come to know each consumer as an individual requires engagement in a deep level of personal and professional reflection (Collins, Arthur, & Wong-Wylie, 2010).

Reflective practice enables rehabilitation counselors to identify their own biases and misunderstandings about emerging disabilities and to seek out opportunities for self-correction to prevent further marginalization of these individuals. The reflective process is initiated by identifying "hitches" in one's practice and posing questions regarding one's own contributions to these problems rather than locating the source of the problem as the consumer (Koch & Arhar, 2002). We have posed self-reflective questions that rehabilitation counselors can ask themselves in various chapters. Perhaps the most important questions that rehabilitation counselors can ask themselves to begin the process of enhancing their understanding of and capacity to work effectively with people with emerging disabilities include the following:

- How do I personally define disability and do I need to rethink and reconstruct my definition in order to work effectively with people with emerging disabilities?
- What biases and misperceptions do I have about emerging disabilities and how can I correct these?
- What are my beliefs regarding whether people whose disabling conditions are less obvious and more difficult to measure should have access to rehabilitation services (Fox & Kim, 2004)?
- Should individuals with medically unexplained symptoms have access to rehabilitation services?
- Am I communicating with consumers with emerging disabilities in a manner that validates or invalidates their experiences?
- Do I have adequate knowledge and expertise to effectively serve individuals with emerging disabilities?

Asking themselves these questions prompts rehabilitation counselors to actively seek out learning experiences; consult with supervisors, health care professionals, medical providers, and individuals with emerging disabilities; and identify other opportunities to mitigate their biases and misunderstandings. Because individuals with emerging disabilities cite the lack of service providers' knowledge and understanding about their conditions as major sources of distress, the willingness of rehabilitation counselors to engage in a process of ongoing reflection and continuing education is paramount. As the universe of disability expands, rehabilitation counselors must assume the role of lifelong learners, continually updating their knowledge and skills by staying current with the rehabilitation literature, joining professional associations, and attending rehabilitation conferences. The reflective process points rehabilitation counselors in the direction of where to expand their expertise. It also indicates areas where rehabilitation counselors can advocate for changes to agency policies and procedures that create barriers to serving individuals with emerging disabilities.

Because emerging disabilities are overrepresented in socially and economically disadvantaged groups, reflective practice is also a critical component in the development of multicultural counseling competencies. Therefore, in addition to identifying potential sources of bias related to emerging disabilities, rehabilitation counselors must also engage in the reflective process to identify and challenge potential biases related to gender, race, ethnicity, sexual orientation, gender identity, age, religion, and other characteristics of individuals that could undermine the ability to provide responsive and effective services to members of culturally diverse populations.

OUTREACH AND ELIGIBILITY DETERMINATION

We have established that many individuals with emerging disabilities may be unaware of the availability of rehabilitation services within their communities; therefore, it is likely that broader outreach and education will become an increasingly prominent task of rehabilitation counselors if they are to increase access to services for contemporary rehabilitation populations, especially underrepresented populations who have the highest rates of emerging disabilities. We have also established throughout this book that, even if they are aware of services, many individuals may not identify themselves as persons with disabilities and are, consequently, unlikely to view rehabilitation programs as potential resources. Thus, outreach is needed to inform these individuals about how various rehabilitation agencies define and conceptualize disability as well as the services these agencies provide. This information can be provided in formats such as educational seminars and workshops to self-help and advocacy groups, sessions at consumer conferences, presentations to community organizations, and outreach to patients of primary care providers and medical specialists.

In outreach efforts, it may be necessary to use language such as "people with chronic health conditions" or "people with health issues that interfere with working" in marketing materials, verbal communications, intake interviews, and eligibility criteria (Koch, Conyers, & Rumrill, 2012). Rehabilitation counselors who provide transition services to youths with emerging disabilities should also be aware that many of these youths do not have individualized education plans (IEPs) or individualized transition plans (ITPs). Thus, outreach to administrators, school counselors, mental health counselors who provide school-based services, teachers, school psychologists, parents, and students may be necessary to ensure that these students are made aware of the availability of rehabilitation services.

We have also established that medical and health care professionals may lack awareness of the availability of rehabilitation services. In addition, as we have discussed in other chapters of this book, physicians often give individuals with emerging disabilities mixed messages about their capacity to enter employment or continue working. Consequently, individuals with emerging disabilities may themselves question their ability to work. Thus, education about the health-related benefits of employment must target both health care and medical providers as well as individuals with emerging disabilities. In communicating the health-related benefits of employment, rehabilitation counselors can cite examples from the research. For example, in addition to wages, salaries, and employee benefits that are needed to purchase nutritious food, receive medical care, obtain safe housing, and participate in health-promoting physical activities (Robert Wood Johnson Foundation, 2013), researchers in vocational and organizational psychology have identified psychological benefits that can improve one's physical and emotional well-being. Work increases social status; provides a daily structure or routine; affords opportunities for social interaction, support, and recognition; connects people with goals and purposes; provides a sense of identity; and provides opportunities for physical and mental activity (Jahoda, 1982; Ross & Mirowsky, 1995). Conversely, unemployment results in a restriction of choices, reduced opportunities to use one's skills, limited social contacts, feelings of reduced control over one's life, and uncertainty about the future. The absence of the socially sanctioned role of worker can undermine the self-esteem of those who are unemployed, particularly in cultures where individuals are defined by their occupational roles.

Accumulating research evidence documents the health benefits of work in samples of individuals with emerging disabilities such as arthritis, autoimmune disorders, and serious mental illness (e.g., Bond et al., 2001; Dunn, Wewiorski, & Rogers, 2008; Grønning, Rødevand, & Steinsbekk, 2010; Hall, Kuarth, & Hunt, 2013; Hergenrather, Zeglin, McGuire-Kuletz, & Rhodes, 2015; Miller & Dishon, 2006; Patti et al., 2007). These studies have linked employment to health outcomes such as improved quality of life, decreased symptoms, improved mental health, decreased hospitalizations, reduced health risk behaviors, reduced health care expenditures, and improved self-reported health status.

Eligibility determination can be a challenge for rehabilitation counselors and consumers, particularly when individuals exhibit less apparent physical disability and/or conditions that are less clearly defined by law or public policies (Fox & Kim, 2004; Koch et al., 2012). Additionally, eligibility criteria that categorize individuals in an "either/or status [as] able or disabled, employable or unemployable" (Vick & Lightman, 2010, p. 76) can exclude individuals whose emerging disabilities are episodic or of unknown etiology. Finally, at the onset of symptoms, individuals with some emerging disabilities may not experience barriers to employment, but these individuals are often in need of rehabilitation services offered in an early intervention framework to prevent permanent work disability when their condition worsens or progresses. Furthermore, youths and young adults with emerging disabilities who acquire disabilities during the career exploration stage of their development (e.g., psychiatric disabilities) may need early intervention services to reassure them that employment is still an achievable goal and to assist them to reengage in important career development activities (i.e., returning to high school or college after withdrawing from courses to treat their conditions). Those with emerging disabilities with onset during career establishment or maintenance phases often require early intervention from rehabilitation counselors to prevent premature departure from the workforce. Determining eligibility, with the aforementioned considerations in mind, will enable rehabilitation counselors and consumers to better document the need for services and to provide concrete evidence for this need when medical documentation is missing, inconclusive, or debated— or when symptoms and functional limitations are not present on diagnosis but will develop over time.

When rehabilitation counselors meet for the first time with consumers who have an emerging disability that is new or unfamiliar, they should conduct preliminary research about the condition before the initial interview. It can be a great source of frustration for an individual with an emerging disability to meet with a health or rehabilitation professional who does not have at least a basic understanding of the condition and to be put in the position of having to educate the professional about the condition in lieu of doing what is necessary to move quickly toward resolution of the consumer's concerns. Good general sources of information include the Centers for Disease Control and Prevention, the National Institutes of Health, the World Health Organization, and the National Organization for Rare Disorders. Information can be obtained through the websites of these organizations, which also provide links to organizations focused on specific emerging disabilities. A caveat to keep in mind is that, in many cases, information obtained from these sources may conflict with the experiences of individuals with emerging disabilities. Therefore, information should also be obtained from consumer self-help and advocacy organizations. At the same time, the rehabilitation counselor wants to recognize that consumers, themselves, are the best experts on their emerging disability and its impact on their lives.

Whereas some individuals with emerging disabilities will state a clear desire to enter or retain work, others may be uncertain, and an important component of eligibility determination and rehabilitation assessment is to assist these individuals with decision making to determine if employment is a desired and feasible goal. The considering work model (Goldblum & Kohlenberg, 2005) provides guidelines for assisting consumers to determine if work is a goal they want to pursue. As we have discussed, for many individuals with emerging disabilities, work can alleviate some of the detrimental effects of their conditions. For others, it can potentially worsen their condition, disqualify them from receiving much-needed disability benefits, and/or require them to devote all of their mental and physical capacities to working, leaving them incapable of participating in other meaningful life activities. Therefore, each case needs to be assessed in an individualized manner wherein the rights and responsibilities to make decisions about work rest solely with the consumer. In facilitating the process of decision making regarding employment, disability factors (e.g., disease course, symptoms, physical capacities, functional limitations, medication side effects) should be considered in a medical assessment of feasibility to work. Potential accommodations for these disability-related barriers should also be explored as part of this medical assessment. The impact of employment on financial security must also be assessed and should take into consideration the impact of employment on government or private disability income and medical benefits. It is important to educate consumers about work incentives at this point in the assessment so that they can make informed decisions about employment. Another focus of the assessment is the impact of employment on other important life domains such as family, community involvement, leisure, and recreation. If employment, even with the provision of reasonable accommodations in a supportive work environment, leaves consumers so exhausted or in so much pain that they cannot participate in these other life domains, employment may not be a reasonable goal. Finally, consideration of the impact of occupational stress on disability and health and strategies to minimize stress at work should be included in this assessment. Examining each of these factors enables the individual to evaluate the risks and benefits of entering employment, returning to work, or continuing to work, with information provided by the rehabilitation counselor to enable informed decision making by the consumer.

For some individuals with emerging disabilities (e.g., individuals who have acquired disabilities from domestic abuse, veterans with disabilities reentering civilian life, individuals with psychiatric disabilities released from jails and prisons, individuals who have acquired disabilities in natural disasters), it will be necessary during intake interviews to determine if their basic needs (e.g., safety, shelter, food, clothing, transportation) are met. If not, referrals and/or rehabilitation services to address these needs will be necessary. Until or unless their basic needs are met, it will be difficult to impossible for these consumers to actively participate in the rehabilitation planning process.

Because rehabilitation counselors must often make medical referrals to establish program eligibility and identify service needs, it is crucial that they identify the most appropriate specialists to ensure an accurate evaluation. Many emerging disabilities are not the result of any one etiology, and the process of evaluation may be fraught with misdiagnoses or disagreements among professionals regarding the presence of a disabling condition or its underlying cause and appropriate course of treatment. Making inappropriate referrals may result in duplicative and unnecessary tests and procedures that exacerbate applicants' stress, further undermine their health, and unnecessarily prolong the time from eligibility determination to plan development. Even further complicating the challenge of making appropriate referral is the presence of co-occurring conditions that is so common among individuals with emerging disabilities.

In identifying and making appropriate referrals to specialists, rehabilitation counselors should seek input from medical consultants. However, it must be kept in mind that these consultants may have their own biases and misperceptions about emerging disabilities. Consumer advocacy organizations can also be consulted to assist with identifying local community providers who are knowledgeable about the various conditions that fall under the category of emerging disabilities. Furthermore, rehabilitation counselors should also be cognizant about screening for secondary conditions (e.g., substance use disorders, depression, anxiety, co-occurring chronic illnesses) because, again, these frequently co-occur with emerging disabilities. Secondary conditions may, in some cases, create greater barriers to rehabilitation goal achievement than the primary condition presented by the consumer.

In conclusion, determining eligibility for consumers with emerging disabilities is unlikely to be a straightforward process. Suggestions for facilitating effective decision making by the rehabilitation counselor–consumer dyad include the following:

- Instead of approaching eligibility determination from a biomedical framework, use an ecological framework to gain a more holistic understanding of the individual's challenges and rehabilitation needs as well as the factors and processes that influence these.
- De-emphasize medical diagnoses and focus assessment questions and evaluations on the individual's symptoms, functional limitations, functional capacities, and the impact these have on their interactions with natural, built, cultural, attitudinal, and social environments.
- Consider both current and future levels of functioning.
- Assess causal factors (e.g., violence, trauma, poverty, natural disasters, unknown etiology, health care inequities) related to reported symptoms and functional limitations and how these shape and influence service needs.
- Determine if the individual's basic needs are met.
- Assess the individual's social supports, resources, and gaps that can be filled by specific rehabilitation services to support maximal functioning.
- For individuals who are uncertain about their desire or capacity to work, the considering work model can be used as a framework for decision making and planning.
- Be sure to make referrals to appropriate medical specialists.
- Screen for co-occurring disorders.

REHABILITATION ASSESSMENT AND PLANNING

In this book, we have introduced various models for the treatment and management of emerging disabilities including patient-centered medical homes, wraparound transition planning models for youths with emerging disabilities, integrated treatment for psychiatric disabilities and co-occurring substance use disorders, trauma-informed care, the biopsychosocial model for pain treatment and management, collaborative documentation, and the recovery model for individuals with psychiatric disabilities. These models encompass the very principles of holistic, individualized rehabilitation planning that emphasize consumer choice and self-determination. In fact, Szymanski, Hershenson, Ettinger, and Enright (1996) proposed an ecological framework for assessment and planning that encompasses the critical components of each of the aforementioned models and incorporates consideration of all the interacting factors and processes impacting the psychosocial and vocational experiences of individuals with emerging disabilities. Table 8.1 provides definitions and examples of the factors and processes affecting the lived experiences of people with emerging disabilities.

The ecological model has been demonstrated to be a useful framework for understanding the psychosocial and vocational impact of emerging disabilities such as HIV (Conyers, 2004) and multiple chemical sensitivity (MCS) (Koch, Rumrill, Hennessey, Vierstra, & Roessler, 2007). In addition to using this model as a framework for rehabilitation assessment and planning, research indicates that rehabilitation counselors should use an integrated, interdisciplinary approach that is ideally provided in a single setting (e.g., medical homes, schools, pain management programs, college counseling centers, mental health agencies). The integrated, interdisciplinary team is likely to include professionals such as school personnel, postsecondary disability service providers, physicians, physical therapists, occupational therapists, psychiatrists, psychologists, mental health counselors, and specialists in complementary and integrative health. Access to rehabilitation services is improved by decentralizing rehabilitation and independent living specialists and stationing these specialists in settings where individuals with emerging disabilities receive health, medical, mental health, and social services (e.g., pain clinics, public health agencies, physicians' offices, community mental health centers, college counseling centers, medical centers, hospitals). Furthermore, an emphasis in the research on treatment and rehabilitation is placed on long-term service provision. Given this need, pooling of resources from multiple agencies and programs is likely to be necessary so that funding is available for providing these prolonged services.

REHABILITATION SERVICES

Identifying services to include in the rehabilitation plan involves the same individualized approach with an emphasis on consumer choice and involvement that is used with all consumers. Likewise, rehabilitation consumers with emerging disabilities stand to benefit from the same services (e.g., counseling and guidance, training, physical and psychological restoration services, maintenance, transportation, tools and equipment, assistive technology, job development and placement) as consumers with traditional disabilities. However, we have identified some key

TABLE 8.1 Application of the Ecological Model to Assessment and Planning With Rehabilitation Consumers Who Have Emerging Disabilities

Constructs	Examples
Individual—attributes of the individual	Disproportionate rates of emerging disabilities among women, racially and ethnically diverse populations, and older Americans
	Chronicity, multitude of symptoms and functional limitations, episodic nature of emerging disabilities
	Range and intrusiveness of symptoms
	Progressive nature of some emerging disabilities
	Co-occurring chronic illnesses and disabilities
	Coping skills
Contextual—situations in which people live or have lived	Overrepresentation of people with emerging disabilities living in poverty
	Family response to emerging disability
	Intimate partner violence
	War
	Climate change and natural disasters
	Overrepresentation of people with psychiatric disabilities in jails and prisons
	Workplace bullying, microaggressions, and incivilities
	School bullying
	Disability legislation
	Violence
Mediating—individual, cultural, or societal beliefs that impact interaction of individuals with their environments	Medical skepticism and invalidation
	Societal stigma, myths, and misunderstandings about emerging disabilities
	Internalized stigma
	Absence of disability identification among many individuals with emerging disabilities
	Self-efficacy in coping with emerging disabilities
	Negative medical and rehabilitation outcome expectations of people with emerging disabilities
	Employer and coworker attitudes
Environmental—elements and structures of environments that impact individuals' behaviors	Physical and attitudinal accessibility of community, school, and work environments
	Air quality of indoor environments
	Unsafe housing
	Organizational culture
	Occupational stressors
Outcome—behaviors or states resulting from the interaction of the other constructs	Recovery
	Symptoms reduction versus symptoms exacerbation
	Quality of life
	Employment versus unemployment and disengagement from the workforce

(continued)

TABLE 8.1 Application of the Ecological Model to Assessment and Planning With Rehabilitation Consumers Who Have Emerging Disabilities (*continued*)

Processes	Examples
Congruence—match or mismatch of individuals with their environments	Match or mismatch with job
	Safety of home environments
	Availability of classroom and job accommodations
	Inclusive versus noninclusive work and school environments
Decision making—processes by which individuals consider options and make decisions	Readiness to change
	Choosing to work
	Disability disclosure
	Illness self-management
	Accommodation planning
	Self-determination and active engagement of youths with emerging disabilities in transition planning
	Making choices about treatment and rehabilitation options
Developmental—changes over time linked with characteristics and perceptions of the individual	Developmental stage at onset of emerging disability
	Stage of readiness for change
	Age-appropriateness of rehabilitation interventions
Socialization—process by which individuals learn life roles	Family and peer supports or lack thereof
	Social isolation
	Opportunities to learn about work
	Socialization into deviant or inferior life and work roles
	Inclusion in communities, schools, and workplaces
Allocation—process by which societal gatekeepers channel individuals into or exclude them from specific life directions	Medical diagnosis versus misdiagnosis or absence of diagnosis
	Lack of availability of transition services for youths with emerging disabilities
	Criminalization of psychiatric disabilities
	Physician recommendations to continue or discontinue working
	Exclusionary eligibility criteria of rehabilitation and disability service organizations
	Health care and rehabilitation inequities
Chance—unforeseen events	Natural disasters
	Chemical exposures
	Random exposure to violence
	Accidents

Adapted from Szymanski et al. (1998).

considerations in implementing these services as well as specific services that have been demonstrated through research to be potentially beneficial to individuals with emerging disabilities. These services focus on assisting individuals to manage their illnesses; reducing the severity of their symptoms and the degree to which these interfere with functioning; treating co-occurring chronic illnesses and psychiatric disorders such as anxiety, depression, and addictions; and improving their overall quality of life.

Counseling, Guidance, and Advocacy

Living with an emerging disability can tax the coping abilities of even the most resilient individuals and those who have unequivocal access to the resources needed to facilitate effective coping. Emerging disabilities and their associated challenges are real and not artifacts of the individual's faulty or unrealistic cognitions. All interactions between the rehabilitation counselor and consumer should be based on this premise. Skepticism on the part of the rehabilitation counselor about the legitimacy of the consumer's disability experience will preclude the establishment of a strong working alliance, effective planning, and positive rehabilitation outcomes.

The process of establishing trust is especially important when working with consumers with emerging disabilities. As we have noted multiple times throughout this book, these individuals have often felt misunderstood and invalidated by medical and health care professionals, family, friends, employers, and coworkers; consequently, they may enter the rehabilitation process anticipating the same response from rehabilitation counselors. Additionally, individuals with emerging disabilities acquired from traumatic events such as war, violence, or natural disasters may have an overarching distrust of others and a sense of unsafety as a result of these traumatic experiences. Therefore, it is imperative that rehabilitation counselors communicate with individuals with emerging disabilities in a manner that emphasizes trust, safety, respect, and validation rather than judgment and skepticism. If during the intake interview, the individual appears guarded, distrustful, or defensive, the rehabilitation counselor should not appraise this demeanor as uncooperativeness or resistant. Rather, the rehabilitation counselor should empathically communicate with the consumer about the consumer's concerns and potentially negative anticipations about the rehabilitation process, the source of these anticipations, and how the rehabilitation counselor and consumer can work together in a manner that transforms negative anticipations into positive anticipations. Most importantly, rehabilitation counselors should strive to instill hope within these consumers.

Rehabilitation counselors should also be conscientious of their language and nonverbal behaviors to ensure that they are communicating in a manner that validates the consumer's experiences. For example, using "we" language instead of "I" language can minimize power imbalances and communicate to consumers that they are not alone and are valued, equal members of rehabilitation teams rather than passive recipients of services. Because individuals with emerging disabilities often do not identify themselves as persons with disabilities, choice of terminology that is consistent with the consumer's terminology is important. For example, many veterans with disabilities do not identify with the "disability" label and prefer the terms "wounded" or "injured" (Frain, Lee, Roland, & Tschopp, 2012). Furthermore, in working with transgender individuals, rehabilitation counselors should always use the individual's chosen name (Gay and Lesbian Alliance Against Defamation [GLAAD], 2015). Some individuals may be able to afford the costs of obtaining a legal name change, but others may not. Still, they should always be referred to by their chosen name. Additionally, transgender consumers should be asked about the pronoun that they would like you to use.

Counseling and guidance should be provided to address the emerging disability, its cause (e.g., violence, aging, natural disaster), and the consumer's reactions to cause of onset; the developmental stage at onset of the disability; the impact of diagnostic uncertainties and medical invalidation on psychological and physical well-being; and the societal stigma associated with the condition and its impact on psychosocial and vocational adjustment. Furthermore, establishing a strong and trusting working alliance with the rehabilitation consumer with an emerging disability will enable the rehabilitation counselor and consumer to identify co-occurring conditions that may interfere with rehabilitation planning and to determine when referrals to other service providers are warranted. Another caveat to keep in mind is that when referrals to mental health professionals are made, the rationale for these referrals should be clearly communicated, and rehabilitation counselors should emphasize that these referrals are not being made because they believe consumers' conditions are "all in their heads," but rather that they are being made to assist individuals to cope with the negative aspects of their disabilities and their experiences of being invalidated and unsupported. Finally, referrals to appropriate mental health professionals, such as rehabilitation psychologists, clinical rehabilitation counselors, or mental health professionals with specific training in other issues such as trauma, may need to be made depending on the consumer's individual circumstances.

One of the primary goals of counseling and guidance is to facilitate psychosocial adaptation to disability. However, psychosocial adaptation takes on a different meaning for individuals with emerging disabilities, and although outcomes such as acceptance of disability, adjustment, and resolution may never be achieved, it does not mean that these individuals are psychosocially maladjusted. For some individuals, particularly those with chronic pain and episodic and/or progressive disabilities, psychosocial functioning can vary from day to day or even from hour to hour, depending on the severity of their pain, the degree to which their symptoms interfere with their functionality, and the quality of their interactions with others in terms of validating or invalidating their symptoms. Likewise, individuals may never "accept" their disability. Given ongoing developments in medical research, a cure is always possible, and belief in this possibility may give them hope and promote their engagement in activities that facilitate management of their symptoms. As another example, it is difficult for many to accept chronic pain as a constant in their life, and some days may require them to "give in" to their pain as opposed to continue functioning despite the pain. From a Western perspective, "giving in" is viewed as a negative, maladaptive behavior. Yet, this behavior allows individuals to use their pain as a guide for needed rest and enables them to "be" with their pain in a way that can lead to improved functioning. Furthermore, satisfaction with life is likely to vary considerably with vacillations in the severity of their pain or other symptoms associated with emerging disabilities. Yet these individuals may still consider their overall quality of life to be quite good. With all of these considerations in mind, the best approach that rehabilitation counselors can take is to set aside their personal theories about psychosocial adjustment to disability and focus instead on supporting each individual consumer's preferences for living life with an emerging disability.

Disability disclosure is another topic that may be of concern for individuals with emerging disabilities because most of their conditions are hidden, and many have encountered negative responses when they have disclosed their disability to medical and health care professionals, significant others, and employers. Counseling and guidance to explore their feelings and concerns about disclosure, past experiences with disclosure, and strategies for disclosing in a manner that reduces the likelihood of negative responses is a critical component of establishing supportive interpersonal relationships and the job accommodations planning process.

In considering the multitude of attitudinal and environmental barriers encountered by individuals with emerging disabilities, the rehabilitation counselor's role in advocating for consumers and equipping them with the skills to self-advocate is likely to expand into new arenas. First and foremost, advocacy is needed to change rehabilitation policies and practices that discriminate against individuals with emerging disabilities. Additionally, rehabilitation counselors can advocate for implementing trauma-informed practices in their agency settings to create environments where consumers who have experienced trauma feel safe. Likewise, they can advocate for policies and practices to make offices more accessible to those with MCS and respiratory conditions. Rehabilitation counselors can take on leading roles to assist communities, schools, postsecondary institutions, and workplaces to develop policies and procedures that are inclusive of individuals with emerging disabilities. Additionally, rehabilitation counselors can join forces with consumer advocacy organizations to eliminate stigma against individuals with emerging disabilities. With the proliferation of social media technologies, they can use these technologies as formats to promote disability awareness and to reduce stigma. Rehabilitation counselors should also consider their roles in joining environmental advocacy organizations to advance policies and procedures to ensure that the needs of individuals with disabilities are included in disaster planning and the development of strategies to mitigate the negative health consequences of climate change.

Treatment and Rehabilitation Approaches

A variety of evidence-based and emerging treatment approaches have been introduced throughout this book. These include medical procedures such as pharmacological and surgical interventions; psychosocial interventions such as cognitive behavioral therapy, mindfulness approaches, and acceptance and commitment therapy; and psychoeducational interventions such as self-determination skills training, illness management and recovery programs, and family psychoeducation. Vocational rehabilitation interventions include counseling and guidance regarding disability disclosure, integrated supported employment and education, and training in the accommodations planning process. Additional interventions include peer support and self-help groups, services provided by peer professionals, and complementary and integrative health approaches.

A theme across treatment and rehabilitation approaches is that they are moderately effective at best and may work for some individuals but not others. We have previously established that individuals with emerging disabilities may exhaust their physical, emotional, and financial resources pursuing an array of treatment approaches, all of which fail to result in desired outcomes. Consequently, rehabilitation counselors and consumers must carefully evaluate what treatment and rehabilitation approaches they have received and their assessment of the effectiveness of these interventions as well as potential approaches they have yet to try that could prove to be beneficial. Along these same lines, services should be culturally appropriate and tailored to the individual's self-determined goals. Consumers should be advised of both the risk and benefits of potential interventions so they can make informed decisions about courses of treatment and rehabilitation to include in the rehabilitation plan. Individuals may become understandably discouraged when treatment approaches fail, and counseling and guidance is a critical service to provide when this occurs. Consumers should also be reassured that the services included on the rehabilitation plan will be periodically appraised with the consumer and that plans can be amended if a particular service is not viewed as helpful to the individual. Finally, many of the interventions described in this book require a substantial time commitment, investment of energy, ongoing practice, and willingness to make significant changes in one's life. Thus, rehabilitation counselors should provide support, encouragement, and reinforcement to consumers as they invest efforts in taking the necessary steps toward change.

Finding well-qualified professionals to deliver these interventions can also be a challenge. The websites of professional associations and licensing and certification bodies are good sources for identifying qualified practitioners. Consultation with interdisciplinary treatment teams can also lead to the identification of qualified providers, as can consumer self-help and advocacy organizations. In some communities, particularly smaller and rural communities, these professionals may not be available, thus restricting options and necessitating exploration of alternatives.

Health Literacy and Illness Self-Management

We have emphasized throughout this book the need for individuals with emerging disabilities to develop illness self-management skills. The adage that "knowledge is power" prevails in rehabilitation philosophy, principles, and ethical standards. Adequate understanding of one's disability or chronic illness is a precondition to illness self-management and involves making informed decisions about one's health, health care, treatment options, and rehabilitation needs. Information that enables individuals to make informed decisions includes the cause, course, and progression of their condition; nutrition; exercise; sleep hygiene; medications and treatment options; intended effects and potential side effects of medications and treatments; treatment settings; qualifications and credentials of health care and rehabilitation personnel; and financial resources for funding treatments. Education about these topics can be provided in a variety of formats including one-on-one sessions, short courses, workshops, lectures, discussion groups, educational and support groups for those who are newly diagnosed, films, YouTube videos, DVDs, pamphlets, newsletters, and websites. Organizations devoted to research and education related to specific disabilities (e.g., the National Organization of Rare Disorders) are also good resources for obtaining this information

Again, it must be kept in mind that individuals with emerging disabilities have struggled to access accurate information about their diagnoses and treatment, and, in many cases, have been misdiagnosed and misinformed. Therefore, rehabilitation counselors must take an active role in assisting consumers with emerging disabilities to access accurate information about their condition. It should also be kept in mind that, although finally receiving a diagnosis can provide relief and validation, it can also create anxiety and emotional distress, especially if the diagnosed condition has an unknown cause, is incurable, and/or is progressive. Counseling and guidance from the rehabilitation counselor can assist individuals to express and cope with these emotionally distressing feelings.

An important skill in illness self-management that we have yet to thoroughly examine in this text is health literacy. Health literacy is the capacity of individuals to acquire, process, and understand basic health information and services so that they can make informed health decisions and take personal responsibility for their health (Briggs et al., 2010; Office of Disease Prevention and Health Promotion [ODPHP], 2016; Sørensen et al., 2012). Health literacy skills include reading and understanding health information provided in pamphlets, brochures, and other publications; understanding verbal and written instructions from physicians and health care providers; comprehending information about prescription medication; reading and understanding consent forms; completing medical and insurance forms; communicating with physicians about their medical histories; and understanding the purposes of assessments and evaluations (National Institutes of Health [NIH], 2015.) Because individuals with emerging disabilities are often treated by a variety of medical and health care specialists, it is imperative that they have health literacy skills. Yet the NIH (2015) has reported that less than half of the U.S. population actually possesses these skills.

Rehabilitation counselors can play a pivotal role in assisting consumers with emerging disabilities to develop health literacy skills. Rehabilitation consumers may become overwhelmed with information provided by the rehabilitation counselor. Therefore, the first step in assisting consumers to develop health literacy skills is to communicate information about health, disability, and the rehabilitation process in a manner that is understandable by consumers and does not overwhelm them. In Table 8.2, we summarize techniques that can be used by rehabilitation counselors to ensure that their communications are understood by consumers.

TABLE 8.2 Rehabilitation Counselor Skills for Facilitating Health Literacy

- Use plain language.
- Avoid using professional jargon and explain technical terms.
- Avoid using acronyms.
- Communicate in a manner that is culturally appropriate.
- Emphasize the most important points first.
- Break down information into smaller chunks.
- Avoid overwhelming individuals with information.
- Observe the consumer's facial expressions and body language for signs of confusion or feeling overwhelmed with information.
- Provide information both verbally and in writing.
- Use visual aids and diagrams.
- Make sure informational materials such as pamphlets and brochures are written in plain language.
- Use the "teach back" method (i.e., the consumer repeats information back to you to ensure understanding).
- Clearly explain the purposes and procedures of any evaluations and assessments that are recommended and get the consumer's input regarding whether these are deemed necessary and potentially helpful. Arrange for visits to various providers if the consumer would like to explore options.
- Suggest that the consumer brings family members, advocates, or friends to appointments to take notes and/or provide support to the consumer.

Source: Briggs et al. (2010); Koo, Krass, and Aslani (2006); NIH (2015); ODPHP (2016).

Rehabilitation counselors can also be instrumental in assisting rehabilitation consumers to develop their own health literacy skills. Specific skills that can be taught to consumers with emerging disabilities are listed in Table 8.3.

In addition to these recommendations, several considerations must be kept in mind. First, rehabilitation counselors should not automatically assume that consumers with emerging disabilities are going to have poor self-literacy skills. On the contrary, many have developed substantial competencies as a result of years of experience interacting with health care and medical professionals. Second, complex terminology used by professionals, both the rehabilitation counselor and the consumer's medical and health care providers, can leave individuals feeling confused, anxious about their ability to manage their conditions, and doubtful about the benefits of treatment and rehabilitation (Briggs et al., 2010). Therefore, the importance of establishing rapport and instilling hope takes precedence. Finally, medically trained sign language interpreters and translators for those with limited English language proficiency should be used whenever they are needed in medical and health care appointments.

A variety of resources are available to rehabilitation counselors and consumers, especially on the websites of consumer advocacy organizations, to assist in

TABLE 8.3 Techniques for Assisting Rehabilitation Consumers to Develop Health Literacy Skills

- Advise consumers to keep their own detailed records so that they can provide accurate and comprehensive information to health care providers. Complete and thorough documentation is not only imperative to accurate diagnoses, but also critical to gaining access to public assistance. These records should include symptoms and dates when they first occurred, triggers of symptoms, family medical history, medications being taken as well as their effects and side effects, results of evaluations and tests, treatments and their outcomes, how symptoms impact daily functioning.

- With electronic records becoming increasingly available to patients, advise consumers to periodically review their records for accuracy and for information they need clarified in appointments with providers.

- Suggest that consumers bring a friend, family member, or advocate to their appointments to take notes, ask questions, and provide the consumer with emotional support.

- Encourage consumers to keep daily diaries to record their symptoms, when they occur, how often they occur, what times of the day they seem to function the best, what factors appear to precipitate symptoms, what helps to alleviate symptoms, when symptoms are most and least severe, how they are responding to medication, and any side effects they are experiencing.

- Encourage consumers to ask how prescribed treatments work and for evidence regarding their effectiveness.

- Suggest that consumers ask for demonstrations of management techniques and technologies that are prescribed (e.g., exercises, use of braces and prosthetics, recommended changes in body mechanics).

- Because consumers may feel intimidated and rushed in their appointments, encourage them to write down questions they have of the health care providers and to bring their questions to the appointments.

- Provide opportunities (e.g., role-plays) for consumers to practice assertive communication with medical and health care providers.

- Discuss with consumers their right to obtain secondary opinions regarding their diagnosis and treatment approaches.

- Assist consumers in developing problem-solving skills to evaluate and decide on various treatment options.

- Teach consumers how to evaluate the accuracy of information obtained on the Internet or through social media and provide them with a list of credible Internet websites (e.g., CDC, NIH, WHO, NIMH, SAMHSA, national disability organizations) to research for accurate health and disability-related information.

CDC, Centers for Disease Control and Prevention; NIH, National Institutes of Health; WHO, World Health Organization; NIMH, National Institute of Mental Health; SAMHSA, Substance Abuse and Mental Health Services Administration.
Source: Briggs et al. (2010); Koo, Krass, and Aslani (2006); NIH (2015); ODPHP (2016).

developing better health literacy skills. Deegan (2013) suggested strategies that can be used by individuals with psychiatric disabilities to change the power imbalance in appointments with psychiatrists. These strategies (e.g., learning to think differently about medications, the role of the patient, and the role of psychiatrists; setting agendas for meetings with psychiatrists; taking charge of meetings) are applicable to consumers with other emerging disabilities who want to change their role as a passive patient and assume greater control of their meetings with health care providers and decisions that are made regarding their health care. This document can be accessed through the National Empowerment Center at http://www.power2u.org.

Peer Supports

The importance of social and peer supports in assisting individuals to deal with the physical and emotional stressors of living with emerging disabilities that are invalidated by others has been emphasized throughout this textbook. Devins and Binik (1996, p. 659) defined social support interventions as consisting of "information exchange in the context of an understanding group that endeavors to provide members with encouragement and mutual support in contending with illness-induced difficulties." One social support intervention that has received significant attention in recent research is peer support and self-help groups. These can be an invaluable resource for individuals with emerging disabilities, providing an opportunity to interact with others who share their experiences and understand what they are going through. A growing trend toward service provision to people with emerging disabilities by peer professionals has also occurred in recent years.

Research on the efficacy of peer support interventions has yielded mixed results in terms of their impact on important outcomes for individuals with emerging disabilities (e.g., symptom reduction, overall physical and mental health, efficacy in illness self-management, coping, life satisfaction). Research has identified the benefits of peer support and self-help groups in assisting individuals to cope with the challenges associated with their disabilities and chronic illnesses. These groups can reduce one's sense of isolation, invalidation, and alienation. Peer support and self-help groups can enhance self-esteem and perceived social supports. They can provide individuals with informational and instrumental assistance that is not available from health care providers. Members have the opportunity to make social comparisons and to observe and model effective coping strategies. For peer leaders and long-term members, advantages are the positive feelings of altruism that accompany helping others that are newly diagnosed or new members of groups.

Peer support and self-help groups also have disadvantages that should be noted. When members of peer support and self-help groups experience setbacks, exacerbation of symptoms, or relapses, it can be distressing for other members of these groups. Members of peer support groups are disproportionately well-educated, middle-class, White females (Borkman, 1997). Disadvantaged groups, particularly those who experience the greatest inequities in health care and rehabilitation, are not adequately represented in research on the outcomes of these interventions. Finally, referral of individuals with emerging disabilities to heterogeneous disability peer support and self-help groups may be ill advised because (a) members of these groups may possess the same damaging misconceptions and stereotypes about emerging disabilities as the general population, and

(b) investigations of the experiences of individuals with emerging disabilities indicate that they feel excluded from the general disability population.

Placement and Follow-Along

Typically, the emphasis in rehabilitation planning has been on the acquisition of employment, with less consideration given to the maintenance of employment. The high rate of disengagement from career development activities and workforce participation that often accompanies the onset of emerging disabilities underscores the need to offer consumers more services focused on academic persistence and job retention (Koch et al., 2012). For individuals with emerging disabilities who acquire their conditions while working, early intervention can reduce the likelihood of premature departure from the workforce and prevent the negative consequences of unemployment (e.g., financial difficulties, psychological stress, isolation, worsening of symptoms, secondary health conditions). For those who are preparing for employment (e.g., participating in postsecondary education) or just entering employment, proactive planning to continue these important career development activities, enter and maintain employment, and advance in one's career will increase the likelihood of career maintenance. Career maintenance services range from periodic checkups for those who are able to retain employment with minimal assistance from the rehabilitation counselor to ongoing supported employment services for those who may need more intensive assistance to maintain employment.

Placement and follow-along services should be tailored to the developmental stage of the individual. For example, integrated supported education and supported employment incorporate consideration of the exploratory career development stage of youths with emerging disabilities. This intervention provides opportunities for these youths and young adults to try out different occupations, develop general work skills, and participate in postsecondary or vocational training to increase their potential for employment. Individuals with emerging disabilities with onset during mid-career or later adulthood are likely to need briefer interventions such as job saves, additional education and training, reasonable accommodations, advocacy, and employer education. Furthermore, job retention services should emphasize consumer empowerment, employer involvement, proactive accommodations planning, anticipatory coping, and illness self-management (Koch et al., 2012). For consumers who are nearing or have passed retirement age, rehabilitation counseling interventions center on making plans for the time when they are no longer working. Rehabilitation counselors can assist these consumers with financial planning, identifying volunteer opportunities and recreational activities, eldercare case management, deciding when it is time for a change in residential circumstance, referrals to Area Agencies on Aging and other eldercare resources, coordination of services with geriatric social workers and nurses, and consultation with family members who may be involved in the consumers' care (Wickert, Dresden, & Rumrill, 2013).

For individuals with episodic and progressive conditions, regular monitoring of changes in their health status, performance of job tasks, and accommodation needs is crucial if these individuals are to maintain their employment and advance in their careers. Immediate changes to the work environment and how job functions are performed can potentially enable individuals to work longer than would be possible without these interventions. Another important consideration in job placement and retention is the effect of occupational stress on the functionality, capacity to perform essential job functions, severity of symptoms, and overall physical and mental health of individuals with emerging disabilities. Recent studies have suggested that chronic workplace stress is a growing problem for American adults and has escalated over the past few decades (Heikkilä et al., 2013; Marin et al., 2011). The increase of job stress, including the perception of having little control over growing demands, has been demonstrated to be associated with increased rates of heart attack, hypertension, and other disorders. There have been estimates of 60% to 90% of medical problems being associated with stress (Collie, 2004). Although stress is a highly personalized phenomenon and can vary widely even in identical situations for different reasons, the amount of stress people feel does have an impact on their physical and psychological well-being. Workplace stress has been linked to a threefold risk for heart and cardiovascular problems (Wolfe, 2004). Stressed employees are also two to three times more likely to suffer from anxiety, back pain, substance abuse, injuries, infections, cancers, and obesity (Wolfe, 2004). Individuals with emerging disabilities are at an even greater risk of experiencing the negative health-related effects of job stress. Also, because of the pervasive stigma that is associated with emerging disabilities, another theme related to accommodations planning is the need to assess the attitudinal accessibility of potential work environments. This assessment focuses on (a) the workplace culture and degree to which diversity is valued, flexibility is provided in how job tasks are performed, and how workers support one another; and (b) workplace policies and procedures that mandate civil and respectful interactions among employees and intolerance of workplace incivilities, micro-aggressions, and forms of covert discrimination.

One model that has emerged from the research that has potential application as a framework for exploring the potential benefits of employment and providing employment services that will lead to improved health outcomes is the Demand-Control-Support Model (DCSM), which was proposed as a framework for conceptualizing the relationship between the work environment and physical and mental health (Karasek & Theorell, 1990). This model has helped to identify psychosocial work conditions that tend to lead to poor physical and mental health, including low decision-making authority, job insecurity, and high psychological or physical demands. It can also be used to identify psychosocial work conditions that are associated with employee psychological and physical well-being, such as high decision-making latitude; employee control over the work process; job demands that allow for use of employees' skills and have intrinsic meaning for employees; support from supervisors and coworkers; clarity regarding work procedures, policies, and tasks to be completed; and opportunities for learning. The DCSM has applications to all phases of the career development process. For example, in exploring career options, the model suggests that only occupations with characteristics that facilitate physical and emotional well-being should be considered as potential career options because, as Merz, Bricout, and Koch (2001) noted, too often people with disabilities are "relegated to the most monotonous, routinized tasks, while being subjected to intense scrutiny and having little autonomy or control" (p. 92).

The DCSM can also be instrumental in helping to guide how vocational out-comes could be monitored and tracked to better assess the health benefits of certain job placements. For example, Merz et al. (2001) illustrated the application of this model to the analysis of psychosocial work environment factors. They suggested that when conducting job analyses, job analysts not only should evaluate essential job functions and worker requirements, but they should also answer questions such as "What are the job demands in relation to the amount of control that the worker has over the demands? How much social support is available on the job? What degree of uncertainty exists in the work environment? Are there conflicting role responsibilities? How might the job be modified to reduce stressors?" (Merz et al., 2001, p. 92). Additionally, because individuals differ in terms of what job factors cause them stress, it is important to also explore with them their vulnera-bilities, coping strategies, and environmental factors that they perceive as stressful and potentially detrimental to their health.

Accommodations Planning

In considering implications for accommodations planning, several themes across this book's chapters span emerging disability populations. First, many individuals with emerging disabilities may not be aware of accommodations or legislation to protect their rights to receive reasonable accommodations in schools, postsecond-ary institutions, and employment because they may not identify as people with disabilities. Educating them about relevant disability legislation and their rights and responsibilities under various laws and how these laws define disability will therefore be necessary. Relatedly, many individuals with emerging disabilities may also be protected against discrimination under other civil rights legislation. Second, because many emerging disabilities are hidden, individuals with these disabilities may have legitimate concerns about disclosure that will need to be sensitively explored with rehabilitation counselors so that these consumers can make informed decisions about disclosure.

The vast majority of emerging disabilities are chronic illnesses that are often episodic with unpredictable vacillations in symptoms and functional capacities, and others are both episodic and progressive. These characteristics require proac-tive planning for the unknown and anticipation of potential future needs for job accommodations. Proactive planning for both classroom accommodations and job accommodations can enhance both academic performance and job satisfactoriness (Rubin, Roessler, & Rumrill, 2016). However, it requires individuals to acquire a unique set of knowledge and skills such as a comprehensive understanding of their disability, knowledge about the anticipated course and progression of the disability, the ability to predict the anticipated impact of their disability on future job performance, and skills in anticipating accommodation needs and requesting accommodations from employers (Koch et al., 2013). Rehabilitation counselors can assist consumers in developing the skills for proactive accommodations planning; however, they must stay attuned to their emotional response to considering their future functioning, provide supportive counseling in dealing with the emotional impact of these considerations, and time proactive planning to coincide with the individual's emotional readiness to consider these issues. After carefully assessing the impact of the consumer's disability on future job performance, the next step is to evaluate the individual's work environment and job demands to determine accommodations that may currently or eventually be needed to support job retention and prevent premature departure from the workforce.

Proactive accommodations planning ideally begins with an assessment of the illness self-management techniques that consumers with emerging disabilities use in their daily lives and how these might transfer to the postsecondary institution or worksite. Rehabilitation counselors can then engage in collaborative decision making with the consumer to identify additional techniques that they can add to their repertoire of self-management skills. This approach can be very empowering because it emphasizes the consumer's capacity to effectively manage his or her condition. Again, as noted elsewhere in this text, many individuals are able to independently develop and practice self-management skills whereas others may need assistance with learning effective strategies.

Shaw et al. (2012, p. 695) emphasized how essential it is for individuals with chronic pain to apply self-management techniques at the job site, noting that chronic or recurrent pain can interfere with occupational function by limiting physical capacity, reducing work productivity, straining relationships with peers and supervisors, and creating a need to alter or modify job tasks to reduce discomfort. To counter these negative impacts, workers must learn to manage pain while maintaining job productivity; judge how and when to disclose pain problems to supervisors and coworkers; find ways to obtain social support and assistance in the workplace; and learn how to initiate or request changes in work habits or physical demands.

Because so many individuals with emerging disabilities experience chronic pain, the rationale provided by these authors for implementing self-management techniques on the job applies to many of these rehabilitation consumers. The authors provide several examples of self-management strategies that can be used on the job (Shaw et al., 2012). Cognitive restructuring can be utilized by countering beliefs that work is detrimental to one's health and can lead to improvements in job performance. Attention techniques can be used to simultaneously focus on both symptoms and work responsibilities to develop self-mastery and functional optimization. This technique can provide evidence to the individual that his or her symptoms do not completely preclude participation in work activities. Effective communication involves learning how to discuss her or his functional limitations and accommodation needs in an effective manner to reduce interpersonal conflict on the job and elicit employer support in providing needed accommodations. Also important is the use of ergonomics, job analyses, modification of job tasks, and making changes in body mechanics to perform jobs in a manner that reduces symptoms such as pain, fatigue, and cognitive limitations. Fears of reinjury or symptom exacerbation can be countered by using systematic problem-solving techniques to identify challenging work activities and organizational constraints and making plans (e.g., job accommodations) to mediate these. Likewise, developing plans for flare-ups, setbacks, and periods of symptom exacerbation can improve the individual's ability to work through these. Constructive use of mini breaks and lunch breaks to practice self-management techniques such as relaxation, meditation, reaching out to mental and physical health providers for support, and stretching can help to minimize symptoms such as pain, fatigue, and cognitive constraints. Time-based pacing can be used to meet production goals by completing the most challenging work tasks when one is feeling the most rested, alert, and in the least amount of pain and relegating less challenging tasks to times when he or she is not feeling his or her best.

Bishop, Frain, Rumrill, and Rymond (2009) studied the relationship between employment status and self-management and disease-modifying strategies in a sample of 175 employees with multiple sclerosis (MS). The researchers found a significant correlation between employment status and use of illness self-management and disease management strategies. Based on this finding, the researchers recommended that rehabilitation counselors incorporate training in illness self-management into rehabilitation plans for employment. This training should comprise (a) an assessment of the consumer's awareness of and participation in self-management; (b) the identification of barriers to self-management; and (c) implementation of strategies to overcome these barriers and actively engage in self-management. Worksite self-management techniques can also be taught to consumers in a group format with each session including a mix of presentations, group discussion, case examples, role-plays, self-assessments, and homework assignments (Shaw et al., 2012). The advantage of providing this training in a group format as opposed to one-on-one training is that it affords the opportunities for consumers to learn from each other and receive support and feedback from others who share work-related challenges similar to their own.

Anticipatory coping is a similar skill to proactive accommodations planning. Anticipatory coping involves both problem solving and behavioral modifications to anticipate and develop appropriate responses to health-related challenges before they arise (Gignac, 2005). The planning and modification of behaviors both at home and at work can improve overall functionality, enabling individuals to continue participating in valued activities and preventing early departure from the workforce. These skills include stretching before getting out of bed in the morning, delegating home chores to others, and giving up less valued activities to free up time and energy to devote to more valued activities such as spending time with family, participating in leisure pursuits, and continuing to work. Anticipatory coping on the job may include behaviors such as completing demanding job tasks when feeling most rested and in the least amount of pain, periodically stretching when sitting for long periods of time, taking frequent short breaks instead of one long break, and alternating rest with activity. Koch et al. (2013) noted that these are accommodations that many individuals can make on their own without having to go through a formal process of requesting accommodations from their employer. The development of anticipatory coping skills on the job does not draw attention to one's disability such as formal accommodations, use of assistive technologies, and ergonomic changes to the work environment do.

CONCLUSIONS

In this chapter, we have summarized some of the unique medical, psychosocial, and vocational challenges faced by individuals with emerging disabilities, and we have further elaborated on treatment and rehabilitation approaches that stand to improve access to and benefit from rehabilitation counseling. It is our hope that, as the constellation of disabilities continues to change and expand, rehabilitation counselors will stay informed through ongoing education on disability trends and advances in treatment and rehabilitation so that they can incorporate these into the rehabilitation planning process. It is also our hope that rehabilitation counseling students will prepare to take on leadership roles in (a) eradicating barriers for individuals with emerging disabilities to rehabilitation programs; (b) advancing policies and procedures to modify eligibility criteria and service delivery patterns that fail to respond to the rehabilitation needs of these consumers; (c) pursuing and providing services in settings where individuals with emerging disabilities receive health care and treatment; and (d) partner with people with emerging disabilities to better educate the general population about emerging disabilities and reduce the widespread stigma associated with these conditions. Rehabilitation counselors, more so than any other professionals, have the knowledge and skills to advance awareness about emerging disabilities and facilitate improved quality of life for individuals with emerging disabilities.

DISCUSSION QUESTIONS

1. We have listed key medical, psychosocial, and vocational issues affecting individuals across emerging disability populations. What do you think are the top five most pressing issues for people with emerging disabilities? Are there any additional issues we have not included in this chapter?
2. What do you think are the most important rehabilitation counseling implications for providing services to individuals with emerging disabilities?
3. As future rehabilitation counselors, how do you plan to stay current with the constantly changing nature and needs of people with emerging disabilities?

REFERENCES

Bishop, M., Frain, M. P., Rumrill, P. D., & Rymond, C. (2009). The relationship of self-management and disease modifying therapy use to employment status among adults with multiple sclerosis. *Journal of Vocational Rehabilitation, 31*(2), 119–127.

Bond, G. R., Resnick, S. G., Drake, R. E., Xie, H., McHugo, G. J., & Bebout, R. R. (2001). Does competitive employment improve nonvocational outcomes for people with severe mental illness? *Journal of Consulting and Clinical Psychology, 69*(3), 489–501.

Borkman, T. (1997). A selective look at self help groups in the United States. *Health & Social Care in the Community, 5*(6), 357–364.

Briggs, A. M., Jordan, J. E., Buchbinder, R., Burnett, A. F., O'Sullivan, P. B., Chua, J. Y.,... Straker, L. M. (2010). Health literacy and beliefs among a community cohort with and without chronic low back pain. *Pain, 150*(2), 275–283.

Collie, D. (2004) *Workplace stress: Expensive stuff.* Retrieved from http://www.emaxhealth.com/38/473.html

Collins, S., Arthur, N., & Wong-Wylie, G. (2010). Enhancing reflective practice in multicultural counseling through cultural auditing. *Journal of Counseling & Development, 88*(3), 340–347.

Conyers, L. M. (2004). Expanding understanding of HIV/AIDS and employment perspectives of focus groups. *Rehabilitation Counseling Bulletin, 48*(1), 5–18.

Deegan, P. (2013). *Reclaiming your power during medical appointments with your psychiatrist.* Retrieved from http://www.power2u.org/articles/selfhelp/reclaim.html

Devins, G. M., & Binik, Y. M. (1996). Facilitating coping with chronic physical illness. In G. M. Devins, Y. M. Binik, & M. Zeidner (Eds.), *Handbook of coping: Theory, research, application* (pp. 640–696). Oxford, UK: Wiley.

Dunn, E. C., Wewiorski, N. J., & Rogers, E. S. (2008). The meaning and importance of employment to people in recovery from serious mental illness: Results of a qualitative study. *Psychiatric Rehabilitation Journal, 32*(1), 59–62.

Fox, M. H., & Kim, K. (2004). Understanding emerging disabilities. *Disability and Society, 19*, 323–337.

Frain, M. P., Lee, J., Roland, M., & Tschopp, M. K. (2012). A rehabilitation counselor integration into the successful rehabilitation of veterans with disabilities. In P. J. Toriello, M. L. Bishop, & P. D. Rumrill (Eds.), *New directions in rehabilitation counseling: Creative responses to professional, clinical, and educational challenges* (pp. 255–281). Linn Creek, MO: Aspen Professional Services.

Gay and Lesbian Alliance Against Defamation (GLAAD). (2015). *Transgender FAQ.* Retrieved from http://www.glaad.org/transgender/transfaq

Gignac, M. A. (2005). Arthritis and employment: An examination of behavioral coping efforts to manage workplace activity limitations. *Arthritis Care & Research, 53*(3), 328–336.

Goldblum, P., & Kohlenberg, B. (2005). Vocational counseling for people with HIV: The client-focused considering work model. *Journal of Vocational Rehabilitation, 22*, 115–124.

Grønning, K., Rødevand, E., & Steinsbekk, A. (2010). Paid work is associated with improved health-related quality of life in patients with rheumatoid arthritis. *Clinical Rheumatology, 29*(11), 1317–1322.

Hall, J. P., Kurth, N. K., & Hunt, S. L. (2013). Employment as a health determinant for working-age, dually-eligible people with disabilities. *Disability and Health Journal, 6*(2), 100–106.

Heikkila, K., Fransson, E. I., Nyberg, S. T., Zins, M., Westerlund, H., Westerholm, P.,… Kivimäki, M. (2013). Job strain and health-related lifestyle: Findings from an individual-participant meta-analysis of 118,000 working adults. *American Journal of Public Health, 103*(11), 2090–2097.

Hergenrather, K. C., Zeglin, R. J., McGuire-Kuletz, M., & Rhodes, S. D. (2015). Employment as a social determinant of health: A review of longitudinal studies exploring the relationship between employment status and mental health. *Rehabilitation Research, Policy and Education, 29*(3), 261–290.

Jahoda, M. (1982). *Employment and unemployment: A social-psychological analysis* (Vol. 1). Cambridge, UK: Cambridge University Press Archive.

Karasek, R., & Theorell, T. (1990). *Healthy work: Stress, productivity, and the reconstruction of working life.* New York, NY: Basic Books.

Koch, L., Conyers, L., & Rumrill, P. (2012). The nature and needs of people with emerging disabilities. In P. J. Toriello, M. L. Bishop, & P. D. Rumrill (Eds.), *New directions in rehabilitation counseling: Creative responses to professional, clinical, and educational challenges* (pp. 116–139). Linn Creek, MO: Aspen Professional Services.

Koch, L., Rumrill, P., Hennessey, M., Vierstra, C., & Roessler, R. (2007). An ecological approach to facilitate successful employment outcomes among people with multiple chemical sensitivity. *Work: A Journal of Prevention, Assessment, and Rehabilitation, 29*(4), 341–349.

Koch, L. C., & Arhar, J. M. (2002). Action research in rehabilitation counseling intern supervision. *Rehabilitation Education, 16*(2), 165–177.

Koo, M., Krass, I., & Aslani, P. (2006). Enhancing patient education about medicines: Factors influencing reading and seeking of written medicine information. *Health Expectations, 9*(2), 174–187.

Marin, M. F., Lord, C., Andrews, J., Juster, R. P., Sindi, S., Arsenault-Lapierre, G.,… Lupien, S. J. (2011). Chronic stress, cognitive functioning and mental health. *Neurobiology of Learning and Memory, 96*(4), 583–595.

Merz, M. A., Bricout, J. C., & Koch, L. C. (2001). Disability and job stress: Implications for vocational rehabilitation planning. *Work: A Journal of Prevention, Assessment, and Rehabilitation, 17*, 85–95.

Miller, A., & Dishon, S. (2006). Health-related quality of life in multiple sclerosis: The impact of disability, gender and employment status. *Quality of Life Research, 15*(2), 259–271.

National Institutes of Health. (2015). *Health literacy.* Retrieved from https://obssr-archive .od.nih.gov/scientific_areas/social_culture_factors_in_health/health_literacy/index .aspx

Office of Disease Prevention and Health Promotion. (2016). *Health literacy and communication.* Retrieved from https://health.gov/communication/?_ga=1.248499844.20845723 87.1469648454

Patti, F., Pozzilli, C., Montanari, E., Pappalardo, A., Piazza, L., Levi, A.,...Pesci, I. (2007). Effects of education level and employment status on HRQoL in early relapsing-remitting multiple sclerosis. *Multiple Sclerosis, 13*(6), 783–791.

Robert Wood Johnson Foundation. (2013). How does employment—or unemployment—affect health? *Health Policy Snapshot: Public Health and Prevention.* Retrieved from http://www.rwjf.org/content/dam/farm/reports/issue_briefs/2013/rwjf403360

Ross, C. E., & Mirowsky, J. (1995). Does employment affect health? *Journal of Health and Social Behavior, 36*(3), 230–243.

Rubin, S., Roessler, R., & Rumrill, P. (2016). *Foundations of the vocational rehabilitation process* (7th ed.). Austin, TX: Pro-Ed.

Schön, D. (1983). *The reflective practitioner: How professionals think in action.* New York, NY: Basic Books.

Shaw, I., & Gould, N. (Eds.). (2001). *Qualitative research in social work* (Vol. 113). Thousand Oaks, CA: Sage.

Shaw, W. S., Tveito, T. H., Geehern-Lavoie, M., Huang, Y. H., Nicholas, M. K., Reme, S. E.,... Pransky, G. (2012). Adapting principles of chronic pain self-management to the workplace. *Disability and Rehabilitation, 34*(8), 694–703.

Skovolt, T. M., & Rønnestad, M. H. (1992). Themes in therapist and counselor development. *Journal of Counseling & Development, 70*, 505–515.

Sørensen, K., Van den Broucke, S., Fullam, J., Doyle, G., Pelikan, J., Slonska, Z., & Brand, H. (2012). Health literacy and public health: A systematic review and integration of definitions and models. *BMC Public Health, 12*(1), 1.

Szymanski, E. M., Hershenson, D. B., Ettinger, J. M., & Enright, M. S. (1998). Career development interventions for people with disabilities. In E. Szymanski & R. Parker (Eds.), *Work and disability: Issues and strategies in career development and job placement* (pp. 255–276). Austin, TX: Pro-Ed.

Vick, A., & Lightman, E. (2010). Barriers to employment among women with complex episodic disabilities. *Journal of Disability Policy Studies, 21*(2), 70. Retrieved from http:// 0-search.proquest.com.library.uark.edu/docview/747126518?accountid=8361

White, S. (2001). Auto-ethnography as reflexive inquiry: The research act as self surveillance. In I. Shaw & N. Gould (Eds.), *Qualitative research in social work: Introducing Qualitative Methods Series* (pp. 100–115). Thousand Oaks, CA: Sage.

Wickert, K., Dresden, D., & Rumrill, P. (2013). *The sandwich generation's guide to eldercare.* New York, NY: Demos Health.

Wolfe, I. S. (2004). The truth about employee stress: Bleeding at the bottom line. *Business2Business.* Retrieved from http://www.super-solutions.com/Thetruthaboutworkplacestress .asp

NINE

New Directions in Emerging Disabilities Research

CHAPTER OBJECTIVES

- *Highlight topic areas in which research is needed to more fully understand the nature and needs of people with emerging disabilities*
- *Examine current trends in rehabilitation counseling research and how investigations with people with emerging disabilities are compatible with these trends*
- *Describe types of emerging disabilities for which health care, community living, and vocational experiences should be investigated more thoroughly in future research*
- *Recommend methodological and data analytic strategies that rehabilitation researchers can use to study the complex, multidimensional needs of people with emerging disabilities*

As we enter the final chapter of this book, we hope that readers have been well acquainted with the characteristics and needs of Americans with emerging disabilities. Disabling conditions that are either new to medical science or growing in prevalence are increasingly evident to rehabilitation professionals, disability advocates, employers, health care providers, and other stakeholders in making our society fully inclusive and welcoming of all people. So, too, are researchers in disciplines such as rehabilitation, psychology, sociology, medicine, health care, law, and political science attending to the emerging disabilities epidemic.

In this chapter, we examine the current status and possible future directions of rehabilitation counseling research for its potential to develop a more thorough understanding of the lived experiences of people with emerging disabilities. We begin by presenting a framework for conceptualizing rehabilitation counseling research in general and emerging disabilities research in particular. Next, we examine subject areas and emerging disability populations that we regard as most fertile for important future research. Finally, we recommend methodological and data analytic strategies for researchers to consider in their efforts to thoroughly evaluate the experiences and outcomes of people with emerging disabilities.

A FRAMEWORK FOR ORGANIZING REHABILITATION COUNSELING RESEARCH INVOLVING PEOPLE WITH EMERGING DISABILITIES

Our framework for organizing emerging disabilities research efforts in terms of primary, secondary, and tertiary contributions to the knowledge base in rehabilitation counseling (Bellini & Rumrill, 2009) is structured by the primary beneficiaries of rehabilitation research—people with disabilities—and the principal goal of federally funded research on disability enhancing the participation of people with disabilities in society. The categories of primary, secondary, and tertiary research reflect the relative proximity or distance of the knowledge claims generated by researchers to the principal beneficiaries and goals of these research efforts. Within the context of this book, *primary* research efforts are those that generate new knowledge that pertains directly to the status/participation of people with emerging disabilities in society. These studies involve descriptive and predictive studies on the outcomes achieved by people with emerging disabilities, research on psychosocial adjustment to various types of emerging disabilities, evaluation of causal models that explain participation outcomes, and intervention research designed to enhance participation.

Secondary research efforts operate one step removed from the central focus of rehabilitation and seek to understand the competencies, attitudes, and dispositions of preservice or practicing rehabilitation counselors who work with people with disabilities. Examples of secondary research include the many studies of roles and functions of rehabilitation counselors in different practice settings, practitioner confidence and competence in specific knowledge domains, and the impact of preservice training on rehabilitation counselor attitudes and behaviors. An example of secondary research focused on emerging disabilities would be an investigation of practitioner competence and confidence in providing rehabilitation services to populations we have described in previous chapters of this book (e.g., older individuals, people with neurodevelopmental disorders, people with mental illness and/or substance use disorders).

Tertiary research efforts contribute knowledge about the professional issues that are relevant to rehabilitation counselors and educators, but they do not center directly on the experiences, perspectives, and concerns of rehabilitation consumers and professionals. Examples of tertiary research topics include ethical standards in rehabilitation; clinical supervision in rehabilitation counseling; evaluation of training modalities in rehabilitation education; and the research productivity of rehabilitation educators, researchers, and programs. An example of a tertiary research study in emerging disabilities would be the impact of specific courses (e.g., psychiatric rehabilitation) on rehabilitation counselors' attitudes and behaviors in providing services to emerging populations of individuals with psychiatric disabilities.

Occasionally, studies will integrate more than one "level" or context in an attempt to develop warranted knowledge. For example, an investigation of the employment outcomes achieved by people with autism spectrum disorders (ASD) being served by nationally certified and noncertified rehabilitation counselors would integrate primary and secondary contexts in the research design. We categorize these cases according to the more proximal context in relation to principal beneficiaries and goals of the research. Hence, the example provided would be *primary* research based on the fact that the knowledge claim pertains to employment outcomes achieved by people with ASD. Our goals in presenting this heuristic framework are to (a) orient rehabilitation counselors and educators to the different contexts in which rehabilitation research efforts are framed, and (b) ensure that future rehabilitation research becomes ever more relevant to people with emerging disabilities.

THE ROLE OF THEORY IN EMERGING DISABILITIES RESEARCH

Theory plays an essential role in the generation of research ideas, and in the development and organization of knowledge within the professional domain of rehabilitation counseling (Bellini & Rumrill, 2009). The history of science teaches us that the advancement of scientific knowledge depends on the development of theory, empirical evaluation of theoretical propositions and models, and refinement of these based on the findings of systematic research programs. Bellini and Rumrill (2009) noted that, to advance the scientific bases of rehabilitation counseling, rehabilitation researchers need to devote more time and energy to theory-driven research programs rather than atheoretical investigations. In recent years, an encouraging number of new or revised theoretical models of disability and related constructs have been advanced, and they have important implications for researchers wishing to more fully understand the characteristics, needs, and outcomes of people with emerging disabilities. These include the International Classification of Function (ICF) model of disability (Frain et al., 2015; World Health Organization [WHO], 2001), the empowerment model (Kosciulek, 1999), the poverty disability model (Strauser, 2013), and the quality of life/disability centrality model (Bishop, 2012). Each of these theoretical models frames disability and the rehabilitation process as a complex interaction of personal, environmental, and systems variables. Each serves to organize and explain hypothesized relationships among personal, environmental, and experiential phenomena in the lives of people with disabilities and/or service providers. It is becoming far more common than in previous decades for rehabilitation investigators to utilize these and other theoretical frameworks to guide the development of their research programs and to design individual studies to test, either wholly or in part, specific theoretical propositions (Bishop, 2005; Bishop, Stenhoff, & Shepard, 2007; Kosciulek, 2005; Kosciulek & Mertz, 2001). The continuing development of the scientific basis of rehabilitation counseling is facilitated by (a) explicit evaluation of the theory-based propositions that follow from contemporary theories and models, and (b) the use of empirical findings to revise theories and models so that they better mirror reality (Bellini & Rumrill, 2009). Theory provides the necessary framework for the advancement of scientific knowledge, but knowledge can only be verified incrementally through successive, individual studies that are relatively narrow in scope. It is important that contemporary theories be complemented, expanded, modified, or replaced by theories grounded in the lived experiences of people with emerging disabilities because, as can be observed throughout the chapters in this book, individuals with emerging disabilities often question or disagree with researcher (outsider)-developed theories that fail to adequately explain their experiences. Other theories go so far as to invalidate their experiences, reinforce myths and stereotypes, and undermine their emotional and physical well-being. That being said, individuals with emerging disabilities, not researchers, are the best experts on the processes and constructs that shape their psychosocial and vocational adjustment as well as their quality of life.

As Serlin (1989) noted, research findings are rarely directly applicable to professional practice. Rather, research contributes to effective practice through the testing, confirmation or disconfirmation, and refinement of causal explanations, which specify what variables are related; how they are related; the nature of the processes that are involved; and the extent to which variable relationships can be generalized across populations, settings, and conditions. Thus, the recent and positive trend toward greater utilization of theories and models in designing and implementing rehabilitation research, along with the increased emphasis on consumer input into these theories and models, has the potential to enhance the relevance of research findings to professional practices. Therefore, we challenge rehabilitation scholars who study emerging disability populations to continue to develop even stronger theoretical bases that are adequately informed by the lived experiences of individuals with emerging disabilities and to translate this new knowledge more effectively into professional practice. Applied research can and should be grounded in theory. This movement will provide our field with stronger warrants for new knowledge claims than has historically been the case in atheoretical investigations. In so doing, it will more rapidly bridge the gap between the profession's need for and utilization of new knowledge, thereby allowing research to keep up with field practice (and, hopefully, vice versa).

Specific rehabilitation research areas that have already begun to benefit from the application of contemporary person–environment interaction models include workplace discrimination, rehabilitation processes and outcomes, family issues in the adjustment to and acceptance of disability, the reciprocal impact of self-perceptions and the perceptions of others in formulating personal responses to disability, and the specific interactions of personal and contextual factors that influence the experiences of people with disabilities across the life span. These research areas have appeared frequently in previous chapters of this book, and their relevance to emerging disability populations is apparent. Moreover, the continued development and testing of theory-based psychosocial and employment-focused interventions have the potential to yield valuable information for both scholars and practitioners about *what* facilitates the achievement of valued social outcomes for people with emerging disabilities and *why*.

Across these various research topics and programs, a stronger focus on the environmental aspects of person–environment interaction models is also needed. We need to know what aspects of the environment present barriers (attitudinal, architectural, systems) to the participation of people with emerging disabilities in various life pursuits and what types of environmental accommodations and supports serve to enhance participation. The causal role of the environment in producing disability outcomes is a central tenet of the disability rights movement and is a cornerstone of the service philosophy of rehabilitation counseling (Rubin, Roessler, & Rumrill, 2016), yet the bulk of research efforts in our field continues to be directed toward understanding the role of the personal dimensions that contribute to the person–environment interaction. A more sophisticated understanding of disability and participation requires greater attention to the role of the environment and the measurement of barriers and supports. Because of the widespread stigmatization of people with emerging disabilities, one environmental factor that is particularly relevant to these populations and warrants greater research attention is attitudinal accessibility and its impact on individuals' participation in schools, postsecondary institutions, communities, rehabilitation programs, and work environments. In particular, there is a need to develop and evaluate instruments for assessing the attitudinal accessibility of these environments and to design and evaluate interventions to remove attitudinal barriers.

EMERGING SUBJECT AND TOPIC AREAS
IN REHABILITATION COUNSELING RESEARCH

The knowledge base in rehabilitation counseling has been built in small increments, with successive studies serving to extend the ones before them along specific lines of inquiry. As we look toward the future, we recognize that the current subject matter of empirical work in our field will be augmented with new research programs designed to build upon what we already know. In that endeavor, issues facing people with emerging disabilities will play an increasingly prominent role. The progressive, linear approach to developing valid knowledge serves many useful purposes, but it also requires vigilance on the part of scientists to avoid "re-hashing" what has already been done and, thereby, limiting the growth of new knowledge.

Numerous studies have given us a thorough understanding of such phenomena as clinical supervision, roles and functions of rehabilitation counselors, practitioner confidence and competence in specific knowledge domains, the influence of preservice training on counselor behaviors, and the scholarly productivity of rehabilitation faculty. In fairness, these lines of inquiry have served and will continue to serve an important evaluative function for the profession, particularly as the populations served and settings in which rehabilitation counselors practice change and expand. However, from a global perspective, these research topics represent second- and third-order investigations, one (or more) step removed from the primary foci of rehabilitation research, which are (a) the interests, skills, values, and experiences of people with disabilities, and (b) how the rehabilitation process facilitates the participation of people with disabilities in all social roles. One problem inherent in devoting too much energy to secondary and tertiary issues (to the exclusion of primary topics) is that rehabilitation research may be viewed as irrelevant to its primary beneficiaries (i.e., people with disabilities). We need to place the focus of our efforts to generate new knowledge squarely where it belongs—on our clients and consumers. That being said, we do recognize the need to investigate how to better promote and ensure the employment of rehabilitation counselors in nontraditional settings where people with emerging disabilities are most likely to receive physical and mental health care services such as medical homes, physicians' offices, specialty clinics, and community health agencies.

Our call for rehabilitation counseling researchers to more explicitly place the primary emphasis of their scientific investigations on the experiences, concerns, perspectives, and outcomes of people with emerging disabilities is consistent with recent research trends in our field. Koch and associates (Koch, Schultz, Hennessey, & Conyers, 2005; Schultz, Koch, & Kontosh, 2007) conducted two investigations on the perspectives of rehabilitation educators regarding future research directions for rehabilitation counseling. The initial study by Koch et al. (2005) used qualitative methods (i.e., focus groups and open-ended Internet surveys) with 63 members of the National Council on Rehabilitation Education (NCRE). The rehabilitation educators were asked to (a) reflect on the history of rehabilitation research and specify those research programs that have had the greatest impact on rehabilitation counselor training and practice, and (b) identify the most important research topics for the future. In the second study, a survey instrument—the NCRE Research Priorities Survey—was sent to all members of the NCRE listserv. NCRE members were asked to rank order eight broad categories and 67 specific research topics regarding the rehabilitation issues that warrant further investigation. The data for this second study were analyzed quantitatively and consisted of 88 usable surveys from NCRE members. The formal purpose of these studies was to establish a consensus-driven research agenda for the field to consider.

In the Koch et al. (2005) study, some of the knowledge domains cited by NCRE members as having the most significant impact in past decades were vocational rehabilitation outcome studies, research on psychosocial issues in adjustment to disability, research that identified inequities in the delivery of rehabilitation services to persons from minority groups, and intervention studies. These research domains all have direct and primary implications for people with emerging disabilities, many of whom have been the subjects of empirical investigations in these broad content areas.

In the Schultz et al. (2007) study, the 88 NCRE members ranked rehabilitation outcomes, rehabilitation interventions, and consumer involvement in rehabilitation as the highest priority categories for future research. All three of these areas pertain to primary research topics according to our criteria, and they represent issues in the lives of people with emerging disabilities that must be more thoroughly understood. Among the 67 specific research topics, the 13 highest-ranked topics warranting further investigation pertained to primary research as we have defined it, with quality of life for persons with disabilities, consumer job retention, and career advancement for persons with disabilities ranked highest overall. These three highest-ranked future research directions have been prominent themes in the other chapters of this book on rehabilitation considerations for people with emerging disabilities.

We share with NCRE members the perspective on what constitutes the most important research topics to be addressed in future rehabilitation research, namely, research that pertains directly to the status/participation of people with disabilities in society. We believe that this broad consensus on future research priorities reflects a fundamental agreement among most rehabilitation educators regarding the primary goals and beneficiaries of rehabilitation research. We believe that this consensus is about the core values of rehabilitation counseling: what we as a profession value in terms of new knowledge and the practice-related values rehabilitation educators seek to instill in their students. Inherent in these values is the need to stay abreast of societal changes that will continue to revise our conception, definition, and treatment of people with disabilities, which is an important theme that recurs throughout this book.

Intervention studies that promote evidence-based practices will be increasingly important in future emerging disabilities research. Fields such as education, psychology, and medicine have adopted guidelines and standards for research findings that constitute evidence-based practices, and we believe that it would greatly benefit the field of rehabilitation counseling to adopt a set of standards for intervention research that guides preservice training and professional service delivery.

Bellini and Rumrill (2009) noted that intervention research must also be designed to address the unique needs of specific populations of people with emerging disabilities such as older individuals with disabilities, people with psychiatric disabilities, injured workers coping with chronic pain, and people with disabilities from racial and ethnic minority groups. We would add to this list of emerging and understudied consumer populations a number of groups whose needs were described in other chapters of this book, including people with:

- Diabetes mellitus
- Multiple sclerosis
- Lyme disease
- Arthritis
- Heart disease
- Asthma
- Allergies
- Stroke
- Polytrauma
- Traumatic brain injuries
- Posttraumatic stress disorder
- Substance use disorders
- Neurodevelopmental disorders
- Lupus
- Multiple chemical sensitivity
- Chronic migraines, fibromyalgia, and other chronic pain conditions
- Age-related visual and hearing impairments
- Dementia

Throughout the chapters in this book, we have introduced a variety of emerging interventions (e.g., integrated supported employment and supported education, rehabilitation case management in college counseling centers, collaborative documentation, trauma-informed rehabilitation counseling) with preliminary evidence supporting their effectiveness in responding to the rehabilitation needs of individuals with the disabilities listed. The need for additional research to further investigate these interventions should also be incorporated into a rehabilitation research agenda that focuses on emerging disabilities. Furthermore, the original consensus research agenda developed by Koch et al. (2005) is more than 10 years old, indicating a need to elicit the current perspectives of rehabilitation researchers on topics of importance to the field. We would anticipate that an updated research agenda would place a greater emphasis on the rehabilitation needs of populations with emerging disabilities. Moreover, we would hope that a contemporary research agenda would include the need for additional research to evaluate psychosocial interventions and community services that address the unique rehabilitation needs of women and minorities with emerging disabilities as well as interventions to assist people with emerging disabilities in developing more effective social networks to enhance participation. Increased attention must be accorded to disabling conditions, the causes of which are related to lifestyle factors, the environment, poverty, and violence.

Some specific studies that are needed to further our understanding of the characteristics, needs, and outcomes of people with emerging disabilities should focus on the Internet as a job placement and career counseling tool for people with emerging disabilities; the applicability of the WHO's International Classification of Function framework to emerging disabling conditions; the validity of self-estimates versus standardized testing in vocational planning and service delivery with people with emerging disabilities; the impact of peer mentoring and role modeling on the employment and long-term career success of people with emerging disabilities; and the relationship of variables such as medical invalidation, diagnostic uncertainties, illness self-management skills, and health literacy to health-related quality of life for people with emerging disabilities.

Also, greater self-advocacy skills is a need that cuts across a number of different topic areas and is central to enhancing the civil rights and participation of people with emerging disabilities in various life areas. Hence, we place a high priority on the need for intervention studies that involve targeted training for people with emerging disabilities who wish to invoke their rights to nondiscriminatory treatment in the workplace under the Americans with Disabilities Act Amendments Act (ADAAA). Whether they are completing job application forms, participating in employment interviews, requesting reasonable accommodations, or redressing discriminatory conduct to which their employers have subjected them, people with emerging disabilities need to know their civil rights as they apply for, enter, and seek to maintain employment, their recourses if those rights are violated, and specific actions they must take to protect the guarantees of fair and equitable treatment that the ADAAA and its predecessor (the Americans with Disabilities Act) has provided since 1992. Additionally, because disability disclosure is a prominent concern among individuals with emerging disabilities, many of whom have invisible disabilities, research is needed to identify practices to facilitate informed decision making about disclosure. Relatedly, there is a need to investigate strategies for evaluating the attitudinal accessibility of work environments because stigma, myths, and misunderstandings about the vocational impact of emerging disabilities, rather than environmental accessibility, are often the greatest barriers to employment for many individuals with emerging disabilities.

Intervention studies are also needed to assist workers with emerging disabilities or their advocates to invoke their federal employment rights under such statutes as the Workforce Innovation and Opportunity Act, the Family and Medical Leave Act, the Age Discrimination in Employment Act, the Civil Rights Act, and the Affordable Care Act. As with most of their legal rights, people with disabilities in general and people with emerging disabilities in particular have historically been underassertive in taking advantage of the considerable benefits of these laws, and rehabilitation counselors must develop and evaluate strategies for improving the self-advocacy skills of our consumers with regard to these federal protections.

Given our society's emphasis on fiscal responsibility and professional accountability in our systems of education, health care, government services, and workforce development, outcome research is a second major future priority for emerging disabilities investigations. We encourage future researchers who study people with emerging disabilities to identify alternative measures of Status 26 (successfully rehabilitated) closures in the State–Federal Vocational Rehabilitation program such as quality of life, improved health and functioning, reduced symptomology, and career advancement. We also believe that future outcome research should address multidimensional outcomes of the rehabilitation process (e.g., various psychosocial benefits associated with receipt of rehabilitation services, benefits to families, employers) as well as other valued participation outcomes beyond employment for people with emerging disabilities (e.g., participation in community settings, access to health care, participation in leisure pursuits).

Speaking of outcomes, the federal government maintains numerous large databases for use in rehabilitation and disability policy research, including the RSA-911 database, the U.S. Equal Opportunity Commission's Integrated Mission System database, the Social Security Administration's database, and the National Longitudinal Transition Study-2 (NLTS2) database. These data sets continue to be underutilized as sources for theory-driven research on rehabilitation outcomes and policy in the rehabilitation counseling literature, especially regarding people with emerging disabilities, and we encourage emerging disabilities researchers to examine and utilize these valuable data sources in their work.

Consumer involvement in rehabilitation was another highly ranked priority for future research according to NCRE members in the Schultz et al. (2007) study, and this subject is still timely for people with emerging disabilities. Involving people with emerging disabilities, and all other stakeholders, for that matter, in all aspects of rehabilitation research and service delivery is the only way to ensure that our complementary research and service delivery efforts are fully responsive to their needs. Moreover, as noted by Bellini and Rumrill (2009), the perceived gap between research and practice will only be bridged when people with emerging disabilities and service providers become more active partners in research efforts.

From our own vantage point as rehabilitation educators and researchers, there are a number of areas of scientific inquiry that seem particularly important in our efforts to more fully understand the nature and needs of people with emerging disabilities. One such area is privatization. Over the past two decades, there has been disappointingly little growth in the knowledge base regarding such private-sector phenomena as the validity of life care planning as a rehabilitation service for people with severe and emerging disabilities such as traumatic brain injuries, polytrauma, age-related blindness, cancer, and amputations related to diabetes; the efficacy and cost–benefits of disability management programs in industry for workers with pain disorders and chronic illnesses; factors that influence return-to-work outcomes for injured employees and those who encounter lifestyle-related health conditions such as diabetes, heart disease, and multiple chemical sensitivity; and applications of vocational assessment and planning strategies in personal injury and workers' compensation litigation involving plaintiffs with emerging disabilities.

The knowledge base in rehabilitation counseling always requires systematic and comprehensive evaluations of disability and rehabilitation policy initiatives, especially as the policies and laws that govern our field change over time with new congresses and presidential administrations and as a result of case law. Specifically, we need to better understand how the ADAAA complements and intersects with other employment laws such as the Affordable Care Act, the Family and Medical Leave Act, and the Workforce Innovation and Opportunity Act (Rubin et al., 2016), especially relative to the coverage of people with emerging disabilities under these laws. We need to more thoroughly understand the disability-related provisions of the Social Security Act—especially the Social Security Disability Insurance and Supplemental Security Income programs, Medicaid, Medicare, and Ticket to Work and other work incentives—regarding how these benefits and incentives apply to people with emerging disabilities. We need to study and understand the impact of amendments and reauthorizations of the Rehabilitation Act and changes in the Rehabilitation Services Administration's programs on access to rehabilitation services for people with emerging disabilities. We need to understand how specific disability policy initiatives and generic social policy initiatives have affected people with emerging disabilities in such fundamental areas of life as housing, transportation, health care, civic participation, education, and access to technology. We need to know whether there is such a thing as the "disability community," and whether people with emerging disabilities consider themselves a part of that group. At the most basic policy level, we need to know what the term "disability" means in contemporary American society. Is it a medical, economic, social status, or situational phenomenon? How does the way we classify people and single them out for services affect their stature and standing in our communities? And to what extent are people with emerging disabilities included in or excluded from those classifications?

Another burgeoning area for emerging disabilities research in the years to come is assistive technology. We need to follow developments in this dynamic facet of our field and systematically study the effectiveness, safety, availability, practicality, and use patterns of new devices as they come on the market, as well as consumers' satisfaction with assistive technology devices. We also look for in-depth inquiries into the interactions between medical technology and assistive technology; in that regard, the interface among health care professionals, rehabilitation counselors, rehabilitation engineers, employers, and people with emerging disabilities will be of paramount interest.

Medical science will continue to have major effects on rehabilitation counseling and research. People with catastrophic injuries and illnesses (e.g., spinal cord injuries, traumatic brain injuries, polytrauma, cancer) are living longer than ever before, and scientifically based research to monitor the medical and psychosocial adjustment of those individuals is needed to continue to improve rehabilitation interventions and outcomes. People with congenital conditions such as spina bifida can now look forward to vocational opportunities and career success, thanks to medical advances that have vastly extended their life expectancies. People with HIV/AIDS are increasingly being viewed as having a chronic, rather than terminal, disease, a classification that brings with it numerous service, research, and policy implications. Medical science has also extended life expectancies for the general population (Wickert et al., 2013), a phenomenon that points to a myriad of scientific and service delivery considerations related to geriatric rehabilitation for people who incur age-related disabilities (e.g., visual impairments, hearing loss, orthopedic impairments, arthritis, cerebrovascular disease).

The processes and outcomes of several intervention strategies and professional specialty areas also need to be examined more thoroughly. Foremost among these is transition from school to adult living for young people with emerging disabilities such as ASD and attention deficit hyperactivity disorder (ADHD)—a process that spans one of the most important developmental periods in people's lives. Applied research is needed to assist special educators and rehabilitation counselors to collaborate more effectively in planning and providing comprehensive services to youths with neurodevelopmental disabilities and emerging chronic illnesses such as diabetes and mental illness who exit public schools and enter the world of work, postsecondary educational programs, and other adult roles (Wehman, 2013). Long-term follow-up data are needed to clarify the service needs of transitioning youth with emerging disabilities and practices that best meet those needs. One of the most important areas for future transition research is postsecondary education. With enrollment rates of students with disabilities having quadrupled on American college and university campuses since 1978 (Rubin et al., 2016) and individuals with psychiatric disabilities and ADHD representing two of the fastest growing groups of students with disabilities (Koch, Mamiseishvili, & Wilkins, in press), increasing interest has been evident in the transition *to* higher education for these students. Less focus has been evident in understanding the in-college experiences of these students that promote or impede academic success (Koch et al., 2016; Mamiseishvili & Koch, 2011) and the transition *from* college and university programs to competitive careers. Comparisons with nondisabled college graduates find alumni with disabilities, especially those with emerging disabilities, at a distinct disadvantage for career entry and job retention (Hennessey, Roessler, Cook, Unger, & Rumrill, 2006). In-depth inquiry is needed to ascertain the precise nature of the difficulties that people with emerging disabilities have in completing postsecondary degrees and translating a college education into a successful career.

Effective employment interventions are needed for people with emerging disabilities that focus on expanding the parameters of rehabilitation service delivery. Primarily, this will involve a commitment to understand the career development needs of people with emerging disabilities after their cases have been closed by rehabilitation agencies. Current rehabilitation practice is replete with sophisticated and proven job development and placement strategies to help people with disabilities secure employment (Strauser, 2013; Wehman, 2013), but there is a glaring lack of effective career maintenance interventions. Numerous studies over the past several years have documented the poor postrehabilitation employment outcomes of people with emerging and traditional disabilities, and most of these investigations point toward the lack of adequate work adjustment services for employed individuals as a primary reason for workforce attrition (Fraser, Kraft, Ehde, & Johnson, 2006). Researchers need to identify the specific reasons that job retention is so difficult for employees with emerging disabilities and tailor interventions to meet those needs.

EMERGING RESEARCH TECHNIQUES AND STRATEGIES

As rehabilitation researchers apply scientific methods to address those emerging issues discussed to this point in the chapter (and many other issues), it is important to note that the way research is conducted is likely to change just as dramatically as the topics under study will. This section examines a number of trends that we anticipate for the foreseeable future in terms of how science is applied in emerging disabilities research.

We have recently begun to see the broad applicability of qualitative research methods in rehabilitation counseling (Koch, Niesz, & McCarthy, 2014). As a means of investigating phenomena that have not been previously examined, identifying variables for theory-building purposes, and providing understanding of the lived experience of emerging disability that is not possible using quantitative methods, qualitative research will play an increasingly prominent role.

Within the qualitative realm, we hope to see a movement toward prolonged engagements with research participants within their natural environments and the application of more rigorous research methods to enhance the credibility of qualitative findings. The grounded theory method of qualitative research (Strauss & Corbin, 1991)—whereby theoretical propositions are developed on the basis of observation and then tested, revised, and refined through prolonged engagement and systematic data analysis—is well suited to investigations that examine people with emerging disabilities. Koch et al. (2005) reported that several rehabilitation educators and researchers identified focus groups as a time-efficient and cost-effective qualitative strategy to gather important data in a small-group format. Focus groups have been used in marketing and advertising for many years, but they have recently made their way to the social sciences as a viable means of eliciting the perspectives of stakeholders in such matters as the future directions of rehabilitation counseling research (Koch et al., 2005), the employment concerns of Americans with chronic illnesses (Roessler, Rumrill, Li, & Leslie, 2015), and the career preparation needs of college and university students with disabilities (Hennessey, 2004).

It is also important that qualitative researchers who investigate the experiences of people with emerging disabilities continue to expand the focus of their inquiries to encompass the experiences of individuals who *are* effectively coping with their disabilities; managing disruptive symptoms and functional limitations; experiencing a high level of life satisfaction; and successfully engaging in postsecondary education, employment, social activities, and other life domains of importance to these individuals. Focusing exclusively on problems in the areas of psychosocial and vocational adjustment may be misrepresentative of the totality of medical, psychosocial, and vocational experiences of individuals with emerging disabilities. Most importantly, assets-focused qualitative research highlights specific factors to facilitate positive psychosocial and vocational outcomes that could be incorporated into the treatment and rehabilitation of individuals who are having difficulties with psychosocial and vocational adjustment.

Furthermore, because there is an extensive base of qualitative research in the health literature as well as a burgeoning qualitative research base in rehabilitation, which has investigated medical, psychosocial, and vocational implications of a vast array of emerging disabilities, there is a need for meta-syntheses of the findings from these investigations. Meta-syntheses are used to summarize, synthesize, and interpret the findings from a multitude of qualitative investigations on a specific topic (Finfgeld-Connett, 2016). Meta-syntheses enable researchers to develop new concepts, frameworks, and theories as well as to expand those that already exist. They offer an empirical foundation for guiding evidence-based practices and fine-tuning these practices to the realities of the research participants. Meta-syntheses also are used to generate research hypotheses and to inform practice guidelines.

Qualitative research designs and procedures continue to evolve to incorporate a multitude of perspectives, designs, and methodologies (Koch et al., 2008, 2014). Furthermore, qualitative approaches have advanced from merely "giving voice" to the research participants to actively engaging them as coresearchers in an emancipatory process to change policies and societal attitudes that further marginalize already disadvantaged groups (Koch et al., 2008). These developments in qualitative research approaches have particular relevance to the experiences of people with emerging disabilities because disability policies and societal practices have so often excluded them. PhotoVoice is one such approach that has the potential to advance knowledge, reduce stigma about emerging disabilities, and influence policies and procedures affecting the lives of people with emerging disabilities. PhotoVoice is a qualitative approach that uses participant-produced photographs and narratives about the photos to obtain an in-depth understanding of their experiences with phenomena such as chronic physical illness, mental illness, stigma, and recovery (Han & Oliffe, 2015). PhotoVoice involves the participants in developing research and interview questions, designing and implementing studies, analyzing and interpreting data, and disseminating research findings. Participants are interviewed about the meanings they attribute to their photographs in either individual interviews, focus groups, or both. Data are analyzed to obtain thick descriptions and understand the nuanced meanings ascribed to the photographs. In many PhotoVoice studies, the researchers and researcher–participants use their photographs and narratives to lobby policymakers, raise public awareness through photography exhibitions, increase empathy among service providers, and destigmatize their conditions. Researchers at the Boston University Center for Psychiatric Rehabilitation (2016, para. 1) have been at the forefront of using PhotoVoice to reduce the stigma associated with mental illness, characterizing this emancipatory research approach as an "empowering tool [that] enables people at the grassroots level without access to decision-makers to represent and define issues of concern, areas of strength, and targets of change—all of which are routinely defined by health specialists, policymakers, or professionals."

For emerging disability researchers who use quantitative research methods, we hope that multivariate outcome analyses will become more prevalent than is currently the case. The constructs that underlie clinical practice and service provision in rehabilitation counseling with people with emerging disabilities are multidimensional, as are the psychosocial factors that influence consumers' participation in the rehabilitation process (e.g., motivation, social supports, socioeconomic status). Why, then, do many researchers persist in operationalizing valued consumer outcomes in dichotomous, "yes or no" fashion (e.g., employed/unemployed, successfully rehabilitated/unsuccessfully rehabilitated, graduated from a training or educational program/failed to graduate)? We need to evaluate outcomes in the lives of people with emerging disabilities as they really are—multidimensional, sometimes complicated, dependent upon multiple factors that vary widely among individuals, and falling along a continuum of successfulness—rather than adhering to an "all or nothing" measurement. We need to examine more than one outcome at a time in the vast majority of research contexts. We also need to evaluate complex variable models that more fully incorporate the complex person–environment interaction models that dominate our theoretical views of disability and the rehabilitation process rather than focusing on simple variable relationships.

To accomplish these aims, Bellini and Rumrill (2009) suggested utilizing a number of specific data analytic techniques. For example, multivariate analysis of variance enables researchers to gauge the interactive effects of different correlated outcomes in a manner that is not possible using univariate analyses. Path analysis and structural equation modeling are data analytic techniques that permit the simultaneous evaluation of theory-driven models of variable relationships in a manner that provides rigorous tests of theory and also permit the revision of theoretical propositions based on the actual empirical data. Rumrill, Cook, and Wiley

(2010) observe that there has been increased use of path analysis and structural equation modeling in rehabilitation counseling research, and this increased use parallels a greater emphasis on theory-driven research.

Another multivariate data analytic technique that provides opportunities to more effectively model the complexity of the real world in which people with emerging disabilities live is multilevel modeling (MLM), also known as hierarchical linear modeling (HLM). MLM is a statistical approach that is appropriate for analysis of "nested" or hierarchically ordered data, as are often encountered in rehabilitation counseling with people with emerging disabilities. For example, consumer outcomes vary as a function of specific consumer characteristics such as ethnicity, education level, motivation, etc. Consumer outcomes may also vary as a function of rehabilitation counselor competency (the next "level" of data in the hierarchy) and state agency characteristics (e.g., amount of funding, specific agency policies). To adequately "model" the rehabilitation process as it really is requires that these different levels of data be taken into consideration. When we analyze consumer outcome at the level of the consumer only, we may be inappropriately ascribing all sources of variability in the service provision process to the characteristics of the consumer, when in fact additional sources may better explain why specific outcomes are achieved. Although to date the use of MLM in the rehabilitation literature has been quite rare, there are a few recent examples of studies that utilized these methods (Kwok et al., 2008; Matrone & Leahy, 2005). Although we advocate here for the use of more sophisticated data analyses in rehabilitation research, we also recognize that sophisticated data analytic techniques are no substitute for a rigorous research design. Quality in the research design, coupled with appropriate data analytic strategies, provides the strongest warrant for a scientific knowledge claim.

Therefore, along with more sophisticated data analytic techniques, emerging disabilities researchers should design more studies that are longitudinal in nature. The vast majority of quantitative rehabilitation investigations utilize a cross-sectional approach to data gathering. That is, data are gathered at one point in time and an attempt is made to infer causal relations from this "snapshot in time." Longitudinal designs may yield much stronger warrants for causal relations because a primary condition of causality—that the cause precedes the effect—is part of the research design. We have observed few examples of longitudinal research designs in recent rehabilitation research.

For rehabilitation outcomes and other data that are not normally distributed, we recommend that emerging disability researchers become familiar with nonparametric statistical analyses that permit comparisons among groups on nominally or categorically coded dependent variables. A growing body of literature in our field is devoted to studies that have used chi squares and other nonparametric techniques to analyze important phenomena in the lives of people with disabilities (McMahon, West, Mansouri, & Belongia, 2006; Unger, Campbell, & McMahon, 2006).

One major development in federal policy and rehabilitation counseling practice that has direct bearing on the techniques and strategies of emerging disability research is the increased emphasis on consumer involvement over the past several decades. Amendments to the Rehabilitation Act in 1992 and 1998 provided strict guidelines for ensuring that people with disabilities take an active role in all aspects of case planning and service delivery in the vocational rehabilitation program (Rubin et al., 2016). Also, there is growing interest among policymakers to involve people with disabilities in all phases of the rehabilitation research process (Rumrill et al., 2010). One such approach to involving people with disabilities in research is known as Participatory Action Research (PAR; Graves, 1991). PAR is defined as "applied rehabilitation research that includes people with disabilities, their families, service providers, scholars, policymakers, and/or other members of the community in the quest of information from the initial conception of the idea through implementation and evaluation of its impact" (19th Institute on Rehabilitation Issues, 1993, p. 16). Given the expanded emphasis on consumer involvement in all aspects of the research process, we expect to see people with emerging disabilities playing an increasingly prominent role in shaping and implementing research projects. By assisting researchers in identifying samples, developing instruments, formulating intervention strategies, analyzing data, reflecting on results, and establishing policy and service agendas, rehabilitation consumers with emerging disabilities will serve as key consultants and real stakeholders in the investigations designed to address their needs.

One PAR approach that has the potential to advance our understanding of issues impacting individuals with emerging disabilities is the concerns report methodology (CRM; Schriner & Fawcett, 1988; Schriner, Roessler, & Johnson, 1992). The CRM is a widely used set of procedures for developing a relevant list of consumer concerns and setting an agenda for needed changes in policy and service delivery based on perceived strengths and problems identified by a particular group of people. This approach has often been applied in disability research, involving people with disabilities and other stakeholders in their success in identifying prominent concerns, setting priorities among the identified concerns for intervention and change, and establishing plans for implementing needed solutions to high-priority problems.

As partners in CRM research, people with disabilities are involved in selecting items for data collection instruments, determining useful data collection procedures, evaluating significant strengths and weaknesses in existing policies and services, and interpreting results. CRM has proven useful with a number of disability groups, some of which qualify as emerging disability populations under the definition used in this book. These groups include people with multiple sclerosis (Rumrill, Roessler, Li, Daly, & Leslie, 2015), individuals with traditional and emerging disabilities (Nary, White, Budde, & Vo, 2004), individuals with blindness or visual impairments (Wolffe, Roessler, & Schriner, 1992), individuals with traumatic brain injuries (Roessler & Schriner, 1992), people with spina bifida (Schriner, Roessler, & Johnson, 1993), deaf people (Schriner, Roessler, & Raymer, 1991), adults with psychiatric disorders (Snyder, Temple, Youngbauer, O'Neil, & Cromwell, 1995), and college students with disabilities (Hennessey et al., 2006; Schriner & Roessler, 1990).

CONCLUSIONS

In an applied social science such as rehabilitation counseling, policy, practice, and scientific inquiry are shaped through an ongoing, reciprocal process. Thus, many of the impending changes in emerging disabilities research about which we have speculated in this chapter stem from changes in disability and rehabilitation policy that have an impact on the profession and practice of rehabilitation counseling. Contemporary rehabilitation counselors are subject to new regulations and policy shifts, heightened certification and licensure standards, and pressures to specialize (to name just a few recent and continuing trends). These trends place heavy demands on rehabilitation counselors to update their knowledge in order to continue to effectively serve people with disabilities. Similarly, rehabilitation researchers must stay current with respect to new developments in the field if the contributions that they make to the knowledge base are to be considered meaningful by policy makers, administrators, counselors, employers, and people with disabilities themselves.

Among the many new developments in the field of rehabilitation counseling, none is more important than the changing nature of disability in contemporary society. People with disabilities that are either new to medical science or increasing in incidence and prevalence are claiming a growing share of the rehabilitation process, and scientific inquiry in the field of rehabilitation counseling must keep step with changes in practice that result from the growing involvement of these individuals.

DISCUSSION QUESTIONS

1. What role does theory play in emerging disabilities research within the field of rehabilitation counseling?
2. What emerging disability populations need to be more thoroughly involved in rehabilitation counseling research?
3. What subject areas in the lives of people with emerging disabilities do you consider most fertile for future rehabilitation research?
4. What research methods and data analytic strategies should future rehabilitation counseling researchers use to gain a more thorough understanding of the needs, perspectives, values, participation, and outcomes of people with emerging disabilities in all aspects of society and across the life span?
5. How important is research in shaping and/or reflecting best practices in the field of rehabilitation counseling vis-a-vis consumers with emerging disabilities?

REFERENCES

Bellini, J., & Rumrill, P. (2009). *Research in rehabilitation counseling* (2nd ed.). Springfield, IL: Charles C. Thomas.

Bishop, M. (2005). Quality of life and psychosocial adaptation to chronic illness and disability: Preliminary analysis of a conceptual and theoretical synthesis. *Rehabilitation Counseling Bulletin, 48,* 219–231.

Bishop, M. (2012). Psychosocial adaptation to chronic illness and disability: Current status and considerations for new directions. In P. J. Toriello, M. L. Bishop, & P. D. Rumrill (Eds.), *New directions in rehabilitation counseling: Creative responses to professional, clinical, and educational challenges* (pp. 25–53). Linn Creek, MO: Aspen Professional Services.

Bishop, M., Stenhoff, D. M., & Shepard, L. (2007). Psychosocial adaptation and quality of life in multiple sclerosis: Assessment of the disability centrality model. *Journal of Rehabilitation, 73,* 3–12.

Boston University Center for Psychiatric Rehabilitation. (2016). *Photovoice.* Retrieved from https://cpr.bu.edu/resources/photovoice

Finfgeld-Connett, D. (2016). The future of theory-generating meta-synthesis research. *Qualitative Health Research, 26*(3), 291–293.

Frain, M. P., Bishop, M., Rumrill, P., Tansey, T., Chan, F., Strauser, D., & Chiu, C. (2015). Multiple sclerosis and employment: A research review based on the International Classification of Functioning. *Rehabilitation Research, Policy, and Education, 29*(2), 153–164.

Fraser, R. T., Kraft, G. H., Ehed, D. W., & Johnson, K. L. (2006). *The MS workbook: Living fully with multiple sclerosis.* Oakland, CA: New Harbinger Press.

Han, C. S., & Oliffe, J. L. (2015). Photovoice in mental illness research: A review and recommendations. *Health, 20*(2), 110–126. doi:10.1177/1363459314567790

Hennessey, M. L. (2004). *An examination of the employment and career development concerns of postsecondary students with disabilities: Results of a tri-regional study* (Unpublished doctoral dissertation). Kent State University, Kent, OH.

Hennessey, M. L., Roessler, R., Cook, B., Unger, D., & Rumrill, P. (2006). Employment and career development concerns of postsecondary students with disabilities: Service and policy implications. *Journal of Postsecondary Education and Disability, 19*(1), 39–55.

Koch, L., Schultz, J., Hennessey, M., & Conyers, L. (2005). Rehabilitation research in the 21st century: Concerns and recommendations from members of the National Council on Rehabilitation Education. *Rehabilitation Education, 19*, 5–14.

Koch, L. C., Mamiseishvili, K., & Wilkins, M. (in press). Postsecondary integration and persistence: A comparison of students with psychiatric disabilities to students with learning disabilities/attention deficit disorders. *Rehabilitation Research, Policy, and Education.*

Koch, L. C., Niesz, T., & McCarthy, H. (2014). Understanding and reporting qualitative research: An analytical review and recommendations for submitting authors. *Rehabilitation Counseling Bulletin, 57*(3), 131–143.

Kosciulek, J. (1999). The consumer-directed theory of empowerment. *Rehabilitation Counseling Bulletin, 42*, 196–213.

Kosciulek, J. (2005). Structural equation model of the consumer-directed theory of empowerment in a vocational rehabilitation context. *Rehabilitation Counseling Bulletin, 49*, 40–49.

Kosciulek, J., & Mertz, M. (2001). Structural analysis of the consumer-directed theory of empowerment. *Rehabilitation Counseling Bulletin, 44*, 209–216.

Mamiseishvili, K., & Koch, L. C. (2011). First-to-second-year persistence of students with disabilities in postsecondary institutions in the United States. *Rehabilitation Counseling Bulletin, 54*(2), 93–105.

Nary, D. E., White, G. W., Budde, J. F., & Vo, H. F. (2004). Identifying the employment and vocational rehabilitation concerns of people with traditional and emerging disabilities. *Journal of Vocational Rehabilitation, 20*(1), 71–77.

Roessler, R. T., Rumrill, P., Li, J., & Leslie, M. (2015). Predictors of differential employment statuses of adults with multiple sclerosis. *Journal of Vocational Rehabilitation, 42*(2), 141–152.

Roessler, R. T., & Schriner, K. (1992). Employment concerns of people with head injuries. *Journal of Rehabilitation, 58*(1), 17.

Rubin, S., Roessler, R., & Rumrill, P. (2016). *Foundations of the vocational rehabilitation process* (7th ed.). Austin, TX: Pro-Ed.

Rumrill, P., Cook, B., & Wiley, A. (2010). *Research in special education* (2nd ed.). Springfield, IL: Charles C. Thomas.

Rumrill, P. D., Roessler, R. T., Li, J., Daly, K., & Leslie, M. (2015). The employment concerns of Americans with multiple sclerosis: Perspectives from a national sample. *Work: A Journal of Prevention, Assessment, and Rehabilitation, 52*(4), 735–748. doi:10.3233/WOR-152201

Schriner, K. F., & Fawcett, S. B. (1988). Development and validation of a community concerns report method. *Journal of Community Psychology, 16*(3), 306–316.

Schriner, K. F., & Roessler, R. T. (1990). Employment concerns of college students with disabilities: Toward an agenda for policy and practice. *Journal of College Student Development, 31*, 307–312.

Schriner, K. F., Roessler, R. T., & Johnson, P. (1992). Employment concerns questionnaire. *Journal of Applied Rehabilitation Counseling, 24,* 32–37.

Schriner, K. F., Roessler, R. T., & Johnson, P. (1993). Identifying the employment concerns of people with spina bifida. *Journal of Applied Rehabilitation Counseling,* 24(2), 32–37.

Schriner, K. F., Roessler, R. T., & Raymer, J. (1991). Employment concerns of deaf university students. *Journal of the American Deafness and Rehabilitation Association,* 25(2), 13–19.

Schultz, J., Koch, L., & Kontosh, L. (2007). Establishing rehabilitation research priorities for the National Council on Rehabilitation Education. *Rehabilitation Education, 21,* 149–158.

Serlin, R. C. (1989). Hypothesis testing, theory building, and the philosophy of science. *Journal of Counseling Psychology, 34,* 365–371.

Snyder, J., Temple, L., Youngbauer, J., O'Neil, T., & Cromwell, R. (1995). *Needs conference for underserved consumers with psychiatric disabilities.* Lawrence: Research and Training Center on Independent Living, University of Kansas.

Strauser, D. (2013). *Career development, employment, and disability in rehabilitation.* New York, NY: Springer Publishing Company.

Strauss, A. L., & Corbin, J. (1991). *Basics of qualitative research: Grounded theory procedures and techniques.* Newbury Park, CA: Sage.

Wehman, P. (2013). *Life beyond the classroom* (5th ed.). Baltimore, MD: Paul Brookes.

Wickert, K., Dresden, D., & Rumrill, P. (2013). *The sandwich generation's guide to eldercare.* New York, NY: Demos Health.

Wolffe, K. E., Roessler, R. T., & Schriner, K. F. (1992). Employment concerns of people with blindness or visual impairments. *Journal of Visual Impairment & Blindness, 86,* 185–187.

World Health Organization. (2001). *International classification of functioning, disability, & health.* Geneva, Switzerland: Author.

Index